SOUTHERN LITERARY STUDIES

JACOBS, Robert D. **Poe: Journalist and Critic.** Lousiana State, 1969. 464p (Southern Literary Studies) 70-80042. 10.95. SBN 8071-0846-4

CHOICE OCT. '70

Language & Literature

English & American

This ambitious study covers a wide range of scholarship. It offers a chronological survey of Poe's practical criticism from 1835 to 1849 — that is, his book reviews in a variety of periodicals. It also formulates the working principles of this activity and relates them to his fiction, poetry, and life in general. Furthermore, it attempts to prove that 18th century rationalism, the new romanticism, and Poe's Southern origins combine to shape the originality of both his journalistic and his theoretical criticism. While the entire undertaking displays Jacobs' perseverance, industry, and dedication, it lacks subtlety and insight. The facts remain facts because his imagination never glows with the vision of new discoveries. But for all its limitations, the study is informative, and supplements Edd Winfield Parks' *Ante-bellum Southern Critics* (1962) and Sidney P. Moss' *Poe's Literary Battles: The Critic in the Context of his Literary Milieu* (1963).

SOUTHERN LITERARY STUDIES

edited by

LOUIS D. RUBIN, JR.

A Season of Dreams: The Fiction of Eudora Welty

ALFRED APPEL, JR.

The Hero With the Private Parts

ANDREW LYTLE

Hunting in the Old South: Original Narratives of the Hunters

CLARENCE GOHDES, EDITOR

Joel Chandler Harris: A Biography

PAUL M. COUSINS

John Crowe Ransom: Critical Essays and a Bibliography

THOMAS DANIEL YOUNG, EDITOR

A Bibliographical Guide to the Study of Southern Literature

LOUIS D. RUBIN, JR., EDITOR

Poe: Journalist and Critic

ROBERT D. JACOBS

POE: *Journalist & Critic*

ROBERT D. JACOBS is Professor of English at
the University of Kentucky. He is co-editor
(with Louis D. Rubin, Jr.) of *Southern Re-
nascence* and *South: Modern Southern Literature in Its Cultural Setting*. He has published articles in various literary journals. A
native of Mississippi, he received his B.A.
and M.A. degrees at the University of Mississippi and his Ph.D. degree at Johns Hopkins
University.

POE

Journalist & Critic

Robert D. Jacobs

LOUISIANA STATE UNIVERSITY PRESS • BATON ROUGE

For Louis D. Rubin, Jr.

Copyright © 1969 by
Lousiana State University Press
Library of Congress Catalog Card Number: 70–80042
SBN 8071-0846-4
Printed in the United States of America by
The Vail-Ballou Press, Inc., Binghamton, New York
Designed by Jules B. McKee

Preface

A T this late date an investigation of the literary criticism of Edgar Poe requires some excuse, if only to provide the investigator with a justification for concentrating his energies for a number of years. I started this study with no more in mind than an interpretation and reconstruction of what Poe actually said as a critic. At the time I began transforming my notes into a manuscript, there were no full-length studies of Poe as a critic, and many of the essays that did explore the subject were concerned exclusively with his aesthetic principles. Taking my cue from Poe's own statement that a theory is only as good as its practice, I intended to examine his book reviews with the purpose of evaluating his success in applying his own literary theories to the work of others. Intentions often change as a study progresses, however, and during the years that passed before this study reached its final form, others anticipated some of my findings with equivalent or superior insights. Consequently the purpose and form of this book changed, as it became necessary to take into account the constantly increasing fund of Poe scholarship and criticism. Even as the pages of my final revision were being typed, significant articles on Poe were appearing in scholarly journals, articles that demanded my consideration and acknowledgment.

Nevertheless, I was able to retain the opinion which motivated this study—that all too often evaluations have been made of Poe as a literary critic that misinterpreted his idiom, failed to consider the often intolerable pressures of a journalistic career, and ignored the application of his theories to the work of others. Conspicuously neglected, though often mentioned in passing, has been the operative effectiveness of the critical theories of the last half of the eighteenth century in determining Poe's approach to the critical act and even in shaping some of his principles. Edward Davidson's brilliant study placed Poe within the context of romantic aesthetics and focused upon his poems and his tales to reveal a unitary principle informing all of Poe's creative work from his youthful poems to his cosmogony, *Eureka.* I have quarreled with few of Professor Davidson's insights, in some respects the most valuable that have ever been offered regarding Poe; instead I have sought to fill in missing data by showing that Poe as a working critic looked backward toward the mechanistic psychological aesthetic of the previous century and forward toward the dynamic organicism of the romantic period. My method, like that of Professor Davidson, is both thematic and chronological, but instead of aesthetic principles I have chosen to examine the operative regulations of Poe's practical criticism.

As a journalistic critic, Poe made his reviews a vehicle for his literary principles. He was a polemicist who sought to enforce his doctrine through the mass media, the journals and lecture platforms of his time. He used the techniques of mass persuasion. One such technique is dogmatic and unqualified assertion, and he used this technique toward a specific end. He was, if you will, a propagandist in the service of art. As a consequence, those who have examined only his most oracular pronouncements out of the context in which they were made have frequently misinterpreted his position. In the context of the occasion for the review, the particular journal in which the review appeared, and the urgency of the issue debated, Poe's more dogmatic assertions may often be seen as growing out of the necessity of polemical emphasis. When "the matter in hand is a dunce to be gibbeted," Poe wrote in his "Marginalia," "Speak out!—or the person may not understand you."

Poe did speak out, but often the rigor of his pronouncements was mitigated upon other occasions when he no longer felt it necessary to press a particular doctrinal issue. Since the initiation of my study, books by Professors Edd Winfield Parks and Sidney P. Moss have done much to reveal the journalist whose voice speaks through the tone of the critic. While I acknowledge a full debt to these prior publications, I believe that my focus is different and that my investigation of the ideological framework within which Poe's opinions found expression allows alternative conclusions or at least emphases.

I have chosen to investigate Poe's criticism chronologically in spite of all the handicaps such a method entails, for I cannot believe that a writer as intelligent as Poe would not exhibit some process of maturation. This method, detailed as it is, requires the tedium of viewing the same topics from different angles as Poe repeated, qualified, or modified his views. Yet only in such a way may we see his development as a critic. The man of 1845 who invoked reason and common sense to guide the artist's taste was not much like the boy of 1831 who claimed that it was the poet's duty to protest, not to think. A restricted examination of Poe's aesthetics obscures this difference, for both the boy and the man declared that the end and the *only* end of art was hedonic value. Still, as Poe matured as a critic, he had to answer such questions as how this value could be transmitted and to what persons. In answering these questions he was inevitably led to an examination of the quality of the aesthetic response as a mode of experience and to speculation concerning its final cause.

Believing that such a development could be traced and described, I have devoted most of this study to Poe's career as a journalist—a book reviewer. Only in my concluding chapters do I fully engage with Poe's aesthetics by attempting to interpret his "philosophy," which was nearly always expressed as fiction, keeping in mind his own premise that a fiction should never bear the burden of truth except in the transcendental sense that the orderly, the consistent, and the symmetrical are *always* true. Order was the principle; disorder was the condition in which the principle must be discovered and revealed. The principle was true under the aspect of eternity, but the "truth" which man acknowledged, the truth of the conditioned and the contingent, could not be expressed by fiction. In his practical criticism Poe dealt with the conditioned and the contingent, the books produced by particular writers with particular temperaments, with varying degrees of skill, for particular purposes that could be lauded or deprecated. Poe railed against inept procedures and irrelevant purposes and refused to consider a work of art validated by its quality of vision. In dealing with the *conditioned*, he refused to invoke the *unconditioned* as a proposition from which value judgments could be deduced. Instead he relied upon the "truth" which his audience could recognize, the truth of nature's laws and of exact demonstration. The ultimate truth, he said in his preface to *Eureka*, would be accepted only by "those who feel rather than . . . those who think," by those who "put faith in dreams as in the only realities."

In Poe as critic, then, we have something of the schizoid condition the characters of his fiction exhibited, insofar as the split was indicative not of mental disorder but of the necessity of accommodation to two kinds of truth, the kind apprehended by the imagination and the kind necessary for conducting the business of life. As a practicing critic, he had to use what he thought of as science, the psychodynamics of stimulus and response and rules grounded in this correlation. He declared that all evaluations must be made in terms of effect, the effect of a work of art upon an audience. Bad grammar, mismanaged figures, incongruous associations, episodic plots, crude versification, failures to maintain the fictional illusion—all must be condemned as injurious to effect. In his practice of criticism Poe was a rhetorician whose rules were as strict as those of one of his sources, the Reverend Hugh Blair; but as a theorist who sought to analyze the nature of beauty and to ascribe a final cause for the hedonic value of art, Poe eventually went beyond all rules and rested his apology for poetry in the imagined nature of an artist-God whose greatest pleasure came from the contemplation of his own perfection, but who had to experience the pain of phenomenal existence before he could fully enjoy his own being.

Poe's work as a critic thus proceeds as a type of dialectic between two kinds of truth, the temporal and the eternal; only toward the end of his life did he achieve a synthesis by attempting to prove that the laws of physics demonstrated the truth that he had imagined. Tracing the course of this development eventually became my intention, although I have endeavored to carry out my original purpose as well by making a historical reconstruction of Poe's work as a practicing critic.

Any investigator of Poe's work has a heavier burden of acknowledgment to prior investigations than he can adequately show without a dismal parade of footnotes. My own notes march in battalions, yet I am aware that my acknowledgments are less than complete. I have resorted to bibliographical and explanatory notes that may not be worth the attention of Poe scholars, but I have tried to make this study useful for the non-specialist. The already published and forthcoming bibliographies of Poe criticism by J. Lasley Dameron obviate the necessity of a listing of secondary sources for any purpose other than to show that I have consulted them, and of any glaring omissions I can only say that when I have been conscious of a debt I have acknowledged it.

To obtain a reliable text for Poe's reviews is a matter of some difficulty. Except when otherwise indicated, I have used the 17-volume edition of Poe's works edited by James A. Harrison, but I have corrected obvious errors by collating with other editions or with the original magazine publications. Since most of Poe's reviews are brief, I have generally confined page references to the entire review, noting particular pages only in a few extended reviews and in *Eureka*. I have not used footnotes for quotations from tales and essays which are available in a number of good modern editions, for in such cases it is easy for the reader to locate the passages for himself. For reviews not in the Harrison edition I have cited the magazines in which they were originally published. The text used for tales, poems, and critical essays is Arthur Hobson Quinn and Edward H. O'Neill (eds.), *The Complete Poems and Stories of Edgar Allan Poe, with Selections from His Critical Writings* (2 vols.; New York, 1946).

My debts for direct and indirect assistance are many. To Louis D. Rubin, Jr., friend and supervisory editor of this series, I owe much for his encouragement, his patience, and his incisive criticism; to Richard Beale Davis, C. Hugh Holman, and Sidney P. Moss, who read my manuscript in its next-to-final draft, for their careful criticism and advice; to the late T. O. Mabbott, for his generosity in sending me a list of the reviews he considered secure in the Poe canon; to Jay B. Hubbell, for the use of notes he made concerning Henry F. Chorley; to J. Lasley Dameron, for the use of his bibliography of Poe criticism prior to its recent publication; to Arthur Wrobel, for making available to me materials on phrenology which he had accumulated in his own research; and to William S. Ward, for materials and bibliographical help on the British periodicals.

A heavy debt for the most practical kind of assistance is owed to the American Council of Learned Societies, for it was during my tenure as an A.C.L.S. Fellow that the actual writing of this study began. I was able to complete my work with the aid of two summer fellowships awarded by the University of Kentucky Research Foundation, which was also responsible for grants that expedited the final preparation of the manuscript.

R. D. J.

Lexington, Kentucky
January, 1969

Contents

POE: *Journalist & Critic*

I · The Matrix

THROUGHOUT his life Edgar Poe thought of himself as a Southerner. He performed his first critical labors as editor of a magazine that had as its announced policy the encouragement of Southern letters.[1] If the destructive zeal of his criticism was soon to dismay the publisher of the *Southern Literary Messenger* and to annoy a few of its contributors, there was nevertheless much about Poe and about his critical stance that was congenial to the South of his time,[2] and a discussion of the development of Poe as a literary critic properly begins with his relationship to the region in which he spent most of his youth.

When Poe returned to Richmond, Virginia, in 1835 to take an editorial post with the *Southern Literary Messenger*, his interests and even his appearance must have created ambivalent reactions. No doubt he was dressed in the funereal black which he customarily wore, partly out of necessity and partly because his theatrical bent made him wish to present the image of a melancholy dreamer, the *persona* that appeared in his poems.[3] He looked like a gentleman down on his luck. Well and good, such a situation would arouse Southern sympathy. But he also looked like a Byronic poet, and Byronism, however much it may have been enjoyed on the printed page, was not a behavioral pattern that was approved. Poe's foster father, John Allan, had been disturbed by the young man's Byronic attitudes, which were not confined to his poetry; and Poe, in order to placate his benefactor and extract some financial sup-

[1] *Southern Literary Messenger*, I (1834–35), 1.
[2] Jay B. Hubbell, "Poe and the Southern Literary Tradition," *Texas Studies in Literature and Language*, II (1960), 157–58.
[3] John Allan, Poe's foster father, gave him a suit of black clothes shortly after the death of Mrs. Allan. For some years this was Poe's best, perhaps his only, suit. N. Bryllion Fagin has made a convincing case for Poe's theatricality, both in his life and in his writings. See Fagin, *The Histrionic Mr. Poe* (Baltimore, 1949).

3

port, once promised to give up Byron as a model.[4] The distinguished Charleston critic Hugh Swinton Legaré had summarized the problem of Byronism in an essay in the *Southern Review*. He appreciated the form of Byron's poems, his classic sense of structure and proportion; but he found in Byron's themes as well as in his life the evidence of a diseased and intemperate imagination.[5] Edgar Poe in his darker humors also presented the symptoms of an imagination colored by the morbid and the misanthropic. He looked like a melancholy misanthrope, and his poems and some of his tales fulfilled the promise of his appearance.

Ironically, Poe was coming to join the staff of a new magazine which had printed on the first page of its first issue a warning from a friendly New Yorker, James Kirke Paulding, to the effect that Southern writers must forget about Sir Walter Scott, Lord Byron, and Thomas Moore before they could be expected to produce anything original.[6] Yet in spite of Paulding's advice one of the first poems published in the *Messenger* exhibited, in the words of a "friend" of the author, "the deep misanthropy of Byron" and "the flowing smoothness and vivacity of Moore."[7] Byronism and all it implied was a literary problem to T. W. White, the publisher of the *Messenger*, but it was more of a moral problem. It was easy for him, when actually confronted by the young man in black with his melancholy poems and morbid tales, to conclude that Edgar Poe

---

[4] Poe to John Allan, May 29, 1829, in John Ward Ostrom (ed.), *The Letters of Edgar Allan Poe* (Cambridge, Mass., 1948), I, 20, hereinafter cited as *Letters*.

[5] "Lord Byron's Character and Writings," in Mary Legaré Bullen (ed.), *Writings of Hugh Swinton Legaré* (Charleston, S.C., 1845), II, 358. Among the better known Southern writers, both William Gilmore Simms and Paul Hamilton Hayne took exception to Byron's character, though they admired much of his work. Terms often applied to Byron's character were "morbid misanthropy" and "licentiousness."

[6] *Southern Literary Messenger*, I (1834–35), 1.

[7] *Ibid.*, 11. The poem had been inscribed in a "young lady's album" and was submitted to the *Messenger* with a letter, from which this quotation was taken. The author of the letter went on to say that the anonymous poet's modesty will probably be somewhat startled at seeing himself in print . . . ." Such devices allowed Southern poets to avoid any taint of professionalism.

was a romantic of the desperate sort, whose wild imagination was loosed in those regions of the macabre where no healthy mind was safe to follow. Calm reason and sturdy common sense were left gibbering at the door that led to the crypt of Berenice. Not only this, when White found that he had on his hands a literary critic as destructively savage as any who wrote for *Blackwood's*, his reactions became anxious and hostile. Poe could be anything, it seemed, except the gentlemanly amateur in letters that Southern mores demanded.[8]

Yet in many ways Poe and his work should have been suited to the Southern temper. He wrote on the subjects popular for lyrical poetry, the only kind for which most Southerners professed any enthusiasm. In politics, about which he never felt much urgency, he expressed the Whig attitude of the Richmond gentry in his opposition to the "democratical mobs." [9] He showed sectional prejudice in his contempt for Boston, that capital city of all the *isms*. He was, with some exceptions, gallant to the ladies, fastidious in dress and manner, proud and sensitive. His one acknowledged vice was his drinking—or rather his inability to hold his liquor—but Southern gentlemen were allowed to have this vice, however much it was disapproved of by the rising middle class, as represented by White, in whose house liquor was not served.[10] In short, Poe did not deviate conspicuously from the Southern norm except in his choice of profession and in his competitive maneuvers to gain professional status. But these deviations were marked enough to cause trouble; the South was no more ready to support a professional critic than it was to support a professional poet.

Still, Poe was of the South, and his taste, at least in poetry, was formed in the South. His beginnings as a poet were in imitation of

[8] For a discussion of the position of the author in the Old South, see Jay B. Hubbell, *The South in American Literature, 1607–1900* (Durham, 1954), 211–14; and Willard Thorp, "The Writer as Pariah in the Old South," in R. C. Simonini, Jr. (ed.), *Southern Writers: Appraisals in Our Time* (Charlottesville, 1964), 3–18.

[9] Hubbell, *The South in American Literature*, 535–36.

[10] See T. W. White to Poe, September 29, 1835, in James A. Harrison (ed.), *Complete Works of Edgar Allan Poe* (17 vols.; New York, 1902), XVII, 20, hereinafter cited as *Works*.

Byron and Moore, and throughout his career as a critic he retained his predilection for lyric poetry that developed the theme of lamentation for love and beauty lost. This was the kind of poetry he wrote himself; it was also the kind written by Edward Coote Pinkney, who preceded him by a little, and by Philip Pendleton Cooke, who followed him by a little. If he made a continuing effort as a critic to validate his preferences, he was doing no more than what Northrop Frye has argued is inevitable for the poet turned critic—projecting a defense of what he liked to read and liked to write. Thus the first question to be considered in a study of Poe as a critic is that of his taste, and he liked the same kind of poetry as did other young romantics in the South.

The "taint of melancholy" which Poe throughout his life associated with the more "soulful" aspects of beauty was, of course, one of the familiar moods of romantics everywhere, but it is somewhat unusual that this particular mood should be so favored by Southern poets. From the defiant anguish reminiscent of Byron to the delicate sadness characteristic of female poets like Mrs. Felicia Hemans, the whole range of melancholy feeling could be found in the pages of the *Messenger* during the 1830's. This is not to say that the magazine published only the poems of Southern poetasters who invoked melancholy. Mrs. Lydia Huntley Sigourney, a valued contributor who was called the "American Hemans," was from the North. The significant point is that the Southern poets whom the *Messenger* did publish were prone to exploit melancholy. White printed what he could get, and since he did not pay for poetic contributions, what he got was mostly from the pens of amateurs who were decidedly squeamish about revealing their names (they used pseudonyms or initials) but not at all hesitant about seeing their effusions in print. Poems on Poe's favorite subject, the death of a beautiful woman, were numerous enough in the *Messenger* to make us feel some retroactive concern about the durability of Southern belles. Perhaps they did die often enough and young enough to inspire reams of elegiac verse. Oddly enough, however, the consolation of the conventional elegy was often absent from these Southern poems, perhaps because the poet was more interested in expressing Byronic despair than in following the conventions of the classical elegy. The focus is upon the feelings of the bereaved lover,[11] who is more concerned with his loss than he is with any possible reunion in Heaven. Such an attitude may sponsor the chilling reply of Poe's raven to the lover's query about future bliss in Aidenn. More than one Southern poet would have answered, "Nevermore."

Since the themes and moods of Poe's own poetry resemble those of many of the *Messenger* poems during the first few years of the journal's existence, it is not unreasonable to conclude that something in the temper of the South made Poe think that sorrow for the passing of the beautiful was the most poetic subject in the world. It was the common romantic mood of transcience that the Southern amateurs seized upon, a mood we can find occasionally in almost any poet during the romantic period but not so frequently as among the Southern poets. The question is, why was this particular mood a little more congenial to the Southern poets than it was, say, to Bryant, Longfellow, Emerson, and Lowell? The most obvious answer is that the Southerners were occasional poets who were moved to expression only by events of crucial personal significance, such as love and death. More debatable but still worth comment is the fact that by the second decade of the nineteenth century some Virginians—and it is chiefly with Virginia that we are concerned—were already looking toward the past with a kind of regret. Historians since W. J. Cash have been busily engaged in de-

---

[11] Edward Davidson has described the significance of burial rituals in nineteenth-century culture, especially Southern culture, and has argued that the eroticism of some of the elegiac poems permitted the age to enjoy what was officially banned. See *Poe: A Critical Study* (Cambridge, Mass., 1957), 105–18. I have no quarrel with this assumption. However, to say that Poe "cleverly capitalized on a popular commodity" and "provided his age with a handbook on how the upper middle class should take care of its dead" raises some questions. The upper middle class of the South (and elsewhere) paid relatively little attention to Poe's tales and poems until the mid-1840's. One would think that a virtual handbook which exploited a popular commodity would win quick popular acceptance. Poe made his reputation as a critic, not as a creative writer. See Hubbell, "Poe and the Southern Literary Tradition," 157–58.

stroying the Cavalier myth of the South, but in questions of literary origins prevailing myths are just as significant as political and economic fact. Clement Eaton and Rollin G. Osterweis have recognized this and have made use of literary materials in analyzing the temper of the antebellum South.[12] There is no need to duplicate their ample evidence, but a citation of prevalent moods that almost certainly affected Poe is in order.

Edward Davidson is probably right in suggesting that Poe may have been influenced by the tensions created in the South by the conflict between the plantation gentry and the rising mercantile class.[13] Reared in a mercantile family, Poe had only the remotest connections with the plantation gentry. In the words of Allen Tate, "A gentleman and a Southerner, he was not quite, perhaps, a Southern Gentleman." [14] No doubt he would have liked to have been. Certainly his brief stay at the University of Virginia, where his gambling and his exorbitant expenditures for clothes earned the disapproval of his foster father, suggests that Poe was capable of imitating the vices of the alleged aristocrats. He was also capable of attempting to create a personal legend that bears striking resemblance to the Virginia cult of chivalry described by Osterweis.[15]

[12] In *The Mind of the South* (1941), Cash states that few of the early colonists of Virginia had any connection with the English Cavaliers and that the Southern plantation aristocracy, always small, took many years to become established. His preface summarizes the legend of the colonial aristocracy. Clement Eaton, in his *Freedom of Thought in the Old South* (Durham, 1940), is chiefly concerned with the decline of liberal thought in post-Jeffersonian days, but he finds a reflection of the predicament of the plantation gentry in some of the literature of the period. Osterweis, in *Romanticism and Nationalism in the Old South* (New Haven, 1949), describes the Southern rejection of those aspects of romantic thought which stressed progress and social reform and the acceptance of the kind of romanticism that glorified the past and found value in a cult of chivalry and a loyalty to caste. Osterweis uses literary sources far more extensively than most historians of the period, and his study is thus valuable for its account of the prevailing myths, whether or not these myths may be verified as social determinants. Much of Osterweis' evidence is taken from the *Southern Literary Messenger*, which of course makes his findings pertinent to Poe.

[13] *Poe: A Critical Study*, 208.

[14] "Our Cousin, Mr. Poe," in *The Forlorn Demon* (Chicago, 1953), 83.

[15] *Romanticism and Nationalism in the Old South*, 82–102.

His romanticized version of his past in a letter to Sarah Helen Whitman, even if we count the fact that all lovers are liars, is only the most striking evidence of his attempt to create a personal legend on Southern terms:

> There is no oath which seems to me so sacred as that sworn by the all-divine love I bear you.—By this love, then, and by the God who reigns in Heaven, I swear to you that my soul is incapable of dishonor—that, with the exception of occasional follies and excesses which I bitterly lament, but to which I have been driven by intolerable sorrow, and which are hourly committed by others without attracting any notice whatever—I can call to mind no act of my life which would bring a blush to my cheek—or to yours. If I have erred at all, in this regard, it has been on the side of what the world would call a Quixotic sense of the honorable—of the chivalrous. The indulgence of this sense has been the true voluptuousness of my life. It was for this species of luxury that, in early youth, I deliberately threw away a large fortune, rather than endure a trivial wrong.[16]

There is no evidence that Poe was ever John Allan's heir, but in the manner of the cult of chivalry he liked to think of himself as one of the disinherited, for honor's sake. If we grant, then, that Poe was capable of imagining himself as a chivalric Southerner of the highest caste, then we can understand how, even in his earliest verse, he was capable of reflecting sentiments that by right should belong only to the members of the first families, brought down in the world by political and economic events beyond their control.

Clement Eaton has argued that the insecurity of the old aristocracy of Virginia would motivate a tendency toward romantic escape, and he finds an illustration in "Florence Vane," the best-known poem of Philip Pendleton Cooke, who can with some justice be considered a member of the plantation gentry. "The theme of unrequited love, the trysting place, a 'ruin lone and hoary,' a dreamlike maiden, and the use of the pathetic fallacy contributed ingredients of sentimental unreality." [17] This poem, and

[16] Poe to Sarah Helen Whitman, October 18, 1848, in *Letters*, II, 393.
[17] *Freedom of Thought in the Old South*, 49.

Cooke's "Young Rosalie Lee," published in the *Messenger* during Poe's connection with the journal, were both on the death of a beautiful woman, and both earned Poe's unqualified approval. An elegiac mood, whatever the subject of its expression, signifies that something valuable is passing, or has gone, and we find the elegiac mood in the South of Poe's youth in sufficient abundance to justify some investigation into just what it was that was passing.

Richard Beale Davis, in a recent study of the intellectual climate of Virginia during the Jeffersonian period, maintains that the prevailing mood, at least until about 1830, was sanguine, and that the nostalgic reverence of men like William Wirt for the Revolutionary generation was not symptomatic of a general pessimism about the future.[18] Historically this is correct. When Wirt in 1812 wrote of the "fallen state of intellect in our country," it was less in a mood of pessimism than it was in a desire to encourage the young people of the time to follow the example of their fathers.[19] A similar attitude was manifested by Jesse Burton Harrison in 1828. He too felt that the state of learning in the upper class had declined from what it was before the Revolution, but he looked forward to "a better destiny" when young men were prepared by appropriate education to be "ornaments to polite society." [20] This is not pessimism but rather a reflection of the confidence of the Enlightenment that education could restore the quality of leadership that Virginia had manifested in the past.[21]

Such statements as the above would seem to have little relevance to a young romantic such as Edgar Poe had he not, in a review in the *Southern Literary Messenger* in 1835, voiced precisely the same opinions:

> The most lukewarm friend of the State must perceive—if he perceives anything—that the glory of the Ancient Dominion is in a

[18] *Intellectual Life in Jefferson's Virginia,* 1790–1830 (Chapel Hill, 1964), 24.

[19] William Wirt, *The Old Bachelor* (3rd ed.; Baltimore, 1818), 135.

[20] Harrison, A *Discourse on the Prospects of Letters and Taste in Virginia* (Cambridge, 1828), 13–26.

[21] See Davis, *Intellectual Life in Jefferson's Virginia,* 29–69, for an account of formal education in Virginia, theory and practice.

fainting—is in a dying condition. Her once great name is becoming, in the North, a byeword for imbecility—all over the South, a type for 'the things that *have been.*' And tamely to ponder upon times gone by is not to meet the exigencies of times present or to come. Memory will not help us. The recollection of our former estate will not benefit us. Let us act. While we have a resource, let us make it of avail. Let us proceed at once, to the establishment throughout the country, of *district schools* upon a plan of organization similar to that of our New England friends. If then, in time, Virginia shall be regenerated—if she shall, hereafter, assume, as is just, that proud station from which her own supine and overweening self-esteem has been the means of precipitating her, 'it will all be owing,' (we take pleasure in repeating the noble and prophetic words of Mr. Minor,) "it will all be owing, under Providence, to the hearkening to that voice,—not loud, but solemn and earnest,—which from the shrine of Reason and the tombs of buried commonwealths, re-iterates and enforces the momentous precept—"ENLIGHTEN THE PEOPLE." ' [22]

One may wonder why Edgar Poe, self-styled aristocrat and avowed romantic, should have taken pleasure in quoting a demo-cratic sentiment that, in good Enlightenment fashion, invokes the "shrine of Reason." The mere fact that he did, however, suggests that his heritage from Virginia was by no means of a piece. This problem will be discussed in some detail, but for the moment let us say that it was incumbent on Poe to praise the speech of Lucian Minor, his employer's friend and trusted adviser. The voice of Minor was a Jeffersonian echo, dedicated to the purpose of making democracy viable by educating the people; and the voice of Edgar Poe, accommodated to editorial responsibility and the policy of the *Messenger*, was for the moment the voice of the rising middle class, impatient with the nostalgia for the past of the planter minority and eager to obtain status in a society in which, regardless of the declining fortunes of the few, upward mobility was more characteristic than downward.

Yet public service, characteristic as it was of the Enlightenment strain, would have had little appeal to an imagination conditioned

[22] *Works*, VIII, 119–20.

by such works as Byron's *Childe Harold* to seek melancholy pleasure in meditation upon the glory of the past. The imagination does not invariably reflect the precise temper of an age—witness how often the urban sophisticates of the age of Queen Anne contemplated the pleasures of rural retirement—but it is vitalized when it encounters a situation that is emotionally appealing, whether or not that situation is characteristic of the society at large. The romantic imagination of the South was vitalized by the predicament of the planter minority, declining in fortune and prestige because of the various reforms instituted by Jefferson to insure the welfare of the majority.[23] In spite of his statements in his review of Minor's address, Poe's imagination was drawn toward the predicament of such men as Philip Cooke. No doubt he would have sympathized utterly with Cooke's despairing cry to his father in 1840: "It is lamentable to see the old families of the land, the first in gentility and caste *reduced*; to see their descendants sinking by marriage and association into humbler classes, and to see mine thus would break my heart." [24] Uncommitted by family ties to the planter caste and thus prevented from finding a locus of value in a specifically Southern past, Edgar Poe still felt enough rapport with the situation of an aristocracy in distress to build himself a fictional world of decayed aristocrats, isolated from the commonplace by their exacerbated sensitivity. His Ligeia belongs to a family "of a remotely ancient date"; his Roderick Usher is a member of a "time-honored race"; even his William Wilson, the man who killed his conscience, comes from an old family and inherits its "imaginative and easily excitable temperament."

Poe, like other romantic Southerners of his time, displayed the elegiac mood, but with a striking difference in subject matter. A comparison with Philip Pendleton Cooke reveals this difference. Cooke's poetic imagination, at first like Poe's excited by the melan-

[23] For an antebellum statement of the predicament of the planters, see David R. Hundley, *Social Relations in Our Southern States* (New York, 1860), quoted in Willard Thorp (ed.), *A Southern Reader* (New York, 1955), 246–47.

[24] Cooke to his father, December 29, 1840, in John D. Allen, *Philip Pendleton Cooke* (Chapel Hill, 1942), 52.

choly theme of love and beauty lost, eventually moved toward an exploration of the chivalric world of Jean Froissart, an appropriate exercise for an inheritor of the Cavalier legend.[25] Cooke's tales presented the life and character of those elements of Virginia society with which he could identify. Poe's poetry, on the other hand, has only minimal reflections of the cult of chivalry and never relinquishes the melancholy theme so attractive to the Southern amateurs. The characters of Poe's tales, though members of ancient families, have little sense of family as Southerners (including Cooke) ordinarily displayed it; and the settings exhibit none of the sense of place abundantly revealed by Cooke and other antebellum writers, whose settings, however idealized, are usually in Virginia. It is as if Poe absorbed a mood and a sense of caste from the Southern subculture but lacked the specific reference that comes from personal relevance.

Let us presume that Poe's imagination undertook its journeys from the same starting point as Philip Cooke's did: a feeling of dissatisfaction with the course of events, an inclination to mourn for something valuable that has been lost, and a desire to let the world know about it. Cooke's imagination could project a situation in which honor, love, and caste were meaningful, either in their preservation or in their loss; but Poe's imagination could not rest there. He went beyond the Southern romance, beyond the borrowed conventions of the Gothic, to hypothecate in his fiction a world running down, a universe in precarious equilibrium before apocalypse. His characters, death-haunted, remain in their darkened rooms while the insensitive world goes on its way to destruction, unknowing and uncaring. Only after the punitive conflagration can man, born again, comprehend the nature of his folly, and only the preternaturally sensitive, the Roderick Ushers, can feel the

---

[25] Cooke's "Proem" to his *Froissart Ballads* (1847) reveals the attractions of his subject:

> In the wells
> Of Froissart's life-like chronicles,
> I dipped for moving truths of old.
> A thousand stories, soft and bold,
> Of stately dames, and gentlemen . . . .

terror of impending calamity. Poe's fiction, it is clear, is not anchored in any consoling myth and does not locate value in a way of life. Philip Cooke did not need a paradise beyond; all he needed was the preservation of status, some recognized activity in the public world, and enough prosperity with its attendant leisure to indulge in his two passions, literature and field sports.[26] The Cavalier myth was enough for Cooke, but it had no personal relevance for Edgar Poe. His imagination could not find comfort in the chivalric past, nor could he devote his energies to any preservation of its semblance in fiction. As a consequence, his fiction exploits aristocratic superiority, aristocratic aloofness, aristocratic disdain of the commonplace; but these qualities are detached from time and place and are presented in an atmosphere of foreboding, as if the very qualities which separated his characters from the common herd were also the agents of their destruction. Son of an itinerant actress and a wayward father, Poe had no claim to status in the South. He could only develop his personal myth, that of a suffering, sensitive aristocrat in a democratic shopkeeper's world.

Though much of Poe's fiction presents a world in decay, he was capable of developing the paradisal theme. As a rule he located his paradise in some unspecified golden age of the past, before science and industry blighted the face of nature and warped the human soul. Unable to hypothecate with full conviction that happy time of the eighteenth century when Virginia gentlemen felt secure in their way of life, he felt that the paradisal estate could have approached reality only in the distant past, and that it would be regained only after the purification of man's heart and soul. Yet the one time that Poe undertook to describe an earthly paradise, he did it in terms that would have been quite congenial to Southerners like Cooke. The topography of "The Domain of Arnheim" is probably drawn from the Hudson River Valley, but Poe's "poet of the

---

[26] Of the two interests, field sports took precedence. Cooke's persistent amateurism is revealed in a letter to Rufus Wilmot Griswold about the *Froissart Ballads:* "I wrote them with the reluctance of a turkey hunter kept from his sport." January 20, 1847, in Allen, *Philip Pendleton Cooke,* 77–78.

landscape," Ellison, speaks as a Southerner committed to the agrarian ideal:

> The ideas of my friend may be summed up in a few words. He admitted but four elementary principles, or more strictly, conditions of bliss. That which he considered chief was (strange to say!) the simple and purely physical one of free exercise in the open air. 'The health,' he said, 'attainable by other means is scarcely worth the name.' He instanced the ecstasies of the fox-hunter, and pointed to the tillers of the earth, the only people who, as a class, can be fairly considered happier than others. His second condition was the love of woman. His third, and most difficult of realization, was the contempt of ambition. His fourth was an object of unceasing pursuit; and he held that, other things being equal, the extent of attainable happiness was in proportion to the spirituality of this object.

Certain elements of the agrarian ideal, or, more specifically, the "conditions of bliss" specified for Southern gentlemen, are obvious in Poe's words, but a passage from the work of David R. Hundley, an antebellum commentator on the social scene, displays the usual aspiration:

> No matter what may be the Southern Gentleman's avocation, his dearest affections usually centre in the country. He longs to live as his fathers lived before him, in both the Old World and the New; and he ever turns with unfeigned delight from the bustle of cities, the hollow ceremonies of courts, the turmoil of politics, the glories and dangers of the battle-field, or the wearisome treadmill of professional routine, to the quiet and peaceful scenes of country life. . . . The old hall, the familiar faces of the old domestics—these all are dearer to the heart of the Southern Gentleman than the short-lived plaudits of admiring throngs, or the hollow and unsatisfactory pleasures of sense.[27]

Poe's Ellison resembles Hundley's gentleman in his enjoyment of retirement, his relish of the peaceful scenes of country life, but there is a characteristic difference. Hundley's gentleman is content

[27] Quoted in Thorp (ed.), *A Southern Reader*, 249.

to live "as his fathers lived before him, in both the Old World and the New," but Poe's poet of the landscape must have, in addition to exercise in the open air and the love of woman (familiar Southern requirements), a spiritual object, an "object of unceasing pursuit." Even when Poe's imagination created an Arcadia in Southern terms, he had to carry it one step beyond to make it an aesthete's dream of perfection. Poe's Ellison does not inherit a way of life. Instead he inherits a fortune of $450,000,000, travels the world over to find an appropriate landscape, and then constructs his paradise from scratch. Once more Poe showed his disaffiliation at the same time that he revealed his Southern origin. Philip Cooke's "retirement" at the Vineyard, an estate his wife inherited from the Burwells (the Burwell family was one of the wealthiest in Virginia), was more typical. He had a splendid view of the mountains and the Shenandoah and the love of his wife, Willianne; he could amuse himself with gardening (although on an infinitely less grandiose scale than Ellison); and he had the spiritual object, his writing of the Froissart ballads. Furthermore, for Cooke as for Ellison, earning freedom from ambition was a difficult achievement. He wrote to his father, "I am becalmed out of the current which the great world of men is moving onward upon; am sunk into inglorious quiet, whilst my temper is for action . . . ." [28] Cooke, except for his temper for action, is very nearly typical of Hundley's Southern gentleman, whereas Poe's Ellison would have been in the South merely a parvenu, a disaffiliate who happened to be fortunate enough to inherit wealth but who created a way of life strictly on his own terms.

Edgar Poe's writing and even his life revealed the tension between what his imagination called for and what his situation permitted, a tension reinforced by his residence in a South committed in part to a romantic cult of chivalry that idealized the past and in part to concepts of improvement derived from the Enlightenment. If various aspects of the cult of chivalry engaged the romantic imagination, the course of events called for action dictated by reason and common sense. As we shall see, Edgar Poe exhibited both

[28] March 7, 1845, in Allen, *Philip Pendleton Cooke*, 65.

strains. As a critic of fiction he defended the romance and censured what he called the "anti-romantic" character of the American public. As a theorist he proclaimed that value resided in the exercise of sensibility afforded by poetry and that the moral suasion of poetry must be subordinate. Few Southern writers of his time stressed the aesthetic purpose of art as did Poe, but a conviction that hedonic value was the primary end of artistic expression was at least possible in a society which tended to think of art as a recreation. It would have been less likely in the New England subculture, where the Puritan tradition caused uneasiness about entertainment which was not morally or socially useful. The moral idea, as Henry James called it, was by no means alien to the Southern literary mind, but it did not receive particular stress in Southern literary criticism.[29]

Forced to become a journalistic critic, Poe became good at it. Almost miraculously, it seemed, he developed competitive ingenuities and employed them in support of T. W. White's inadequately financed magazine. He studied the tactics of successful periodicals and introduced into those areas of the *Messenger* for which he was responsible a professionalism that some Southerners, amateurs in

[29] Of the better-known Southern writers, Henry Timrod and Paul Hamilton Hayne, both a generation younger than Poe, did exhibit a moral bias. To Timrod truth was a nobler aim than beauty in a poem, and Hayne was prone to make moral judgments. See Edd Winfield Parks, *Ante-Bellum Southern Critics* (Athens, Ga., 1962), 203, 230. Even Hayne, however, was calling for analytical criticism as late as 1859. See Richard James Calhoun, "Literary Criticism in Southern Periodicals" (Ph.D. dissertation, University of North Carolina, 1959), 11–12. And Hayne praised E. P. Whipple as the one Northern critic who always judged on aesthetic grounds. Most Northern reviewers had dispensed with judicial criticism by 1840 in favor of what Harry Hayden Clark has called "sympathetically reproductive criticism." Professor Clark recognized that Poe's judicial method was characteristic of "contrasting Southern standards." See Clark, "Changing Attitudes in Early American Literary Criticism, 1800–1840," in Floyd Stovall (ed.), *The Development of American Literary Criticism* (Chapel Hill, 1955), 43–52. Whatever the moral bias of the particular critic, emphasis upon analysis and judgment would compel him to examine style and structure in order to make a competent evaluation. Moral judgments were not lacking in Southern criticism, even in that of Poe, but there was relatively more concern for aesthetic qualities than in the criticism of the North.

spirit, found difficult to understand. Poe's poems may bear a resemblance to those of the Southern occasional poets, but his criticism advanced standards equivalent to those of the most formidable British quarterlies. Other critics in America might wish to elevate the morals and manners of a raw new nation, but Edgar Poe drew upon the critical tradition of an older country in his concentration upon matters of taste.

His effort to improve taste was developed along lines familiar to the South, although many Southern writers were hostile toward stringent book reviews. Still, Southerners who read anything at all read the harsh reviews of the British quarterlies and recognized the tactics of the so-called "tomahawk" review when Poe employed them in the *Messenger*. Many of them approved, for Southerners were prone to sanction the validity of the rhetorical approach and, as Richard James Calhoun has shown, stressed the analytical method. Calhoun argues that the nature of Southern criticism reflects the "legalistic bent of the cultivated Southern mind." [30] Over thirty years ago Margaret Alterton maintained that the influence of the law helped shape Poe's practice as a critic,[31] and in principle she was correct, though her assumption that William Wirt, a famous jurist, acted as a mentor for the young Poe was subsequently disproved.[32] Poe's tendency as a book reviewer was to make judgments and to amass evidence to prove that they were valid.

Equally important, however, was the strain of literary conservatism in the South, something to be expected in a predominantly rural region. Publishing centers and opportunities for literary debate were mostly in the North, and though Poe spent a few of his formative years in Baltimore, he started reviewing books in Richmond, which was not much more than a village in 1835; and his first distinctive maneuver in the critical arena was an assault upon a member of a New York literary clique. Romantic in his taste and in

[30] "Literary Criticism in Southern Periodicals," 11–37, 71–72.
[31] *Origins of Poe's Critical Theory* (Iowa City, 1925), 46–67.
[32] Richard Beale Davis, "Poe and William Wirt," *American Literature*, XVI (1944), 212–20.

his creative efforts, Poe showed the conservative strain in his book reviews. We will find in his practical criticism what have been generally recognized as eighteenth-century tendencies. These tendencies, however, should be traced not to the Age of Pope, with its stress upon rules allegedly drawn from the practice of classic writers, but to the late eighteenth century, when critical constants were derived from what were considered to be the laws of human nature, discovered by psychological investigation. A complex of traditional ideas were instrumental in the formation of Poe's critical theory and practice, particularly in his modification of romantic aesthetics to serve his own needs and convictions.

2

No critic works in an intellectual vacuum. However he may concentrate on the technical aspects of art, as Poe was prone to do in his book reviews, he will still owe something to the prevalent epistemologies of his time and place; and in a period of transition conflicting tendencies are inevitably present. Poe's only advanced schooling was at the University of Virginia, where, because of the influence of Thomas Jefferson, the ideas of the Enlightenment were still predominant.[33] As has already been indicated, the Enlightenment strain was evident in Lucian Minor, one of the most influential members of the *Messenger* circle. Accordingly, it is not surprising that Poe as a literary critic often made use of the kinds of arguments and proofs characteristic of the Enlightenment. He rarely acknowledged his Enlightenment sources, as he did when he was using the authority of the romantic critics, such as Coleridge and August Wilhelm Schlegel, who were not as familiar to the American public, yet the substratum of Enlightenment thought

[33] This point was made by Philip A. Bruce, in *The History of the University of Virginia* (New York, 1920–22), but for a more recent account of the way in which Jefferson attempted to establish a liberal, republican institution, see Davis, *Intellectual Life in Jefferson's Virginia*, 62–66. For Jefferson's thought, see Adrienne Koch, *The Philosophy of Thomas Jefferson* (New York, 1943); and Herbert W. Schneider, "The Enlightenment of Thomas Jefferson," *Ethics*, LIII (1943), 246–54.

and Enlightenment method is evident in most of his work as a critic. As a youthful romantic it was incumbent on him to protest; it was the proper role for a poet. When he became a critic, however, and found it necessary to validate his claims, he began to use the kind of proofs that had been repugnant to the young poet, the proofs of reason, common sense, and what he thought of as scientific demonstration—the proofs of the Enlightenment.

When we speak of the Enlightenment in America, we must speak of the Scottish common-sense school of philosophers, for theirs was the most significant philosophical tradition in America between the time of the Revolution and the time Poe began to write book reviews.[34] Moreover, the literary critics who were either affiliated with the Scottish school or whose ideas were derived from it were very influential in America. As William Charvat has shown, the most popular periodicals in America during Poe's youth were the *Edinburgh Review*, the *Quarterly Review*, and Campbell's *New Monthly Magazine*, all of which were edited by Scots in the critical and philosophical tradition of the common-sense school.[35] Lord Kames, better known as a literary critic than as a philosopher, has been considered by one historian as a founder of the Scottish school.[36] Hugh Blair's famous *Lectures on Rhetoric and Belles Lettres* may be regarded in part as an application of Kames's theories. The less well-known but still influential work of Archibald Alison was in the Scottish tradition, and Lord Jeffrey of the *Edinburgh Review* was strongly influenced by Alison. These men were, with the possible exception of Edmund Burke and Dr. Johnson, the most frequently cited authorities; and two of them, Kames and Blair, produced books that were as ubiquitously studied in secondary schools and colleges as the texts of Cleanth Brooks and Robert Penn Warren have been in our own time.[37]

[34] Herbert W. Schneider, A *History of American Philosophy* (New York, 1946), 246.

[35] *American Critical Thought, 1810–1835* (Philadelphia, 1936), 29.

[36] Henry Laurie, *Scottish Philosophy in its National Development* (Glasgow, 1902), 103.

[37] This fact has been documented almost too many times to require reference. David Potter, in the Foreword to a recent facsimile edition of Blair's

It would be surprising, indeed, if Poe had remained unaffected by the most popular philosophical and critical traditions of his time, but this influence, so far as it may be detected, is covert, representing as it does a body of opinion that was taken for granted. Nevertheless the influence is there, and it furnished Poe with some of his basic arguments about the nature of the human mind and, in turn, about the origin and effect of aesthetic feeling. Poe's more specific literary applications of these authorities will be examined in the context of his criticism; here only the general attitudes and widely adopted psychophilosophical premises will be discussed.

Commentators on Poe from Woodberry to Feidelson have noted his attempts to reconcile materialism and idealism.[38] In this context it would be more precise to say that he sought to bring those intuitive agencies of truth and beauty posited by both the Scottish philosophers and the post-Kantian transcendentalists within the scope of a materialistic psychology. Poe never discounted suprarational experiences, but in order to prove that such experiences had value, he felt that he had to locate their origin in faculties of the human mind. If this could be done, they would be regarded as natural and hence necessary. It was in this endeavor that the psychology of the Scottish common-sense school and phrenology, which must be regarded as a physiological extrapolation from the premise of discrete mental powers, fell readily to Poe's hand.

The Scottish realists opposed both the idealism of Berkeley and the skepticism of Hume; such "metaphysical reasoning," they felt, rashly ignored nature's laws and the constitution of the human mind. Nature is real, said the Scottish philosophers. The senses, whether they are the external senses by which man perceives the

---

Lectures, stated that "at least one hundred and thirty editions were issued, the last in 1911." Hugh Blair, *Lectures on Rhetoric and Belles Lettres,* ed. Harold F. Harding (2 vols.; Carbondale, Ill., 1965), I, v. For the popularity of Kames, see Helen Whitcomb Randall, *The Critical Theory of Lord Kames,* Smith College *Studies in Modern Languages,* XII (October, 1940–July, 1941), 85. For the popularity of both critics, see Charvat, *American Critical Thought,* 30–33.

[38] George E. Woodberry, *The Life of Edgar Allan Poe* (New York, 1909), II, 250; Charles Feidelson, Jr., *Symbolism and American Literature* (Chicago, 1953), 38.

world or the internal senses by which he apprehends the beautiful and the good, give us valid information about the objects of perception.

John Witherspoon, one of the first proponents of the Scottish philosophy in America, emphasized its dislike for metaphysics. "The truth is," he wrote, "the immaterial system is a wild and ridiculous attempt to unsettle the principles of common sense by metaphysical reasoning." [39] Samuel Stanhope Smith, president of the College of New Jersey (Princeton) from 1795 to 1819, defined the method of the Scots as "an investigation of the constitution and laws of nature, both in the physical and moral worlds, as far as the powers of the human mind, unaided by the lights of revelation, are competent to discover . . . ." [40] Dugald Stewart, who was influential on Thomas Jefferson and fairly well known in the South,[41] wrote of the "frivolous and absurd discussions which abound in the writings of most metaphysical authors . . . ." He was much kinder to the materialists: "Instead, therefore, of objecting to the scheme of materialism, that its conclusions are false, it would be more accurate to say, that its aim is unphilosophical . . . , since matter and mind, considered as objects of human study, are essentially different; the science of the former resting ultimately on the phenomena exhibited to the senses; that of the latter, on the phenomena of which we are conscious." [42]

The Scottish philosophers, insofar as Stewart is typical, thought that speculation concerning final causes, if it were based upon an

[39] Quoted in Jay Wharton Fay, *American Psychology before William James* (New Brunswick, 1939), 61.

[40] Quoted *ibid.*, 62.

[41] Margaret Alterton made a case for Poe's familiarity with Dugald Stewart on the basis of an article entitled "Genius" which appeared in the *Southern Literary Messenger* in 1836 (II, 297). Poe did not write the article, as Miss Alterton assumed (*Origins of Poe's Critical Theory*, 97), but as assistant editor he would have had to read it. In fact, the editorial note appended to the article and disagreeing with some of the assumptions is almost certainly by Poe. The author was "evidently no phrenologist," Poe wrote. *Southern Literary Messenger*, II (1836), 300.

[42] *Elements of the Philosophy of the Human Mind* (Albany, 1821), I, 9–14 *passim*.

examination of natural laws, was not inconsistent with their method. Stewart quoted Newton's *Optics* in support of his position and threw in a good word for the French Physiocrats (the source of many of Jefferson's ideas), who considered "the physical and moral laws of Nature as the unerring standard which the legislator should keep in view in all of his positive institutions." [43] Purely rational speculation, however, or a blind reliance upon supernatural revelation, as in the literalist interpretation of the Bible, were equally chimerical in comparison with the common-sense method. It is very probable that the distaste for metaphysics and mysticism apparent in many American reviews of Coleridge during the 1820's owes much to the Scottish tradition.[44] Later chapters of this study will show that Poe himself, after his initial enthusiasm for Coleridge, began increasingly to rely upon what he considered the laws of nature, as revealed by science and interpreted by common sense. Like Stewart, he took "the physical and moral laws of Nature as the unerring standard." The construction of the universe and the constitution of the human mind became the bases for Poe's literary principles.

The chief significance of the Scottish philosophy, as far as literary criticism was concerned, was that it emphasized an investigation of consciousness. The method was not scientific, in the sense of modern experimental psychology, for it had little to do with physiology. Still, it opened the door for physiological investigation by its hostility toward "metaphysical reasoning" and by the presumption that there must be in the human mind certain natural powers or faculties responsible for intuitive cognitions—those things which we appear to know without having to think about them. In general this intuitive knowledge was called "common" sense, common because everybody had it to some degree. Two particular categories of intuitive knowledge with which the Scottish philosophers were concerned had to do with the beautiful and the good. One did not have to *think* about whether an object was beautiful or ugly or whether an action was good or bad; one just *knew*, and such knowledge appeared to have the immediacy of

[43] *Ibid.*, 240.   [44] Charvat, *American Critical Thought*, 21–22.

sense perception. Accordingly, "inner" senses were posited, and they were called the "taste" and the "moral sense." Sometimes the taste and the moral sense were thought of simplistically as functioning in much the same way as the external senses, except that the stimuli were different. By the second half of the eighteenth century, however, it was recognized that these intuitive capacities were complex in their operation, and though the old terminology was still used, the references were metaphorical and did not designate specific organs. Nevertheless the activity of these faculties remained a subject for empirical investigation, and it was concluded that these seemingly intuitive capacities could be nurtured. According to Lord Kames, for instance, the moral sense was innate, but it remained rudimentary among savages. It was educable, however, and could be improved until the finest and most delicate moral discriminations could be made.[45]

Historically, the third Earl of Shaftesbury was the first British writer to emphasize this "inner" sense as a guide to conduct; but Shaftesbury, something of an aesthete, came so close to identifying the good with the beautiful that he regarded a response to the beauty of an action as a moral feeling. Francis Hutcheson, one of the forerunners of the Scottish school, followed the lead of Shaftesbury in combining reflections on beauty and morality and stressed the beauty of right actions and feelings as an element in their appeal. However, Hutcheson considered the moral sense and the sense of beauty as separate faculties, and thenceforth the distinction was taken for granted among the Scottish philosophers. The interest in the aesthetic aspects of goodness remained strong, and it was thought that there was a close connection between good morals and good taste. As Lord Kames expressed it, "a taste in the fine arts goes hand in hand with the moral sense, to which indeed it is nearly allied." [46]

It was easy for Americans, particularly for those who inherited the Puritan attitude that art could be validated only by its moral

[45] Henry Home, Lord Kames, *Sketches of the History of Man* (Glasgow, 1818), I, 105.
[46] *Elements of Criticism*, ed. Abraham Mills (New York, 1858), 13.

usefulness, to argue from Kames that because of the close association of the taste with the moral sense, whatever was good was
beautiful, and that an art which was productive of sound morality
automatically fulfilled any aesthetic requirements. Even Thomas
Jefferson, who could scarcely be considered an heir of the Puritans,
claimed that moral action was beautiful: "When any signal act of
charity or of gratitude, for instance, is presented either to our sight
or imagination, we are deeply impressed with it's [sic] beauty and
feel a strong desire in ourselves of doing charitable and grateful acts
also. On the contrary, when we see or read of any atrocious deed,
we are disgusted with it's [sic] deformity, and conceive an abhorrence of vice." [47] Thus for Jefferson the arts could be morally useful by depicting acts "of charity or of gratitude" to be emulated.

A more surprising account of the moral usefulness of the taste
may be found in the writings of the Reverend Asa Burton, a Congregationalist minister of Jefferson's generation. He broadened the
concept of the taste so that it was responsible for all reactions of
gratification or disgust and proclaimed it the primary faculty of
the mind: "The faculty of taste is the most important property
of the mind. It is the seat of all our pleasures and pains; contains
all the principles of action, which govern men; it is the fountain of vice and virtue, and according to its nature when we bid
farewell to life, such will be our endless state beyond the grave." [48]
Burton was trying to reinforce the religious psychology of Jonathan
Edwards by proving that nothing could take the place of a genuine
sense of the beauty of virtue; he was by no means trying to claim
that aesthetic appreciation could supplant religion. Nevertheless,
his view of *taste* as the "fountain of virtue and vice" illustrates the
dilemma of the American theorists who wished to use the aesthetic

---

[47] Thomas Jefferson to Robert Skipwith, August 3, 1771, in Julian P.
Boyd (ed.), *The Papers of Thomas Jefferson* (Princeton, 1950), I, 76.

[48] Burton was a Congregationalist minister whose division of the faculties
into the understanding, the will, and the taste was based on his reading of
Kant. His definition of the faculty of taste as the seat of all feelings of pleasure and pain was much broader than that of the Scottish philosophers. Extensive quotations from Burton's work may be found in Fay, *American Psychology before William James*, 75–90.

sense to validate morally useful art. Emerson gave a characteristically American solution when he declared in his essay "Nature" that a noble moral action confers beauty upon its attendant circumstances.

These examples of speculation about the function of the aesthetic sense in relation to morals are cited merely to show that when Poe undertook to define the province of art he was engaging in a well-established debate about the role of the separate faculties in governing or influencing human behavior. As we shall see, he reversed the usual priorities. If a Burton or an Emerson could argue that what was good had to be beautiful, Edgar Poe could counter with the argument that what was beautiful had to be good and that beautiful art had an indirect effect upon behavior simply because it was beautiful.

Poe separated the faculty of taste from the moral sense just as Kames and Thomas Jefferson did,[49] and he asserted that if man's education had been governed by the sense of the beautiful instead of by the practical reason, he would have been better and happier. However much he may have preached against the heresy of the didactic, Poe did not eliminate moral beauty from the proper concerns of poetry. As will be shown in a later chapter, he merely wished to limit the mode of thematic expression. In poetry virtue should be depicted, not explicitly developed as a thesis. It should be beautifully presented to the imagination in order that the aesthetic sense might perform its function properly in influencing behavior. When a moral thesis is a mere exemplum, without the

---

[49] Jefferson made the distinction in a letter to Thomas Law, dated June 13, 1814: "The *To Kalon* . . . is founded in a different faculty, that of taste, which is not even a branch of morality. We have indeed an innate sense of what we call beautiful, but that is exercised chiefly on subjects addressed to the fancy, whether through the eye in visible forms, as landscape, animal figure, dress, drapery, architecture, the composition of colors, etc., or to the imagination directly, as imagery, style, or measure in prose or poetry, or whatever else constitutes the domain of criticism or taste, a faculty entirely distinct from the moral one." Andrew A. Lipscomb and Albert L. Bergh (eds.), *The Writings of Thomas Jefferson* (Washington, D.C., 1903), XIV, 141.

conditioning attributes of beauty, it appeals to the conscience as duty. When a moral thesis is *argued*, it is up to the reason to decide on its validity. Morality can be properly presented by the fine arts only when the aesthetic quality of the presentation is a governing consideration.

These matters will be examined in detail in appropriate contexts; however, it should be made clear at the outset that Poe's validation of his principles depended in large measure upon a well-established psychological tradition. On the face of it, any sharing of ideas between the epigones of the Scottish common-sense school and the ultraromantic Poe, whose imagination wandered in the wild and the weird, would seem absurd. Yet as a literary critic Poe was eclectic and sought to have the best of both worlds, that of the soaring imagination and that of a practical methodology based upon "mental science." [50] His excursions into conflicting epistemologies remind us in a way of William James, whose radical empiricism allowed him to concede the possibility of pragmatic truth to any aspect of experience, the most visionary or the most mundane. Though no transcendentalist went further in acknowledging the claims of a suprarational experience of beauty, Poe, especially during the 1840's, expressed contempt for metaphysical speculation, just as did the Scots, and he was prone to sneer at the transcendentalists as perverters of a noble philosophy.

Increasingly, as he grew older, Poe began to demand reason and common sense as mediators between the imaginative vision and its revelation in a work of art. Accordingly, it would appear that when he began to grapple with the problems of criticism, he felt it necessary to find rational explanations of the mental and emotional phenomena of the creative act. Such explanations, he hoped, would allow him to control the creative experience and to validate his lit-

[50] Léon Lemonnier exaggerated Poe's dedication to science by claiming that Poe resembled doctors who refused to believe in the soul because they could not discover it by dissection, but the discussion of science and materialism in his study of critical reaction to Poe in France is well worth reading. See Lemonnier, *Edgar Poe et la critique française de 1845 à 1875* (Paris, 1928).

erary judgments scientifically. As a literary critic, Poe wanted a clear and simple system of psychology which he could regard, in Enlightenment fashion, as the laws of human nature. The Scottish philosophers provided such a system, which may be illustrated from the writings of Dugald Stewart.

Stewart hoped to achieve an understanding of the human mind that would enable him to suggest ways of controlling its aberrant tendencies. Today his *Elements of the Philosophy of the Human Mind* would be called a textbook in educational psychology, for he believed that proper educational methods, developed by an "accurate analysis of the general principles of our nature, and an account of the most important laws which regulate their operation," would eliminate the possibility of overemphasizing one talent or tendency at the expense of the others. For Stewart an unbalanced mind was quite literally a mind whose faculties existed in disproportionate strength. Such disproportion, even though it might result in what appeared to be original genius, was inimical to the happiness of the individual and the welfare of society. In opposition to primitivistic concepts of natural genius, Stewart wrote: "happiness, in so far as it arises from the mind itself, will be always proportioned to the degree of perfection which its powers have attained; but that, in cultivating those powers, with a view to this most important of all objects, it is essentially necessary that such a degree of attention be bestowed upon all of them, as may preserve them in that state of relative strength, which appears to be agreeable to the intentions of nature." [51]

Edgar Poe also believed that mental perfection was represented by a proportionate development of the powers of the mind, as is revealed by one of his discussions of genius: "what is the fact, as taught us by analysis of mental power? Simply, that highest genius . . . is but the result of generally large mental power existing in a state of absolute proportion—so that no one faculty has undue predominance." [52] Stewart apparently believed that hereditary weak-

[51] *Elements of the Philosophy of the Human Mind*, I, 22.
[52] "Fifty Suggestions," *Works*, XIV, 176.

nesses could be corrected by appropriate education, and accordingly he opposed specialization.[53] Poe was very little concerned with public education, but the few remarks he did make, even in the context of fiction, indicate that he thought that most of the unhappiness in the world was caused by emphasis upon practical knowledge—the reason—at the expense of the taste, or the aesthetic faculty.[54] The poetical faculties, Poe was to insist, are not at war with the mathematical faculties, and a true genius would give evidence of both. In his tales which depict neurosis Poe showed what happens when certain faculties have hypertrophied as others have withered; and in his criticism he used the psychological principle of a mental "balance of powers" in accounting for certain excellences and defects. There are many men of genius in terms of native endowment, he said, but few works of genius, because a work of genius requires the proper employment of the full mental equipment, each faculty being exerted at will in the appropriate stages of composition. The greatest error in the composition of po-

[53] *Elements of the Philosophy of the Human Mind,* I, 18–22. Stewart did not want to discourage a natural talent in a particular activity, say the "abstract sciences." This would be frustrating the intention of nature. What he wanted to do by education was to develop other talents so that the individual would be a whole man instead of an unhappy and neurotic genius remarkable, say, in mathematical ability, but "deficient in vivacity, in imagination, and in taste." If Poe's tales were a projection of his personal situation, as is frequently suggested, then the attractions of "mental science" are easily explained. Stewart's psychology offered some hope in that it stressed the correction of hereditary weaknesses by the "exercise" of the subnormal faculties. Phrenology was even more attractive in this respect, for it provided the means for an easy self-analysis together with suggestions for a sort of self-administered therapy. It may be that Poe's pride in his mathematical abilities and in his capacity for analysis was a rationalization of his fear that, like Roderick Usher's, his sensibility was abnormally developed at the expense of "moral energy." This would account for the *doppelganger* motif in his tales and also for his eagerness to be a man of universal erudition, a type of true genius whose faculties were proportionally developed.

[54] This complaint appears in "The Colloquy of Monos and Una" in the context of a polemic against applied science. As Poe explained in a footnote, he was recommending a general education of the sensibility, which he referred to elsewhere as the capacity to appreciate beauty and loathe deformity in whatever context they might appear.

etry, he would assert more than once, was to use the reason or the moral sense in a mental activity appropriate to the aesthetic sensibility; but since a genius possessed a full complement of mental powers he would be equally averse to using the sensibility alone in an activity appropriate to the reason.[55]

Throughout his career as a critic Poe insisted that the greatest art could be produced only by an artist whose faculties existed in the balance and proportion that was the intention of nature. Although imagination and taste were characteristic of the creative mind, it took more than creative talent to produce a great work of art. Judgment, reason, patience, and the capacity for labor, Poe was to affirm on a number of occasions, were necessary to produce a good poem. Shelley was an artist with great imaginative power, but in Poe's opinion he relied too much on natural genius. As a consequence, Poe said, Shelley's poems were merely rough drafts or notes to himself; they were not finished works of art.

Poe constructed his critical theory upon a psychological basis, and the psychological systems he used reflected the Enlightenment premise that human nature in perfection would exhibit the balance and proportion of the physical universe. There were laws for mental activity as precise as the laws of physics, and to obey these laws was to carry out the intention of nature. In this he resembled Emerson, but he differed from the Concord sage in that he did not conceive of the creative mind as a relatively passive medium through which a vitalizing current of inspiration poured. Like the Scottish philosophers, Poe was prone to confine his investigation to the activity of the conscious mind and had relatively little to say about inspiration, although what little he did say was sometimes transcendental enough to enable a number of investigators to dis-

---

[55] In other words, nature should be followed by using each faculty according to the purpose for which it was "designed." The faculties were allowed to cooperate, but priority should be assigned for teleological reasons. Writing a critique, for instance, is an analytical activity which occurred *after* the initial impression of a poem on the sensibility. Poe gave "Christopher North" (John Wilson) as an example of a critic who depended too much on his sensibility. Review of Wilson's *Critical and Miscellaneous Essays*, in *Graham's Magazine*, XX (1842), 72.

cover similarities between Poe's theory and that of Emerson. As a practicing critic, however, Poe concentrated on the mental activities that permitted conscious control. Even poetic vision, he once speculated, could be brought under the domination of the will if the proper conditions could be established.

Poe's first significant use of a psychological approach in criticism appears to have little to do with the traditional faculty psychology. His chief resource was phrenology, which the nineteenth century called the "science of mind," and he amplified his phrenological concepts of various mental organs with a quasi-Coleridgean account of the imagination and the fancy. This is the subject of a later chapter, however, and phrenology is discussed here only because its premises about the mind are not so alien to the Scottish faculty psychology as they might appear. Phrenology was popularized in America chiefly through the books of George Combe, whose works went through many editions in America between 1830 and 1845. Combe, a Scot himself, claimed that his writings were nothing more than an extension and refinement of the old faculty psychology. His was a "humble attempt" to enlarge the "mental philosophy" of Hutcheson, Adam Smith, Thomas Reid, Stewart, and Thomas Brown "with the aid of the new lights afforded by Phrenology." [56] Poe knew of Combe's work in 1836 and mentioned it in his review of the *Phrenology* of Mrs. L. Miles. Edinburgh, Poe asserted, was the "stronghold of faith in phrenology," [57] and he gave every evidence of having faith in it himself.

It has already been mentioned that the Scottish philosophers, though they neglected physiology themselves, had left the way open for physiological investigation. They had written somewhat vaguely of a few faculties or "active principles" and had designated them as the reason, the taste, the moral sense, the imagination, and so forth. The phrenologists took the inevitable next step by ascrib-

[56] *The Constitution of Man Considered in Relation to External Objects*, ed. Joseph A. Warne (9th American ed.; Boston, 1839), ix. Poe mentioned Combe several times in his reviews and in 1841 praised him highly as a "candid reasoner" who "reasons to discover the true." *Works*, X, 158.
[57] *Works*, VIII, 252–53.

ing all mental activities to various "organs" of the mind. They invented names for these organs and claimed to be able to analyze character by measuring the prominences on the human skull. Just as the Scottish philosophers had claimed that they were investigating the "constitution and laws of nature in both the physical and moral worlds," so did George Combe claim to be investigating the constitution of the human mind and the fixed laws by which it was regulated.[58] He was as certain as was Dugald Stewart that by learning the natural laws of the intellect man could direct his activities in accordance with nature's intentions.

Clearly phrenology developed out of Enlightenment assumptions about man's relation to the universe, and it made use of the traditional teleological argument: one assumes the benevolence of the Great Designer and confirms the assumption by examining his designs. Poe, whose head was filled with Enlightenment science, was delighted with phrenology because it purported to validate the teleological argument with proofs as precise as those obtained in the physical sciences. The fact that the phrenologist could actually locate the organ for aesthetic feeling seemed to Poe adequate proof that there was not only an immediate cause for art but a final cause as well. The Great Designer *intended* for man to respond to the beautiful in nature and in art. Eventually Poe became dubious about the validity of the phrenological method because it was based upon a priori assumptions, but then he resorted to the old faculty psychology to support his claims about the nature of the aesthetic response and its final cause, and his proofs remain equally unscientific to our eyes today.

Poe's criticism as a whole falls into two categories: literary criticism and rhetorical criticism. When he was writing as a literary critic, he attempted to discover universal validating principles and made occasional ventures into aesthetics. As a rhetorical critic, however, he concerned himself with the effect of a literary work and examined the means by which appropriate or inappropriate effects were produced. Not that he would have made any such distinction, for most of his effort was devoted to transforming what

[58] *The Constitution of Man*, 28.

was essentially rhetoric, or the calculation of effects, into universal procedures which he considered equally valid for composition or for judgment. In this he is reminiscent of the British psychological critics of the late eighteenth century, who had rejected the rules in favor of an analysis of the response to a work of art. As Edward N. Hooker observed, "It was undoubtedly in the minds of these essayists that from observations of the general reaction to works of art, principles of beauty could be deduced, in a manner more or less scientific, which should have the certainty of mathematics." [59] This is precisely what Poe sought—the certainty of mathematics in the calculation and the judgment of effects—even though he made use of the postulates of Platonic metaphysics to support the value of a relatively pure aesthetic response. There was nothing unusual about this. Even the phrenologist George Combe did the same thing, as did some of the Scottish philosophers. As a rule Poe refused to accept the old neoclassic test of universal approval, the *consensus gentium*, for, like Lord Kames and Sir Francis Jeffrey before him, he considered only the cultivated taste capable of making correct discriminations. Even with this opinion, however, he did not want to neglect the needs of a general audience. Believing that the proper test of art was its effect, he felt that it was possible to appeal to both the cultivated and the uncultivated taste.

3

The theorists referred to in the preceding pages are not "sources" in the sense that Coleridge was a source for Poe. I have used them here only as illustrations of an intellectual ambience to which he was, in part, responsive. Poe's wide and often superficial reading of current journals and of popular compendiums of "universal" knowledge makes the task of identifying the exact sources of his opinions difficult and often unprofitable. Because he was eclectic and not highly discriminative in his choices, we cannot justifiably claim that he was a disciple of any particular critic or school of criticism.

[59] "The Discussion of Taste from 1750 to 1770, and the New Trends in Literary Criticism," PMLA, XLIX (1934), 581.

W. K. Wimsatt's generalization that "Poe's ideas are Kantian and Coleridgean aesthetic undergoing the fate of M. Valdemar" [60] is no more adequate than John Paul Pritchard's assertion that Poe's "final definition of art . . . is substantially Aristotle's doctrine of *mimesis* or artistic imitation." [61] Categorical assignments, untrustworthy at best, are especially unreliable in reference to Poe.

Eventually Poe proposed a theory of the universe which would reconcile the conflicting epistemologies that appear by intimation or by direct reference in his work. This effort at a synthesis was his *Eureka*, which he presented in lectures during the last year of his life, but which was published only after his death. A discussion of *Eureka* is reserved for the last chapters of this study. It is inconceivable that Poe would have learned nothing in the eighteen years between his first critical essay and his final statement. We shall follow from here the development of his thought and his critical method, showing his enthusiasm when he encountered what seemed to him to be a new and superior mode of validation, but also showing his rejection of that mode when it proved inadequate to his needs.

[60] William K. Wimsatt, Jr., and Cleanth Brooks, *Literary Criticism: A Short History* (New York, 1966), 479.

[61] *Criticism in America* (Norman, Okla., 1956), 72.

II · "Letter to Mr. —— ——"

BEFORE 1831, when Edgar Poe published his third book of verse, he had wanted only to be a poet; but his first two publications, *Tamerlane and Other Poems* (1827) and *Al Aaraaf, Tamerlane and Minor Poems* (1829), had met the usual fate of a poet's first efforts. It was necessary for him to attract the attention of an indifferent public, so, as Wordsworth had done before him, he composed a preface designed to explain his own concept of poetry and to discredit theories that supported a different kind of verse. The preface, which he called "Letter to Mr. —— ——,"[1] appeared in his *Poems, Second Edition* (1831). This "letter" appears to be a spontaneous protest against the dullness and pedantry of the Lake School of poets. It was the duty of a poet to protest, Poe announced, not to engage with metaphysical subtleties in the manner of a philosopher. He was a young man of feeling like the late John Keats, and he wanted the world to know it. Yet Poe was being somewhat less than candid. A close examination of the "letter" will show not only that he had a well-defined concept of the purpose of poetry but also that he had read enough criticism to support it. His supporting argument is largely covert, however, for it was necessary for him to preserve the stance of a young man of sensibility proclaiming his affection for the muse.

A question occasionally debated is whether or not Poe matured as a critic. Some have held that his aesthetic ideas never developed beyond this earliest expression, and one reliable authority has argued convincingly that Poe's critical theory is implicit in his early verse.[2] This position is defensible if we say "some aspects of his

[1] I have used the 1831 version of this essay with its less familiar title because the "Letter to B——," as printed in the *Southern Literary Messenger* for July, 1836, omits one significant statement. The text of the 1831 version may be found in Poe's *Poems, Second Edition*, Facsimile Text Society (New York, 1936).

[2] Davidson, *Poe: A Critical Study*, 2.

theory," for the "letter" expresses several convictions about the nature and purpose of poetry that Poe never abandoned. Poe arrived at his idea of the priority of aesthetic value very early in his career, but his development of an argument to support aesthetic value required frequent reassessment of his proofs. Poe's general attitude was common among romantic poets, but as he began to justify it his difference from most of his contemporaries emerged; for his polemical strategies resulted in an emphasis on expressive form that was relatively uncommon in America, though it was familiar enough in Europe.[3]

One subject which has attracted the attention of scholars for many years has been the nature and extent of Poe's borrowings from other critics. Coleridge has been considered a major influence, and rightly so.[4] Yet even in the "Letter to Mr. ———— ————," where Poe appropriated almost exactly Coleridge's distinction between poetry and science, he claimed to dispute the authority of both Wordsworth and Coleridge, while at the same time professing his admiration for Coleridge's "towering intellect" and "gigantic

---

[3] M. H. Abrams has described the development of the concept of the lyric as poetic norm in British criticism but has then gone on to show that the expressive theory, which exalted music as the pure expression of feeling, reached an extreme among the German *Frühromantiker*. See *The Mirror and the Lamp* (Norton Library ed.; New York, 1958), 84–94. It is possible that Poe, even at the age of twenty-two, had learned something of German aesthetics from his reading of British journals, but it is unlikely that he had more than a marginal acquaintance, if any at all, with the pertinent texts. Henry A. Pochmann has listed Poe's references to Herder, Novalis, Tieck, Hoffman, and A. W. Schlegel, but the references were all made later. See *German Culture in America* (Madison, Wis., 1957), 393–97, 722. Poe's interest in German literature might have been aroused by George Blaetterman, professor of modern languages at the University of Virginia and a native of Germany, but the best evidence points toward Poe's having studied only Latin and French, and possibly Italian and Spanish. See Arthur Hobson Quinn, *Edgar Allan Poe: A Critical Biography* (New York, 1941), 99–101. The troublesome problem of Poe's knowledge of German language and literature has been handled by a number of competent specialists, and I will limit myself here to the background in British aesthetics that was almost certainly familiar to him.

[4] See Floyd Stovall, "Poe's Debt to Coleridge," University of Texas *Studies in English*, X (1930), 70–127.

power." The grounds of his disagreement with Wordsworth were made very clear, but the only charge he brought against Coleridge was that the critic "goes wrong by reason of his very profundity. . . ." Ordinarily we would need to explore no further. Romantic anti-intellectualism has been discussed too many times to require additional exegesis. Poe's statements in the "letter" remind us of Rousseau's indictment of reason: "C'est que quand l'homme commence á raisonner, il cesse sentir." At about the same age at which Poe wrote his "letter," Keats had written letters to Richard Woodhouse condemning Wordsworth and Coleridge for philosophizing instead of being content with feeling. It is from the fragmentary remarks in these letters, as explained by subsequent scholarship, that we know Keats's literary theory. A similar procedure may be employed with Poe in an attempt to reconstruct from his "Letter to Mr. —— ——" not only what he thought about poetry at the time but also the various assumptions, psychological and aesthetic, that would have supported him in his argument. By this means Poe's dispute with Coleridge and Wordsworth, if it is reflective of anything more than a young man's protest against his elders, can be understood and placed in historical perspective.

The concluding paragraph of Poe's "letter" begins with a close paraphrase of a statement in Chapter XIV of the *Biographia Literaria:* "A poem, in my opinion, is opposed to a work of science by having, for its *immediate* object, pleasure, not truth . . . ." Then Poe omits the second half of Coleridge's sentence, which distinguishes the poem from other pleasure-giving literary forms (the novel and the romance), and substitutes a distinction of his own. The difference is crucial to our understanding of Poe.

In the omitted passage Coleridge stated that a poem could be distinguished from other pleasurable genres "by proposing to itself such delight from the *whole,* as is compatible with a distinct gratification from each component *part.*" The only reason that Poe would have left Coleridge at this point would have been that he thought Coleridge's distinction inadequate. Poe's substitution must be quoted in full because his terminology provides clues to his assumptions about the way the mind works in perceiving beauty; and these assumptions, in turn, provide grounds for his opposition to Coleridge and, in a different sense, to Wordsworth.

> A poem . . . is opposed . . . to romance, by having for its object an *indefinite* instead of a *definite* pleasure, being a poem only so far as this object is attained; romance presenting perceptible images with definite, poetry with *indefinite* sensations, to which end music is *essential*, since the comprehension of sweet sound is our most indefinite conception. Music, when combined with a pleasurable idea, is poetry; music without the idea is simply music; the idea without the music is prose from its very definitiveness.

Poe's proposition in this passage is simple enough. He thought that poetry, being in metrical form, should not attempt to express clear and definite ideas but should be limited in its aim to some sort of vague pleasure. Still, any proposition, however naïve, has something back of it. We can better understand Poe's unsupported assertion if we examine the aesthetic theories which at twenty-two, in his time and place, he would have been most likely to encounter —and we should remember that he had spent much of the time between the ages of eighteen and twenty-two in the army and at West Point, situations hardly conducive to literary study.

Poe used the term "sensation" in reference to what is felt from the "perceptible images" of both the romance and the poem.[5] If he was using the term in its strict significance and not loosely as a synonym for feeling or emotion, there can be only one assumption about the aesthetic response that justifies the usage. This assumption, which has been described briefly in Chapter I, was that an internal sense was responsible for aesthetic feeling, and that it was analogous in a certain way to the external senses. According to Gordon McKenzie, the notion of an internal sense of taste was

[5] We must understand the romance as a highly imaginative prose narrative, not as a metrical romance. Sir Walter Scott had given currency to the distinction between the prose romance and the novel, and it was employed in America by Hawthorne and Simms, as well as by Poe. Coleridge referred to the romance *and* the novel, but Poe omitted the novel, probably because he thought that the romance differed from the poem only because it was in prose, whereas the novel was so different that it was not worth consideration. Poe's opinions of the novel and the romance will be examined in the context of his book reviews.

archaic by the end of the eighteenth century.[6] Sir Francis Jeffrey, the famed critic of the *Edinburgh Review,* dismissed it somewhat contemptuously in 1811.[7] Yet archaic opinions have a habit of lingering with all the semblance of authority in popular textbooks, and we have to look no further for such authority than the *Lectures on Rhetoric and Belles Lettres* of Dr. Hugh Blair, the first Regius Professor at the University of Edinburgh. Blair was and would continue to be considered authoritative in America, possibly because he was conservative and offered no challenging or disturbing theories.[8]

Blair presented all of the old definitions. There was an internal sense for the perception of beauty and it was called the taste. It was common to all mankind and it enabled "the philosopher and the peasant; the boy and the man" to receive "pleasure from the beauties of nature and of art." Since it was "founded on a certain natural and instinctive sensibility to beauty," the taste was autonomous in its activity and had nothing to do with the "operation of Reason," although reason could be brought in a posteriori to explain why certain objects pleased and others did not. It was recognized that some had finer taste than others, partly because of innate differences in sensitivity, but more significantly because of differences in cultivation. Any sense, internal or external, was improved by exercise, so it was safe to conclude that experience of the beautiful would lead to a finer or more delicate taste, which, when corrected by the reason, would provide the standard for aesthetic discrimination.[9]

In perfection, taste would exhibit both delicacy and correctness, which could be defined as the ability of the judgment to reject

[6] *Critical Responsiveness: A Study of the Psychological Current in Later Eighteenth-Century Criticism* (Berkeley, 1949), 30.

[7] Review of Archibald Alison's *Essays on the Nature and Principles of Taste,* in Francis Jeffrey, *Contributions to the Edinburgh Review* (New York, 1869), 13–15.

[8] Jeffrey disposed of Blair summarily by classing him with "a whole herd of rhetoricians" who did not "pretend to have any new or original notions." *Ibid.,* 20.

[9] Blair, *Lectures,* I, 16–19.

"spurious beauties." Unfortunately, however, these capacities did not exist in equal measure. A naturally "strong sensibility" might be impressed by "coarse" beauty, if not refined by constant experience of the beautiful. A strong judgment, which is employed in the detection of faults, might be overbearing in its disapprobation unless softened by the "power of Delicacy." Of a person of good taste it could be said that "Delicacy and Correctness, mutually imply each other," and if there were "any one person who possessed in full perfection all the powers of human nature, whose internal senses were in every instance exquisite and just, and whose reason was unerring and sure, the determinations of such a person . . . would be . . . a perfect standard for the Taste . . . ." However, there is no such person, Blair concluded wistfully, and the best we can do in arriving at a standard is to consult the feelings of all mankind—by which he meant, along with Lord Kames and most of the other theorists on taste, the feelings of cultivated gentlemen. Blair emphasized sensation, for reason, in his opinion, must ultimately refer to "sense and perception" as the basis for all speculation on beauty.[10]

This summary of Blair's remarks on taste explains the assumptions that lay behind Poe's attack on Wordsworth in the "letter." His attempt to refute Coleridge is covert, however, and may be more easily understood if we examine the supposed characteristics of the aesthetic response as sensation.

When Shaftesbury and Hutcheson posited the "sixth sense" of taste, they knew that the response to beauty was as immediate as an organic sensation of pleasure or pain, but that it could be traced to no simple cause. Locke had argued that all ideas in the mind could be ascribed to sensation or reflection, but he had said little about the aesthetic response. To correct this deficiency the proponents of internal senses made room for intuitive perception of the beautiful (and of the good, of course), but they did not progress so far from Locke that they could account for these intuitions without assigning the responsibility to special sense organs. Still, the post-Lockean theorists of taste found it difficult to define

[10] *Ibid.*, 20–31.

the sensations of the beautiful. Some, such as Edmund Burke, who denied the existence of an inner sense, attributed the pleasures of taste to qualities in objects. Beautiful objects were small, smooth, gently curved, delicate or fragile, and colored in pastel. The sublime, a source of more significant pleasure, was characterized by greatness, roughness, power, and somber colors. Burke, however, was too simplistic; he failed to make enough allowance for previous experience—the influence of prior associations—in accounting for aesthetic responses.[11]

In 1749, eight years before Burke published his *Enquiry*, David Hartley had brought out a psychophysiological examination of perception and response that eventually discredited Burke's objectivism. Although Hartley, as a physician, was chiefly concerned with the way impulses moved from the sense organs to the brain, he attributed most of the pleasures of taste to the association of ideas. Not so extremist as his follower, Archibald Alison, Hartley did admit that simple musical sounds afforded an organic pleasure to the ear and even went so far as to speculate that discords, originally unpleasant sounds, could be pleasing to those sophisticates who were bored with the "sweetness of Concords." He made only a minimal effort to trace the effect of association on the pleasure of music, but he did acknowledge that certain kinds of music were associated with "affections and passions" and could be said to express them.[12] Hartley, like his followers in the association theory, did not propose an inner sense of taste.

The next "psychologist" who was strongly influential on aesthetic theory was Lord Kames, whose *Elements of Criticism* (1762) was second only to Blair's *Lectures* as an authoritative reference. Kames mediated between the objectivist and subjectivist

[11] Edmund Burke, A *Philosophical Enquiry into the Origins of Our Ideas of the Sublime and Beautiful*, ed. J. T. Boulton (London, 1958), 64, 116–17, 124. What Burke failed to recognize was that a complex evaluation, such as the recognition of beauty, is largely a cognitive process and cannot be successfully described as a physiological reaction to the stimulus. The association psychologists, however elementary their assumptions, were aware of the cognitive process and tried to explain it.

[12] *Observations on Man*, facsimile reproduction, 2 vols. in one (Gainesville, 1966), I, 425–26.

positions by assuming that many emotions resemble their causes, but that the process of association is also operative.[13] The quality of an object or of an event produces a correspondent feeling in the mind, but after this "primary" emotion is excited, a "secondary" emotion may be aroused by association. Kames's concept of the taste was equally mediatory. He did not describe it as an internal sense specifically, but he claimed that everyone was born with a taste for natural beauty. A taste for artificial beauty (works of art) was acquired. Those objects that have intrinsic beauty appeal only to the senses, but in works of art the beauty is relative, and the response to complex art is difficult to define.[14] Nor did Kames really attempt to define it. He could be quite specific about the pleasures derived from sights and sounds, but the best he could do when speculating upon beauty itself was to analyze it into its constituent parts, such as color, shape, size, and motion.[15] Kames still demanded the neoclassic aesthetic properties of "regularity, uniformity, proportion, order, and simplicity," and he was quite suspicious of the "complex forms and profuse ornaments" of the most recent art. As for the psychological origin of aesthetic feeling, Kames could do no more than say that it "depends on the percipient as much as on the object perceived" and that it "cannot be an inherent property in either." [16]

Kames concerned himself very little with music, which was troublesome to British aestheticians of his period because it did not create images in the mind that could be examined for their emotion-producing qualities. However, he anticipated Alison by claiming that music produced a feeling that was neither an emotion nor a passion.[17] It was not an emotion, because it was productive of desire, but it was not a passion, because the desire had no object. Here Kames provided a psychological basis for the romantic attachment to music, but he showed little affection for lyric poetry because he did not think it appropriate for serious subjects.[18] Like

---

[13] *Elements of Criticism*, 22–23, 28, 94–95.   [14] *Ibid.*, 42–43, 103–108.
[15] *Ibid.*, 102–61 *passim*.   [16] *Ibid.*, 108.   [17] *Ibid.*, 38–39.
[18] *Ibid.*, 320–23. Kames was a strict moralist, and while he admitted that music could "humanize and polish" the mind, he was obviously afraid that

most of the British theorists of his century and afterward, Kames preferred vocal music, for music that accompanied words was very effective in enhancing such general emotions as love or pity.[19]

As deficient as he was in pure aesthetics, Kames could still be very emphatic in describing the moral effect of sight and sound, for he thought that these impressions were almost exclusively mental and that they detached us from the sensual delights of the "inferior" senses. The fine arts depended exclusively upon sight and sound and thus contributed nothing to sensual gratification. The pleasures of the taste, then, were ethereal pleasures of the mind. Music was especially productive of pleasure, for no disagreeable combination of sounds could be legitimately termed music.[20]

Kames's theories at the moment seem to have little relevance to Poe's "letter," but Kames's psychology was used by Blair with results that are more obvious. Blair made the customary statement that music enhances feeling, but he went one step farther by asserting that under the influence of strong feeling "objects do not appear . . . as they really are, but such as passion makes us see them." [21] With Blair's enormous influence, generations of students would assume that when words were joined with music, verbal images would not resemble the objects of reference but would appear only as highly stimulated feeling dictated. Blair, something of a chronological primitivist, admired the bards of old who sang to the harp; and he expressed some regret that music should have been separated from poetry. It is not surprising, then, that he showed an affection for the lyric which was not too com-

---

it could "promote luxury and effeminacy" because of its inherent charms. An undue emphasis upon instrumental music would result in a kind of wallowing in pure hedonic value; therefore music should be used to accompany words that expressed the ethically sanctioned feelings.

[19] *Ibid.*, 74–75. Even in song Kames found certain disadvantages. Songs, in his opinion, could not express "important" emotions. He deprecated French and Italian opera because one's pleasure at a performance was derived more from the music than from the "sentiments," which he defined as thoughts that are aroused by strong feeling. Music, to Kames as to Poe, was feeling without thought; it was only a stimulant without a proper cause or object. It had to be combined with an idea to produce a poem.

[20] *Ibid.*   [21] Blair, *Lectures*, II, 315.

mon among British critics of his generation—he was matched only by Thomas Gray, who can scarcely be considered a critic. In fact, he drew close to Poe when he wrote, "There is no agreeable sensation we receive, either from Beauty or Sublimity, but what is capable of being heightened by the power of musical sound." [22]

Blair, a rhetorician rather than a philosopher or a psychologist, was not much concerned with the question of whether beauty was a quality of the object or something that happened in the mind, but his assumption of an internal organ of taste indicates that he was even more conservative than Kames. He frequently referred to "agreeable sensations" in the old-fashioned way, and he dismissed beauty that expressed "qualities of mind," particularly in regard to the human face, as a subject too difficult to explore. [23] Certainly one would never expect, if he read Blair's *Lectures* when they appeared in 1783, that within seven years a work would be published which would make Blair seem as antique as Quintilian (incidentally, one of Blair's favorite authorities). Archibald Alison's *Essays on the Nature and Principles of Taste* (1790) completed the shift to subjectivism initiated by Hartley. That Blair's work continued in use for more than half a century simply illustrates the truism already mentioned—archaic ideas stay with us long after the premises upon which they are based have been discredited.

For Alison the response to beauty was a "peculiar emotion" that developed by an associative process from "simple emotions," such as joy, grief, or sympathy. The origin and nature of this peculiar emotion were hard to describe: "It is often . . . difficult to say what is the quality of the object which produces the emotion of beauty, and it is sometimes difficult, in the case of complex objects, when different qualities unite in the production of emotion, to define the exact nature of the emotion we feel . . . ." [24] In fact, Alison continued, analytical criticism, by attempting to define the beauties of a composition, usually succeeded in "destroying the

---

[22] *Ibid.*, I, 92.   [23] *Ibid.*, 87.

[24] *Essays on the Nature and Principles of Taste*, ed. Abraham Mills (New York, 1844), 63. Hereinafter cited as *Essays on Taste*.

sensibility of taste." [25] At last we appear to have arrived at the idea that lies behind Poe's assertion in the "letter to Mr. —— ——" that exercise of the judgment impairs the sensitivity to beauty. If his argument had been governed strictly by Blair's premise of an inner sense of taste, Poe would have had to invoke judgment—an analytical activity—to separate genuine from spurious beauties and thereby correct the vagaries of instinctive appreciation. Yet, as we shall see, Poe employed an Alisonian argument against Wordsworth, even though his terminology was Blair's. Poe's eclecticism was uncritical; he appropriated the ideas that he needed either without knowing or without caring that they were based on conflicting accounts of mental activity.

Poe had stated that music—metrical form [26]—was essential to the pleasurable effect that was the object of a poem. As we have seen, theorists from Shaftesbury to Alison had acknowledged that the response to a work of art was different from the simple pleasures of the senses. The earlier psychologists, through Kames, had been inclined to attribute this pleasure to representation in an artificial medium of the sights and sounds that were naturally pleasing, but they had made the qualification that there was an additional pleasure in the recognition of design or purposefulness in an art form. Those who were closer to Locke tended to think that the more vivid the representation, the greater the resultant pleasure; and hence there was an eighteenth-century development of what has been called the rhetoric of sensation. Kames was especially emphatic in describing the effect of vivid description, claiming that "a lively and accurate description of an important event, raises in me ideas no less distinct than if I had been originally an eye-

---

[25] *Ibid.*, 73.

[26] Poe's term was "music," but it is obvious that he was referring to poetry instead of song. Consequently he could only mean metrical form. This usage was conventional. Kames had employed the terms "music" and "melody" in reference to versification, for it was assumed that poetry was read aloud and that the psychological effect of similar sounds, as in rhyme, approximated that of recurrent musical phrases. The effect of meter corresponded to that of musical measure.

witness." [27] However, emotions are not felt until the "ideal" spectator is thrown into a kind of "waking dream" or "reverie" by
"lively and distinct images" and imagines himself actually present
at the event. Obviously what Kames wanted in a poem was just exactly the opposite of what Poe wanted, yet there are critical commonplaces in Kames that would eventually be used in Poe's
arguments, by implication in the "Letter to Mr. ⸺ ⸺" and
directly in some of his reviews.

Kames had noted perfunctorily that a "more perfect melody of
articulate sounds is what distinguishes poetry from prose" and had
gone on to affirm that the chief end of prose was instruction.[28]
Both Coleridge and Poe had distinguished poetry from science on
grounds of purpose, but only Poe had retained the Kamesian distinction between poetry and prose in general. Elsewhere Kames,
who disliked rhyme and pronounced rhythmical effects, had commented disparagingly that the melody of verse "so powerfully en-
chants the mind, as to draw a veil over very gross faults and imperfections." [29] By this he did not mean stylistic defects, but failures
in logic and probability. In other words, poetry by its very quality
of delight is an inefficient means of conveying truth, however effective it is in making us feel. Blair followed Kames by asserting that
music raises feeling to such an intense level that feeling actually
modifies perception. It remained for Alison to add the last word,
starting with the effect of instrumental music and then describing
the effect of music joined with words, as in song.

Music, said Alison, is a succession of sounds which resemble
spoken words in that, like tones of voice, these sounds are general
signs of feeling which do not express "any particular passion." He
supported his point by quoting James Beattie's striking description
of music as an "unknown tongue" which "conveys no determinate
feeling." Beattie and Alison agreed that words were necessary to

[27] *Elements of Criticism*, 52.

[28] *Ibid.*, 291. As Gordon McKenzie has explained, Coleridge did not distinguish between poetry and prose because any such distinction would be
on the basis of superficial form. The poetic experience could occur in either.
See McKenzie, *Organic Unity in Coleridge* (Berkeley, 1939), 69.

[29] Kames, *Elements of Criticism*, 323.

make music express either ideas or emotions; and Alison, like Blair before him, thought that the union of music and words represented the "most expressive species of composition," the *only* kind which affected the "minds of uninstructed men." [30]

The rationale of Poe's assertion that music is essential to the pleasurable effect of poetry is now complete. An objection could be made that Blair and Alison were describing folk ballads which were actually sung, whereas Poe was referring in his "letter" to poetry in general. To Poe's mind, however, this would be a needlessly artificial distinction, for eventually he was to state what now he was only implying, that the ballad was the most effective kind of poetry and that something had been lost when words were separated from musical accompaniment.[31] The pleasurable effect could be retained, but only in part, by metrical form.

The theoretical commonplaces of the past half-century do not fully account for Poe's insistence that poetry aims at indefinite pleasure. To equate Alison's "complex pleasure of taste" with Poe's "indefinite pleasure" would be to violate Alison and perhaps to misread Poe. However, no one would be likely to deny the young poet the ability to arrive at his own conclusions and to use what he knew of critical theory to support them. Then, too, he was engaging with a problem that had not been particularly important to the critics of the eighteenth century. Prior critics had not needed to defend metrical form; they had taken it for granted. When Kames distinguished poetry from prose on the ground that it exhibited a "more perfect melody" and that its chief end was to please, he was simply expressing what everyone knew. Coleridge had introduced a challenging and disturbing discrimination when he had separated poetry not only from science but also from the novel and the ro-

[30] *Essays on Taste,* 160–67. James Beattie, professor of moral philosophy at Marischal College, was closely associated with the Scottish common-sense school. His essay on *Poetry and Music as They Affect the Mind* was published in 1776 and was for some time considered authoritative. Adam Smith, better known as an economist, also had something to say on the subject. He agreed with Beattie that instrumental music conveyed no ideas or definite emotions. In fact, pure sound did not signify anything.

[31] Poe made this suggestion a number of times in his reviews, but he stated it unequivocally in "The Poetic Principle."

mance. The analysts of taste were not concerned with prose fiction because it was not an art form. The fine arts to Kames and Blair and Alison were poetry, drama, music, sculpture, painting, architecture, and landscape gardening. Therefore, when they discussed the pleasure derived from a poem as aesthetic pleasure, they did not have to distinguish it from the pleasure gained from a novel. For all practical purposes the problem did not exist. It did exist for Wordsworth, who had to explain why he wrote in verse instead of prose; [32] it existed for Coleridge, and perhaps, as a consequence, for Edgar Poe. In Poe's naïve aesthetics, however, the distinction was as simple and obvious as it had been for Kames. Poetry was different from prose fiction because it was fine art. Metrical form, like music, created indefinite feelings which modified the ideas derived from a perception of real objects or of a representation of real objects. Prose fiction, on the other hand, being less "artificial," presented "perceptible images" that aroused definite sensations. That's all there was to it. Poe never forgot the Kamesian dictum that emotions resembled their causes, and given this premise his logic is impeccable. Poetry as a fine art raised the peculiar feeling of taste, which previous authority had established as different from

[32] See the Preface to the second edition of the *Lyrical Ballads* (1800). Wordsworth was very much aware of prior speculation on the effect of meter and rhyme in casting a veil of unreality over objects and events; and he knew that with his purpose of presenting, as nearly as possible, the real passions of man in a state of nature, many would wonder why he did not write in prose. Prose was considered a less artificial form of discourse, better suited for the imitation of real life—which appeared to be Wordsworth's object. Yet in spite of the charges of didacticism made by his detractors, Wordsworth professed commitment to the hedonic value commonly attributed to poetry and explained his decision to write in verse on a perfectly conventional basis. It was "the tendency of metre to divest language, in a certain degree, of its reality, and thus to throw a sort of half-consciousness of unsubstantial existence over the whole composition . . . ." Accordingly, the pain of pathetic situations would be "overbalanced" by the pleasure derived from meter and the situation itself would seem less real. This much of Wordsworth's argument would have been acceptable to Poe, had it not been invalidated by the elder poet's insistence on distasteful subjects and low diction. Coleridge, of course, had located certain fallacies in Wordsworth's argument and had exposed them in several chapters of the *Biographia Literaria*, which Poe had just read.

ordinary sensation.[33] Feelings are like their causes; therefore the indefinite pleasure of taste must arise from indefinite sensations caused by metrical form. Nothing of the kind could be said of the romance or the novel, so the young Poe thought he had caught Coleridge in an obvious error. Poetry was different from prose because it was directed exclusively at the taste.

As has been already mentioned, Coleridge in Chapter XIV of the *Biographia Literaria* had distinguished the pleasure of a poem from that of prose fiction not in kind but in degree. The poem, being an organized whole, demanded close attention to its parts not merely as isolated elements but in their relatedness to each other in a total construct. If we assume that Poe read more than one chapter, he would have found Coleridge arguing in Chapter XVIII that metrical form was not essential to the pleasurable effect of poetry but was only a conditional pleasure dependent upon thought and expression. Coleridge agreed with the traditional commonplace that meter stimulated feeling, but he was not prepared to admit that this intensified feeling necessarily blurred our perceptions. Instead, he wrote, "it tends to increase the vivacity and susceptibility both of the general feelings and of the attention." In itself metrical form is useless; it is valuable only as a stimulant. Meter is the proper form of a poem, Coleridge conceded, not because metrical form is essentially poetic (Poe's position), but because poetry implies "an excited state of the feelings and faculties" and meter helps provide this excitement. Coleridge always urged, and Poe denied, that though the *immediate* object of a

---

[33] It is worth noting that Jeffrey, in his attempt to account for the peculiarity of the pleasure of taste, used the term "vague" to describe the effect of the perception of beauty. See *Contributions to the Edinburgh Review*, 31. Aesthetic feeling was indescribable, but Alison and Jeffrey argued that it came from perception as modified by previous experience and by the activity of the imagination. Kames and Blair had placed more emphasis upon the evocative medium than upon the imaginative activity of the observer. Poe, confining himself strictly to hedonic value in the "letter," referred only to the kind of pleasure attributable to a work of art. His use of "indefinite pleasure" as a description of the emotion of taste would be considered accurate. In later essays he sometimes used "vague" as a synonym for "indefinite."

poem is pleasure, its *ultimate* object ought to be truth, "either moral or intellectual." Even in compositions designed to give pleasure, Coleridge affirmed, the "mere superaddition of metre, with or without rhyme," would not entitle prose compositions "to the name of poems."

It is obvious that Coleridge attributed value to poetry not because it was a fine art and aroused the peculiar pleasure of taste, but because, in the words of Walter Jackson Bate, "beauty is a *way of approaching* the true and the good; it is a way of rendering truth *realizable* to the total mind . . . ." [34] The difference between Poe and Coleridge is fundamental, not simply a superficial qualification made by a young man trying to attract attention to himself by quarreling with an authority. Edgar Poe, in the "Letter to Mr. ———————" and in all of his subsequent criticism, argued that poetry as a fine art appealed only to the sense of beauty, that metrical form was essential to this appeal, and that (perhaps remembering Kames) it had nothing to do with sensual gratification or "passion" directed toward an object. Poe was to develop various strategies of proof in later years, but eventually he returned to the premises of the analysts of taste—that there was a separate faculty for the recognition of beauty, and that the operation of the reason in its pre-Kantian definition as the power of analysis was alien to and even destructive of aesthetic feeling. Poetry, Poe was to say eleven years later, "is the handmaiden but of Taste," a statement which admits no ambiguity but which can be understood as Poe meant it only if we have recourse to the psychological premises upon which the statement rests.

2

Perhaps my excursion into an aspect of literary history that has been more thoroughly investigated by others is permissible if it helps illuminate Poe's critical practice as well as some of the obscurer references of his theory. If my reconstruction of the premises that underlie his concluding argument in the "letter" is accurate,

[34] *Prefaces to Criticism* (Garden City, 1959), 161.

then Poe's reproof of Coleridge for profundity and his high contempt for Wordsworth are not quite so irresponsible as they may seem. Most of his essay is polemical, but he would have felt reasonably safe in assaulting a poet whose subjects and diction had outraged conservative critics and a "philosopher" whose opinions were as yet understood by only a few in America. As we have seen, Poe had behind him the covert authority of the theorists best known to his potential audience. His strategy was not without guile, for he indirectly validated his own kind of poetry by discrediting theories that would implicitly or explicitly oppose it, a procedure which indicates that Poe knew very well what he was about. An examination of this strategy will be helpful, for it prefigures a method that he was to employ with increasing skill in his book reviews.

Poe began the "letter" by making an indirect attempt to qualify himself as an expert in judging poetry. He asserted with seeming boldness that a good poet was *necessarily* a good critic, dismissing the obvious argument that a poet is likely to favor the kind of poetry that he himself writes. Poe's easy disposal of such a crucial question was not without precedent. It was assumed that a *good* poet would have a cultivated taste, refined, as Kames and Blair had said, by experience with works of art. After Alison had invalidated the use of the analytic reason, which Kames and Blair had both found necessary for criticism, Sir Francis Jeffrey, in a review of Scott's *The Lady of the Lake*, had made the same claim as Poe: that a good poet was a good judge because in addition to natural sensibility he would have a cultivated taste.[35] Such a judge would not have to think about an object of art before pronouncing it beautiful, for, as Jeffrey affirmed in a review of the 1811 edition of Alison's *Essays*, "the perception of beauty . . . we hold to be, in most cases, quite instantaneous, and altogether as immediate as the perception of the external qualities of the object to which it is ascribed."[36] Because of the prestige of Jeffrey and the *Edinburgh Review*, we can be certain that this opinion was widely circulated, particularly since his review of Alison was subsequently published in the *Encyclopaedia Britannica* (1824) as the article on Beauty.

[35] *Contributions to the Edinburgh Review*, 368.   [36] *Ibid.*, 21.

Jeffrey had emphasized "long experience" of the beautiful, however, and such a qualification, it would appear, would virtually eliminate the youthful Poe. Alison himself would have been more to Poe's purpose, for Alison had declared that sensibility diminished with age, a premise which Poe was about to use against Wordsworth.

Almost immediately in the "letter," by stating that a good poet would have an "intimate acquaintance with the subject," Poe protected himself against the possible charge that he was making innate talent the only qualification for criticism. If his remark were interpreted to mean that studying the subject is all that is required, Poe would be on shaky ground indeed, for a bad poet could study as much as a good one and thus would have an equal capacity for making a just critique—a possibility which Poe categorically denied. However, cultivating the taste, in Poe's sense, did not mean immersing oneself in theoretical considerations. It meant experiencing the beautiful in nature and in art. By such experience delicacy or refinement of taste is acquired, and since by Jeffrey's time taste could be regarded as a discriminative as well as a perceptive faculty, all a critic really needed was cultivated taste. That Poe was thinking in such terms is indicated by his analogical argument: "Poetry, above all things, is a beautiful painting whose tints, to minute inspection, are confusion worse confounded, but start boldly out to the cursory glance of the connoisseur." [37] Here we have Jeffrey's "instantaneous" recognition of the qualities of the beautiful combined with Alison's hostility toward close analysis. Cultivated taste is implied by the word "connoisseur."

That Alisonian aesthetics were common enough in America needs no demonstration, but a pair of opposite reactions from the South are significant. George Tucker, professor of moral philosophy

[37] Poe omitted this sentence from the version he published in the *Messenger* in 1836, probably because he recognized that his analogy with painting was carelessly chosen and would suggest to his readers that he retained the old neoclassic concept of poetry as an imitation of nature: *ut pictura poesis*. Fully committed to the romantic doctrine that poetry was like music in its expression of feeling, Poe by 1836 would admit that a short tale could be like a painting, but a poem could not.

at the University of Virginia, was one of the few Americans who wrote on the subject of taste. His essays were first published in the *Port Folio* in 1814 and 1815, and were issued as a collection in 1822 under the title *Essays on Various Subjects of Taste, Morals and National Policy*. Tucker, considering beauty a quality of the object, was so opposed to the new subjectivism that he devoted a portion of his satirical fantasy *A Voyage to the Moon* (1827) to an attack on Jeffrey's associationism, no doubt inspired by the article in the *Britannica*. It has been suggested a number of times that Tucker's work was influential on Poe. If so, the influence was minimal as far as aesthetic theory is concerned. Much more relevant to Poe's argument was a review published in 1829 in the *Southern Review*. The anonymous critic had obviously read Alison and Jeffrey and then had ventured to propose his own definition of taste: "Taste does not represent a single idea, nor a composition of ideas, but only an abbreviation of terms designating ideas, which occur simultaneously. It is in relation to the heart and to the senses of discipline, the eye and the ear, what judgment is in reasoning, and honour is in morals—the rapid perception of those ultimate results, which repeated development has so completely ascertained, as to render it no longer necessary to expand and exhibit their elements in detail."[38] Here are the familiar psychological assumptions: the faculties—the taste, the reason, and the moral sense— are allowed their discrete functions; a seeming immediacy of judgment is described, for both perception and feeling have been trained by appropriate exercise; detailed analysis is unnecessary for the discriminative act of the taste. More obviously relevant to Poe's statement is the author's explanation of the way in which a poet is able to detect the qualities of a poem. There is a similarity, the author claimed, between the quick decisions of a "practiced reasoner" in regard to familiar subjects and the quick judgments of a poet on poems. These instantaneous decisions seem marvelous to the uninitiated, yet the reasoner himself "is at no loss to trace out the ladders and the scaffolding, which enabled him, gradually, to reach

[38] Review of De La Motte Fouqué's *Kleine Romane*, in *Southern Review*, III (1829), 32.

the vantage ground of truth." In like manner the poet's eye perceives "at a glance, a multitude of nice appliances, linked together on a chain of gossamer," which the ordinary observer could not "detect, distinguish, or detail." [39] So it is with Poe's connoisseur, who perceives at a "cursory glance" those details of execution that are meaningless to the "minute inspection" of the analytical judgment.

Having qualified himself as a connoisseur, a poet intimately acquainted with his subject, Poe was now in a position to prosecute his general attack on the use of reason in matters of taste and his detailed assault on Wordsworth. The generalized charges came first: "Against the subtleties which would make poetry a study—not a passion—it becomes the metaphysician to reason—but the poet to protest." Wordsworth, Poe insinuated, had behaved like a metaphysician instead of a poet. Intellectual activity does not produce poems: "I feel, from the bottom of my heart, that learning has little to do with the imagination—intellect with the passions—or age with poetry." Why? Because the recognition of beauty is instinctive, like that "moral mechanism by which the simplicity of a child may overbalance the wisdom of a man." Thus far Poe was preaching the gospel of Blair, and, as Blair had to do before him, he had to rescue himself from the implications of a naïve primitivism. It is at this point, therefore, by inserting his example of the connoisseur, that he reinforced his earlier proposition that a good poet would know his subject. What we are to understand is that in terms of wisdom a poet may be like a child, but that his taste is highly developed.

Far from being a naïve protest, Poe's criticism of Wordsworth

[39] *Ibid.* It is significant that in "The Philosophy of Composition" Poe was to make a similar claim for the ability of the poet to reconstruct the rational processes of composition. He even used cognate metaphors, though his own were drawn from stagecraft instead of from building construction. Compare Poe's "wheels and pinions—the tackle for scene shifting—the step-ladders and demon traps" with the *Southern Review* author's "ladders and scaffolding." Disciples of the Scottish school would not think it extraordinary for a man of cultivated taste to know what he was doing. He would have learned from experience. Only primitives were supposed to depend on blind inspiration.

has the weight of familiar authority behind it. His terminology was Blair's, but the psychology he used was Blair improved by Alison and, more remotely, by Dugald Stewart. "As to Wordsworth, I have no faith in him. That he had, in youth, the feelings of a poet I believe—for there are glimpses of extreme delicacy in his writings —(and delicacy is the poet's own kingdom . . .)—but they have the appearance of a better day recollected . . . ." "Delicacy" is the key term here, and it should be rescued from the effeminate connotations it has gathered since the eighteenth century. Several critics had associated delicacy in one way or another with the aesthetic response. Burke had used it to refer to a quality of beautiful objects and Alexander Gerard had employed it in reference to a refined sensibility, but Hugh Blair was the familiar authority who had declared that delicacy represented "the perfection of that natural sensibility on which Taste is founded." [40]

The presumption that sensibility declined with age, though a truism scarcely worth examining, was particularly prominent in Alison, who attributed it not only to the diminishing warmth of imagination but also to the habits of reason and reflection acquired in maturity. This idea is evident in Poe's next statement: "He [Wordsworth] was to blame in wearing away his youth in contemplation with the end of poetizing in his manhood. With the increase of his judgment the light which should make it apparent has faded away. His judgment consequently is too correct." If we read Poe's last sentence without benefit of Blair, we are annoyed by his apparent illogic. How can a judgment be correcter than correct? Blair had defined the operation of judgment in taste as having to do chiefly with the detection of faults. All Poe meant was that Wordsworth was too assiduous in finding fault and was more or less blind to beauty. Blair himself had been too conservative to disparage correctness of judgment. He went only so far as to admit that delicacy and correctness never existed in perfect balance in the taste of a single individual and that error could be expected on one side or the other. Alison had few neoclassic inhibitions and asserted flatly that habitual exercise of analytical judgment would destroy

[40] Blair, *Lectures*, I, 23.

the sensibility. This, according to Poe, was Wordsworth's predicament. Having desiccated his sensibility by too much speculation on art in his youth, the mature Wordsworth had had to "reason us into admiration of his poetry." This was an absurd procedure, for beauty was self-evident to the refined taste.[41] Poe, of course, was referring to Wordsworth's prefaces, and he was now ready, having accounted for the elder poet's lack of taste, to demonstrate that Wordsworth had lost the ability to write good poems and appreciate others. Wordsworth was equipped only to detect faults.

The case in point was James Macpherson's "Ossian," which had been admired extravagantly for its sublimity by Blair and Kames. Poe echoed their judgment by finding in the Ossianic poems "gorgeous, yet simple imagery, where all is alive and panting with immortality, than which earth has nothing more grand, nor paradise more beautiful." Still, it should have taken more than an affection for Macpherson's poems to provoke an extended diatribe against Wordsworth in the context of Poe's preface to his own poems. Wordsworth had criticized Macpherson's images in his "Essay, Supplementary to the Preface" of the *Poems* of 1815, and it would appear that Poe, who had read all of Wordsworth's prefaces more carefully than he was admitting, had detected a threat to his own kind of poetry. The discussion hinges on the nature of poetic imagery, and we should remember that images, in the terminology of the late eighteenth century, signified not figures of speech but the pictures called up in the mind by descriptive passages. We should remember also that Poe concluded his essay with an account of what he considered to be the proper effect of images in poetry, as these images were rendered in metrical form.

In the passage to which Poe referred, Wordsworth alluded to Macpherson's "spurious imagery" and asserted that everything in "Ossian" which was not stolen was "defined, insulated, dislocated, deadened," and that it would always be so when "words are substi-

---

[41] The inner sense of taste, according to Blair, enabled us to feel immediate pleasure in a work of art. The reason could explain *why* we were pleased (*ibid.*, 22), but pleasure came first. No one could reason us into liking tasteless compositions.

tuted for things." [42] This statement exhibits what was sometimes called Wordsworth's "peculiar theory," which required concrete diction, or specific words instead of the normal "poetic" style. Poe was offended for two reasons, first because Wordsworth had said that Macpherson's images were defined, whereas to Poe they were grandly indefinite, and secondly because Wordsworth's requirement of specificity, of things instead of words, invalidated Poe's own "vague and indefinite" poems.

The other aspects of Poe's criticism of Wordsworth can be summarized briefly; Poe simply repeated the charges made by hostile critics for the past two decades and even aped their manner. The most notorious assault on Wordsworth's poetry was Sir Francis Jeffrey's review of *The Excursion* in 1814. Jeffrey, using the premise of taste, had been harsh in condemning Wordsworth's verbose didacticism, his mysticism, his low diction and subjects, and his "peculiar system," arguing that these "blemishes" represented a combination of bad taste and "self-partiality." [43] Poe included the whole list of faults, directly or indirectly. Jeffrey had spoken of the disproportion between Wordsworth's taste and his genius (power of execution). Poe went a step further by implying that the poet had lost both powers, and quoted, somewhat inaccurately, lines from "The Idiot Boy" and "The Pet Lamb" as self-evident proof. He also referred contemptuously to *Peter Bell* and made a veiled allusion to *The Waggoner*; these two works had provoked a flurry of hostile criticism when they were published in 1819. [44]

It is apparent that Poe's specific charges against Wordsworth were as commonplace in 1831 as were the assumptions about taste which supported them. His employment of direct ridicule is worth

[42] "Essay Supplementary to the Preface," *The Complete Poetical Works of William Wordsworth* (Cambridge, 1904), 813.

[43] *Contributions to the Edinburgh Review*, 457–69. See also Jeffrey's review of *The White Doe of Rylstone, ibid.*, 469–72.

[44] William S. Ward, "Wordsworth, the 'Lake' Poets, and Their Contemporary Magazine Critics," *Studies in Philology*, XLII (1945), 94. Professor Ward's survey indicates that, except for "die-hards like Jeffrey," Wordsworth had won acceptance among the magazine critics by 1820. Poe was clearly following the line of Jeffrey and the earlier reviewers.

noting, however, for it anticipates one of the methods he employed in reviewing books. Poe concluded his diatribe by quoting a passage from the Preface to the *Lyrical Ballads* and interpolating parenthetical guffaws:

> 'Those who have been accustomed to the phraseology of modern writers, if they persist in reading this book to a conclusion (impossible!) will, no doubt, have to struggle with feelings of awkwardness; (ha! ha! ha!) they will look round for poetry (ha! ha! ha! ha!) and will be induced to inquire by what species of courtesy these attempts have been permitted to assume that title.' ha! ha! ha! ha! ha!
>
> Yet let not Mr. W. despair; he has given immortality to a wagon, and the bee Sophocles has eternalized a sore toe, and dignified a tragedy with a chorus of turkeys.

This was the kind of ridicule which Poe was to use in some of his early book reviews and which he defended in 1835 in a letter to Beverley Tucker. Its use here shows that he was already familiar with the tactics of British reviewers and that the distance between the romantic poet of 1831 and the "tomahawk" critic of 1835 is not so great as might be supposed.

On the larger issue of hedonic value Poe was on safer ground, at least as far as posterity is concerned, than he was in his protest against Wordsworth. The analysts of taste, however they differed among themselves as to the operation of taste, were in agreement that the faculty was concerned only with the recognition of beauty. Fine art, they all said, appealed to the taste, and only indirectly to the moral sense or the reason. This was the aesthetic to which Edgar Poe subscribed, and if its proponents enlisted hedonic value in the service of virtue, some of them still knew where art stopped and preaching began—witness Jeffrey's impeachment of Wordsworth's didacticism. Throughout his career Poe asked no more than this, that taste come first, and in his most characteristic statement in "The Poetic Principle" he declared that taste served virtue by depicting its beauty, causing us to loathe the "deformity" of vice. Poe was far less of an aesthete than some critics would have us believe, but the ground of his dispute with Coleridge indicates that even at the age of twenty-two he was able to understand that the British critic considered insight more valuable than pleasure and estimated the worth of metrical form accordingly. Poe took his stand on the side of form, for it was form alone that separated fine art from the practical art that had truth as its object.

Taken as a statement of theory, Poe's "Letter to Mr. ⸺ ⸺" is a jejune performance, disorganized and irresponsible in asserting what a mature critic would have attempted to argue in detail; but taken for what it is, a defense of poems intended to make us feel instead of think, it is well enough managed to anticipate the polemicist who in five years was to attack a New York literary clique and thereby attract nationwide attention to an obscure Southern periodical. America needed an apologist for art; moralists lurked behind every bush, particularly in New England.

Poe never developed an aesthetic system that could withstand intensive scrutiny, which is the reason why Wimsatt and Bate, among others, have dismissed him summarily.[45] He advanced no new propositions, and he chose from the old whatever he needed to establish his proofs. He did not write to the "selectest of the wise of many generations," as Shelley would have it, but to the American mass audience. A mob, Poe once said, had to be led by its nose, and he led it by dangling carrots of familiar arguments and pseudo-scientific demonstrations. He cajoled, he threatened, he lied, and sometimes he raved, but always in the service of what he considered art. Popular didactic poets, like Longfellow, became the inoffensive targets of his abuse, but poets like Keats and Shelley and the early Tennyson, whose didacticism was less overt, received a full measure of praise. Yet to Poe's mind it was Keats alone who never erred in his appeal to the sense of beauty.

Within five years Poe was to reverse his attitude toward critical analysis, for after he became a reviewer he learned through trial and error that protests were not proof and that it was more effective to blast literary sin with evangelical fervor than it was to empathize with the "spirit" of each author, an approach that was cur-

[45] Wimsatt and Brooks, *Literary Criticism: A Short History*, 478–80; Bate, *Prefaces to Criticism*, 149–51.

rently recommended. He learned to describe "blemishes" in graphic detail, occasionally ridiculing them but more often patiently analyzing them by whatever principle he was able to apply, whether it was Coleridge's definition of the imagination or a rhetorical rule for figures.

Poe reviewed fiction as well as poetry, and since the prose romance could not be examined adequately by the aesthetic of taste, he had to devise his own standards, borrowing or adapting principles formulated for other genres.[46] Such a procedure was effective in producing a rationale for the short tale, but Poe could never accommodate the novel to his conviction of what art should do—appeal to the taste. Eventually he decided that the value of a novel depended on thought, not on form, which made it a practical instead of a fine art.

[46] This was a common problem for the magazine critics. Sir Archibald Alison, son of the critic referred to in these pages, dated the appearance of the new genre, the historical romance, from the publication of Scott's *Waverly* in 1814. For the first time a prose form had appeared that could appeal to the imagination and taste. Alison denigrated both the eighteenth-century novel and the Gothic romance, declaring that they were now (1842) almost unreadable. The historical romances, on the other hand, rivaled the epic and the drama; they were "the ballads of a civilized and enlightened age." *Essays, Political, Historical, and Miscellaneous* (Edinburgh and London, 1850), III, 533.

III · The Apprenticeship of a Critic

JUST when Edgar Poe began reviewing books for the *Southern Literary Messenger* is not certain. His letter to White late in April, 1835, indicates that he considered himself a regular contributor.[1] Some bibliographers believe that his first book review for the magazine appeared in the February issue.[2] However, "Berenice," his first short story for the *Messenger*, was published in March, and the first book review that can be established as his by external evidence appeared in the April number. All that can be said positively is that at some time between January and March, 1835, Poe, through the good will of John Pendleton Kennedy, established a connection with the Richmond magazine. He had no editorial prerogatives. He was simply a contributor, paid by the column. Yet Poe was displaying somewhat more than the usual contributor's interest in the *Messenger*; he was inserting notices of the magazine, a form of advertising, in Baltimore newspapers.

Unquestionably Thomas Willis White, the publisher, needed the help of an editor who was capable of intelligent discrimination. Formerly a printer, White was handicapped by his limited education and his acknowledged incapacity to make literary value judgments. From the beginning of his enterprise he sought advice and contributions from his more sophisticated friends, and without their help the *Messenger* would probably have foundered before Poe arrived to make it famous—or notorious, as some contemporaries thought.

White's first editor, who evidently served without pay, was James E. Heath, who was at the time auditor of the Commonwealth of Virginia. Heath had had no journalistic experience, but

[1] *Letters*, I, 57–59. Poe indicated that he would send White one tale a month but said nothing about poems or book reviews.
[2] For a summary of the evidence see William Doyle Hull, "A Canon of the Critical Works of Edgar Allan Poe with a Study of Poe as Editor and Reviewer" (Ph.D. dissertation, University of Virginia, 1941), 61.

he had written a novel called *Edge-Hill; or, The Family of the Fitzroyals,* which White himself had published in 1828. Furthermore, Heath was the first recording secretary of the Virginia Historical and Philosophical Society, which had been organized in 1834. As literary men were reckoned in the Virginia of 1834, Heath was well qualified for the position, and, more important, he belonged to a group of intellectuals who had status and influence. How he found the time to edit the magazine is another question.

White did not depend solely upon Heath. He also called upon his friend Beverley Tucker. A professor of law at William and Mary, Tucker had yet to publish the two novels upon which his literary reputation would rest.[3] A third friend from whom White received advice and contributions was Lucian Minor. Minor, like Tucker, was a respected lawyer for whom literature was an avocation. When Heath wanted to resign in February of 1835, White had tried to persuade Minor to become his editor at an annual salary of $800.00, telling him that he would be expected to work only thirty hours a week;[4] but Minor declined. Perhaps White was fortunate (though he would have been unlikely to admit it), because less than a year later he employed Edgar Poe for $520.00, and one suspects that Poe's working week was often considerably longer than thirty hours.

The chief point of interest here is that White was aiming at a thoroughly respectable provincial publication and that he was seeking help from Virginians of status—professional lawyers with literary inclinations. Thus the *Messenger,* in White's vision, was to be primarily a magazine which served sectional interests. It would be an outlet for what Southern men of letters apparently assumed was the vast, untapped storehouse of local literary treasure, a treasure strangely undiscovered by the money-grubbing publishers of the North.

[3] *George Balcombe* and *The Partisan Leader,* both published in 1836.

[4] T. W. White to Lucian Minor, February 17, 1835, in David K. Jackson, *Poe and the Southern Literary Messenger* (Richmond, 1934), 93–95. The pertinent letters from White to his advisers, Lucian Minor and Beverley Tucker, are in Jackson, 93–115, and hereafter in this chapter will be cited by date only.

To understand what Poe confronted when he assumed the "assistant" editorship of the *Southern Literary Messenger* it will be helpful to survey the magazine before his pen and his authority, limited though it was, made themselves felt. When White undertook to publish a magazine in Richmond, he knew that the odds were against him. Magazines had not flourished in the South, even in Charleston, the most "literary" of the Southern cities. Hugh Swinton Legaré's *Southern Review,* a somewhat ponderous quarterly modeled after the *Edinburgh Review,* had survived only four years, 1828–32. It had been a review only, impressive in its learning and conservative dignity, but unlikely to succeed with the general reading public. The *North American Review* was well established in the North, but Southerners were prone to read British publications, which were available at bargain rates.

White wanted to publish a monthly "variety" magazine, with articles, stories, poems, and reviews. That such a journal could have tremendous popularity had already been proved by *Blackwood's* in England. Then, too, White hoped to gain subscriptions by playing upon the South's sensitivity to its literary backwardness in comparison with the North. The first issue of the *Messenger* in August, 1834, called for a "Southern" literature: "Are we to be doomed forever to a kind of vassalage to our Northern neighbors—a dependence for our literary food upon our brethren, whose superiority in all the great points of character,—in valor—eloquence and patriotism, we are no wise disposed to admit?"

It was assumed by many that Southern literature had languished because most of the publishing houses and journals were in the North and displayed sectional bias in rejecting Southern offerings. It was also assumed that many educated Southerners had manuscripts stacked in their closets and that urging from patriotic editors would bring them to light, since Southerners were too gentlemanly to engage in the vulgar business of trying to persuade Northern publishers. That most of this was an aspect of the Southern chivalric myth is likely, but certainly Philip Pendleton Cooke would never have published his one book without the encouragement of Poe, John Pendleton Kennedy, and Rufus Wilmot

Griswold.[5] As far as the *Messenger* was concerned, however, White's call to literary arms perhaps had more than the desired effect.[6] Many of the unpublished poems of the South had been written on odd scraps of paper, as Cooke described his own habit, or they were inscribed in the albums in which every genteel young woman kept her sentimental memorials. Emily Dickinson to the contrary notwithstanding, not much good poetry is produced this way. When White and Heath called for Southern contributions, the albums yielded their treasures, presumably over the dead bodies of the protesting authors. An attempt at anonymity was usually made, some contributors allowing their effusions to be sent in by a "friend," others modestly concealing themselves behind single or multiple initials or pseudonyms. Frequently the disguises were transparent. John Collins McCabe signed his verse "M'C," and Alexander Beaufort Meek went so far as to give his address— "A. B. M. of Tuscaloosa."

Philip Cooke, the best of the *Messenger* poets except for Poe, called himself "Larry Lyle," but formed his *l*'s so peculiarly that the editor printed the pseudonym as "Zarry Zyle." Cooke almost gave his identity away, however, by writing an indignant protest against a criticism of his "Song of the Seasons" by an anonymous correspondent who simply gave his address—Shepherdstown, Virginia. The critic had objected in a mild way to the "obscurity" of the poem (this was the usual charge in America against anything less pellucid than Gray's "Elegy"). In his rebuttal Cooke quoted an attack that Editor Heath himself had made against critics in general, implying that the Shepherdstown correspondent must be, as Heath had described critics, "one of the little great men in the world, who have the vanity to conceive that their taste and judgment, (if they have any) is the standard for all mankind, and who snap and bark like the curs which infest our streets, and annoy the byways . . . ."[7]

---

[5] Allen, *Philip Pendleton Cooke*, 67–71.

[6] In July of 1835 Edward Sparhawk, White's second editor, printed this remark: "The quantity of rhyme poured in upon us, is indeed a matter of admiration. The effusions which we consign to outer darkness monthly, are past enumeration." *Southern Literary Messenger*, I (1834–35), 652.

[7] *Ibid.*, 388.

Cooke's defense is not particularly significant as literary criticism, but it does show how easily the ire of an American author, particularly a Southern amateur, could be aroused by hostile criticism. Harsh criticism, particularly of the sort that had been in fashion a few years earlier in the British quarterlies and in a few American journals, would have seemed especially out of place in a new provincial journal.[8] White had invited contributions from friends and acquaintances in Virginia, and no doubt some contributors thought that the *Messenger* would be a kind of organ for a mutual admiration society of unpublished Southern authors. The Shepherdstown correspondent had been very tactless in speculating that the bad poems printed in the *Messenger* must have come from White's friends. "I know that you have too much taste to have printed them through choice," [9] Shepherdstown hastened to add. Literary logrolling was the order of the day, and the correspondent simply assumed that it was going on in the *Messenger*.

The reputation for publishing too much bad verse continued to dog the *Messenger* even during Poe's editorship, but even so he sometimes found it necessary to apologize for rejecting contributions from friends, either his or White's. Too, it must have been a

---

[8] This opinion was expressed within a year by a Southern newspaper, the Newbern *Spectator*, after Poe's criticism had become well known. The *Spectator* charged that there was not enough talent in the South for the *Messenger* to adopt the tone of Jeffrey, *Blackwood's*, or Walsh. See Chapter VII, note 3. Robert Walsh, a Philadelphia journalist, was the only American before Poe who had earned a reputation as a harsh critic. William Wirt had been angered by Walsh's criticism but in 1829 had advised Poe to get advice from Walsh about publishing his poems, and Poe had done so. See *Letters*, I, 20. One of the reviewers for Walsh's journal, Dr. James McHenry, learned that punishment for an overly harsh review could be swift. His assault upon William Cullen Bryant and Nathaniel Parker Willis in 1832 had aroused the enmity of the New York *Knickerbocker*, and the *Knickerbocker* rebuttal had destroyed him as a critic. See Sidney P. Moss, *Poe's Literary Battles* (Durham, 1963), 64–67, for an account of the McHenry affair and its relevance as a forecast of what would happen to Poe a few years later. Regional rivalries were too intense for a journal to permit an "outside" attack upon a local author to go unpunished. For an account of these rivalries, see Frank Luther Mott, *A History of American Magazines, 1741–1850* (New York, 1930); and Perry Miller, *The Raven and the Whale* (New York, 1956).

[9] *Southern Literary Messenger*, I (1834–35), 324.

frustrating experience for Poe simply to wade through the mass of anonymous contributions that appeared in response to White's call. Occasionally these contributions appeared with covering letters such as the following: "I send you these lines without the writer's name. It is one of many instances in proof of what I have long believed, that selections might be made from the unpublished writings of Virginians, composing a volume of which any country might be proud. The writer of the above throws off such scraps at idle times, without effort and without pretension. With so much of the inspiration of poetry, he has nothing of its madness, and will never consent to be known to the world as an author." [10] This communication speaks for itself about the uneasiness that writing poetry caused among Virginians. A poet was quite likely to be a mad fellow, and the only way for a gentleman to compose poetry was to "throw off scraps" at idle times. The scrap thrown off in this case was called "Beauty Without Loveliness," a poem neither worse nor better than dozens of others White published during the first year of his magazine.

Thus one of Poe's problems after he became editor had to do with accepting or rejecting the contributions of Southern poetasters, who could be very superior in refusing to acknowledge themselves as authors but who could also be furious when their literary offspring were mistreated. Each author who had some personal claim had to be handled as a special case, as Poe's several letters of apology indicate.[11] And there was always the editorial embarrassment of refusing a Southern contribution after Heath and White had announced that the chief purpose of the journal was to awaken the slumbering Southern muse.

[10] *Ibid.*, 255.

[11] In March, 1836, Poe wrote to the Richmond minister, John Collins McCabe, about the difficulty of making selections from the "mass of MSS." and acknowledged his embarrassment at having to read contributions from friends. *Letters*, I, 86. He overcame his embarrassment enough to reject McCabe's poem, "The Consumptive Girl," not on the grounds of its hackneyed subject (an astonishing number of poems were written about tuberculosis), but because of its defective versification. Poe also had to apologize to Beverley Tucker and Lydia Huntley Sigourney, and it is very probable that there were letters to unknown contributors that have been lost.

From the first, however, the *Messenger* had several regular contributors, some of them from the North, who were a little better
than most of the Southern amateurs. Notable among these were
Mrs. Lydia Huntley Sigourney and Mrs. E. F. Ellet (with whom
Poe was to have an unpleasant involvement ten years later). To
modern taste the moralistic melancholy of Mrs. Sigourney, who
was called the "American Hemans," is scarcely preferable to the
death-and-damnation despair of the Byronic tribe, but at least she
was a professional writer, highly esteemed in both North and
South.

The prose selections in the *Messenger* during the first year, except for articles reprinted from other journals and Poe's tales, were
not much better than the poems. Apparently Virginians doted (or
at least Heath thought they did) on descriptions of visits to the
Virginia Springs, which he published with monotonous regularity.
Then there was a fairly steady diet of moral tales, frequently of revenge, jealousy, or some other "low passion," but invariably ending
with an exhortation to the audience to take heed from the horrible
example presented in such frightening detail. For heavy reading the
subscriber to the *Messenger* had a few articles on aesthetic subjects, such as George Cooke's series called "The Fine Arts," and
speeches, most of which had been delivered before the Virginia
Historical and Philosophical Society. George Tucker's "Discourse
on the Progress of Philosophy" was greatly admired, but then
Tucker was professor of moral philosophy at the University of Virginia and had already achieved a reputation as a writer. Other
speeches were somewhat less instructive. The most impressive
piece of fiction was a serial novel called "Lionel Granby," which
proceeded on its deadly course through number after number.

This, then, was the journal to which Poe was contributing and of
which he was to become the editor. A more formidable problem
than the quality of the contributions (over which Poe never had
complete editorial control) was the journal's opinion, probably
originated by Heath but assented to by White, that literature must
be moral and instructive in purpose. In this the policy of the
Messenger approximated that of the other American journals of
the day, and it was against such a policy that Poe was to mount his

strongest attack, basing his own critical standards on art instead of morality.

Heath soon made it clear that he could not approve of what he called "fairy tales," that he had no liking for "German *diablerie*," and that if a writer did not display "good sense, sound morality, and correct taste," [12] he could expect short shrift from the editor of the *Messenger*. And short shrift he usually got, although Heath had no scruples against condemning a writer such as Edward Bulwer, who was enormously popular, and then filling his pages by pirating in its entirety one of the tales that he had condemned. William Beckford's *Vathek*, an oriental Gothic novel which Byron had liked and which Poe was rather fond of himself, aroused Heath's deepest indignation: "We should pronounce it . . . to be the production of a sensualist and an infidel—one who could riot in the most abhorred and depraved conceptions and whose prolific fancy preferred as its repast all that was diabolical and monstrous, rather than what was beautiful and good. We shall not even attempt a detailed account of this volume . . . ." [13]

But Heath never gave a detailed account of *any* volume. Excuses were usually made, giving one reason or another for failing to analyze the contents of the book being reviewed. Actually Heath had sufficient reason: he was a busy man, and the work he did for the *Messenger* was done out of friendship.

Beverley Tucker was also a reviewer for the *Messenger* during its first year; his reviews are superior to Heath's both in style and criti-

---

[12] *Southern Literary Messenger*, I (1834–35), 324. Heath had received some verses from a poet who signed himself "Fra Diavolo," and he seized upon the occasion to make editorial remarks not only about the bad taste of writing poems featuring "lover fiends" but also about the folly of imitating such "vicious models as Byron, Shelly [*sic*], and other gentlemen of the 'Satanic School.'" Several times he proclaimed his dislike for "fairy tales," and he advised contributors to "throw aside the trammels of foreign reading." *Ibid.*, 64, 125, 377. Heath's attitude was precisely that of conservative British reviewers of some twenty years earlier. Southey and others had condemned the "Satanic School" and "lover fiends"; see William S. Ward, "Some Aspects of the Conservative Attitude Toward Poetry in English Criticism, 1798–1820," *PMLA*, LX (1945), 397.

[13] *Southern Literary Messenger*, I (1834–35), 189.

cal objectivity. In fact, some of them have been mistaken for Poe's.[14] Tucker found less fault with Bulwer than Heath had. *The Last Days of Pompeii*, Tucker averred, had raised the popular British author 50 per cent in his opinion. But even with Tucker Bulwer did not get off scot-free: "Mr. Bulwer's pictures, in all his works that we have read, are too gaudy,—too highly wrought,—and therefore too much above nature,—and want the delightful repose and serene features which distinguish the great Scottish magician [Sir Walter Scott]." [15] Thus, according to this Southern critic, Sir Walter followed nature's simple plan, whereas Bulwer was too prone to artifice. Even Bulwer's "vivid and powerful fancy," his "extensive learning," his "fine imagery and impassioned eloquence" did not redeem him from the fault of imposing art too strenuously upon unpretentious nature. After such generalizations, however, Tucker was no more willing than Heath to undertake an analysis of the book being reviewed, for that would deprive the reader "of much of that exquisite pleasure which attends the progressive development of the plot."

In spite of Tucker's fairly favorable review, we can conclude that the *Messenger* was hostile to Bulwer until Poe took over, for immediately after Tucker's review, as if to atone for his leniency, a long diatribe by the poet Sumner Lincoln Fairfield was printed which accused Bulwer of having stolen the idea for his novel and some of his scenes from Fairfield's narrative poem, "The Last Night of Pompeii." [16] Fairfield was bitter over the fact that Bulwer's novel was immensely popular while his own poem had lan-

---

[14] Tucker's reviews of Paulding's *Slavery in the United States* and of Manzoni's *I Promessi Sposi* are both printed in the Harrison edition of Poe's works. For the identification of *Messenger* authors other than Poe, I have been guided by David K. Jackson, *Contributors and Contributions to the Southern Literary Messenger* (Charlottesville, 1936).

[15] *Southern Literary Messenger*, I (1834–35), 241.

[16] *Ibid.*, 246. Fairfield was also a journalist, having founded the *North American Magazine* in Philadelphia in 1832. The *Messenger* established closer relations with Baltimore and Philadelphia journals than with the New York and New England publications. It might have been predicted that Poe, after being rejected by New York, would go to Philadelphia, where he found a post in 1839.

guished and died. Such treatment, he trumpeted, drives American poets "far away from the barren realm of Parnassus." Plagiarism, native versus foreign authors—these were problems to which Poe was to address himself later; but they appeared in the *Messenger* before Poe made them his special concern.

Probably the greatest difficulty Poe was to encounter after his connection with the *Messenger* became official was the announced editorial opposition of the journal to harsh analytical criticism. In the "Editorial Remarks" of the March, 1835, issue Heath had stated: "We can fearlessly recommend the *poetry* in this number, —if not faultless, as at least superior to the carpings of illiberal and puerile criticism." Obviously he meant to forestall *any* criticism of the poems, because he went on to attack the critics who "snap and bark" like curs. This was the editorial statement that Philip Pendleton Cooke quoted in his own defense after being assailed by the Shepherdstown correspondent. Even after Heath left the journal, White continued to be wary of harsh criticism, and that Poe did manage to publish some scathing reviews of worthless books is as much a tribute to his nerve as to his perceptiveness as a critic. Publisher White apparently shuddered many times during 1836 over the occasional savagery of Poe's book reviews.[17]

The April, 1835, number of the *Messenger* was the last one published under Heath's supervision. He was growing restless from the demands of his unsalaried position and found it necessary to devote full time to his own affairs. In the May issue White happily proclaimed that he had secured "a gentleman of approved literary taste and attainments, to whose especial management the editorial department of the 'Messenger' has been confided." Poe was still on the sidelines, a mere contributor, and this new editor was Edward

[17] See White to Lucian Minor, October 1, 1835, and November 23, 1835, for an expression of his reservations about Poe's reviewing methods. In a letter to Beverley Tucker dated April 26, 1837, White showed contempt for Poe's reviews and accused him of failing to read the books he reviewed. He was evidently afraid that Poe would make him legally liable and said as much concerning Poe's proposed inclusion of Cooper in the "Autography" series. White to Poe, September 29, 1835, in *Works*, XVII, 21. Cooper's habit of suing calumniators was well known. Poe was "no lawyer," White exclaimed in the letter to Minor of November 23.

Vernon Sparhawk. His literary attainments were a volume of verse he had published at the age of twenty-two and writing he had done as a reporter for the New York *American*. For some reason Sparhawk did not get along well with White. His journalistic experience, plus the fact that he was to devote full time to the editorial task, should have augured well for White's magazine, but Sparhawk remained at the post for only three months. The May, June, and July issues of the magazine were under his guidance, yet the superiority of a few of the reviews during this period can be credited to Tucker and Poe. Sparhawk's own reviews, when they can be identified, are brief and perfunctory. White must have had problems with Sparhawk from the beginning, because within a month after the new editor had been employed, the publisher was inviting Poe to come to Richmond and join his staff, *if* there should be occasion for his services during the coming winter.[18]

Poe did come to Richmond, but only on a temporary basis. White wrote to Minor on August 18 that he had discharged Sparhawk as "regular editor" but that he would continue to receive assistance from Sparhawk and from Poe, who had promised to remain for one month. Evidently this arrangement was unsatisfactory, however, for early in September White wrote again to Minor, saying that he was acting as his own editor and that he had put together the July number himself. Poe had written several reviews, but, for reasons that we shall see later, he had not been entrusted with the editorship.

The problems Poe was to face when he did become a full-time member of the *Messenger* staff in October are reasonably clear. The owner and publisher, though he was unqualified as an editor, was determined to keep the editorial management of the journal as much as possible in his own hands. Then too, as we have seen, the journal's policy of encouraging Southern writers placed a restriction upon the editorial prerogative to accept contributions on the basis of merit. Finally, the *Messenger* under Heath's management had announced editorial opposition to harsh criticism, obviously with

[18] See Poe to White, June 22, 1835, in *Letters*, I, 63; Poe paraphrased White's offer in his reply.

White's sanction; yet Poe's first fully authenticated review in the magazine employed the type of satire we have noted in the "Letter to Mr. ——— ——." Even against these odds, within one year Poe managed to transform the *Messenger* from an innocuous provincial journal into a nationally known publication, primarily if not entirely through his literary criticism. There were other difficulties of a more personal nature with White, but discussion of these will be reserved while an examination is made of the reviews attributed to Poe before he achieved some measure of editorial authority.

2

As might be expected, Poe's first reviews—if indeed they are his —show little of the quality that was to make him famous. The earliest one which with some reason can be attributed to him is a review of Robert Montgomery Bird's *Calavar; or The Knight of the Conquest*. The review appeared in February, 1835, and there is no external evidence connecting Poe with the *Messenger* before March, but Bird was reviewed three times in the journal, apparently by the same critic, and the last review is certainly Poe's.[19] The first review is distinctive only because the style is better than that of the other *Messenger* reviews in the first few numbers and because it sticks fairly well to its subject. Tucker was the only other *Messenger* reviewer who was capable of writing so well, and he was addicted to the essay-type review that was becoming common in American journals—discoursing at length on whatever struck his fancy, even if it was not directly connected with the book being reviewed.

[19] The three novels reviewed were *Calavar, The Infidel,* and *The Hawks of Hawk's Hollow*. The author of the second review acknowledged the authorship of the first, and the author of the third indicated that he had already expressed his opinion of the previous two. However, he used the editorial "we," and it is possible that he was simply acknowledging the fact that the two previous books had been reviewed by the *Messenger*. The third review is unquestionably Poe's, and the first two have been accepted by a number of bibliographers, including William Doyle Hull, Killis Campbell, David K. Jackson, and C. F. Heartman and J. R. Canny. Professor T. O. Mabbott, however, has written to me that he considers the two earlier reviews doubtful.

It makes little difference, except for bibliographical accuracy, whether this review is accepted in the Poe canon or not; it can neither add to nor detract from his reputation. It is useful, however, as an illustration of the standards applied to the novel. The reviewer examined the work in terms of verisimilitude, characterization, and style, and concluded that, although "it is certainly the very best American novel, excepting one or two of Mr. Cooper's . . . ," it fails in one respect because it is "too unnatural even for romance." [20] This sounds like Tucker, but Poe also employed the standard of nature in regard to the novel. Since there were no rules for the novel, the critic had to borrow his criteria from other genres. If the novel departed too obviously from verisimilitude, or if it made use of what William Gilmore Simms called "the wild and the wonderful," [21] it could be considered as a romance and the demand for verisimilitude was mitigated. If it were a novel of manners, it was supposed to depict with fidelity the society upon which it focused. Journalistic critics were calling for lifelikeness long before the advent of realism, yet the fidelity to nature demanded by the critics of Poe's time was as different from the realism of William Dean Howells as Howells' realism was different from the naturalism of Norris and Dreiser. What Poe and his fellow journalists demanded in a novel was Aristotelian probability in both action and character. Although Bird's *Calavar* was supposed to be a historical romance, the critic complained of its lack of probability: "There is too much improbability and miraculous agency in the various life-preserving expedients, and extraordinary rescues which are constantly occurring . . . they impart to a tale founded on historical truth, an air of oriental fiction which is not agreeable."

Characters too should be true to nature, and Bird, the reviewer thought, was no more qualified "to depict the female" than was Fenimore Cooper. Today we object to Cooper's idealized heroines because they do not come to life: they wander through the forests, unmussed in clothing and deportment, swooning at frequent inter-

[20] *Southern Literary Messenger*, I (1834–35), 315.
[21] For a discussion of Simms's theory of the romance, see Edd Winfield Parks, *William Gilmore Simms as Literary Critic* (Athens, Ga., 1961), 10–22.

vals, and voicing only the proper sentiments. The reviewer of the 1830's was also annoyed by the somnambulism of Cooper's females, but he had no objection per se to their exemplary behavior. When Poe and his contemporaries came to judge a fictional character, they measured not by life itself but by what they thought people *should be*. We will find in later reviews that when Poe applauded fidelity to nature in character portrayal, he was speaking of idealized human nature, not the sweaty actual. Neither he nor his contemporaries approved of inconsistency in behavior—which is of course characteristic of real life. A female character in fiction should behave according to her station in society, her education, and the received moral standards of her class. If her behavior were inconsistent with these, she was considered unnatural.

An essay which appeared in a later number of the *Messenger*, though it is not Poe's, is worth quoting at length because it illustrates the attitude of many American critics toward fiction. After discoursing on the amount of moral good that could be achieved by a novel which observed the usual pieties, the anonymous essayist stated:

> The novel is only valuable as illustrating some peculiarities, defects, or excellencies of character—passages of historical interest, or the manners and customs of a class; and its success must depend upon the ability with which it is adapted to the end desired to be accomplished. . . . The whole class of romances viewed as a means of forming individual character, must assume in the eyes of the moralist and statesman, an importance far beyond their intrinsic value, as literary works; and it is the forgetting of the ulterior and vastly more interesting purpose which they serve, in the general economy of society, that has misled many virtuous and even able men, to undervalue and despise the whole species as frivolous and worthless.[22]

Thus the novel had value, but not aesthetic value. It was likely to be viewed as social history or, if a romance, as an instrument formative of character. This attitude underscores the necessity, as conceived by the critic of the 1830's, of characters being consis-

[22] *Southern Literary Messenger*, I (1834–35), 479.

tently good or evil. The idealized heroes of romances were models for emulation; the villains were dramatized warnings of the penalties of vice. To neglect this moral assessment in favor of intrinsic literary value, as Poe was increasingly prone to do, was thought by many to be an abdication of the critic's primary responsibility.

The review of *Calavar*, whether it is Poe's or not, is conventional enough in its approach. Here and there it follows the pattern set by Heath and Tucker, particularly in the apology for not examining the work closely: the critic would "forbear making quotations from the work, or entering into a more minute analysis of the story." Unlike the Poe of later years, who was not provincial in his attitudes, this reviewer betrayed American self-consciousness by claiming that *Calavar* would not "shrink from competition with the very best European works of the same character." If the review is Poe's, he was not yet sure enough of himself to deviate from the norms of American journalistic criticism. An American critic was *expected* to scrabble industriously among American publications to find something with which to answer Sydney Smith's contemptuous query, "Who reads an American book?"

Although William Doyle Hull lists several brief reviews in the April number as Poe's, the only one for which there is external evidence is the review of *Confessions of a Poet*.[23] This review is the first of the type that gained Poe the reputation of a literary hatchet man. In it some of his pet prejudices, which later were proposed as critical principles, first manifested themselves; chief among these was his distaste for any form of affectation. He was quick to point it out in this review: "The author has very few claims to the sacred name he has thought proper to assume. And indeed his own ideas on this subject seem not to satisfy himself. He is in doubt, poor man, of his own qualifications, and having proclaimed himself a poet in the title page, commences his book by disavowing all pretensions to the character. We can enlighten him on this head.

[23] *Works*, VIII, 2–3. The author of the *Confessions* was Laughton Osborn, a minor New York poet whose satire *A Vision of Rubeta* was also reviewed severely by Poe in 1845. Poe's letter to Osborn in 1845 professing admiration for the *Confessions* and denying authorship of the second review appears to be dishonest on both counts. See *Letters*, I, 294–95n.

There is nothing of the *vates* about him. He is no poet—and most positively he is no prophet. He is a writer of notes." Explanatory notes were to be Poe's special abomination. Later he was to formulate the dictum that a poem should contain within itself all that was necessary for its comprehension; but as yet he merely ridiculed the author's method: "Lest his book should *not* be understood he illustrates it by notes, and then lest the notes *should* be understood, why he writes them in French. All this is very clear, and very clever to say no more." What Poe would have said about Eliot's *The Waste Land* is alarming to contemplate.

Less forgivable, if we think that a literary critic should exercise *caritas* toward his subjects, is Poe's application to the unfortunate author of the mordant humor he had learned from his study of the reviews in *Blackwood's Magazine:*

> The author avers upon his word of honor that in commencing this work he loads a pistol, and places it upon the table. He farther [*sic*] states that, upon coming to a conclusion, it is his intention to blow out what he supposes to be his brains. Now this is excellent. But, even with so rapid a writer as the poet must undoubtedly be, there would be some difficulty in completing the book under thirty days or thereabouts. The best of powder is apt to sustain injury by lying so long "in the load." We sincerely hope the gentleman took the precaution to examine his priming before attempting the rash act. A flash in the pan—and in such a case—were a thing to be lamented. Indeed there would be no answering for the consequences. We might even have a second series of the Confessions.

Today we are likely to think that the author of the *Confessions* got no more than he deserved, but Thomas Willis White, who was afraid of offending anyone who might be in a position to injure his young journal, did not think so. Poe had to defend his review to White because an article in the Richmond *Compiler* charged that he had not read the book that he reviewed.[24]

It is difficult to understand American journalists' uneasiness about harsh reviews without reference to reviewing practices in England for the preceding quarter-century. The British quarterlies had

[24] Poe to White, May 30, 1835, in *Letters*, I, 59–60.

a reputation for savage reviewing. It was thought that Keats had been "killed" by criticism.[25] Everyone who kept up with literature was familiar with the fact that a lashing given to Byron's *Hours of Idleness* had provoked the hot-tempered lord's retaliation in "English Bards and Scotch Reviewers." Sydney Smith, notorious for his contempt for American literature; William Gifford, who though not guilty was generally credited with the destruction of Keats's "Endymion" in the *London Quarterly* in 1818; Christopher North; and Francis Jeffrey had been feared, respected, or sometimes detested in America for years before Poe tried the "tomahawk" method.

Distaste for the harsh criticism of the early reviewers had been marked in the South. In 1816, Thomas Jefferson had written to William Wirt, upon publication of Wirt's biography of Patrick Henry: "You must expect to be criticized; and by a former letter I see you expect it. By the Quarterly Reviewers you will be hacked and hewed, with tomahawk and scalping knife. Those of Edinburgh, with the same anti-American prejudices, but sometimes considering us as allies against their administration, will do it more decently." [26] Jefferson, an experienced politician, cynically expected political bias to control the tone of a review, but, like a few other Southern writers, he disliked analytical criticism. In the same letter he went on to say: "I have always very much despised the artificial canons of criticism. When I have read a work in prose and poetry, or seen a painting, a statue, etc., I have only asked myself

[25] The first sentence of Poe's "The Duc De L'Omelette" is "Keats fell by a criticism," a statement so out of place in the tale that it can be understood only by reference to Poe's intention in his projected "Tales of the Folio Club" to burlesque journalistic criticism. See Poe to Joseph and Edwin Buckingham, May 4, 1833, in *Letters*, I, 53. One of the members of the Folio Club was to be named Mr. Blackwood Blackwood. The irony is that in 1833 Poe was disposed to satirize criticism, while two years later he was defending satirical criticism in a letter to Beverley Tucker, December 1, 1835, *ibid.*, 77. Poe's attitude toward criticism remained ambivalent for some time—until his necessary profession muted the protesting voice of the young poet.

[26] In Paul Leicester Ford (ed.), *The Works of Thomas Jefferson* (New York, 1905), XII, 36.

whether it gives me pleasure, whether it is animating, interesting, attaching?"

Wirt, one of the most professional of the Virginia writers before Poe, fumed at a review of his book of essays, *The Old Bachelor*, by the American critic Robert Walsh. Walsh had charged Wirt with "extravagance of fancy," but Wirt defended himself in a letter to Francis Walker Gilmer, asserting that Walsh's "fancy has no *retina* in common with mine; it does not reflect the same colours, nor the same objects." But, he continued, "because this critic's auditory nerves are of lead, his eye dim, and his sensibility comparatively cold, my language is foolishness and hyperbole to him. This I verily believe is the chief ground of his censure." [27] The fact that Wirt defended himself is not important—all writers are prone to do that. It is the nature of his defense that is revealing. Apparently he considered as the chief qualification of a critic the sensibility of genius. He goes on to say of Walsh:

> He has . . . acquired the dashing, dissertating style of the Edinburgh Reviewers. He knows, too, the just principles by which criticism should be regulated towards the author: that it is the business of the critic to praise as well as to censure, whenever they are due. He understands, also, the mechanical rules of criticism. But all this cannot supply that native want of sensitive delicacy without which a man can never be a great critic. It has been said that genius is not necessary to a critic; it is enough that he has taste. I doubt the possibility of the seperation [sic], in literature. For they seem to me to depend upon an identity of organization which qualifies a man equally for either task—to write or to judge.

Wirt's opinions remind us of Poe's insistence upon natural sensibility as a qualification for the critic, as well as of his early hostility toward criticism. Such opinions put into practice would result in appreciation, not analysis, and Poe's "letter" of 1831 was much more consonant with the attitude of Jefferson and Wirt than were the reviews he wrote after he became a journalist.

In order to understand the taboos Poe was violating when he re-

[27] In Richard Beale Davis, *Francis Walker Gilmer: Life and Learning in Jefferson's Virginia* (Richmond, 1939), 130.

viewed *Confessions of a Poet,* it is necessary to examine the grounds upon which harsh criticism was usually based in the American journals of the 1830's. It was perfectly safe to be venomous toward a book, as Heath was in his review of *Vathek,* if atheism, irreverence, or immorality were either explicit or implicit in it. It was equally safe to condemn a book if it contained ideas that were considered daring, radical, or dangerous. The Southern distaste for transcendentalism, which Poe professed to share, had to do with the political, social, and religious implications of the philosophy. Among the transcendentalists were abolitionists, social levelers, and pantheists. Furthermore, transcendentalist jargon was "mystical" and "obscure." Most good Americans thought that the truth should be clearly expressed and easy to understand.[28]

There were also the idiosyncrasies of individual editors or publishers. Heath's opposition to "fairy tales" and "German *diablerie*" was not based upon any aesthetic or philosophical consideration. He objected to the first because he considered fairy tales, like *The Arabian Nights,* trivial and childish and not fit "for the intellectual appetite." He objected to the second on grounds of good taste and morality, often considered almost synonymous in American criticism.

Hostility toward a book on purely literary grounds was comparatively rare. "Affectation" and "striving for effect" were pejorative terms occasionally used in critiques, but these really had as much to do with the character of the author as with his work, for the work was an index to character. The demand for sincerity was normally made.[29] In the criticism of poetry, when an attempt was made to invoke an aesthetic standard, it was usually derived from the premises of taste. The critic simply held up the "beauties" and "sublimities" of the work for admiration. When he censured, he quoted the faulty passages, as Poe did in the "letter," pronouncing them bad in *ex cathedra* fashion. Occasionally an American critic during the 1830's pointed out imaginative or fanciful passages of a

[28] Charvat, *American Critical Thought,* 7–26.
[29] For a discussion of the criterion of "sincerity" in romantic and Victorian criticism, see Abrams, *The Mirror and the Lamp,* 298, 317–20.

poem, but not often did he follow Coleridge's lead and attempt to make a psychological distinction between the two. In fact, now and then a critic objected to "overheated" imagination or to "extravagant" fancy, echoing neoclassic opinion. There is no evidence of distrust of the imagination in the *Messenger*, however. Even Heath extolled the imagination in the manner of the Scottish critics when it obeyed the conventional moral sanctions. Reviewing the *Sketches* by Mrs. Sigourney, Heath wrote: "Though highly gifted with the powers of imagination, and of course capable of exciting that faculty in others, her object seems to be rather to touch the springs of the heart and awaken the moral feelings of our nature. . . . She is an example altogether worthy of imitation among the professors of literature, in enlisting all its allurements in the great cause of human virtue." [30] Heath never forgot that the chief value of literature was moral edification, and he could never bring himself to believe that Poe's excursions into the horrible served any useful purpose. The critic, as well as the creative writer, was supposed to direct his efforts according to the accepted criteria of social value, to enlist in "the great cause of human virtue."

These, then, were the critical practices Poe was expected to observe, the practices hallowed by custom and safe to follow. As we shall see, Poe followed some of them. He felt his way for a time, but as soon as he gained experience and assurance he began to search for viable aesthetic principles upon which to base his decisions, principles by which he could demonstrate literary merits or faults.

There is some evidence that Poe was called upon to furnish a number of reviews for the April issue other than that of *Confessions of a Poet*; but those that may be attributed to him are brief notices such as any reviewer might have written. His contributions to the May number, the first issue under Sparhawk, were reviews of John Pendleton Kennedy's *Horse-Shoe Robinson* [31] and Mrs. Frances Anne Butler's *Journal*. In reviewing *Horse-Shoe Robinson* Poe confronted the difficulty any critic faces when handling the

---

[30] *Southern Literary Messenger*, I (1834–35), 22.
[31] *Works*, VIII, 4–11.

work of a friend and benefactor. It would have been standard for a journalistic critic to praise the novel without reservation, perhaps comparing it favorably with the work of Scott. Actually, Poe's commendation is quite measured. He acknowledged that the "spirit of imitation" had been visible in Kennedy's first book, *Swallow Barn*, and had, "in great measure, over-clouded its rare excellence." *Horse-Shoe Robinson* was original, however, and should, in Poe's opinion, "place Mr. Kennedy at once in the very first rank of American novelists." If this statement appears exaggerated, we should remember that the only major American novelist at this time was Cooper. Simms and Bird were just beginning to attract attention.

Poe followed the journalistic norm for reviewing novels, giving copious extracts from the book and commenting on character and style. As Heath and Tucker did before him, he made an excuse for omitting consideration of the plot: "We do not wish to attempt any analysis of the story itself—or that connecting chain which unites into one proper whole the varied events of the novel. We feel that in so doing, we should, in some measure, mar the interest by anticipation; a grievous sin too often indulged in by reviewers, and against which, should we ever be so lucky as to write a book, we would protest with all our hearts."

Perhaps there is more here than meets the eye. Poe made the same excuse as did Heath, but one suspects that with Heath the motivation was either lack of time or ability. Poe, however, as he was to prove shortly, did examine plot construction, although in the novel he did not consider it an absolute desideratum. Kennedy's plots were anything but well constructed, so Heath's old evasion served Poe well if he wished to avoid censuring the work of his benefactor. He did praise the character of *Horse-Shoe Robinson* without reservation: "He is the life and soul of the drama—the bone and sinew of the book—its very breath—its every thing which gives it strength, substance, and vitality." Here Poe was sound enough, and he has been sustained by subsequent opinion. Nor did he find fault with Kennedy's style: "Its general character, as indeed the general character of all that we have seen from the same pen, is a certain unpretending simplicity, nervous, forcible, and altogether devoid of affectation. This is a style of writing above all others to be desired, and above all others difficult of attainment." Poe was making a perfectly standard comment. "Simplicity," with the overtones it carried of "nature's truth," was admired by Poe's contemporaries.[32] A complicated, rhetorical style, on the other hand, was likely to be considered affected or obscure. Poe's statement that Kennedy's style was devoid of affectation would have been very meaningful to the *Messenger* reader. In the March number an essay entitled "Thoughts on Affectation" had expressed the conventional attitude. The essay begins with the definition from Dr. Johnson's *Dictionary*: "Affectation . . . is 'an artificial show, an elaborate performance, a false pretense, . . . affected—studied with overmuch care, or with hypocritical appearance.'" It is the opposite of "the most captivating of all graces—*simplicity and truth*." Thus affectation was not simply a harmless mannerism to the critic of Poe's time, as the essay goes on to indicate: "Of all the diseases of the mind or the heart, affectation is the fittest subject of ridicule—since we are ridiculous not for what we are, but for what we pretend to be . . . *la belle nature* is loveliest when embellished, not prostituted, by art, in its most vulgar form, viz: *affectation*." [33] Sincerity and plainness were virtues Americans tended to arrogate to themselves, in contrast to sophisticated, "affected" Europeans. Thus, by saying Kennedy's style was devoid of affectation, Poe was paying him a high compliment both as a man and as a writer.

The chief fault that Poe found with *Horse-Shoe Robinson*, once

[32] Poe, oddly enough, had just written a letter to White (April 30, 1835, *Letters*, I, 58) disparaging simplicity as a literary virtue: "Nobody is more aware than I am that simplicity is the cant of the day—but take my word for it no one cares any thing about simplicity in their hearts. Believe me also, in spite of what people say to the contrary, that there is nothing easier in the world than to be extremely simple." By the evidence of this statement Poe adopted the "cant of the day" in order to say something good about the style of his friend.

[33] *Southern Literary Messenger*, I (1834–35), 365. The author was John H. Bernard, of "Caroline," according to a letter from T. W. White to Lucian Minor dated April 18, 1835. White disparaged the essay, probably because it was more platitudinous than most.

he had ruled out consideration of the plot, was the punctuation. Even here he hedged a bit by saying that he did not know whether to blame the author or the printer. Kennedy used the dash to excess, a fault Poe dwelt upon at some length; he even rewrote one of Kennedy's paragraphs without dashes to prove that it would read as well with normal punctuation. In conclusion he commended, after the manner of Heath, the "high tone of morality, healthy and masculine," that "breathes throughout the book," but he took exception to the "too scrupulously rigid poetical justice" that was dealt out to all the "great and little villains of the story." In this objection Poe revealed a difference from most American journalistic critics. As a rule the critic did not cavil at poetic justice. In fact, in the very same issue of the *Messenger* an article, probably by Sparhawk, declares a certain novel defective because the villains receive the same reward as the virtuous characters.[34] Poe, though not averse to praising the high moral tone of a piece of fiction, was concerned with technique. Ordinarily he deplored the wrenching of plot that was sometimes necessary to reward virtue and punish vice. The denouement of a tale, he was to insist in later years, should be a consequence of previous action and character development.

A review of the *Journal* by Frances Anne Butler (the actress Fanny Kemble), which also appeared in the May issue, has been attributed to Poe.[35] Mrs. Butler's work was one of those criticisms of America by an English traveler that aroused resentment among sensitive citizens. The *Messenger* reviewer displayed a far more liberal attitude toward foreign criticism than did most of his countrymen. Patriotic outrage was discarded in favor of common sense: "To be indignant at gross misrepresentation of our country is an exhibition of patriotism in one of its most laudable forms. But the sentiment may be carried too far, and may blind us to evils and de-

[34] *Southern Literary Messenger*, I (1834–35), 481.
[35] Several bibliographers have listed this review in the Poe canon, but I have considered it doubtful on the basis of style and attitude. In response to my query, Professor T. O. Mabbott indicated that it was probably not Poe's.

ficiencies in our condition, when pointed out by a foreigner, which it would be well for us rather to consider with a view to their amendment." [36] Although he was open-minded toward Mrs. Butler's attitudes, the reviewer showed typical American prudishness in regard to her language: "the style and language is often coarse, we might say vulgar; and her more impassioned exclamations are often characterized by a vehemence which is very like *profanity*, an offence that would not be tolerated in a writer of the other sex. We cite a few from among the many passages which we have noted, as specimens of undignified, unfeminine, and unscholarlike phraseology . . . ." [37] This "unscholarlike phraseology" consisted of such expressions as *dawdled, gulped, walloped,* and *pottered,* which would have been objected to by Dr. Johnson on grounds of taste but without the overtones of moral reprehension that we sense in the American critic.

Unquestionably Poe could be prudish. He shared the attitudes of his time toward coarse language and the delicacy expected of "females," but if the May review of Mrs. Butler's *Journal* was his, he soon changed his mind about her coarseness. In the December number of the *Messenger,* the first issue under his editorship, he dismissed the charge of vulgarity in a review of the *Edinburgh Review,* pointing out that the British journal "defends her from the ridiculous accusation of vulgarity (there is positively not an iota of vulgarity in the composition of Fanny Kemble) and very justly gives us a rap over the knuckles for our overweening vanity, self-sufficiency, and testiness of temper." [38] The December review is definitely in the pungent Poe manner. If the May review was his, he was feeling his way, diplomatically displaying current attitudes toward gentility of language and female behavior (Tucker thought it disgraceful for the "sacred name" of a woman to be "profaned by the public breath"). In the December number, however, Poe was primarily responsible for the editorial criticism and, as we shall see, this new authority made a difference. If the earlier review was not his, it is quite possible that his defense of Fanny Kemble in December was an open challenge to the previous editorial standards.

[36] *Works,* VIII, 25.   [37] *Ibid.,* 22.   [38] *Ibid.,* 86.

By the end of 1835 a new critical voice was speaking in the *Messenger*, and Poe wanted the world to know it.

Two reviews in the June, 1835, number of the *Messenger* are Poe's; the first is of Robert Montgomery Bird's *The Infidel*,[39] and the second, too perfunctory to discuss, is of Eliza Leslie's *Pencil Sketches*. Poe approves of *The Infidel* in measured terms, using the normative formula of praising exciting incidents, well-drawn characters, and enchanting descriptions of natural scenery. He impressed his own stamp on the review by a careful analysis of the author's style, finding fault only in the overuse of one "inelegant" word—*working*—used to describe the "convulsions of the countenance, under the influence of strong passions: as, his *working* and agonized visage . . . ." Poe preferred high-style, "elegant" language in all contexts except the humorous, but he was more concerned with taste than with verbal morality. Heath and Tucker, on the other hand, as was customary with American journalistic critics, had conceived it their duty to attack any expression that might ruffle the placid surface of linguistic gentility.

3

Although two reviews in the July, 1835, number of the *Messenger* were printed by Harrison in Poe's *Works*, a letter from White to Lucian Minor states that all the criticism in that issue was by Sparhawk; [40] but then Sparhawk was discharged and White called for help from Poe. At some time between July 20 and August 18, 1835, Poe came to Richmond. All of the book notices for the August number were his, but they were brief paragraphs obviously rushed through to meet a deadline. As yet Poe had no editorial authority, and White was reluctant to give him any, perhaps for the reason that appears in his letter to Minor on September 8. "Poe is now in my employ—not as Editor. He is unfortunately rather dissipated,—and therefore I can place very little reliance upon him. His disposition is quite amiable. He will be of some assistance to me in proof-reading—at least I hope so." So much paper has been

[39] *Ibid.*, 32–37.   [40] August 18, 1835.

expended on Poe's drinking habits that it is supererogatory, to use one of his own favorite terms, to drag forth the matter again. But the letter quoted above was written *before* White should have developed any reservations about Poe on other grounds. True, he had objected, as did Heath, to the "horror" of Poe's "Berenice," [41] and he had been a little alarmed at the reaction of the Richmond *Compiler* to Poe's first attempt at a satirical review; but, as he said, Poe was quite amiable. His only uneasiness about Poe in September of 1835 appears to have concerned his reliability; a man with a hangover is not at his best during office hours. This, on the face of it, accounts for his reluctance to extend editorial authority to Poe; it seems unlikely that White was so stupid as to fail to recognize the young man's flair for journalism.

On September 21 White wrote to Minor again: "Poe has flew [*sic*] the track already. His habits were not good.—He is in addition the victim of melancholy. I should not be at all astonished to hear that he had been guilty of suicide. I am now alone." White was not in error about Poe's tendency toward melancholia. In a letter to Maria Clemm, his aunt, Poe revealed that he was extremely depressed by August 29, evidently because Mrs. Clemm was considering sending his cousin Virginia to live with Neilson Poe, a prosperous relative. This letter, full of the self-pity with which Poe was generously endowed, does hint at suicide. "Oh God have mercy on me. What have I *to live for?* Among strangers with *not one soul to love me.*" [42] Two weeks later Poe wrote to his friend Kennedy in the same vein, but without fixing a cause for his melancholy: "Excuse me, my dear Sir, if in this letter you find much incoherency. My feelings at this moment are pitiable indeed. I am suffering under a depression of spirits such as I have never felt before." [43]

As he was prone to reveal his agony, Poe had probably expressed his feelings to his employer in equally vivid terms. Thus White was

[41] Poe to White, April 30, 1835, in *Letters*, I, 57–58. Poe admitted that "Berenice" was too horrible but undertook a defense of exaggerated effects in short tales and claimed that magazines had owed their success to such tales.

[42] *Ibid.*, 69–71.   [43] *Ibid.*, 73.

able to diagnose Poe as temperamental, and, sober citizen that he was, he feared to entrust the editorship of the *Messenger* to one so unstable. Evidently White had planned to offer Poe some form of permanent employment; [44] but between September 11, when Poe admitted his depression to Kennedy, and September 21, the date of White's second letter to Minor, Poe "flew the track," and in spite of his urgent need for a literary editor White discharged him—or Poe returned to Baltimore on his own initiative. Before he left Richmond, Poe wrote all the reviews for the September number, but after his departure White's journal was in trouble. No October issue was published, and the November one was delayed until December, when it came out as Number 1 of Volume II. Thus Poe's undependability cost the *Messenger* two issues.

White had made up the August number, as he put it in a letter to Minor, "out of his wits," but by September 29 he was at his wits' end. On that date he wrote Poe the now famous letter censuring his drinking habits but holding out a conditional promise of re-employment. The letter seems to be in response to solicitations by Poe:

> That you are sincere in all your promises I firmly believe. But Edgar, when you once again tread these streets, I have my fears that your resolves would fall through,—and that you would again sip the juice, even till it stole away your senses. Rely on your own strength, and you are gone! Look to your Maker for help, and you are safe!
>
> How much I regretted parting with you, is unknown to anyone on this earth, except myself. I was attached to you—and am still,—and willingly would I say return, if I did not dread the hour of separation very shortly again . . . .
>
> You have fine talents, Edgar,—and you ought to have them respected as well as yourself. Learn to respect yourself, and you will very soon find that you are respected. Separate yourself from the bottle, and bottle companions, for ever . . . !
>
> If you should come to Richmond again, and again should be an

[44] In the letters cited above, Poe told Mrs. Clemm that White was going to pay him $60 a month, but he told Kennedy that the salary would be $520 a year.

assistant in my office, it must be expressly understood by us that all engagements on my part would be dissolved, the moment you get drunk.

No man is safe who drinks before breakfast! No man can do so, and attend to business properly . . . .[45]

Unless White was being completely hypocritical in this letter, he admired Poe's talents, regretted losing him, and found fault only with his drinking—for moral and business reasons. Admirers of Poe's genius may fume over the patronizing tone used by a dull man to a brilliant one; but so is it ever when the dull man is in charge and the brilliant one has his problems. The upshot of the matter was that Poe did come to Richmond again, within a week after the date of White's letter. White wrote to Minor on October 20 stating without comment that Poe was with him again. Four days later he again wrote to Minor, outlining his strategy for making Poe a sort of editor without title:

> Suppose you send me a modest paragraph—mentioning that the gentleman [Sparhawk] announced as my assistant in the 9th No. of the Messenger retired from its editorship with the 11th No.—that the paper is now under my own editorial management, assisted by several gentlemen of distinguished literary attainments.—
>
> You may introduce Mr. Poe's name as amongst those engaged to contribute for its columns—taking care not to say as editor. All this I wish you to manage with great care for me. Let it come in a separate letter to me—directed to 'T. W. White.'

Why all this excess of caution? Did White simply wish to take credit for everything that happened in the magazine? Or was he afraid that Poe, who had demonstrated both his unreliability and a penchant for satirical reviews, would offend someone? If the latter, he could displace the blame by an editorial reminder that Poe was, after all, only a contributor. Obviously he did not want Poe to open the letter, for he directed Minor to address it to him personally. Why, above all, ask Minor to phrase an editorial notice for him? The "modest paragraph" should have been simple enough to write.

[45] In *Works*, XVII, 20–21.

The only answer which seems to make much sense is that Minor was a lawyer and would exercise legal caution. It seems that White wanted Poe to be editor in fact but not in title, and he wanted Minor to manage the public statement with great care because he distrusted Poe and wished to avoid any possibility of legal difficulty.

Poe had written the critiques for the September number, we may presume, in the state of depression that prompted his drinking bouts. Nevertheless, one of them shows traces of his mature approach in that it makes an effort to condemn on principle. The book he was reviewing was *Mephistopheles in England, or The Confessions of a Prime Minister*, anonymous, of course, as such pieces were likely to be. "The author," Poe wrote, "whoever he may be, is a man of talent, of fine poetical taste, and much general erudition." Having allowed this much, he proceeded to demolish the book itself: "It abounds with the coarsest and most malignant satire, at the same time evincing less of the power than of the *will* for causticity—and being frequently most feeble when it attempts to be the most severe. In this point it resembles the English Bards and Scotch Reviewers. The most glaring defect, however, in the structure of the book, is its utter want of *keeping*. It appears, moreover, to have no just object or end . . . ." [46] The last sentence shows that Poe was moving toward his most distinctive approach in criticism—the appraisal of a work as a teleological construct. In saying that the work had no "keeping," he meant that it lacked the congruous association of various elements which would make it a harmonious whole. Furthermore, no controlling purpose or end was manifest. In his later criticism Poe showed an almost obsessive interest in the "pre-established design" of a work and the means by which the design was carried out, but in this brief review there is only a hint of what he was eventually to call a principle grounded in nature.

The only other review in the September issue worth mentioning is one of a translation of Euripides by the Reverend R. Potter.[47] In this review we can observe the difficulty which Poe was to have

[46] *Ibid.*, VIII, 42.   [47] *Ibid.*, 43–47.

many times during his career as a professional critic: that of reviewing on short notice a book he really was not qualified to evaluate.
Poe had a brilliant, absorptive mind, and his preparatory schools
had been good ones. After his year at the University of Virginia he
was undoubtedly better equipped to discuss Greek drama than
even the most precocious sophomore of today, but he was certainly
no expert in the field. Accordingly, he did what many another professional book reviewer has done, cribbed wholesale from the work
of an acknowledged scholar. August Wilhelm Schlegel's *Lectures
on Dramatic Art and Literature* had been translated into English
and was available, so Poe used it liberally. He did give credit to
Schlegel for the few direct quotations he used, but the indirect
quotations and paraphrases were another matter. Almost the entire
review was adapted from Lectures IV, V, and VIII of Schlegel's
book, Poe merely rephrasing and reorganizing as he saw fit. Even in
this borrowing, however, Poe did no more than one of the critics of
the *North American Review,* who, in an essay entitled "Present
Literature of Italy," followed Schlegel slavishly for several pages
with acknowledgment as scanty as Poe's.[48]

Some effort was made by journals to farm out books to reviewers
who had special qualifications in the appropriate fields. Thus the
Messenger often assigned books on law, history, and biography to
Beverley Tucker, professor of law at the College of William and
Mary. Frequently, however, a professional reviewer like Poe was expected to handle any book that turned up, whether the subject
were oriental antiquities or medical jurisprudence. Poe reviewed
these specialized studies as a matter of course, displaying a semblance of scholarship whenever he could. Much of the paraded
learning of his reviews (and of his fiction, for that matter) came

---

[48] That such acknowledgment was not considered necessary, even by
scholars, is indicated by the fact that James Marsh, author of this essay,
was a professor of languages and eventually became president of the University of Vermont. He did give Schlegel credit in a single footnote, but
his use of Schlegel's *Lectures* is far more extensive than the footnote implies. See James Marsh, "Present Literature of Italy," *North American Review,* XV (1822), 104–130, for the material on Italian drama that resembles Schlegel's work.

from the "research" he was forced to do as a reviewer. Fake erudition did not fool everyone, and then as now it was one of the marks of the hack. It was even satirized as such in a piece of fiction published in the *Messenger* for February, 1837, a month after Poe had left. The contempt expressed in this story for the harsh criticism and fake scholarship of the critic makes it worth quoting at length because it conveys the atmosphere in which a critic had to work in Poe's time.

> A person who wrote the most bitter and reckless of all the critical anathemas of which my employer's magazine was the receptacle, and whose effusions, at the same time, were most crowded with classical allusions and quotations, frequently came into the store and amused himself (if such a red-hot-pepper-pod-and-vinegar-cruet sort of animal could be amused,) with looking over and taking notes from the books upon the shelves. He bore the appearance of the shabby-genteel; but he was, beyond doubt, the most morose, snappish, unsocial, cross-grained, author I ever saw. . . . He passed by the voluminous classical works with which the shelves groaned, and spent hours in poring over and taking notes from the "Universal Gazetteer," the "Biographical Dictionary," the "Classical Dictionary," and, above all . . . the "Dictionary of Quotations."

This unkind description shows the attitude a "gentleman" frequently displayed toward the literary hack. Poe might have felt the projected image of the critic uncomfortably like his own, had he not possessed a somewhat lordly attitude himself. His publication of "Pinakidia" indicates that he wished to forestall this sort of criticism. It was the *other* American journalists who pilfered wholesale from such works as D'Israeli's *Curiosities of Literature*, not Poe. Much of the erudition displayed in periodical literature, he claimed, was derived from "either piecemeal cullings at second hand, from a variety of sources hidden or supposed to be hidden, or more audacious pilferings from those vast storehouses of brief facts, memoranda, and opinions in general literature, which are so abundant in all the principal libraries of Germany and France." [49]

[49] *Works*, XIV, 38.

Poe had published the "Pinakidia" only five months before the attack upon fake erudition appeared in the *Messenger*. Perhaps he
had come to the conclusion, which would be in accord with his
temperament, that the best defense was an attack, yet his own
pilfering has been established beyond question. We are entitled to
suspect that there was a motive other than self-aggrandizement behind the paraded erudition of Poe's reviews and fiction, particularly
in view of the anti-intellectualism he displayed in the "Letter to
Mr. —— ——" and in such tales as "The Colloquy of Monos and
Una." David K. Jackson is probably correct in his suggestion that
the 175 items in "Pinakidia" had originally been intended as fillers
in the *Messenger*.[50] It was already an established policy in the
journal to use such materials, and in later years Poe found a ready
market for similar items, some original but many, as various investigators have shown, culled from the handbooks of universal
knowledge popular in both Europe and America. It was obviously
Poe's intent in the "Pinakidia" to point out to the gullible public
that the information and ideas so readily available in the journals
and handbooks did not represent true scholarship on the part of
the authors but only assiduity in the use of encyclopedias.

Americans, self-conscious about the shortcomings of the nation's
culture, could never quite assume the bland contempt of pedantry
characteristic of the British gentleman, even though some of them,
including Poe himself, pretended to. American journals were making strenuous efforts to become purveyors of culture,[51] and Poe, although occasionally he was ironic about it, committed himself as a

[50] "Poe Notes: 'Pinakidia' and 'Some Ancient Greek Authors,' " *American Literature*, V (1933), 258–59.

[51] One of the curious byproducts of these efforts to educate the public
was the "knowledge" magazine, which Mott has noted as existing in England and France as well as in America. The *Magazine of Useful and Enter-
taining Knowledge* was founded in New York in 1830, the *Weekly Abstract of General Knowledge* in 1833, and the *Monthly Abstract of General
Knowledge* in 1834. Mott, *A History of American Magazines*, 363–65. Poe's
"Pinakidia" was a timely journalistic endeavor, but, more than that, his
prefatory note was an honest appraisal of the situation. Erudition was a
salable commodity in a society that offered unparalleled opportunity for
social mobility, and Poe was a professional journalist.

journalist to raising the American literary tone. His display of erudition, then, was not merely self-advertising but was related to the attempt of American journalism to educate a public that still manifested a colonial sensitivity to European charges of ignorance and vulgarity.

The difficulties Poe encountered as editor-sans-title for the *Messenger* were formidable. Considering his temperament and attitudes, one can safely say that some of these difficulties would have been present had he worked in any other region; but others may be associated with the peculiarly provincial nature of the Southern subculture. White had wanted to found a magazine, but he had wanted it to be a Southern, even a *Virginian*, magazine. As he wrote to Beverley Tucker in January of 1837, "I feel proud of the Messenger. I feel proud to believe that I have been the humble instrument of rearing up a publication which shall be a credit to my native State and Country." But no credit, his letters to Tucker clearly indicate, was to be given to that scurrilous critic Edgar Poe. White's magazine had to put the South's best foot forward, which meant that it had to observe the customary pieties of Virginia society. How Poe earned a national reputation as a critic in spite of these inhibitory circumstances is our next topic.

IV · The Zoilus of the Messenger

THE December, 1835, number of the *Messenger* was the first issue under Poe's editorial guidance. On page one appeared the publisher's announcement that the "intellectual department of the paper is now under the conduct of the proprietor, assisted by a gentleman of distinguished literary talents." This gentleman, of course, was Edgar Poe, and though he did not have the title of editor he was, for all practical purposes, the primary resource of the "intellectual department." The announcement also lauded Poe as a writer: "Every side has rung with praises of his uniquely original vein of imagination, and of humorous, delicate satire."

Poe's editorial influence upon the magazine, if he had any at this point, is not immediately apparent. The articles and poems of this first number of Volume II are very much like those of Volume I. Since the last two numbers of Volume I had not gone to press, the December issue would have been made up of contributions received earlier and accepted by Sparhawk or White. There is a striking difference, however, in the size of the book review section. Book reviews occupy twenty-eight pages of this issue, whereas there had been only five pages in July, two in August, and three in September. If the book review section had not continued to be large while Poe was overseeing it, it would be logical to conclude that the expansion of the "intellectual department" was caused by the backlog of books that had accumulated during October and November. But throughout Poe's tenure in 1836, the space devoted to criticism averaged fifteen pages. Only in the November, 1836, issue, the last one under Poe's supervision, did the number of pages drop to the previous average. Furthermore, after Poe left the *Messenger* in January of 1837, the "intellectual department" almost disappeared for a time. White's friends simply could not supply the criticism that Poe had furnished largely by himself. It was as a lit-

94

erary critic that Poe made his weight felt on the *Southern Literary Messenger.*

Most of the reviews in the December number were undistinguished, and not all of them were written by Poe; but in one review he seized the opportunity he had probably been waiting for and catapulted the *Messenger* and himself into notoriety. This was a review of *Norman Leslie,* a novel by Theodore Sedgwick Fay, associate editor of a well-known journal, the New York *Mirror.*

During his years in Baltimore on the fringes of the journalistic set, Poe must have learned about the literary cliques and cabals which controlled magazine publication and, to a certain extent, journalistic reputations in America.[1] We can also assume that, with his reading of British magazines, Poe had gathered some idea of the nature of magazine publishing in England. No doubt he was aware that the earlier periodicals in England were sometimes thought of as "booksellers' organs" which merely praised those books the booksellers wanted to push. Also he must have known—it was common knowledge—that the great quarterlies of England represented political parties and that literary opinion was often controlled by political attitudes.[2] His own favorite, *Blackwood's Edinburgh Magazine,* had been founded as a Tory journal in opposition to the Whig *Edinburgh Review.* In America periodicals were scarcely more independent in their opinions. Thus there was a need, sometimes described by editors in the tone of voices crying in the wilderness, for unbiased criticism, which Edgar Poe somewhat quixotically undertook to supply.

The initiation of a campaign for independent criticism is very much to Poe's credit, as Sidney Moss has amply demonstrated; and one would be inclined to award Poe appropriate laurels were there not evidence of other and less worthy motivations. The British reviewers were notorious for their harsh condemnation of works they did not like for either political or literary reasons. Although Jeffrey,

---

[1] For an account of journalistic cliques during this period, see Miller, *The Raven and Whale,* 23–35, 104–117; and Moss, *Poe's Literary Battles,* 3–37.

[2] Ward, "Some Aspects of the Conservative Attitude," 386–98.

the great Cham of the *Edinburgh Review,* was probably sincere enough in his attack upon the Lake School, the reviewers of *Blackwood's* might sometimes be accused of pure journalism or pure deviltry (or both) in their ridicule of the "Cockneys." [3]

As an example of the *Blackwood's* type of review that Poe had read, we may take one from the March, 1823, number. This particular review is worth quoting because the tone of jocular contempt is similar to that which Poe employed:

> We have been long looking about for some person or other to immolate to our fancy—some victim to break upon the wheel, and to whom we might give, with soft reluctant amorous delay, the coup-de-grace. But it is amazing what difficulty there is in laying hands upon a suitable culprit. It is not a mere blockhead we are in search of; for in that case we should only have to go into the Phrenological Society, and, without any selection, take the first member we met,—a blockhead, no doubt, of the first magnitude. Neither is your obsolete knave the man for our purpose; otherwise a radical or a Cockney would come quite pat. . . . We have in our eye six criminals, two in verse, and four in prose, whom we intend to put to death in a few months. Three of them know whom we mean; and three of them are like the silly sheep,
>
> > "Pleased to the last, they crop their flowery food,
> > And kiss the hand just raised to shed their blood." [4]

[3] The term "The Cockney School" was contemptuously applied by John Gibson Lockhart to a number of London writers. Lockhart was a reviewer for *Blackwood's* who was so vitriolic that he was called "the Scorpion." He became editor of the *Quarterly Review* in 1825, but derision at the expense of the "cockneys" was associated with *Blackwood's.* In a letter to Beverley Tucker in December, 1835 (*Letters,* I, 77), Poe defended his own "levity" in reviewing by alluding to a *Blackwood's* review of "an Epic Poem by a cockney tailor." Tucker's reply (*Works,* XVII, 23) reveals his own attitude toward satirical criticism: "As to Blackwood; I admire Wilson, but he is an offence unto me by the brutal arrogance of his style of criticism. I have no doubt he demolished the poor Tailor. But 'who breaks a butterfly upon the wheel?' Supported by the powerful party whose organ he is, he may never feel that he injures himself by such things; but he does. His criticisms will have the less weight with the impartial."

See John Louis Haney, *Early Reviews of the English Poets* (Philadelphia, 1904), xxiv–xlvi, for an account of British reviewing practices, particularly those of *Blackwood's* in assailing the "Cockney School."

[4] *Blackwood's Edinburgh Magazine,* XIII (1823), 321.

Apparently this kind of reviewing appealed to Poe. He had begun his career as a writer of prose by burlesquing current modes of popular fiction, and throughout his life he displayed a liking for the kind of hoaxes, satires, and conundrums which attracted public attention. This aspect of Poe's character has been obscured beneath his romantic agony, but it is indisputably there. Of course it is possible that Poe challenged the author of *Norman Leslie* and his supporting clique in the name of high literary principles and was subsequently bruised in spirit by the retaliation of a gross, brutal world; but it is equally possible that, in the manner of the *Blackwood's* critic, he was looking for a dunce to gibbet, anticipating the probable literary war with confidence that as a journalistic critic he would thrive on the attention it would attract. People *read* Lockhart, Gifford, and Wilson, even when they professed to despise their methods.

Poe's first review of this type, his annihilation of *Confessions of a Poet*, had been premature. His position with the *Messenger* had not been secure enough for protracted warfare, but, perhaps fortunately for Poe, the only reaction to the review had been a mild rebuke by the Richmond *Compiler*. In attacking the editor of the New York *Mirror*, however, Poe encountered organized opposition. The novel had been receiving advance publicity ("puffs") in the *Mirror* for months, and excerpts from it had been printed, Poe felt, *ad nauseam.* Poe had found a proper adversary, and he must have thought his new position was firm enough to withstand a counterattack. The first lines of his review were an open challenge: "Well! —here we have it! This is *the* book—*the* book *par excellence*— the book bepuffed, beplastered, and be-Mirrored: the book 'attributed to' Mr. Blank, and 'said to be from the pen' of Mr. Asterisk: the book which has been 'about to appear'—'in press'—'in progress'—'in preparation'—and 'forthcoming': the book 'graphic' in anticipation—'talented' *a priori*—and God knows what *in prospectu.* For the sake of everything puff, puffing, and puffable, let us take a peep at its contents!" [5]

Not one word of qualification mitigates Poe's scorn. He ridiculed the plot, asserted that the characters had "no character," and

[5] *Works*, VIII, 51.

claimed that the style was "unworthy of a schoolboy." Further, to make it perfectly clear that he was inviting retaliation, he exposed Theodore Fay as the author (the novel bore the customary anonymity), and emphasized his position as the editor of the New York *Mirror*, the journal responsible for most of the advance publicity. All in all, said Poe, *Norman Leslie* was "the most inestimable piece of balderdash with which the common sense of the good people of America was ever so openly or villainously insulted."

This review established Poe's reputation as a literary polemicist —many in his own time used a less neutral term. An account of his journalistic conflicts has been given in scrupulous detail by Sidney P. Moss and need not be repeated here, but the effect of Poe's method upon his employer White has been either neglected or glossed over by Poe's biographers. The evidence is not extensive, but it is sufficient. White, previously disturbed by Poe's satirical reviews, became quite alarmed. The possibility of a lawsuit must have crossed his mind, for he wrote to his adviser, Lucian Minor: "You are altogether right about the Leslie critique.—Poe has evidently shown himself *no lawyer*, whatever else he may be. The Editor of the Metropolitan has fallen into the same error.—Well that blunder cannot be repaired.—It will pass undetected, I hope." [6]

But White's hope was not fulfilled. The New York clique retaliated first covertly and then directly, not only through the *Mirror* but also through the New York *Commercial Advertiser* and the Philadelphia *Gazette* of Willis Gaylord Clark. The affair eventually created lifelong enemies for Poe, among them Lewis Gaylord Clark, brother of Willis; [7] but there was one immediate salutary effect—White's magazine became a phenomenon. Attention had been attracted to an obscure Southern publication, and attention in the journalistic world meant subscriptions.

Still, White was worried. His advisers took exception to Poe's satirical method. His previous editor, Heath, had been contemptu-

---

[6] November 23, 1835, in Jackson, *Poe and the Southern Literary Messenger*, 105.

[7] Moss has described this feud in detail. *Poe's Literary Battles*, 85–131.

ous of harsh criticism, which he assumed was mean-spirited. A few Southern newspapers published adverse editorial comments. Had White been a professional journalist, he might have been delighted at the publicity the *Messenger* was to receive during the next few months; but the amateur spirit ruled in the South, and White was concerned with his public image. The publisher had at least one consolation, however. On December 25 he confided to Minor that Poe, "I rejoice to tell you, still keeps from the bottle." [8]

With the amount of work Poe was doing, he *must* have been keeping from the bottle. In addition to his numerous reviews he was preparing the "Autography" series for the *Messenger*. Pretending to be one Joseph Miller,[9] Poe wrote to as many of the famous or near-famous men of the day as he could and then professed to analyze their personalities from their autographs, which were duplicated in the *Messenger*. The hoax was a clever piece of journalism that immediately became a hit, but Poe's analyses sometimes contained a sting, and White was wary.

In comparison with the review of *Norman Leslie*, Poe's other critiques in the December issue are tame, but three should be mentioned. He examined *The Hawks of Hawk Hollow*, the third of Robert Montgomery Bird's novels to be reviewed in the *Messenger*.[10] In the two earlier critiques, already discussed, measured approval of the novelist's works had been expressed, but in this review, which is more secure in the Poe canon, Bird was accused of imitating Scott and of producing an inferior imitation at that. Poe found no fault with the style of the novel but objected to the character development. The hero, Hyland, was inconsistently portrayed, and "although to be inconsistent with one's self, is not always to be false to Nature," Bird allowed his hero to change character completely. This criticism was conventional. To Poe and

[8] In Jackson, *Poe and the Southern Literary Messenger*, 105.

[9] *Joe Miller's Jests*, by John Mottley, an eighteenth-century playwright, had been first published in 1739. "Joseph Miller" had been an actor in the Drury Lane company noted for his humor. "Joe Miller" was slang for a trite jest, so it should have been easy for both Poe's victims and his audience to detect the hoax.

[10] *Works*, VIII, 63–73.

his contemporaries, "following Nature" did not necessarily mean the reproduction of empirically verifiable traits. Conformity to social type was preferable, a literary propriety observed quite successfully by Cooper but less faithfully by Simms and Bird.

Poe was not prepared, in this review or in later ones, to make any significant contribution to the theory of the novel. To him it was not a true art form and could not be properly examined as an artistic structure, for, as Poe said of the epic or long narrative poem, a composition that could not be immediately apprehended as a total design did not stimulate aesthetic pleasure, however much it might please on other grounds. However, when he came to review the short tale, Poe invoked what he considered to be an indispensable aesthetic principle. In his analysis of *Tales of the Peerage and the Peasantry*, allegedly "edited" by Lady Dacre, he made a statement which anticipated his mature theory of the short tale. After accusing Lady Dacre of an "unpardonable piece of affectation" in pretending to edit the tales she had actually written (Poe disliked the anonymity practiced by most authors of the day), he praised her artistry in achieving "unity of effect": "An every day writer would have ended a story of continued sorrow and suffering, with a bright gleam of unalloyed happiness, and sunshine—thus destroying, at a single blow, that indispensable unity which has been rightly called the unity of effect, and throwing down, as it were, in a paragraph what, perhaps, an entire volume has been laboring to establish." [11]

Unity, of course, was one of the oldest standards of literary criticism, but in the past it had been conceived in terms of form. It was Archibald Alison who had advanced the most persuasive argument in British aesthetics for what he called the "unity of expression" or "unity of emotion." Basing his argument upon the subjective reaction of an audience, he claimed that throughout a composition a single emotional tone should be preserved. A historian would be forced to include "trifling and uninteresting events," but a poet, treating the same material, should exclude everything that did not contribute to the general emotion he wished to arouse in his reader.[12]

[11] *Ibid.*, 74–75.   [12] *Essays on Taste*, 100–103.

In the criticism of fiction Poe's contemporaries sometimes demanded a unity of action, as they did in the drama, but standards for the short tale had not been established, and Poe's statement that unity of effect was necessary represented an innovation. Obviously he meant the same kind of unity that Alison had demanded in all of the fine arts, and, had he wished to do so, he could have cited Alison, Coleridge, and Schlegel in his support.[13] This was Poe's first expression of the theory of the single effect which he was to develop more fully in later reviews.

His only other criticism in the December issue which is worthy of comment is a detailed examination of various periodicals. Before Poe became editor, the *Messenger* had occasionally reviewed other journals, but usually in brief paragraphs. Poe, however, devoted a paragraph to each article in the *Edinburgh Review* for July, 1835, and, following the current practice of reviewing reviews, called for a reform in journalistic criticism: "This article is written with great ability; but why call that a Review which is purely a dissertation on the state of the Irish Church?" [14] Then, in examining a review of Wordsworth's *Yarrow Revisited and Other Poems* in the *Quarterly Review*, he continued in the same vein of disapproval: "Here is one of those exceedingly rare cases in which a British critic confines himself strictly to his text—but this is nearly all that can be said in favor of the article. A more partial, a more indiscriminate or fulsome panegyric we never wish to see, and surely 'Yarrow Revisited' is worthy of a better fate." [15] Next Poe turned his attention to the *North American Review*, a quarterly which he later called "that ineffable buzzard." The issue for October, 1835, he found guilty of "puffing" American writers: "The North American, in its last number, considered Southey a fine writer, but Washington Irving a much finer, and indeed 'the best living writer of English

---

[13] In Chapter XV of the *Biographia Literaria*, Coleridge discussed the ability of the imagination to reduce "multitude into unity of effect." Schlegel examined the dramatic unities in his *Lectures on Dramatic Art and Literature* and concluded in Chapter XVII that a "deeper, more intrinsic, and more mysterious unity" than the Aristotelian unity of action was required in dramatic art.

[14] *Works*, VIII, 89.   [15] *Southern Literary Messenger*, II (1836), 62.

prose': having, however, to review Mr. Channing in the present number, its opinions are conveniently modified to suit the occasion, and *now* the English of William E. Channing is declared *coram populo* to be 'equally *elegant,* and a little more pure, correct, and pointed than that of Mr. Irving.' There is surely something very absurd in all this." [16] What Poe objected to here was both national and sectional bias in criticism. It was bad enough for the *North American* to exhaust superlatives upon Irving, an internationally recognized stylist, but to claim that Channing's prose was superior to that of Irving was simply uncritical admiration of a son of New England by a New England journal. Furthermore, the *North American* was guilty of deprecating its betters in the person of Coleridge. He challenged the magazine to prove its claim that " 'Coleridge shews an almost total want of precision and clearness of thought.' " Coleridge's works are available, Poe stated, and "we greatly prefer proof to assertion." Poe's position is obvious. He was demanding an unbiased criticism which examined the text and did not employ unsupported generalizations.

Poe used these reviews of other journals not as perfunctory notices (equivalent to cooperative advertising), but as a means to reform current reviewing methods; and, as we have seen, he did not hesitate to challenge the most powerful critical voice in America, the *North American Review.* He envisioned a review as a review and nothing more, thus eliminating, at least as critiques, the long, elaborate essays of the quarterlies.[17] If a review were to be genuine

---

[16] *Southern Literary Messenger,* II (1836), 64. The review Poe condemned was by A. H. Everett, a conservative critic who did not admire Coleridge.

[17] Poe's opposition to discursive essays did not go unchallenged. The Washington *Telegraph* defended the current practice in these terms: "We do not agree with the reviewer [Poe] in condemning every thing under the name of a 'Review,' to which that name, in its strictest sense, does not apply. He who under the name gives an essay on the subject of the article professed to be reviewed, does not break faith with the public, because for more than thirty years, the word has been understood to include such essays. Now he who gives a good essay, gives a good thing, and when he does this, . . . we have no right nor mind to complain." Quoted in *Southern Literary Messenger,* II (1836), 136.

criticism, it could not be guilty of overestimating the quality of native sons, and it had to rid itself of sectional bias. Eventually Poe was to demand what he called for now only by implication: an analytical review that examined merits and defects and made judgments on the basis of principles. For several years Poe was compelled to smuggle his program for reform into his own reviews. It was not until 1841 that he found an opportunity to express it at length in an article published in *Graham's Magazine.*

2

The December number of the *Messenger*, with its large quota of criticism, attracted attention both North and South, and many journals reviewed it. It was Poe, we must assume, who collected these reviews and published some of them in a supplement to the January, 1836, issue of the *Messenger*. No doubt White approved, but, having little of Poe's flair for journalism, he probably did not originate the idea.

Some of Poe's biographers, following his own interpretation, have claimed that his methods of criticism gained practically universal approval, except from the New York clique incensed by his *Norman Leslie* review. But even if Poe's supplement contains a fair cross-section of opinion, the most we can claim is that the press approved more frequently than it disapproved.[18] Those who liked Poe's reviews commended his candor, impartiality, and independence of spirit; but other journals found fault with his severity and his tone of derision. The New York *Courier and Enquirer* thought that the review of *Norman Leslie* evinced "personal hostility" not only toward Mr. Fay, the author, but also toward "all who may be supposed to favor or admire him." The Washington *Telegraph* objected to Poe's satirical method, although it found his severity justifiable. The Baltimore *American* censured the tone of Poe's notice of the *North American Review* and warned him that, though there was much matter for "cutting up," he had better take a les-

[18] The following quotations may be found in the Supplement, *Southern Literary Messenger*, II (1836), 133–40.

son from the meat carver and not smear his own fingers; "Mr.
White and his editor should keep the tone and bearing of the Messenger elevated and cavalier-like."

This last must have annoyed White considerably. A Virginian
having to take a lesson in journalistic deportment from a Baltimore paper! White wanted his magazine to do honor to his native
state. A journalistic war, however profitable it was commercially,
would scarcely fit the image he wished to project.

Sectional feeling, which was already running high in the thirties,
may have been responsible for some of the Southern satisfaction
with Poe's method, but even in Virginia not all of the papers were
so eager to take the starch out of the Yankees that they joined
Poe's cause. The Norfolk *Beacon* felt that in general the critical
notices were "in bad taste, particularly the reviews of the North
American and the British Reviews," but the editor went on to admit that the good outweighed the bad. The Lynchburg *Virginian*
was more severe; several of the notices, the Lynchburg editor maintained, were "too dogmatical and flippant." Such reviews as that of
Norman Leslie would be read, he continued, because people "will
always be attracted in crowds to behold an infliction of the Russian
knout or to see a fellow creature flayed alive." Though Mr. Fay undoubtedly deserved a "blistering" for publishing such a book as
Norman Leslie, he did not deserve a flaying. The implication of the
Lynchburg editor was that Poe was making a deliberate bid for
notoriety.

Though White must have been disturbed by the mixed reaction
to Poe's reviewing tactics, at least he did not force the young editor
to hold back—not yet. The January, 1836, number of the *Messenger* contained sixteen pages of criticism, a considerable drop
from the twenty-eight of the previous number, but still more than
the *Messenger* had ever had before Poe became editor.

The lead review in the issue was of the poetry of a triumvirate
which Beverley Tucker, in a letter to White, called "a leash of
ladies"—Mrs. Lydia Huntley Sigourney, a valued contributor to
the *Messenger,* Miss H. F. Gould, and Mrs. E. F. Ellet.[19] Only

[19] *Works,* VIII, 122–42.

the critique of Mrs. Sigourney merits comment. Poe, usually the perfect Virginian in his tenderness toward females, was in something of a dilemma. Ordinarily he employed different standards in reviewing the works of women, but he must have felt that honesty required him to suggest that Mrs. Sigourney's reputation was not justified by her poems. Quite tactfully, if we remember how Poe's gorge rose every time he contemplated, perhaps enviously, an undeserved reputation, he described how mediocre writers managed to achieve recognition by the careful manipulation of publicity, "or by appealing continually with little things, to the ear of that great, overgrown gander, the critical and bibliographical rabble." Then, perhaps feeling that he was going too far in implicating Mrs. Sigourney, he inserted a qualification: "But it must not be thought that we wish to include Mrs. Sigourney in the number. By no means. She has trod, however, upon the confines of their circle. She does not *owe* her reputation to the chicanery we mention, but it cannot be denied that it has been thereby greatly assisted."

Next Poe brought up what for him was a frequent charge—imitation:

> We have watched, too, with a species of anxiety and vexation brought about altogether by the sincere interest we take in Mrs. Sigourney, the progressive steps by which she has at length acquired the title of the "American Hemans." Mrs. S. cannot conceal from her own discernment that she has acquired this title *solely by imitation.* The very phrase "American Hemans" speaks loudly in accusation: and we are grieved that what by the over-zealous has been intended as complimentary should fall with so ill-omened a sound into the ears of the judicious.

Poe, now rarely content to make a general charge without supplying the evidence, catalogued the particulars in which Mrs. Sigourney imitated Mrs. Hemans—in subject matter, in the elements of her versification, in "peculiar terms of her phraseology" (such as in overuse of yea! and alas!), and in "an invincible inclination to apostrophize every object, in both moral and physical existence," and to prefix to nearly every poem mottoes and quotations "of which the verses ensuing are, in most instances, merely a paraphrase." Such mannerisms in Mrs. Hemans herself were "gross and inartistic," but as imitated mannerisms they were absolutely inadmissible.

Poe's criticism is sound. Imitation of an author's stylistic eccentricities suits only parody or burlesque, but Mrs. Sigourney was in dead earnest. Still, the justice of Poe's charges counted for little when they were levied against the divine Lydia, who, like Mrs. Hemans, could do no wrong.[20] The retaliation was immediate. Mrs. Sigourney's friends rose indignantly to her defense, and the lady herself announced sorrowfully that she could no longer contribute to the *Messenger*. White, alarmed, had Poe write a letter of apology, which turned out to be not particularly apologetic. Instead, Poe defended his review:

> I am vexed to hear that you have not received the Messenger regularly, and am confident that upon reception of the January number . . . you will be fully convinced that your friends, in their zeal for your literary reputation, have misconceived the spirit of the criticism to which you have alluded. To yourself, personally, we commit our review, with a perfect certainty of being understood. That we have evinced any "severity amounting to unkindness" is an accusation of which you will, I sincerely hope, unhesitatingly acquit us. We refer you, especially, to the concluding sentences of the critique.[21]

The concluding sentences which Poe hoped would mitigate his criticism state that when Mrs. Sigourney throws "aside the petty shackles which have hitherto enchained her, she will assume, at once, that highest station among the poets of our land which her noble talents so well qualify her for attaining."

Poe's apology was not enough, for the poet's literary honesty had been impugned. Maintaining the air of modesty and piety which constituted her public image, Mrs. Sigourney answered Poe at length. She had a deep consciousness of her own imperfections and

[20] For the astonishing popularity of Mrs. Sigourney, see E. Douglas Branch, *The Sentimental Years, 1836–1860* (New York, 1934), 135–38; and Mott, *A History of American Magazines*, 499.

[21] April 12, 1836, in *Letters*, I, 89–90.

knew that "the courtesy of the publick" had exceeded her deserts. Aware of this, she should not be oversensitive about a review, but—

> At the same time I confess that there are points in yours for which I was not perfectly prepared.—The exposition, however severe, of any faults in style, spirit, or construction, which I might have reformed,—would have been held cause of gratitude. But the character of a determined imitator,—and one whose reputation has been greatly assisted by chicanery,—seem to impeach both intellectual and moral integrity.—If founded in justice, they truly demand a "purgation with euphrasy and rue."—I would be the last to invade your right of fully expressing these opinions, or to cherish the least resentment towards you for holding them.—I simply regret, even to grief, that any course of mine, could have induced you to form them.—I would not for a moment admit the idea that there is aught of equality between my writings, and that of the most gifted poet of the age, so recently claimed to her native sphere.— The resemblance, which my friends have imagined to exist, I have resolved into their partiality. The contents of a volume of poems, published in 1814 & selected by a friend from journals, written in early youth, without a thought of publication, & another in 1821, were composed before I had heard of Mrs. Hemans, and likewise one in 1827,—most of whose poems were in existence, before I had the pleasure of perusing any of hers,—can therefore not be classed as imitations of that pure model.[22]

If Mrs. Sigourney was telling the truth, she had the better of the argument, and Poe, who thought of himself as an impartial critic, was diminished to a mean-spirited hack who assailed an author's character instead of concentrating, as Mrs. Sigourney demanded, on "faults in style, spirit, and construction." There were grounds for Mrs. Sigourney's indignation. Sincerity was part of the romantic credo. An imitative poet, since he was not expressing *himself*, was culpable from both a literary and a moral perspective, the first because an imitation is rarely as good as an original, and the second because, as Poe pointed out, the imitative author improved his

[22] April 23, 1836, in *Works*, XVII, 34–35.

status by trading on another's ability and reputation. Knowing these implications, Mrs. Sigourney was right in feeling that her integrity had been impeached.

Originality, that traditional sign of poetic genius, Poe made one of his own criteria. Originality not only affirmed that the poet possessed innate sensibility, a necessary requirement; it could even testify to what Keats had called the "holiness of the heart's affections," because originality precluded the use of someone else's feelings—borrowed emotions could scarcely be holy. Poe, however, placed as much emphasis upon originality of expression as he did upon originality of sentiment or of thought. Stealing another poet's *idea*, a charge which he was to make against Longfellow, deserved condemnation because the consequent expression could not be sincere; but stealing a poet's *manner*—his stylistic signature—was equally to be condemned because the thief used a skill not his own. As for stealing mannerisms which had no virtue in the first place, this denoted not only dishonesty but a profound lack of taste.

Thus we can understand the bases of Poe's obsession with plagiarism. Unfortunately he brought his accusations against second-rate poets who were doing no more than writing about conventional subjects in the period style. Poets of this sort usually sound pretty much alike. Even Poe's own poetry, in spite of his efforts at originality, is superficially similar to that of other poets of the time, including Edward Coote Pinkney and Thomas Holley Chivers. A few years later Poe achieved some understanding of the imitativeness likely to be found in a bookish poet who wrote in the period style, but this was only after he had engaged in the unpleasant "Longfellow war" and had incensed Longfellow's friends in much the same way as he had Mrs. Sigourney's. One thing he was beginning to learn from these experiences, however, was that it was safer and indeed more virtuous for a reviewer to stick to the text than it was to indulge in either the savage or jocular attacks of the earlier British reviewers. This was already his theoretical position, but he was unable to maintain it whenever he was riding his hobbyhorse of plagiarism or finding it necessary to take vengeance on a literary enemy.

Pressure from White required Poe to placate Mrs. Sigourney and, if possible, induce her to continue her contributions to the *Messenger*. On June 4 he wrote again, expressing his fears that he had forfeited her good will and requesting her to forgive him to the extent of resuming her contributions.[23] Her answer of June 11 was quite amiable. She assured Poe that she cherished no resentment, and that if she had, his favorable review of her friend Grenville Mellen's poems would have removed it. (Fortunately she did not know that this review in the April issue was not by Poe.) Having thus delicately cleared herself of the possible imputation of un-womanly anger, Mrs. Sigourney acquiesced: "I send at your request, what I happen to have by me,—and as you will have it to be a peace offering, you can thus view it, though there is in reality, no truce to be made between us. Do not, however, assume a more lenient style with regard to me, in consequence of any little aid I may have afforded the 'Messenger,' since no traffick in civilities is as valuable in my opinion as sincerity." [24] So the Sigourney affair was smoothed over, with the honors, if there were any, going to the lady. Preserving the approved moralities of the age and maintaining sweetness and light even in this private correspondence, she vindicated her character if not her poetry. Some of Poe's other victims were less high-minded.

Though Mrs. Sigourney was mollified, Thomas Willis White was still uneasy. As early as January White had begun to doubt Poe's capacity as a critic and had let him know it. Disturbed, Poe had written to Beverley Tucker for support, and Tucker responded immediately with a letter to White:

Last night I received a letter from Mr. Poe by which I learned that you may not feel as much confidence in his capacities for the duties of his station as is necessary for your mutual comfort. This doubt he attributes in part to what must have been a misconstruction by you of one of my letters. . . . I only mention this to say that Mr. Poe's review of a leash of these ladies, in your last number, is a

23 Poe's letter of June 4 has been lost, but it may be reconstructed in part by Mrs. Sigourney's reply on June 11.
24 In *Works*, XVII, 38.

specimen of criticism which, for niceness of discrimination, delicacy of expression, and all that shows familiarity with art, may well compare with any that I have ever seen . . . .[25]

Tucker was one of White's trusted advisers, and this statement should have been reassuring enough. In January of 1836, with the *Messenger's* reputation booming and new subscriptions pouring in, White should have been happy with Poe, but a letter to Tucker reveals an ambiguous attitude: "My right-hand man Poe thinks it [the January number] superior [to the others]—This is natural. . . . I shall on some suitable occasion, tell you a great deal about my young friend and editor.—It will be for your private ear." [26]

Unfortunately we do not know what White told Tucker in his "private ear," but cloistered praise like cloistered virtue rarely makes a noise in the world. If White had had something good to say about Poe, why would he be secretive about it, especially since Tucker was engaged in Poe's defense? On the basis of other letters about Poe, which shall be taken up in due course, we must suspect White of some irony in his phrase, "my young friend." Still, Poe *was* his right-hand man, no question about that. As a rule White deferred to Poe in decisions about contributions, as his letter to William Scott of August 25, 1836, indicates: "Courtesy to Mr. Poe, whom I employ to edit my paper, makes it a matter of etiquette with me to submit all articles intended for the Messenger to his judgment,—and I abide by his dicta. What he might decide . . . it is impossible for me to say." [27] However, in January of 1837, when Poe was on his way out, White wrote again to Scott saying that Poe had accepted his manuscript after striking out the first and the two concluding paragraphs, which White had taken upon himself to restore.[28] Unquestionably White reserved to himself the privilege of overruling Poe, but more than likely Poe put up an

[25] Quoted in Hull, "A Canon," 60.
[26] White to Tucker, February 6, 1836, *ibid.*, 52.
[27] Hull, "A Canon," 57. Scott was probably the "Englishman from New York" who wrote an article entitled "Rights of Authors" published in the January, 1837, issue of the *Messenger*. He may have been William Cowper Scott, a New York journalist, but David K. Jackson has not listed William Cowper Scott as contributing anything prior to 1845.
[28] *Ibid.*

argument whenever it happened. Despite White's misgivings, however, for nearly a year Poe was to have virtual control of the "critical department," and he made the most of his opportunities.

3

The squabble with Mrs. Sigourney and White's reaction have
been described in detail to illustrate the difficulties encountered by
an "independent" critic. But the review which occasioned the
quarrel has even more significance, for in it Poe made his first considered statement of what unity in a poem meant to him. With the
theories of both Schlegel and Coleridge in mind, he brought up the
question of unity in reference to the epigrams which Mrs. Sigourney customarily prefixed to her poems. This topic was only an excuse, however, for Poe's principle is much broader than the particular practice he condemned by it:

In poems of magnitude the mind of the reader is not, at all times,
enabled to include in one comprehensive survey the proportions
and proper adjustment of the whole. He is pleased—if at all—with
particular passages; and the sum of his pleasure is compounded by
the sums of the pleasurable sensations inspired by these individual
passages during the progress of perusal. But in pieces of less extent
—like the poems of Mrs. Sigourney—the pleasure is *unique,* in the
proper acceptation of that term—the understanding is employed,
without difficulty, in the contemplation of the picture *as a whole*—
and thus its effect will depend, in a very great degree, upon the
perfection of its finish, upon the nice adaptation of its constituent
parts, and especially upon what is rightly termed by Schlegel, "the
unity or totality of interest." Now it will readily be seen, that the
practice we have mentioned as habitual with Mrs. Hemans and
Mrs. Sigourney is utterly at variance with this unity. By the initial
motto—often a very long one—we are either put in possession of
the subject of the poem; or some hint, historic fact, or suggestion is
thereby afforded, not included in the body of the article, which,
without the suggestion, would be utterly incomprehensible. In the
latter case, while perusing the poem, the reader must revert, in
mind at least, to the motto for the necessary explanation. In the
former, the poem being a mere paraphrase of the motto, the inter-

est is divided between the motto and the paraphrase. In either
instance the *totality* of effect is annihilated.[29]

This passage must be examined with some care because it ex-
presses the concept of artistic form which Poe retained throughout
his career and for which he was to advance a teleological argument.[30] He never made any essential modifications of the concept,
yet in different reviews he shifted his emphasis from structural unity
to the unity of emotional effect—Alison's unity of emotion—as the
situation demanded. Such a shift is apparent in this passage. In
reference to "poems of magnitude" Poe concentrated on hedonic
value, "the sum of . . . pleasure," and typically employed his
hedonistic calculus in assuming that, since the mind cannot immediately grasp the design of a long poem, the peculiar pleasure derived from an immediate recognition of purpose would be lacking.
Such a proposition could be derived logically from the premises of
taste advanced by Jeffrey and Alison, although neither critic went
so far as to say that poems should be brief.[31] Nor did Poe at this
particular time; it was in later years that he argued that poems
should be brief because the intensity of the effect could not be long
endured, an assumption he shared with John Stuart Mill and some
others.[32] The point here is that Poe, like the Scottish aestheti-

[29] *Works*, VIII, 125–26.
[30] Poe repeated this passage with minimal revision six years later in his
review of Longfellow's *Ballads and Other Poems*.
[31] Alison discussed at length the influence of design, or the recognition
of purposeful skill, in arousing the "emotion of beauty," concluding, as
was typical of the Scottish philosophers, with a proposition about the final
cause of art, which was to create from the raw material of nature forms
"more pure and more perfect than any that Nature herself ever presents
to them," thus imitating the creativity of God and reinforcing religious
feeling. *Essays*, 453–54, 458. Our first impression of a beautiful scene, Alison argued, was that of design, or the effect of workmanship. Jeffrey had
insisted upon the immediacy of the aesthetic response. Poe's deduction is
logical. If the mind could not grasp an artistic structure without extensive
study, then the aesthetic pleasure aroused by the immediate recognition of
design would be lacking, although other pleasures might be experienced
from separate details.
[32] Abrams has pointed out that J. G. Sulzer had anticipated Poe in an
encyclopaedia of aesthetics published in 1771–74 and that John Stuart

cians, sought to analyze effects and then to validate those effects
teleologically, a procedure he was to employ much more extensively three months later.

In accounting for the proper effect of a short poem, Poe shifted
from hedonic value to what he called "totality of effect," making
use of the term "understanding," in either a Lockean or a Coleridgean sense,[33] to indicate that the intellectual as well as the emotional faculties must be engaged in the total apprehension which
prior authority had declared characteristic of cultivated taste.[34]

By 1836 Poe had read both Coleridge and August Wilhelm
Schlegel, and there are evidences of this reading in the passage under consideration. His proposition about the pleasure derived from
a long poem reminds us of Coleridge's statement that in any poem
the pleasure derived from the whole is that which is "compatible
with a distinct gratification from each component part." More
pertinent to Poe's criticism of Mrs. Sigourney is Coleridge's next
paragraph.

> . . . if the definition sought for be that of a *legitimate* poem, . . .
> it must be one, the parts of which mutually support and explain
> each other; all in their proportion harmonizing with, and support-
> ing the known influence of metrical arrangement. The philosophi-
> cal critics of all the ages coincide with the ultimate judgment of all

---

Mill had said the same thing in 1838. Abrams, *The Mirror and the Lamp*,
90, 136–37. Poe advanced the argument in "The Philosophy of Composition" (1846) and in "The Poetic Principle" (1848).

[33] Locke had used the term for the reasoning faculty of the mind, but
Coleridge, following Kant, had classified the understanding as a lower
power, directed toward the comprehension of ordinary experience, whereas
the reason was an intuitive power with insight into the universal. If Poe
was using Schlegel accurately, he may be interpreted as saying that the understanding is employed in apprehending the formal structure of a short
poem, its adaptation of means to the end; but in this review he virtually
ignored what Schlegel considered more significant, the organic unity which
was apprehended intuitively.

[34] From the time of Blair and Kames through that of Alison and Jeffrey
to the time of Coleridge and Schlegel, the complexity of the response to
art was increasingly recognized. A "cultivated taste" implied appreciation
of artistic skill, a capacity to interpret meaning, and the ability to express
value judgments as well as a sensitivity to emotional nuance.

countries, in equally denying the praises of a just poem, on the one hand, to a series of striking lines or distiches, each of which absorbing the whole attention of the reader to itself, disjoins it from its context, and makes it a separate whole, instead of an harmonizing part; and on the other hand, to an unsustained composition, from which the reader collects rapidly the general result, unattracted by the component parts. The reader should be carried forward, not merely or chiefly by the mechanical impulse of curiosity, or by a restless desire to arrive at the final solution; but by the pleasurable activity of the mind excited by the attractions of the journey itself.[35]

It is easy to see why this passage might have come to Poe's mind when he was confronted with Mrs. Sigourney's mottoes, which, in his interpretation, forced the reader to refer to a "separate whole" for matter that should have been integrated into the body of the poem itself. He and Coleridge were describing different phenomena, but the principle of unity of effect would apply to each. Poe invoked it to demand autonomy for the poem itself, Coleridge in the service of organic unity.

It is strange that Poe referred to Schlegel in this passage, for Coleridge's remarks are much more pertinent. Probably it was because he had just been reading Schlegel's lectures, and it may have been five years since he had consulted the *Biographia Literaria*. Even at that he borrowed only a phrase from Schlegel, took it out of context and applied it in a way not completely compatible with his source. The German critic was not referring to poems at all but was trying to establish a more comprehensive principle for the drama than the traditional unity of action. Even the phrase, "unity of interest," was not Schlegel's, as Poe implied, but had been taken from a French critic: "De La Motte, a French author who wrote against the Unities in general, would substitute for Unity of action, the *Unity of interest*. If the term be not confined to the interest in the destinies of some single personage, but is taken to mean in general the direction which the mind takes at the sight of an event,

[35] *Biographia Literaria*, ed. J. Shawcross (London, 1907), II, 10–11.

this explanation, so understood, seems most satisfactory and very near the truth." [36]

Poe's own explanation of the pleasurable effect of a short poem hinges upon two separate but related phenomena: (1) total design, as recognized by "perfection of . . . finish" and "nice adaptation of . . . constituent parts," those elements of a composition which can be apprehended by the rational faculty; and (2) unity of interest, which must mean "unity of impression." That this explanation could have been derived from Schlegel's lecture on unity is easily substantiated.

Like Coleridge, Schlegel insisted upon organic unity instead of the formal unity of the neoclassicists, which he considered lifeless. The mechanical unity of a watch, Schlegel wrote, consists in its function of measuring time, but this unity can be apprehended by the understanding. On the other hand, the organic unity of a living form consists in the idea of life, which we possess only by "inward intuition." This vitality cannot be recognized through a mere analytical examination of parts. In a work of art, which Schlegel, like most other romantics, took to be analogous to a living thing, unity is apprehended not by the eye and ear alone, nor by the understanding alone, but by a comprehensive act of the mind which he called "intuition." All of the parts of an art work, Schlegel maintained, are "subservient to one common aim . . . to produce a joint impression on the mind." For Schlegel as for Coleridge, one could not separate feeling from ideas, as the faculty psychologists had been prone to do, for the intuitions of the mind produce ideas: "This is all one; for the feeling, so far as it is not merely sensual and passive, is our sense, our organ for the infinite, which forms itself into ideas for us." [37]

[36] A. W. Schlegel, *Lectures on Dramatic Art and Literature*, trans. John Black, ed. A. J. W. Morrison (2nd ed.; London, 1904), 340. For a discussion of Poe's debt to Schlegel, see Albert J. Lubell, "Poe and A. W. Schlegel," *Journal of English and Germanic Philology*, LII (1953), 1–12. My own interpretation of Poe's use of Schlegel will appear both in my text and in explanatory notes.
[37] Schlegel, *Lectures*, 244.

The organic concept, then, was there for Poe's use in the same lecture from which he borrowed one phrase, but his reductionism was apparent in the way he used that phrase. He did not really invoke organic unity, that "deeper, more intrinsic, and more mysterious unity" which Schlegel called for in a work of art, but used the principle of a unified effect to demolish Mrs. Sigourney's mottoes. A poem would not produce a unified effect if the reader had to go outside the poem for information to clarify its import. It would be unfair to say that Poe did not understand the organic principles of Coleridge and Schlegel, for, as was typical of his practical criticism from this time forward, he advanced the general proposition and then applied it to the case at hand. He is more to blame for fixing his attention upon a defect so trivial as Mrs. Sigourney's epigrams, but we must realize that to Poe it was not an inconsequential error. He was to continue to insist that a poem should contain within itself all that was necessary for its comprehension, a corrective so necessary that it was revived by the "new" critics of the twentieth century.

A more serious limitation was his denial of unity of effect to long poems. His declaration that the mind of the reader cannot grasp "the proportions and proper adjustment of the whole" would make sense only if he retained the notion that the "design" or formal structure of a poem is analogous to that of the visual arts, which indeed he implied by his phrase, "one comprehensive survey." We should not be misled by Poe's usual correlation of poetry with music as a nonrepresentational art; for not only are his poems and his tales pictorial in many ways, but, as we shall see, he continued for some time to emphasize pictorial effects in his theoretical propositions. It was six years before he was to limit the length of a poem on the ground of the intensity of its effect, an entirely different psychological principle from the one he used here. No doubt he was still remembering the theories of the psychologists of taste, who had made the recognition of design one of the chief intellectual pleasures to be derived from a work of art.

In evaluating Poe as a literary critic we should keep in mind the requirements of his profession. He was forced to review an incredible amount of bad but popular writing, the kind that might have been condemned out of hand on the basis of taste. Yet in striving to establish a critical method based upon principles instead of taste, he often had to employ principles suitable for the evaluation of works of literature upon writings that were beneath the level of art. A literary critic would feel disposed to be satirical about a hopelessly bad book because he could not treat it seriously. As we have seen, Poe had just tried the satirical method, but the reaction was perhaps stronger than he was prepared for. Beverley Tucker had warned him a month earlier about the possible reaction: "I did not mean to deny the efficacy of a certain style of criticism in demolishing scribblers. . . . It may make the critic as formidable to the rabble of literary offenders as Jack Dalgliesh or Jack Portious himself, but it makes him odious too, and adds nothing to his authority in the estimation of those whose approbation for his sentence cuts off the sufferer from the poor privilege of complaining, and the poor consolation of sympathy." [38]

Perhaps this admonition from a man he respected influenced Poe to start trying to criticize on the basis of science instead of spleen during the coming year; but, as we shall see, he did not relinquish the satirical method. Beginning with the review of Mrs. Sigourney, however (a review which won Tucker's approbation), Poe began to introduce literary theory into his reviews more and more in order to furnish a basis for his allocation of merits and defects.

[38] December 5, 1835, in *Works*, XVII, 23.

v · *Conflicting Aims: Journalist or Critic?*

POE had disposed of Mrs. Sigourney by an aesthetic principle, but his review of *The Partisan*,[1] by William Gilmore Simms, was not only a reversion to his satirical method but also a violation of the *Messenger* policy to encourage Southern authors. To White it must have seemed that his young editor was deliberately kicking the Southern muse in the teeth, not to mention alienating a contributor (Simms did send some poems to the *Messenger* which were published later in the year). To cause difficulty with Mrs. Sigourney, already a contributor, was bad enough, but to endanger support from the leading author of the South[2] was sheer perversity.

Poe's review *was* perverse. He spent two columns making fun of Simms's four-line dedication of the novel to a friend, a dedication which certainly seems harmless enough, even modest:

To Richard Yeadon, Jr., Esq., *of South Carolina*

DEAR SIR, My earliest, and, perhaps, most pleasant rambles in the fields of literature, were taken in your company—permit me to remind you of that period by inscribing the present volumes with your name.

THE AUTHOR

[1] *Works*, VIII, 143–58.

[2] Simms had already published several books of verse and three novels, which Poe listed, along with Simms's best long poem, *Atalanta* (1832). The Charleston author was by far the most successful writer in the South, having earned six thousand dollars from his books in 1835. Hubbell, *The South in American Literature*, 582. It is quite obvious that Poe knew of Simms's reputation both North and South. He would have been equally aware that to offend Simms was potentially damaging to the *Messenger*, for Simms could have contributed poems, short stories, and book reviews which, except for Poe's own work, would have been superior to anything as yet published.

Poe, with mordant humor, created a verbal picture of the supposed presentation of this dedication to Yeadon, ridiculing Simms's close punctuation in the process. He concluded with this sentence: "Mr. Y. feels it his duty to kick the author of 'The Yemassee' down stairs." Then, to contrive a point for such apparent malice, he wrote: "Now, in this, all the actual burlesque consists in merely substituting things for words. There are many of our readers who will recognize in this imaginary interview between Mr. Yeadon and Mr. Simms, at least a family likeness to the written Dedication of the latter. This Dedication is, nevertheless, quite as good as one half the antique and lackadaisical courtesies with which we daily see the initial leaves of our best publications disfigured."

Poe used Simms's brief inscription to attack the florid dedications sometimes found in books of the time. These he construed as hypocrisy designed to curry favor. Simms's dedication was obviously not of this type, however, and Poe was out of order.

Nor did Poe stop with the dedication. In the remainder of his review he rebuked Simms for a faulty plot, for vulgarity of language, for bad taste in characterization, and for "shockingly bad English," concluding that the Charlestonian had the eye of a painter and should sketch landscapes instead of writing novels. Simms's reaction, which appeared in a letter to Evert Duyckinck some years later, is quite understandable:

> Poe is no friend of mine. . . . He began by a very savage attack on one of my novels—The Partisan. . . . he was rude & offensive & personal, in the manner of the thing, which he should not have been, in the case of anybody,—still less in mine. My deportment had not justified it. He knew, or might have known, that I was none of that miserable gang about town, who beg in literary highways. I had no clique, mingled with none, begged no praise from anybody, and made no condition with the herd. He must have known what I was personally—might have known & being just should not have been rude.[3]

[3] William Gilmore Simms to Evert A. Duyckinck, March 15, 1845, in Mary Simms Oliphant, Alfred Odell, and T. C. Duncan Eaves (eds.), *The Letters of William Gilmore Simms* (5 vols.; Columbia, S.C., 1953), II, 43. After this complaint Simms paid tribute to Poe's "remarkable power" and

This review furnishes evidence that Poe's war against the New York literati was not his only reason for writing satirical critiques. Among his less worthy motivations must have been the desire to attract attention. It would be difficult to explain his ridicule of Simms's dedication to Yeadon on any other ground. Yet there is still the possibility that he thought *The Partisan* an inferior work, and, as he had written to Tucker in December, to have treated an inferior work seriously "would have defeated the ends of the critic, in weakening his own authority by making himself ridiculous." [4] Poe was a young unknown, trying to gain authority in a hurry, and the kind of authority he had in mind was that of Jeffrey, Christopher North, William Gifford, and J. G. Lockhart, not that of the typical journalistic critic in America. In later reviews Poe was to make amends to Simms, and he and the Charleston novelist became quite friendly some ten years later. [5]

Other reviews in the January number are no more significant as literary criticism than Poe's review of Simms, but in them is evidence that Poe was trying to develop a psychological approach, a direction that would be almost inevitable in the light of the background already discussed, British aesthetics from Kames to Coleridge. In a notice of a new edition of *Robinson Crusoe* he called attention to the "potent magic of verisimilitude" achieved by Defoe, but he went a step farther than the ordinary journalistic critic (Defoe's "verisimilitude" was a critical commonplace) in

---

showed a certain amount of insight by suggesting that Poe said "bitter things through a wanton consciousness of power."

[4] *Letters*, II, 77.

[5] This reconciliation occurred after Poe had said some good things about Simms's later books, but it came about partly because Simms joined with Duyckinck and Poe in a hot literary war against Lewis Gaylord Clark of the New York *Knickerbocker*, a war which, as far as Poe was concerned, had begun with his review of *Norman Leslie*. Sidney Moss has described this affair in detail in *Poe's Literary Battles*, but Perry Miller's *The Raven and the Whale* gives a fuller account of the various personalities involved. Simms's letters to Duyckinck during 1845 and 1846 are pungent with hostility toward Clark. See especially those dated October 19, 1845, and November 13, 1845, in Oliphant, Odell, and Eaves (eds.), *The Letters of William Gilmore Simms*, II, 105–108, 116–19. Sympathy and understanding are shown in his letter to Poe of July 30, 1846. *Ibid.*, 174–77.

attempting to account for it: "Indeed the author of Crusoe must have possessed, above all faculties, what has been termed the faculty of *identification*—that dominion exercised by volition over imagination which enables the mind to lose its own, in a fictitious individuality." [6]

What Poe called the "faculty of identification" was the sympathetic imagination that some British critics had considered necessary for literary genius. Coleridge had described how Shakespeare "darts himself forth, and passes into all forms of human character and passion." [7] Hazlitt, also in reference to Shakespeare, had written, "The poet may be said, for the time, to identify himself with the character he wishes to represent, and to pass from one to another, like the same soul successively animating different bodies." [8] More than Coleridge and far more than Hazlitt, however, Poe emphasized the dominion of the will over the activity of the imagination. To Coleridge the imagination was a power that could be guided by the artistic will but was not dominated by it. To Hazlitt it was strongly emotionalized perception, an awareness of the object so intense that consciousness of the perceiving self was eliminated. Identification with the object was possible only in a state of strong feeling, and feeling could not be turned on or off by the dominion of the will. Hazlitt found little value in technical skill unless it was preceded by this heightened awareness. Poe, on the other hand, was already beginning to emphasize technique, for neither insight nor feeling had value unless they could be transmitted to others.

We must interpret Poe's emphasis upon conscious art in relation to his journalistic polemics. There were apologists enough for "natural" genius among the romantic critics, but there were few for technical skill. Poe would correct the situation by providing the necessary purgative for bad art. Accordingly, in the February *Messenger* he announced his intention and administered his purge in a review of another subliterary novel:

[6] *Works*, VIII, 169–73.   [7] *Biographia Literaria*, II, 20.
[8] Hazlitt, "On Shakespeare and Milton," *Collected Works*, ed. A. R. Waller and Arnold Glover (New York and London, 1902), V, 47–48.

. . . when we called Norman Leslie the silliest book in the world we had certainly never seen Paul Ulric. *One* sentence in the latter, however, is worthy of our serious attention. "We want a few faithful laborers in the vineyard of literature, to root out the noxious weeds which infest it."

In itself, the book before us is too purely imbecile to merit an extended critique—but as a portion of our daily literary food—as an American work published by the Harpers—as one of the class of absurdities with an inundation of which our country is grievously threatened—we shall have no hesitation, and shall spare no pains, in exposing fully before the public eye its four hundred and forty-three pages of utter folly, bombast, and inanity.[9]

We can see from this that Poe did not dispose of all books he considered worthless with a perfunctory notice. Here he condemned on principle, at least part of the time, and made quotations from the book itself to bear out his charge of folly and bombast. Morris Mattson's *Paul Ulric* was an amateurish imitation of the novels of D'Israeli, and Poe was ruthless in pointing it out, along with detailing the absurdities of plot and style.

Though Poe often condemned where the cliquists might praise, this was not the only way he moved against the tide of American journalistic criticism. He was also capable of commending authors (usually foreign) whom American critics were likely to condemn. The novels of Edward Bulwer-Lytton had given many reviewers opportunities for dissertations on immorality in fiction.[10] Poe, on the other hand, reviewing *Rienzi*,[11] praised Bulwer for some of the very qualities other critics had found objectionable:

We have long learned to reverence the fine intellect of Bulwer. We take up any production of his pen with a positive certainty that, in reading it, the wildest passions of our nature, the most profound of our thoughts, the brightest visions of our fancy, and the most en-

[9] *Works*, VIII, 178–79.
[10] Charvat, *American Critical Thought*, 152–53. This opportunity had not been neglected by the *Messenger*. Bulwer's *The Pilgrims of the Rhine* had been damned for immorality in the third issue of the magazine. *Southern Literary Messenger*, I (1834–35), 54.
[11] *Works*, VIII, 222–29.

nobling and lofty of our aspirations will, in due turn, be enkindled within us. We feel sure of rising from the perusal a wiser if not a better man. In no instance are we deceived. From the brief tale— from the "Monos and Daimonos" of the author—to his most ponderous and beloved novels—all is richly, and glowingly intellectual—all is energetic, or astute, or brilliant, or profound. There *may* be men now living who possess the power of Bulwer— but it is quite evident that very few have made that power so palpably manifest. Indeed, we know of *none*. Viewing him as a novelist—a point of view exceedingly unfavorable (if we hold to the common acceptation of "the novel") for a proper contemplation of his genius—he is unsurpassed by any writer living or dead.

There are two points in this statement worth consideration. First, Poe praised the intellectual power of Bulwer and delighted in what other critics deprecated, Bulwer's portrayal of the "wildest passions of our nature." Poe was not concerned with the social effect of such stimulation, it appears, and was capable of assuming that wisdom was its own reward. Second, he stated flatly that novels do not afford the best opportunity for the contemplation of Bulwer's genius. By genius, Poe could only mean artistic genius, and, as has been previously pointed out, he did not consider novels to be works of art. That Bulwer was capable of artistry, he hastened to affirm: "In a vivid wit—in profundity and a Gothic massiveness of thought —in style—in a calm certainty and definitiveness of purpose—in industry—and above all in the power of controlling and regulating by volition his illimitable faculties of mind, he is unequalled—he is unapproached." Poe never wasted his superlatives. He was attributing to Bulwer the qualities that were completely lacking in Morris Mattson—thought, clearly defined purpose, industry, and "above all" the artistic will. We need only to compare Poe's excessive praise of Bulwer with the concluding paragraph of his review of *Paul Ulric* to detect his strategy. Mattson's book was "despicable in every respect." And, Poe continued, "Such are the works which bring daily discredit upon our national literature. We have no right to complain of being laughed at abroad when so villainous a compound, as the thing we now hold in our hand, of incongruous folly, plagiarism, immorality, inanity, and bombast, can command at any moment both a puff and a publisher." Since both of these reviews appeared in the same issue of the *Messenger*, Poe was administering his corrective by example and by comparison. He was rebuking uncritical literary nationalism, informing the public that it had been misled about Bulwer, and administering a purgative for bad American writing; but he was also emphasizing certain requirements for an artist: a definite purpose, together with the industry and the will to carry it out. Sensibility was not enough, he was to affirm a number of times in later reviews.

As far as the art of the novel was concerned, however, Poe was somewhat at a loss. A genre critic, he had difficulty fitting *Rienzi* into the conventional categories. It was a historical novel, but it stayed too close to the facts for Poe to regard it as a romance.[12] It could have been a history instead of a novel, and as such it was "essentially Epic rather than Dramatic." This classification enabled Poe to make an Aristotelian pronouncement that *Rienzi*, as epic, was "History in its truest—in its only true, proper, and philosophical garb." In addition, he wrote, it had the "delineations of passion and character" proper to the romance and gave a "profound and lucid exposition" of the philosophy of government!

No significance can be attached to Poe's evaluation of *Rienzi*; the real interest of the review lies in his challenge to contemporary attitudes. He could not have lauded Bulwer in such terms without full knowledge that he was going against the current of American criticism. He would have known, too, that he would be annoying

[12] Poe was having difficulty accommodating his conception of the romance to the historical novel. In his review of *The Partisan*, he had stated that the "interweaving of fact with fiction is at all times hazardous," for he could not conceive of a successful union of truth with fable in the novel any more than he could in poetry. A romance to him was a product of the imagination, not a manipulation of historical fact into a story. Simms, less inhibited by genetic theory than Poe, felt no such difficulty. A writer of historical romances should stick to the facts as far as possible but should not be confined by them: "He must be free to conceive and to invent—to create and to endow;—without any dread of crossing the confines of ordinary truth, and of such history as may be found in undisputed records." Quoted in Parks, *William Gilmore Simms as Literary Critic*, 16.

White and perhaps even Beverley Tucker. In the January, 1837, issue of the *Messenger*, after Poe had left the magazine, Tucker reviewed Bulwer's play *The Duchess de la Valliere*. This review was as severe as any of Poe's, but White was delighted. He wrote Tucker: "For myself, individually, I am in rapture with the drubbing you have given Mr. B.—The only fault I find with it, that you have handled him half so severely as he merited.[13]

White could be happy about a severe review by Tucker because it was based upon the sacrosanct principle of morality. The play, Tucker claimed, could have "taken its turn upon the stage, with the obscene comedies of Congreve and Farquhar." He did not profess to know how the larger cities of Europe or America would react to such "exhibitions of splendid villainy and alluring sensuality," but he was *"absolutely sure*, that, in our unrefined, unenlightened, unpretending, uncanting community of white and black, no such dramas as this of Mr. Bulwer's would draw together audiences as would pay the candle-snuffer. We have," he continued, "and again we say thank God!—We have no titled libertines, no demireps of quality, no flaunting divorcees—none either rich, or great, or noble, who seek their wives from the stage or the stews." [14] Furthermore, Tucker was sure that Bulwer's drama simply would not be tolerated among the ladies of Virginia!

Tucker's review was Standard American and, more important to White, Standard Virginian, with its patent distrust of the morals of great cities and its provincial smugness about the ladies of Virginia. The easy morality of European society had been the object of American abuse for nearly half a century, and villains in the sentimental novel and on the stage were often British officers. English travelers since the War of 1812 had aroused American resentment by their remarks about Yankee crudeness, vulgarity, and ignorance, and the American journals had retaliated in kind. Sensitive to such charges, Americans took pride in the sturdy honesty and moral elevation of their nativist heroes, whose mere presence on the stage was a rebuke to the licentious follies of Chesterfieldian fops.

[13] Quoted in Jackson, *Poe and the Southern Literary Messenger*, 111.
[14] *Southern Literary Messenger*, III (1837), 90.

Tucker's tirade was typically provincial, and it was precisely this provincialism that Poe challenged in the name of universal standards. He had been a good student, and the authorities of the past had declared that the ultimate test of a work of art was universality.[15]

This is not to say, however, that Poe was about to become an objective critic—to evaluate by invariable principles was an ambition he cherished but never achieved. He could extol his friends and berate his enemies just as the cliquists of New York did. In the February number there was a review of a novel by Lambert A. Wilmer, *The Confessions of Emilia Harrington*.[16] Wilmer had been friendly to Poe during his difficult period of near starvation in Baltimore, and Poe had conceived with him the plan of publishing a monthly magazine. Wilmer had even written a poetic drama, *Merlin*, based upon Poe's youthful love for Sarah Elmira Royster.[17] Poe would have had to be either a disloyal friend or the most dis-

---

[15] Kames, for example, had been disturbed by the apparent variability of taste, not only among individuals but also among different nations and periods; but he relied upon his assumption of a common human nature to resolve the dilemma: "By the principles that constitute the sensitive part of our nature, a wonderful uniformity is preserved in the emotions and feelings of the different races of men; the same object making upon every person the same impression, the same in kind, if not in degree. There have been, as above observed, aberrations from these principles; but soon or late they prevail, and restore the wanderer to the right track." *Elements of Criticism*, 473. Alison's subjectivism seemed to remove any possibility of a universal standard, but even he assumed that members of a given society or class would have similar experiences and hence similar associations and that the diversity of taste could be corrected by cultivation. The standard, then, would be the approbation of cultivated gentlemen, with the only observable variance being that which derived from temperamental differences. Poe's position was similar to Alison's, but, like Kames, he assumed a common human nature governed by laws that could be analyzed and applied. He agreed with Blair that "in every composition, what interests the imagination, and touches the heart, pleases all ages and all nations. There is a certain string, which, being properly struck, the human heart is so made as to answer to it." Blair, *Lectures*, I, 34. Poe advanced this particular proposition in his later criticism, where occasionally he echoed Blair's metaphor.

[16] *Works*, VIII, 234–37.

[17] T. O. Mabbott (ed.), Introduction, *Merlin*, by Lambert A. Wilmer (New York, 1941), 26.

passionate of judges had he given the book the criticism it deserved. Being neither, he resorted to a method which violated his code as a critic—discussing a number of things other than the book itself, chiefly the power of verisimilitude in *Robinson Crusoe*, which he had treated in an earlier review. He credited Wilmer with the same power, which by the standards of the time was no small praise. More unusual for Poe, he went on to claim that *Emilia Harrington* would "render essential services to virtue in the unveiling of the deformities of vice." This, he wrote, "is a deed of no questionable utility." Ordinarily Poe wasted little space on the moral utility of a novel—he left that to his journalistic confreres—but, since Wilmer's book catered to the public appetite for sensation, this was about the most tactful commendation Poe could give. Quickly getting off the subject, Poe praised Wilmer's poem, "To Mira," which had appeared in the December issue of the *Messenger*, as showing "exquisite tenderness of sentiment, . . . deep and unaffected melancholy . . . and high polish of versification." Finally, he had some kind words for Wilmer's *Merlin* and for his editorial writings in the *Saturday Evening Post*. All this without any actual criticism indicates that Poe was for a moment doffing his mantle as the "Zoilus" of the *Messenger* in order to do a favor for a friend.

Yet if Poe could praise the inferior work of a friend, we must not conclude that he was always being kind when he became excited about a book that has since been forgotten. He was evidently sincere in his admiration for Henry F. Chorley's *Conti the Discarded* (a collection of tales),[18] though Chorley is remembered today, if at all, only by the specialist in nineteenth-century English literature. "Conti the Discarded" was a tale on a subject that titillated the romantic mind—the misunderstood genius. The place of art and artistic genius in society was Chorley's special concern throughout his literary career,[19] and the subject was of unusual interest to Poe, who already had, and was to continue to have, his own difficulties with the public. Chorley's tales, Poe wrote, "have a noble,

[18] *Works*, VIII, 229–34.
[19] Hubbell, *The South in American Literature*, 539.

and to us, a most thrillingly interesting *purpose*." He continued in an adulatory vein: "In saying that our whole heart is with the author—that the deepest, and we trust, the purest emotions are enkindled within us by his chivalric and magnanimous *design*—we present but a feeble picture of our individual feelings as influenced by the perusal of Conti." Then Poe paraphrased from Chorley's preface a passage concerning the way the world degrades the work of the artist into "a mere plaything" and the way the artist, perhaps in consequence, brings "his own calling into contempt by coarsely regarding it as a mere engine of money getting." Poe continued to paraphrase Chorley freely, changing the English writer's words to make them more emphatic. Chorley wrote: "That genius is not to be bound by vulgar rules, is a maxim which, however true, has been too often repeated; and there have appeared on earth enough spirits of the loftiest and most brilliant order who have worthily taken their part in life as useful citizens, affectionate husbands, faithful friends, to deprive of their excuse all such as hold that to despise and alienate the world is the inevitable and painfully glorious destiny of the highly gifted!" [20] The first clause of this passage Poe changed to, "That genius should not and indeed cannot be bound down to the vulgar common-places of existence is a maxim . . .," and then went on to repeat Chorley verbatim to the end of the passage.

Although we may not approve of Poe's practice of changing quotations to suit his own purpose, we can at least try to understand his motives. Poe admired Chorley because the English writer was trying to create a more generous public attitude toward the creative artist by refuting the popular notion that the artistic genius was inevitably alienated from the world by his egotistic insistence upon unconventional behavior. Poe had a personal stake in the matter. His early poetry had revealed a posture of alienation and somewhat morbid pride. His behavior—his youthful drinking and gambling—had been censured in the middle-class business milieu of John

[20] *Conti the Discarded: With Other Tales and Fancies* (American ed.; New York, 1835), I, x.

Allan; and he was currently having difficulties with the equally conventional Thomas Willis White.

Too, the notion that the artistic genius was unbalanced because some of his faculties were exaggerated at the expense of others was widely current in Poe's day, and more than once Poe felt called upon to defend genius by maintaining that the highest genius exhibited a complete development of all the faculties. A sympathetic treatment of genius would thus command Poe's immediate interest. Although Chorley argued that a genius did not necessarily despise the conventions of the world, he gave in *Conti* a sympathetic account of behavior that would be outrageous in American eyes.

In *Conti* Madame Zerlini, an Italian prima donna, falls in love with Colonel Hardwycke, an Englishman, and becomes his mistress for twelve years, bearing him a son. When Colonel Hardwycke decides to marry someone else, Madame Zerlini promptly expires, dying for love in proper romantic fashion. The "vulgar rules" which Chorley referred to in his preface apparently had less to do with art than with moral conventions. Poe's audience was used to the notion that genius could snatch a grace beyond the reach of art —could masterfully violate the rules of composition. Chorley could have been interpreted along these lines, but Poe wanted his readers to receive the intended meaning, so he substituted "vulgar commonplaces of existence," which could not so easily be misunderstood. He did not want the "noble purpose" of understanding the behavior of genius to be frustrated by an ambiguous phrase in Chorley's preface. Madame Zerlini, of course, receives her comeuppance; she is properly punished for her transgressions. The significant thing is that she was treated sympathetically.

Poe's admiration of Chorley, however, was not based solely on the fact that he and the English author were interested in the same subject. In Chorley's description of the demise of Madame Zerlini, sex and death are deliciously mingled in a way which Poe must have found attractive. He quoted the appropriate passage:

> He went in. Madame Zerlini was there—flung down upon a sofa, in an attitude which, in life, it would have been impossible for her to

maintain for many moments. Her head was cast back over one of the pillows, so far, that her long hair, which had been imperfectly fastened, had disengaged itself by its own weight, and was now sweeping heavily downward, with a crushed wreath of passion flowers and myrtles half buried among it. Everything about her told how fiercely the spirit had passed. Her robe of scarlet muslin was entirely torn off on one shoulder, and disclosed its exquisitely rounded proportions. Her glittering neglige was unclasped, and one end of it clenched firmly in the small left hand, which there was now hardly any possibility of unclosing. Her glazed eyes were wide open—her mouth set in an unnatural, yet fascinating smile; her cheek still flushed with a more delicate, yet intense red than belongs to health . . . .

It is possible that this passage, which describes the embrace of death almost as if it were a sexual struggle, prefigures Poe's own description of the fierce effort of Ligeia to preserve her life by an effort of the will; but in Poe's tale there are no exquisitely rounded shoulders for the delectation of the reader. Sex is almost completely sublimated in Poe, unless it appears in the form of necrophilia. On the other hand, as his admiration for Bulwer and Chorley indicates, he was not nearly so prudish about such matters as Heath and Tucker. His taste for the sex-death motif has occasioned a number of psychopathological studies, such as that of Madame Bonaparte, which attempt to examine Poe's neurosis through his writings. Yet if we extend the evidence to include the writing he liked, we would see that at least one aspect of his neurosis could be linked to a period taste. Readers in the 1830's relished morbidity; and it was in the Gothic tradition for sex to be smuggled in with the terror.[21]

2

The February issue of the *Messenger* contained thirty-one pages of criticism, the greatest number during Poe's editorship, but in

[21] For an illuminating discussion of this point, see Davidson, *Poe: A Critical Study*, 105–20.

March only nine pages of critical notices appeared. Whether anything had happened beyond the normal variation of books received, it is difficult to say. White had written to Lucian Minor on December 25, 1835, that Poe still "kept from the bottle," but whether that happy state of affairs continued throughout January and February of 1836 we do not know. Since Poe was writing nearly all of the critical notices, any fluctuation in his state of health, emotional or otherwise, would have been directly reflected in the amount of criticism published. Mrs. Clemm and Virginia had joined him in Richmond in October of 1835, but as he did not marry Virginia until May 16 of the following year, the obligations of being a family man should not have interfered with his work. Furthermore, his letters during January and February of 1836 were cheerful and businesslike. He wrote to Kennedy on January 22, "My health is better than for years past, my mind is fully occupied, my pecuniary difficulties have vanished, I have a fair prospect of future success—in a word all is right." [22] On the face of it, then, the relatively small number of notices for the March issue was not caused by Poe's personal situation. Probably fewer books were received, or space was limited.

Of the criticism in the March number only two reviews have any bearing on Poe's development as a literary critic. The first was of a brief study guide to the "science" of phrenology, compiled by a Mrs. L. Miles from the works of the founders of phrenology, J. K. Spurzheim and F. J. Gall.[23] Poe, like many other Americans, was tremendously excited by the potentialities of the phrenological system. It seemed to be useful for self-analysis, mental therapy, educational theory and practice, and even literary criticism.[24] American magazines had been publicizing phrenology since 1809, and a short-lived quarterly called the *Annals of Phrenology* had begun publication in Boston in 1834. Spurzheim himself had visited

---

[22] *Letters*, I, 81.   [23] *Works*, VIII, 252–55.

[24] Articles in American journals were quick to point out these uses. One such article was entitled "Application of Phrenology to Criticism" and appeared in *Annals of Phrenology*, I (1834), 200–23. Five years later the *American Phrenological Journal* ran a series called "Predominance of Certain Organs in the British Poets." II (December, 1839–June, 1840).

America and in the course of his visit had died somewhat spectacularly in 1832. A public autopsy was held, his brain was removed and weighed, and Harvard University made a special effort to commemorate his loss.[25] An alert reader of all the journals he could get his hands on, Poe would certainly have encountered many articles on phrenology. It had been a topic of special interest in the *New-England Magazine* between 1833 and 1835, and Poe had tried to sell a tale to that journal in 1833.[26] It was discussed in many other magazines, including Lewis Gaylord Clark's *Knickerbocker*.[27] Poe's familiarity with the background of phrenology is suggested by his repeating the story of Spurzheim's gaining five hundred "converts" by lecturing with a brain in one hand and a copy of the *Edinburgh Review* in the other. He also mentioned the Scottish phrenologist George Combe, whose works went through many editions in the 1830's and 1840's and who was immensely popular in America.

Poe claimed that the "most salutary" use of phrenology was "self-examination and self-knowledge" and that "through the science, a perfectly accurate estimate of . . . moral capabilities" might be obtained.[28] There were other uses too numerous to mention in a brief review, Poe said. Two which he did not mention, but which he was soon to put into practice, were characterization in fiction and psychological criticism.[29]

[25] John D. Davies, *Phrenology: Fad and Science* (New Haven, 1955), 17. A biographical sketch of Spurzheim, prefixed to the third American edition of his *Phrenology*, published in 1836, gives a full account of his death and subsequent events. In accordance with his own wishes, Spurzheim's skull was preserved by the Boston Phrenological Society. The sketch also describes Spurzheim's Edinburgh triumph. See *Phrenology*, ed. Nahum Capen (Boston, 1836), 50, 152.

[26] See Poe to Joseph T. and Edwin Buckingham, May 4, 1833, *Letters*, I, 53.

[27] A defense of phrenology was published in the *Knickerbocker* for August, 1833, but the editors became skeptical of the "science" in a few years. Mott, *A History of American Magazines*, 449–50.

[28] The term "moral" in Poe's statement should be interpreted as roughly equivalent to "mental."

[29] For Poe's specific use of Mrs. Miles's work, see Edward Hungerford, "Poe and Phrenology," *American Literature*, II (1930–31), 209–31.

The only other review in the March issue which is worthy of comment is of A. B. Longstreet's *Georgia Scenes.* In this review Poe demonstrated that he was capable of commending a type of American humor different from his own "grotesques." He made no attempt to analyze the humor or express a theory of the comic. He simply praised the work for its quality of producing sheer enjoyment and concluded that it would make the writer's fortune if it were published in England. For if Poe, who professed himself "not of the merry mood," enjoyed Longstreet's tales, "what would Christopher North say to them?—ah, what would Christopher North say? that is the question. Certainly not a word. But we can fancy the pursing up of his lips, and the long, loud, and jovial resonation of his wicked, uproarious ha! ha's!" [30]

Poe gave credit to Longstreet for his ability to draw character, Southern character in particular, and regarded the book as "a sure omen of better days for the literature of the South." This was an accurate forecast, for Longstreet's book was the first in a line of publications of Southwestern humor which were to catch the public fancy for the next half-century. Of equal interest, however, is Poe's visualization of the reaction of Christopher North to *Georgia Scenes.* It gives us some idea of the image he had of the famous critic. Certainly to Poe, North was not, as he seemed to Beverley Tucker, the sinister figure who took sadistic pleasure in flaying poor-devil authors. Instead, Poe saw him as a jovial imp, characterized more by "wicked" good humor than by cruelty. And it is not hard to imagine that Poe, in his own satirical reviews, had attempted to project a similar image of himself but had succeeded only in evoking the charge of flippancy from American journalists who were not sympathetic toward mordant humor—particularly when it was directed at their friends.

By the time he had written the reviews for the March number of the *Messenger,* Poe had developed patterns which he was to follow, more or less regularly, throughout his career, for he had learned what he had to do to survive as a journalistic critic. The competition in the magazine world was vicious. Magazines were

[30] *Works,* VIII, 258.

started with little capital and inadequate subscription lists, and most of them expired within one to five years. The thing to do was to secure contributions from the best-known writers [31]—Irving, Cooper, Bryant, Bird, and a few others esteemed in the 1830's— but few publishers could manage more than token payments. White most certainly could not afford to pay established authors,[32] and Poe had to employ other tactics to attract attention. He had proved himself to be a tough competitor, but this does not mean that he relinquished standards. On the contrary, he thought that courageous book reviews, unqualified by fear or favor, were as necessary for the reputation of a magazine as the quality of merchandise was for a retail establishment. Whatever qualms he may have had as a "Southern" gentleman were quickly overcome by his recognition that he was in a business and that his competitors in New York were not hampered by scruples. Yet they had been the first to utter cries of outrage when Poe assaulted one of their own. This alone would not have been likely to deter him, but when White and his advisers had failed to appreciate the shrewdness of Poe's tactics, he knew that ridicule, however much it was justified in his own mind, would not gain respect for him as a critic. He had to become what was then called a "philosophical" critic and validate his claims on psychological or even metaphysical grounds, as Coleridge had before him. His first "philosophical" criticism appeared in April, 1836, in a review which most Poe scholars have taken to be the most significant of his *Messenger* period, his double review of *The Culprit Fay*, by Joseph Rodman Drake, and *Alnwick Castle*, by Fitz-Greene Halleck, two poets whose reputations were much higher in 1836 than they are today.

[31] At White's request, Poe wrote to Robert Montgomery Bird twice, to Cooper once, and to Fitz-Greene Halleck once, soliciting contributions. See *Letters*, I, 75–76, 93, 94–96.

[32] See White to Tucker, January 19, 1837, in Jackson, *Poe and the Southern Literary Messenger*, 112–13, for a description of his financial problems.

VI · The Final Cause of Art

THE review of Drake and Halleck [1] illustrates the three aspects of Poe as a critic which must be correlated before any assessment can be made of his place in the history of criticism: (1) the competitive journalist, (2) the critic who examined books for their literary quality, and (3) the psychological aesthetician who sought to define the response to art and to establish its final cause. It was this last endeavor which would qualify him to his contemporaries as a philosophical critic.

The first pages of the review show Poe as a journalist, answering his detractors and making prescriptions for the "health and prosperity" of American literature. Next he attempted to define aesthetic feeling, the sentiment of poesy. Finally, he made a detailed examination of the works at hand, with only a minimal display of the levity which had attracted readers but had made formidable enemies. Only the first part of the review can be considered irrelevant to the act of criticism, for the last two correlate in the sense that Poe was trying to formulate valid generalizations about the origin and end of poetic feeling and to apply them to the works under consideration.

Poe opened his review with a lengthy denunciation of the state of American journalistic criticism. "There was a time," he wrote, "when we cringed to foreign opinion—let us even say when we paid a most servile deference to British critical dicta," yet only the "excess of our subserviency was blamable." It was reasonable to recognize a supremacy that only "prejudice or ignorance" would deny. Now, he continued, Americans go to the opposite extreme, and "so far from being ashamed of the many disgraceful literary failures to which our own inordinate vanities and misapplied patriotism have lately given birth, and so far from deeply lamenting that these daily puerilities are of home manufacture, we adhere

[1] *Works*, VIII, 275–318.

pertinaciously to our original blindly conceived idea, and thus often find ourselves involved in the gross paradox of liking a stupid book the better, because, sure enough, its stupidity is American." However correct Poe was in his opinion, this was scarcely the kind of statement that would go unchallenged. Too many feathers would be singed among the literary nationalists. Yet Poe's great concern for American letters at large was perhaps disingenuous, for he was using it as a defense for his own book-reviewing methods: "Deeply lamenting this unjustifiable state of public feeling, it has been our constant endeavor, since assuming the Editorial duties of this Journal, to stem, with what little abilities we possess, a current so disastrously undermining the health and prosperity of our literature."

It appears that the occasion for Poe's discussion of the state of literary criticism in America was the reaction of the New York clique to his *Norman Leslie* review. Colonel William L. Stone, editor of the *Commercial Advertiser,* had printed in his own newspaper an attack made on Poe by Willis Gaylord Clark in the Philadelphia *Gazette.* Clark, as Poe was quick to point out, was an editor of the New York *Knickerbocker.* Clark's charge against Poe was puerile; he merely stated that the "critical department" of the *Messenger* was "quacky" and that the critic could not write the works he condemned. Stone's own comment, which follows, would have to be taken more seriously because he invoked the alleged ethics of book-reviewing:

> The Duty of the critic is to act as judge, not as enemy, of the writer whom he reviews; a distinction of which the Zoilus of the Messenger seems not to be aware. It is possible to review a book severely, without bestowing opprobrious epithets upon the writer: to condemn with courtesy, if not with kindness. The critic of the Messenger has been eulogized for his scorching and scarifying abilities, and he thinks it incumbent upon him to keep up his reputation in that line, by sneers, sarcasm, and downright abuse; by straining his vision with microscopic intensity in search of faults and shutting his eyes, with all his might, to beauties. Moreover, we have detected him, more than once, in blunders quite as gross as those on which it was his pleasure to descant.

It is to Poe's credit that he printed the charges against him, but those made by Colonel Stone must have been too close for comfort, even though they exaggerated Poe's practice. When Beverley Tucker had questioned the levity of his satirical reviews, Poe, in a rather superior tone, had answered by citing the example of *Blackwood's*. Young and inexperienced, he had thought the critic had a perfect right to ridicule a ridiculous work. By April, however, he had learned that it was necessary for a book reviewer to be as well established as a Jeffrey or a Christopher North to be able to publish satirical reviews with impunity. He *had* gained notoriety, but at the expense of being charged with a deliberate attempt to gain it. To defend himself against Stone's charge, Poe stated his book-reviewing code and invited his detractors to employ the same standard:

> While in our reviews we have at all times been particularly careful *not* to deal in generalities, and have never, if we remember aright, advanced in any single instance an unsupported assertion, our accuser has forgotten to give us any better evidence of our flippancy, injustice, personality, and gross blundering, than the solitary *dictum* of Col. Stone. We call upon the Colonel for assistance in this dilemma. We wish to be shown our blunders that we may correct them—to be made aware of our flippancy, that we may avoid it hereafter—and above all to have our personalities pointed out that we may proceed forthwith with a repentant spirit, to make the *amende honorable*. In default of this aid from the Editor of the Commercial we shall take it for granted that we are neither blunderers, flippant, personal, nor unjust.

Poe's legalistic rejoinder, which amounted to saying that he was innocent until proved guilty, was really an evasion. He had been flippant, sarcastic, and personal in more than one review. His motive may have been, as he claimed, to reform reviewing practices in America by being contemptuous of "stupid books," but even his friend Tucker had intimated that the end did not justify the means. Poe had become notorious; he was admired in many quarters, but he had yet to prove that he was a philosophical critic instead of a hack reviewer. The review of Mrs. Sigourney had been a beginning, and now, in the remainder of the review of Drake and Halleck, Poe undertook to demonstrate that he could make judgments based upon principles.

2

Before the review of Drake and Halleck, Poe had made little attempt to use a psychological approach in his criticism, although he had the example of Coleridge and, more remotely, Kames, Blair, and Alison before him. Nor had he attempted to express a metaphysical basis for his theories even though Coleridge, his chief guide, had applied both philosophical and religious principles to poetry. In this review, however, Poe did both, possibly because he wished to be a critic instead of a book reviewer and almost certainly because he knew that "philosophical" criticism was secure against the Colonel Stones and the Willis Gaylord Clarks of the journalistic world.

Poe began by attempting, as Coleridge had in Chapter XIV of the *Biographia Literaria*, to formulate a definition of poetry, taking poetry, as Coleridge had, in its larger sense as embracing all genres of art. Then, still following Coleridge's method, Poe undertook to define poetry in psychological terms; but unlike Coleridge, who focused upon the creative mind of the poet, his power of reconciling opposites, Poe focused upon poetic feeling, which he claimed could be described distinctly enough "for all the purposes of practical analysis." Before attempting to analyze this feeling, however, he provided a teleological explanation of its existence:

To look upwards from any existence, material or immaterial, to its *design*, is, perhaps, the most direct, and the most unerring method of attaining a just notion of the nature of the existence itself. Nor is the principle at fault when we turn our eyes from Nature even to Nature's God. We find certain faculties, implanted within us, and arrive at a more plausible conception of the character and attribute of those faculties, by considering, with what finite judgment we possess, the *intention* of the Deity in so implanting them within us, than by any actual investigation of their powers, or any speculative deductions from their visible and material effects. Thus, for example, we discover in all men a disposition to look with reverence upon superiority, whether real or supposititious. In some, this disposition is to be recognized with difficulty, and, in very peculiar cases, we are occasionally even led to doubt its existence altogether, until circumstances beyond the common routine bring it accidentally into development. In others again it forms a prominent and distinctive feature of character, and is rendered palpably evident in its excesses. But in all human beings it is, in a greater or less degree, finally perceptible. It has been, therefore, justly considered a primitive sentiment. Phrenologists call it Veneration. It is, indeed, the instinct given to man by God as security for his own worship. And although, preserving its nature, it becomes perverted from its principal purpose, and although swerving from that purpose, it serves to modify the relations of human society—the relations of father and child, of master and slave, of the ruler and ruled—its primitive essence is nevertheless the same, and by a reference to primal causes, may at any moment be determined.

This passage has been quoted at length because it illustrates Poe's tendency to make a teleological justification of aesthetic feeling. What he gave was nothing more than the old argument from design, commonly used in post-Newtonian religious apologetics but derived here from the phrenological description of the human mind. The use of such an argument in aesthetic speculation had been characteristic of the analysts of taste, for none of them had been quite prepared to permit hedonic value to be its own justification. It had to lead to something more worthy, religious feeling, and the Scottish philosophers did not hesitate to employ a quasi-Platonic argument when they discussed taste, in spite of their dislike of metaphysics.[2] This tendency was most obvious in Archibald Alison. Acknowledging that his opinion coincided with that of the "Platonic school"—Shaftesbury, Hutcheson, and Reid [3]—Alison concluded his *Essays* with an account of the final cause of aesthetic

[2] For the Scottish rejection of metaphysics, see Chapter I, Section 2, of this book.

[3] *Essays on Taste*, 444. Alison was a close associate of Thomas Reid, one of the founders of the Scottish common-sense school; the *Essays* were dedicated to Reid.

feeling. The beauties and sublimities of the material world, he said, did not exist as actual qualities, but only as signs of such qualities, intended to awaken in us a hunger for more perfect beauty than any existing in nature. Aesthetic feeling would lead us at last to religious sentiment. The mind, seeking perfection, eventually would rest in God.[4]

Such speculation would seem entirely alien to phrenology, the "science of mind," and Poe's own statement that it is more instructive to inquire into God's intention than to investigate the mental powers would appear to be a renunciation of scientific procedure. The phrenologists had employed dissection and had actually examined the brain and the skull. Yet George Combe, an admirer of the Scottish philosophy before he undertook to improve upon it with the findings of Spurzheim, displayed his intellectual heritage by an emphasis on moral feeling characteristic of the Scots.[5] Nor did he neglect aesthetics; his account of the purpose of Ideality, except for his terminology, is identical with Alison's account of the purpose of taste. No vulgar utilitarianism or selfishness contaminated the pure pleasure generated by Ideality. As Combe expressed it, "IDEALITY delights in perfection from the pure pleasure of contemplating it. . . . the picture, the statue, the landscape, or the mansion on which it abides with the intensest rapture, is as pleasing, although the property of another, as if all its own. It is a spring that is

---

[4] *Ibid.*, 457–58.

[5] Combe acknowledged the affiliation in the preface to his most popular work, *The Constitution of Man;* he claimed that his method of inquiry was essentially that of the Scottish philosophers. In reviewing Combe, the *Knickerbocker* pointed out that the findings of the "new science" resembled the "brilliant metaphysical discoveries of Hutcheson, and Reid, and Stewart." *Knickerbocker*, I (1833), 316. The use of the term "metaphysical" in this quotation is likely to be confusing, for both the Scottish philosophers and the phrenologists strenuously opposed metaphysical speculation as such. The term, however, was frequently used in the sense of "psychological." Poe exhibited this ambiguity in his reviews, praising "metaphysical" ability in one context but disparaging "metaphysical" speculation in another. For the hostility of the phrenologists toward metaphysical speculation, see David Bakan, "Phrenology Is Foolish?" *Psychology Today*, I (1968), 45–46.

touched by the beautiful wherever it exists; and hence its means of enjoyment are as unbounded as the universe." [6]

What Poe would have learned from Combe, then, even if he had not already learned it from the analysts of taste, was that the sense of the beautiful was one of the higher sentiments of the mind, closely associated with religious feeling. As Combe explained, Ideality had a capacity for "endless moral and intellectual refinement . . . by which we may arise in the scale of excellence, and, at every step of our progress, reap direct enjoyment from this sentiment. Its constant desire is for something more exquisite still." [7] This pleasure was to Combe, as it had been to Alison, a moral sentiment, an ideal pleasure. It had nothing to do with sensuous pleasure or passion; other faculties took care of these.[8] Poe's use of this essentially moral justification of aesthetic feeling is immediately apparent:

[6] *The Constitution of Man*, 66.   [7] *Ibid.*, 78.

[8] These were the "lower faculties" common to man and animal; they included "amativeness" (sexual feeling), "philoprogenitiveness" (desire for offspring), and the external senses, which Combe classified as Genus I of the "Intellectual Faculties." These faculties were supposed to be responsible for simple perception (Genus I), for elementary ideas of shape, form, color, size, weight, and existence (Genus II), for the perception of relationships in the physical environment (Genus III), and for the discovery of abstract relationships such as the cause-effect nexus, analogies, and ideational differences (Genus IV). This last category was called the "Reflecting Faculties" and would correspond to the eighteenth-century "reason." Genus II and Genus III would correspond to what the Scottish philosophers called "common sense." The phrenologists had no "Intellectual Faculties" equivalent to Coleridge's higher "Reason," but certain of the "Moral Sentiments" operating in conjunction with the "Intellectual Faculties" enabled the individual to desire the ultimate truths of revealed religion but at the same time to accept only such truths as met the tests of observation and experience. The result, so Combe explained, would be a viable "natural religion." See Combe, *The Constitution of Man*, 75–81, for an explanation of the uses of the faculties.

Because Poe used the phrenological jargon, his terminology is difficult for us to interpret today. "Intellectual," in Poe's vocabulary, did not necessarily signify rational, but merely something that happened in the higher faculties, as opposed to the feelings or propensities common to man and animal.

Very nearly akin to this feeling [veneration], and liable to the same analysis, is the Faculty of Ideality—which is the sentiment of Poesy. This sentiment is the sense of the beautiful, of the sublime, and of the mystical. Thence spring immediately admiration of the fair flowers, the fairer forests, the bright valleys and rivers and mountains of the Earth—and love of the gleaming stars and other burning glories of Heaven—and mingled up inextricably with this love and this admiration of Heaven and of Earth, the unconquerable desire—*to know*. Poesy is the sentiment of Intellectual Happiness here, and the hope of a higher Intellectual Happiness hereafter.

It is obvious from this passage that Ideality to Poe's mind was little more than the old faculty of taste, commonly called the "sense of the beautiful." The fact that Ideality could be considered one of the imaginative faculties, along with Hope and Marvellousness,[9] allowed Poe to employ next what he had learned from Coleridge: "Imagination is its [poetry's] soul. With the *passions* of mankind—although it may modify them greatly—although it may exalt, or inflame, or purify, or control them—it would require little

[9] Mrs. Miles, whose work Poe had reviewed, classified "Ideality" as an imaginative faculty; Combe called it a moral sentiment. A confusion of terminology is evident among the phrenologists, for the term "faculty" implies creative ability, whereas "sentiment" implies a capacity for feeling. There was also a difference in the number of propensities, sentiments, and faculties, depending upon which phrenologist one read. F. J. Gall, originator of the system, had listed twenty-six organs of the mind, Spurzheim and Combe thirty-five. The Fowler brothers, most prominent of the American phrenologists, had expanded the list to forty-three. To be accurate, "Ideality" should be called a faculty if it were to be considered as creative, but a sentiment in respect to the appreciation of beauty. Gall, writing in French, had named the organ "Poésie" after having noted its prominence in the busts of several poets. "Phrenology," *Encyclopaedia Britannica* (11th ed.), XXI, 534–40. Poe's term "poesy" may have come from Gall, and he was being phrenologically accurate when he defined it as "the sentiment of Intellectual Happiness here." It would have to be combined with the moral sentiment, "Hope," however, if it were to give "the hope of a higher Intellectual Happiness hereafter." Combe had explained that "Veneration" plus "Hope" and "Wonder" gave us religious feeling. Mrs. Miles classified "Hope" and "Marvellousness" with "Ideality" as imaginative faculties, enabling Poe to consider all three as aspects of the imagination, while at the same time interpreting them, in their passive aspect, as sentiments.

ingenuity to prove that it has no inevitable, and indeed no necessary co-existence." [10] Except for the first sentence, however, this
passage owes little to Coleridge, who was not so insistent upon
idealization that he would banish passion from poetry. Instead, as
his admiration of Shakespeare's "Venus and Adonis" indicates,
Coleridge recognized the unifying power of passion, which stimulated the imagination to its proper business of "reducing multitude
into unity of effect." [11] Poe, however, struggling to arrive at a
philosophical definition of aesthetic feeling as an *intellectual* delight, drew upon the Platonic tradition for his teleological principle
and used the phrenological description of Ideality as his "scientific"
proof.[12] This may seem to us today to be the most naïve of eclectic

[10] Combe had declared that the passions, or "animal propensities," must
be guided by the moral sentiments before true happiness could be achieved.
"No faculty is bad," Combe wrote, "but each has a legitimate sphere of
action, and, when properly gratified, is a fountain of pleasure . . . ." *The
Constitution of Man*, 97. In other words, it is a law of human nature, instituted by a benevolent God, for us to enjoy our feelings. Since the response
to beauty is a legitimate moral sentiment, no opprobrium should be attached to the hedonic value of art. Poe's argument that passion does not
necessarily co-exist with the imagination is phrenologically correct, for in-
dulgence of the animal propensities requires no imagination; furthermore,
the imagination is abused when it is allowed to "inflame" the passions. It
should be used only to "purify," "exalt," or "control" them.

[11] *Biographia Literaria*, II, 15–16. Coleridge's argument is complex and
requires summary. He did not deny even the "animal impulse" as a subject for poetry, as Poe was increasingly prone to do, but explained that
Shakespeare's feelings as an artist were "aloof" from the passions depicted
in the poem. Then, using "passion" in a different sense, Coleridge gave an
example of its unifying power. Poe apparently referred only to the animal
passions (using phrenology instead of Coleridge) in his attempt to prove
that poetry was concerned only with the ideal. The difference is more in
application than in theory. Poe sought to achieve the ideal in part by a
restriction of subject matter. Coleridge did not restrict subject at all but
remarked that a genius would not use his "personal sensations and experiences." In other words, it is not *Shakespeare's* "animal impulse" in *Venus
and Adonis*, but an imaginative presentation of sexual love, a feeling "of
which he is at once the painter and the analyst." Even this would have
been rejected by Poe, who eventually claimed that a poet should treat only
ideal love.

[12] Marvin Laser, who discussed phrenology briefly in connection with
Poe's aesthetic theory, argued that the Platonic teleology appeared in Poe's

procedures, but it would not have seemed naïve in Poe's time. Phrenology, particularly as it was popularized by Combe, appeared to validate scientifically the kind of secular idealism cherished by most Americans and previously supported only by the imprecise faculty psychology of the Scots. The existence of an actual organ for man's capacity to idealize was an exciting proposition even for the transcendentalists,[13] and to be able to use it in his defense of poetry was exciting to Edgar Poe.

After the "philosophical" portion of his review was complete, Poe undertook to discuss the practical result of poetic feeling as it was expressed in language, poetry itself. The only proper test of a poem, he affirmed, was "its capabilities of exciting the Poetic Sentiments in others." At first glance this would appear to be equivalent to A. E. Housman's gooseflesh symptom as the measure of poetic excellence. If a poem makes you feel the shiver down the spine or the prickling of the scalp that are the neurological indices of poetic feeling, then the poem is a good one. Poe was not so naïve as to eliminate the act of criticism, however. Instead his words suggest an anticipation of I. A. Richards' early experiments with the evaluation of student responses.[14] The response to a poem can be

---

criticism after he had read Shelley's A *Defence of Poetry* when it appeared in 1840. See Laser, "The Growth and Structure of Poe's Concept of Beauty," *English Literary History*, XV (1948), 69–84. Certainly Poe's idiom thereafter resembled Shelley's, but this idiom was common to romantic aesthetics. The attempt to validate the response to beauty as a moral sentiment was equally characteristic of both the Scottish critics and the phrenologists, however, as was the use of a quasi-Platonic argument. Poe thought he had found an illustration of the argument in Shelley's "Hymn to Intellectual Beauty." *Works*, VIII, 283n. This is not surprising, since Shelley's head gave phrenological tokens of "large" Ideality. See "Predominance of Certain Organs in the British Poets, No. 6," *American Phrenological Journal and Miscellany*, II (1840), 461.

[13] Emerson called Combe's *The Constitution of Man* "the best sermon I have read for some time." Ralph Rusk (ed.), *The Letters of Ralph Waldo Emerson* (New York, 1939), I, 291.

[14] *Practical Criticism: A Study of Literary Judgment* (Harvest Book ed.; New York, n.d.). Richards' method involves an assessment of appropriate and inappropriate responses to poetry. Poe's "poetic sentiment" would be an appropriate response; any feeling that arose from a lower level of apprehension would be inappropriate.

measured, Poe asserted, by the use of observation, experience, "ethical analysis," and common sense. Only the term "ethical analysis" is troublesome. As Poe used it, it could hardly refer to moral behavior; he must have been using the word in its original Greek sense as having to do with character, and we may substitute "character analysis" in a manner appropriate to the phrenological approach.

Poe's next statement may seem to be one of the most outrageous ever made by a supposedly responsible critic, for he went on to say that a poet "highly endowed with the powers of Causality," even if "deficient" in Ideality, would compose a finer poem than the poet who had Ideality without Causality. This jargon must be interpreted. Poe defined Causality as "metaphysical acumen," which out of context makes as little sense today as Causality, but his illustration—that a metaphysician can analyze the responses of others—makes it clear that he meant something like psychological discernment. Causality was one of the "Reflecting Faculties" and had to do with the comprehension of cause and effect relationships; this, in terms of stimuli and responses, would have been a branch of metaphysics for Poe.[15] What Poe was saying, then, was that an unimaginative poet with great ability in practical psychology would produce a finer poem than an imaginative poet without such ability. He "proves" his point by appropriating a story told about Coleridge's being analyzed by Spurzheim; the phrenologist had concluded that Coleridge was deficient in Ideality but quite well developed in Causality. Poe passed this off as his own interpretation, but the incident was well known among enthusiasts of phrenology.[16] His point was that Coleridge's poems, the "purest of all poems," appealed exclusively to the imaginative faculties in spite of the poet's personal lack of imagination, as evidenced by the shape of his skull! Accordingly, he could only have written these poems as a metaphysician would, by using the psychology of effect.

[15] Gall had named this faculty "Esprit Métaphysique" and had found it very prominent on the busts of Fichte and Kant.

[16] *The American Phrenological Journal* saw fit to mention it twice: II (1839–40), 168, 359.

Seen in the phrenological context, Poe's argument may seem ridiculous, but we should try to understand his purpose in making it. In his attempt to rescue American literature from the amateurs, he had already begun to emphasize, as we have seen, the artist's purpose and his dedication to his art. The popular romantic notion, that a poet needed only genius, was to Poe a fallacy that must be exposed. As he put it, "the *Poeta nascitur,* which is indisputably true if we consider the Poetic Sentiment, becomes the merest of absurdities in reference to the practical result." This much of his argument would have been acceptable even to T. S. Eliot, who was no admirer of Poe.[17] Unfortunately, however, Poe confined himself to the test of effect and implied that a good grasp of audience psychology was about all that a poet needed to produce good poems. This reduces the poet at best to a rhetorician, at worst to a popular hack. Yet Poe meant to do neither, as is evidenced by his teleology of art. To him poetic feeling was next in the hierarchy of value to religious feeling, and to arouse it, by whatever means, was an inestimable service to all mankind. Although he contradicted himself blatantly by declaring in one paragraph that imagination was the soul of poetry and in the next that a poet deficient in imagination could still stimulate the Ideality of others if he understood psychology, all that he was really doing was distinguishing between means and ends. In terms of its *end,* imagination is the soul of poetry. In terms of *means,* one needs far more than imagination if he is to write good poetry; he needs to know how to appeal to an audience, a necessity which the great romantic poets, in Poe's opinion, sometimes forgot. Poe was a practical American and a journalist, and he was very dubious about the value of expression for its own sake. He overstated his case, as he did frequently, but his subsequent examination of the poems of Drake and Halleck reveals that, far from thinking of the poet-psychologist as a popularizer, he was trying to correct the popular taste by showing how easy it was to

[17] Cf. Eliot's famous statement in "Tradition and the Individual Talent" that it is not "the intensity of the emotions . . . but the intensity of the artistic process . . . that counts." Generally speaking, this was Poe's position.

mistake the power of comparison for imagination, the sponsor and agent of "Ideality."

Without reference to Poe's phrenological sources, we would find his shift back and forth from Ideality to imagination very confusing. In the phrenological system, as has already been noted, there was more than one imaginative faculty, but it was Ideality that was peculiarly concerned with transforming sense impressions into mental images. In other words, it "idealized" perception by making objects into ideas, but it did more than this; it also organized associated feelings into a unified response as did Alison's faculty of taste.[18] Thus in its passive aspect it recognized beauty, as Poe claimed, but since, like the faculty of taste, it was capable of refinement, it had an active heuristic function in leading the soul toward perfection. The faculty seemed enough like Coleridge's imagination, as Poe interpreted Coleridge, to warrant using the terms synonymously. Poe made an unacknowledged appropriation from Coleridge in a footnote, defining imagination as "in man, a lesser degree of the creative power in God." [19] This probably means that

[18] According to Combe, the higher sentiments—Veneration, Hope, Wonder, and Ideality—could work together in a unified response, such as that manifested in religious adoration, but the rational faculties had to be employed to validate revealed truth before a natural religion would be possible or even desirable. *The Constitution of Man*, 95–97. It is obvious that some of the phrenologists, like the deists before them, considered that a natural religion, validated by science, could be the only true religion. Combe did not scoff at revelation, as did the radical deists of the eighteenth century; but he thought that revelation had to be subjected to the tests of science and experience, as did the men of the Enlightenment. It is worth noting that, like the Scottish philosopher-psychologists, the phrenologists did not consider a natural imbalance of the faculties an unalterable hereditary endowment. Instead, they thought the faculties could be exercised for improvement just as could the muscles. See Bakan, "Phrenology Is Foolish?" 48. Of course, a man with a complement of fully developed faculties would be a universal genius—and to Poe the only true genius was a universal genius, good at everything he tried. With his fear of hereditary mental imbalance, Poe attempted to become a universal genius or at least to pass himself off as one, equally gifted in imagination, reason, science, and even field sports. In the light of his unstable personality, his attempts at self-development should earn our compassion and our admiration.

[19] This borrowing from Coleridge was exceptionally naïve, for it created a problem of definition that Poe ignored. On one page he defined "poesy"

Poe was considering Ideality as an active power, creative in the sense that it provides glimpses of a more nearly perfect nature than is revealed to the physical senses. With this meaning in mind, one can understand Poe's criticism of Drake and Halleck. In spite of his confusing phrenological jargon, it is a reasonably competent application of Coleridge's distinction between the imagination and the fancy.

Drake's *The Culprit Fay* was a narrative poem, so Poe first summarized the plot, as was his custom when space permitted. Then he undertook to examine the poem for evidence of imaginative power and declared that, contrary to popular opinion, the poem was "utterly destitute of any evidence of imagination whatever." All Drake had done was provide "mere specifications of qualities, of habiliments, of punishments, of occupations, of circumstances . . . which the poet has believed in unison with the size, firstly, and secondly with the nature of his Fairies." These specifications, Poe asserted, indicated that the poet had only a "very moderate endowment of the faculty of Comparison—which is the chief constituent of *Fancy* or the powers of combination." The Coleridgean provenance of Poe's last clause is obvious, as is his denigration of fancy.[20] In phrenology, fancy, like Causality, was one of the "Reflecting Faculties" and had nothing to do with Ideality, so Poe uses Coleridgean and phrenological opinion as mutual reinforcement.

To illustrate Ideality in poetry, Poe had to leave Drake and cite a greater poet—Shelley, who had also described a fairy, Queen Mab. Poe quoted a passage and made an appropriate commentary: "It will be seen that the Fairy of Shelley is not a mere compound of incongruous natural objects, inartificially put together, and unaccompanied by any *moral* sentiment—but a being, in the illustration of whose nature some physical elements are used collaterally

---

as a sentiment and claimed, quoting Coleridge, that "Imagination is its soul" and, again quoting Coleridge, that it is "creative." *Works*, VIII, 283. On the very next page, using the term "Ideality" as synonymous with imagination, he asserted that Ideality alone cannot create, unless aided by Causality. This last would be sound according to Combe—a sentiment does not create unless aided by certain faculties or powers.

[20] See *Biographia Literaria*, I, 202, for Coleridge's exact words.

as adjuncts, while the main conception springs immediately *or thus apparently springs* from the brain of the poet, enveloped in the moral sentiments of grace, of color, of motion—of the beautiful, of the mystical, of the august—in short of *the ideal*." Again Poe's language needs to be translated. Under "moral sentiments" both Combe and Mrs. Miles had included "Benevolence," "Veneration," and "Imitation," but "Form" and "Color" were classified under "Observing Faculties," a subdivision of the "Intellectual Faculties." If Poe was adhering to the phrenological description of the mental activity necessary for creative work, he would have known that a great many "organs" of the mind must cooperate to produce works of art. The "grace, color, and motion" he listed in the quotation above would be perceived in the natural world by the "Observing Faculties" and would arouse the moral sentiment of Ideality. Thus "idealized," this raw material would be appropriate for artistic expression, but still other faculties must be employed before the conception could be enacted in an art form that would arouse the moral sentiment in others. Combe had listed Coloring, Time, Tune, Constructiveness, Form, Locality, Ideality "and other faculties" as being necessary for the fine arts.[21] Poe, as we have already seen, added Causality, a "Reflecting Faculty," which was supposed to trace "the relation of cause and effect." [22] In brief, art was the end product of feeling *plus* intellectual effort, and the mere fact that Shelley's poems aroused the "sentiment of beauty" gave evidence of the intellectual activity of the poet: "the main concept springs immediately *or thus apparently springs* from the brain of the poet, enveloped in the moral sentiments . . . ." The "ideal" in a poem, then, would be essentially what is defined in aesthetics as meaning or significance, as contrasted with the formal or sensuous elements of the work of art. It is not the changeless archetype of Platonic metaphysics.

The fact that Poe chose "grace, color and motion" as moral sentiments suggests that he was not strict in observing the phrenological classification, for the phrenologists would have placed all of

---

[21] *The Constitution of Man*, 81.   [22] *Ibid.*

these under the "Intellectual Faculties" of perception.[23] If we turn to Archibald Alison, however, we find these qualities treated as effects, and it was as emotional effects that Poe used them. To Alison, no color or motion was beautiful unless it aroused moral feeling or suggested moral ideas.[24] If we examine the passage from *Queen Mab* which Poe quoted, we will see how completely it fulfills Alison's definition of moral beauty.

> The Fairy's frame was slight; yon fibrous cloud
> That catches but the faintest tinge of even
> And which the straining eye can hardly seize
> When melting into eastern twilight's shadow,
> Were scarce so thin, so slight; but the fair star
> That gems the glittering coronet of morn,
> *Sheds not a light so mild, so powerful,*
> *As that which, bursting from the Fairy's form,*
> *Spread a purpureal halo round the scene,*
> *Yet with an undulating motion,*
> *Swayed to her outline gracefully.* [Italics Poe's.]

The "purpureal halo" would inevitably be associated with royal dignity,[25] and since it radiated from the fairy, it would have to be regarded as a moral quality of the Queen, an aspect of character rather than merely clothing. Drake, in contrast, had used colors in *The Culprit Fay* without regard for their associational value.

As for "grace," Alison had explained that the qualities of grace and beauty in a human form were different, and that the sentiments aroused by these qualities were different. Grace "seems to demand some higher and more uncommon requisites than those which are necessary to mere beauty." It arouses respect and admiration, for it implies "something dignified or exalted in the mind of the person" whose attitudes or gestures are graceful.[26] This feeling is entirely appropriate when associated with Queen Mab. Drake's

---

[23] Poe stated his dissatisfaction with Mrs. Miles's classification in his review: "This classification is arranged with sufficient clearness, but it would require no great degree of acumen to show that to mere perspicuity points of vital importance to the science have been sacrificed." *Works*, VIII, 254. Unfortunately he did not suggest any improvement.

[24] *Essays on Taste*, 443–48.   [25] *Ibid.*, 180.   [26] *Ibid.*, 425.

Ouphe, on the other hand, becomes ludicrous not only in his appearance but also in character; for he commits the egregious error of falling in love, as Poe put it with a touch of his customary levity, "with a mortal maiden, who may, very possibly, be six feet in her stockings." The Ouphe is one inch tall!

Alison devoted an entire chapter to the effect of motion in arousing the sentiment of beauty. Motion in curves was beautiful, whereas rapid motion in straight lines expressed power, an aspect of sublimity. Since the light radiating from Queen Mab undulates and sways with her graceful motion, it could be said to wave gently, which according to Alison was expressive of "tenderness, interest, and affection"—all moral sentiments.[27] All of these expressive qualities, then, constituted the Ideality of Shelley's concept. He had not merely provided "specifications," which would imitate the hypothetical physical form of a fairy; instead, as Poe claimed correctly, he had used the physical elements as "adjuncts" to enact an idea. Such a procedure was the proper evidence of imagination, evidence not to be found in Drake's poem.

Poe quoted passage after passage to demonstrate that Drake was "inartificially" (inartistically) putting together incongruous elements by means of the fancy. He even resorted to a Coleridgean device—substituting other elements for the ones specified [28]—to prove that there was no necessary connection among these elements and that almost anyone could write as well "without exercising in the least degree the Poetic Sentiment, which is Ideality, Imagination, or the creative ability." Only once did Poe find a measure of imagination in Drake's poem, in the line, "The earth is dark but the heavens are bright." Poe explained that here Drake suggested the "moral sentiment of the brightness of the sky compensating for the darkness of the earth—and thus, indirectly, of the happiness of a future state compensating for the miseries of the present." It would appear by this that Poe was endorsing a kind of

[27] *Ibid.*, 331–36.

[28] Coleridge had said that "whatever lines can be translated into other words of the same language, without diminution of their significance, either in sense or association, or in any worthy feeling, are so far vicious in their diction." *Biographia Literaria*, I, 14.

free-floating symbolic import suggestive of religion but uncommitted to any specific frame of symbolic reference. Lacking a sense of value in the concrete, he wanted moral feeling to be aroused by a collocation of semantic elements with rich connotative significance but minimal specification. By a process of abstracting such elements from the welter of experience and using them pictorially, the artist could control his effects and achieve relatively pure feeling, which was obviously what Poe wanted. On the other hand, if the artist specified by imitating the actual, or by hypothesizing a nonexistent actual and then imitating it, as Drake did, the associative processes of the audience would be uncontrolled and unity of effect would be lost. Poe's unity of effect is quite different from that of Coleridge, for Coleridge saw the imagination as reconciling opposites, whereas Poe, like Alison before him, insisted that a unity of emotion should be achieved by a selection of terms or objects that have similar connotations. Accordingly, he preferred the use of loaded phrases like "the heavens are bright" to an exact description of a sun-lit sky. This was the basis of his condemnation of Drake. Drake gave details without considering their connotative import, and Poe quoted copiously to illustrate:

> He put his acorn helmet on;
> It was plumed of the silk of the thistle down:
> The corslet plate that guarded his breast
> Was once the wild bee's golden vest;
> His cloak of a thousand mingled dyes,
> Was formed of the wings of butterflies;
> His shield was the shell of a lady-bug queen,
> Studs of gold on a ground of green;
> And the quivering lance which he brandished bright
> Was the sting of a wasp he had slain in fight.

Then he rewrote the passage, substituting other specifications, to prove that if a poet did not take account of associations, any details would serve so long as they fit a fairy one inch tall.

Such a fanciful description as the one just quoted at least had a certain merit of congruity, Poe admitted, but it had no meaning. Even worse were the passages in which Drake, no doubt trying to imitate Shelley's cosmic imagery, described the beauty of a "Sylphid queen."

> But oh! how fair the shape that lay
>   Beneath a rainbow bending bright
> She seem'd to the entranced Fay
>   The loveliest of the forms of light;
> Her mantle was the purple rolled
>   At twilight in the west afar;
> 'Twas tied with threads of dawning gold,
>   And button'd with a sparkling star.

It would appear that this description, which used the same physical elements as Shelley's, should have been equally appealing, but Drake had specified details of clothing—mantle, threads, buttons —whereas Shelley had generalized his description, allowing the connotations of his cosmic images—clouds, stars, and light—to function unimpeded by what to Poe would have been the vulgar associations with buttons and threads.

Poe quoted other passages, italicizing lines and even words and phrases that he considered imaginative. Most of the italicized lines would appear to us no better than the others if we examined them without reference to Poe's theory of the value of association. How, for instance, can the single word "lonely," taken out of context, indicate imagination? Or the expression, "glimmers and dies"? This last comes from the lines, "And through their clustering branches dark / *Glimmers and dies* the fire-fly's spark." Poe's explanation was that the phrase exalted the imagination "by the moral sentiment of beauty heightened in dissolution." But it does so only out of context. In context the purity of the moral sentiment would have been violated by the specific reference to fireflies. Poe was bothered throughout by Drake's attention to insects, leeches, shrimps, crabs, and bullfrogs, and he made a list of them to illustrate Drake's departure from the Ideality that should arouse the poetic sentiment. Bugs and small animals did not gratify that faculty which yearned for a beauty more perfect than any to be found in nature, nor did they have associative value in arousing moral feeling.

The remainder of the review of Drake merely adds further illustrative material, and the only point of interest is Poe's objection to "the thunderdrum of Heaven" as bathetic. His concept of bathos was that of the eighteenth-century rhetoricians, a "sinking" from the sublime by making a comparison between the grand and awe-inspiring and the mean and contemptible. Thus to compare Heaven's sublime thunder to a drum was an inexcusable violation of figurative propriety.

Poe's review of the poems of Halleck is similar in its unilateral approach. He pointed out a few passages which he considered imaginative, invariably choosing those which employed such loaded abstractions as melancholy, glory, legend, and solitary. He objected strenuously to words with vulgar associations, claiming that no poet could "unite in any manner the low burlesque with the ideal, and not be conscious of incongruity and of a profanation." Halleck made this tasteless error:

> Men in the coal and cattle line
> From Teviot's bard and hero land,
> From royal Berwick's beach of sand,
> From Wooler, Morpeth, Hexham, and
> Newcastle upon Tyne.

One shudders to imagine what Poe would have said about Eliot's typist and her carbuncular young man.

3

This review was Poe's first attempt at "philosophical" criticism, and it exhibits the reductionism that was his greatest weakness as a critic. He formulated a single first principle—that all poetry must be ideal—and defined idealism as a desire for pure hedonic value dissociated from any context which would make it meaningful. "Intellectual happiness" divorced from knowledge and construed as a sentiment evoked by a marshaling of effects denied any value to poetry except that of a stimulus to feeling. That Poe at least partially recognized this limitation is indicated by his conventional attempt to confer an aura of religious value on art by his psychological analysis of final causes and his quasi-Platonic argument that a recognition of ideal beauty leads us toward the perfection that is Heaven. Thus far, he was not conspicuously at odds with Shelley and Keats, but neither British poet displayed such a dislike for the phenomenal as did Poe, who tended to eliminate words that name and specify and retain those general terms that elicit responses without designating the details of perception. This flight from the real can be explained on psychological grounds, but it can scarcely be justified as a first principle of art. If the poet does not make some engagement with the human context, his symbols lose all vitality; they evoke nothing, for they have nothing to evoke. The moral sentiments Poe demanded as an added dimension of meaning are as barren of significance as his poetic sentiment, for they do not arise from any condition in which moral feeling has particular relevance. Poe wanted, via art, to move from becoming to being; but he wanted to do it all at once, without climbing Plato's ladder from the specific to the ideal.

A wish to escape the flux of the phenomenal world does not necessarily produce abstract diction—witness Yeats's "Sailing to Byzantium," in which the desire to be gathered into the "artifice of eternity" is communicated in the humanly relevant symbols of physical decay. Yet an escapist temperament can manifest itself in a revulsion against the concrete and an inclination to experience feeling without the engagement with reality that ordinarily stimulates the feeling. Poe wanted moral feeling to be a psychic phenomenon divorced from ethical considerations. Experienced in such a way, the moral sentiment becomes pure hedonic value, uncontaminated by any utilitarian motive or, except indirectly, by any utilitarian consequence. Such a theoretical formulation is logical if one starts with the premise that the *only* purpose of art is to give pleasure, and, by the evidence of the "Letter to Mr. —— ——," Poe did start with this premise. An even greater reductionism in artistic value concepts would be brought about by the use of a primitive psychology that assumed a particular faculty as the seat of aesthetic emotion. If the critic calls this faculty "taste," then he would be able to argue that an artist must eliminate from consideration all subjects and diction that do not conform to a hypothesized standard, which, as we have seen the argument applied, meant the refined taste of cultivated gentlemen. If the faculty is called "Ideality," then the artist would be restricted to depicting the ideal, which in Poe's words meant the beautiful, the "mystical," and the "august." In later years Poe dropped the term "Ideality" and referred to the poetic faculty in the traditional way as the "taste," but his teleology of art remained unchanged. The imagination was restricted, at least in poetry, to a pictorialization of the ideal, and ideal beauty remained for him the aim and test of a poem.

Poe's application of his first principle of art is not without merit, considering the quality of the poems he reviewed. He at least knew that a poem should be meaningful on a higher level of apprehension than that required for a response to the verse of Drake and Halleck; but even with this knowledge he made no effort in this particular review to determine whether or not this extended import was developed organically through correlated symbolic modes. Instead he retained the Longinian habit of looking for impressive words, phrases, and lines that were touchstones of beauty or sublimity. Had the provenance of his method been thoroughly Coleridgean—or Schlegelian, for that matter—he would have known that a single word or phrase detached from its context no more demonstrates imagination than a single color illustrates beauty. It is the organization that counts. Poe had read both Coleridge and Schlegel in reference to organic unity and had used them to disqualify Mrs. Sigourney's mottoes, but he ignored the question in this review. Unity to him appears to have been a unity of tone, achieved by the management of connotative import. The lines he praised were devoid of any quality except that of a hackneyed "poetic" suggestiveness; but again, in fairness to Poe, we should remember that he was reviewing third-rate poets and that he cited Shelley as an illustration of pure Ideality, along with (in a footnote) Aeschylus, Dante, Cervantes, Milton, Pope, Burns, Coleridge, and Keats.[29] We would hardly expect Drake and Halleck to be welcomed into this company.

In spite of its defects as literary criticism, Poe's review of Drake and Halleck was the most impressive he had yet written for the *Messenger*, and it was well received, except by some of his New York enemies.[30] He had now demonstrated that he could write "philosophical" criticism and make evaluations on the basis of principle instead of prejudice. His range was not to remain so narrow as it was in this review, and eventually he developed a better understanding of the cognitive potentialities of the poetic enterprise, but unfortunately he continued his journalistic practice of seeking a "lead" for each review. That is, he would pick out a single merit or defect attributed to an author by allegedly popular critical

[29] *Works*, VIII, 299. Poe's list of "imaginative poems" is highly selective. The "poems of the purest ideality" are *Prometheus Vinctus*, by Aeschylus; the *Inferno*, by Dante; *Destruction of Numantia*, by Cervantes; *Comus*, by Milton; "The Rape of the Lock," by Pope; "Tam O'Shanter," by Burns; "The Ancient Mariner," "Christabel," and "Kubla Khan," by Coleridge; and especially "The Sensitive Plant" by Shelley and "Ode to a Nightingale" by Keats.
It is easy to see why Poe would consider the last four of his choices as specimens of "purest ideality." Both by his criteria and by his taste, they would have to rank very high. "The Sensitive Plant" continued to be his favorite poem. It advanced what Poe considered the most proper theme for a poet, the yearning for immortal beauty. His other choices are more difficult to explain. His objection to the "low" should have eliminated Burns's poem, for it was written in Scots idiom. Pope's "The Rape of the Lock" should have seemed too frivolous for Ideality, although it could have been offered as an example of the Fancy. It is likely that the selection of Cervantes' play derived from Schlegel's praise of "its unconscious and unlaboured approximation to antique grandeur and purity." Schlegel, *Lectures*, 491. And it may be that his citation of Aeschylus came from Schlegel's opinion that Aeschylus was the "creator" of tragedy and that "terror is his element." Schlegel also singled out *Prometheus Bound* as representing "Tragedy herself: her purest spirit revealed." *Ibid.*, 93.
[30] Joseph Rodman Drake, a native New Yorker, had been dead for sixteen years, but Fitz-Greene Halleck, also a New Yorker, was associated with the Knickerbocker group, the members of which were published in Clark's *Knickerbocker* during the 1830's. Some New York journals praised Poe's review, but it must be assumed that his enemies, the Clark brothers, were incensed. For the generally favorable reception of this review, see Moss, *Poe's Literary Battles*, 55–56, 69–70.

opinion and then focus his analysis upon this particular point. In only a few reviews do we find Poe broadening his approach. As a rule he is guilty of the charge Ronald S. Crane once levied against Cleanth Brooks—"critical monism."

During the months to come, Poe failed to maintain even the relatively low level of "philosophical" criticism that he reached in this review. He soon reopened his campaign against New York by destroying a book by Colonel William L. Stone. Perhaps for this reason, among others, the confidence of his employer steadily declined. Poe had only eight more months to remain with the *Messenger*.

VII · *Toward Standards*

A professional book reviewer for an American monthly magazine had little opportunity to practice philosophical criticism, for he had to hammer out notices of the subliterary material that piled up on his desk. Poe did attempt to examine this material by literary standards, however. In May of 1836 he reviewed a travel book, *Spain Revisited*, by a Lieutenant Slidell, and revealed his dislike for fulsome dedications and bad grammar.[1] Poe considered himself an expert in matters of syntax and usage; and of all grammarians, he was one of the most prescriptive. The slightest ambiguity of reference or deviation into colloquialism provoked him into rewriting the passage to demonstrate correct English.[2] His reconstructions, however, did not always go unchallenged. The editor of the *Newbern* (North Carolina) *Spectator* deplored the tone of his reviews in general, and his penchant for demolishing dedications and his hypercriticism of grammar in particular. Poe answered the charge at length, not only defending himself as a grammarian but also subjecting his critic to a personal attack: "We are at a loss to know who is the editor of the Spectator, but have a shrewd suspicion that he is the identical gentleman who once sent us from Newbern an unfortunate copy of verses. It seems to us that he wishes to be taken notice of, and we will for the once, oblige him with a few words. . . . If the editor of this little paper does not behave himself we will positively publish his verses." [3]

[1] *Works*, IX, 1–13.

[2] According to Charvat, this had been a routine practice of American reviewers some years earlier. *American Critical Thought*, 87–88.

[3] *Works*, VIII, 336–37. No doubt Poe singled out this particular criticism for rebuttal because the *Spectator* had implied that Poe's assumption of the "tone of a Walsh, a Blackwood or a Jeffries [*sic*]" was *Messenger* policy. There was not enough concentration of talent in the South, the *Spectator* editor continued, to warrant support of a journal that pretended to such superior standards. Nevertheless, "the Messenger has boldly put itself

Poe was feeling his power. He had received letters of praise from Professor Charles Anthon, Mrs. Sigourney (now mollified), and James Kirke Paulding. Even Halleck, whose poems Poe had criticized severely, had complimented the *Messenger* and Poe. Furthermore, Poe's review of Drake and Halleck had been hailed as "one of the finest pieces of criticism ever published in this country." All this praise was quoted or referred to in the July Supplement to the *Messenger*,[4] and if the notices that were published are a fair sampling of opinion, Poe's criticism was already respected, even feared, from Natchez to Boston; and his fiction was drawing almost equal praise. Yet it was disturbing to find a hometown newspaper, the Richmond *Courier and Daily Compiler*, objecting to the gloom of his tales: "Mr. Poe is too fond of the wild—unnatural and horrible! Why will he not permit his fine genius to soar into purer, brighter, and happier regions? Why will he not disenthrall himself from the spells of German enchantment and supernatural imagery? There is room enough for the exercise of the highest powers, upon the multiform relations of human life, without descending into the dark, mysterious, and unutterable creations of licentious fancy."[5]

This had been the opinion of White's first editor, James Heath, and of White himself, and it illustrates a conventional American attitude that Poe found a perpetual source of frustration. Earlier American critics had wanted cheerful, optimistic accounts of the human condition, not morbid analyses of the darker recesses of the human soul.[6] Thus far, however, Poe gave little evidence that such opposition disturbed him. He wrote the kind of tale he wanted to write, and his inclination was reinforced by his knowledge of the

---

forth as an arbiter whose dicta are supreme; and with a severity and indiscreetness of criticism,—especially on American works,—which few, if any, of the able and well established reviews have ventured to exercise, has been not only unmerciful, but savage." In order to make a detailed reply, Poe quoted the entire criticism of the *Spectator* in the July Supplement of the *Southern Literary Messenger*, II (1836), 517. White would have been disturbed both by the accusation that undue severity to American authors was his journal's policy and by the hint that the South could not support a magazine with such relentless standards.

[4] *Southern Literary Messenger*, II (1836), 517–24.   [5] *Ibid.*, 345.
[6] Charvat, *American Critical Thought*, 17–18, 153–55.

success tales of psychological horror had had in British magazines. Accordingly, he was not disposed to heed the warnings of a few moralists in Richmond, Virginia. If his letter to Philip Pendleton Cooke three years later is honest, it was enough for him that the discriminating few appreciated tales like "Morella" and "Ligeia." "As for the mob—let them talk on. I should be grieved if I thought they comprehended me here." [7]

Meanwhile there were books to be reviewed, and Poe continued in his self-appointed task of reforming journalistic criticism in America. In May he challenged American provincialism by praising Mrs. Trollope, whose *Domestic Manners of the Americans* had offended the national sensitivity by intimating that those manners left much to be desired. "We have no patience with that atrabilious set of hyper-patriots," wrote Poe, "who find fault with Mrs. Trollope's book of flumflummery about the good people of the Union." A book should be judged as a book, he asserted, not as a national affront: "That our national soreness of feeling prevented us, in the case of her work on America, from appreciating the real merits of the book, will be rendered evident by the high praise we find no difficulty in bestowing upon her *Paris and the Parisians*—a production, in whatever light we regard it, precisely similar to the one with which we were so irreparably offended." [8] In this vein Poe might appear to us as the champion of literary America, challenging the dragons of stupidity, false pride, and provinciality; but all too often he deviated from the path of principle to gratify a personal pique. He had been lying in wait for Colonel William L. Stone, editor of the New York *Commercial Advertiser*, ever since that gentleman had used his newspaper to reprimand the "Zoilus" of the *Messenger* for the scathing *Norman Leslie* review. In June the victim was at hand, in the form of *Ups and Downs in the Life of a Distressed Gentleman*. No doubt Colonel Stone's book deserved to be "used up" (as Poe was fond of calling his destructive method), but, as usual when he was gratifying a grudge, Poe's review was splenetic rather than critical.

The first two pages of the review prodded what is always a tender

[7] September 21, 1839, in *Letters*, I, 118.　　[8] *Works*, IX, 17–18.

spot, the potential market for the book. Poe announced the price, counted the pages, and concluded that purchasers would be bilked, intimating that the book was so worthless that it should be measured by its size only. A single issue of the *Messenger*, Poe claimed, was six times as long as Stone's book and cost less than half as much. Therefore, unless *Ups and Downs* were sixteen times as high in quality as the *Messenger*, Stone was presuming upon the "excessive patience, gullibility, and good nature" of the public. Poe added insult by naming the anonymous author and stating that the book "should have been printed among the quack advertisements in a space corner of his paper." [9]

Poe had very little else to say about *Ups and Downs*. The stinging but amusing satire of his earlier destructive reviews is less marked in this one, which may indicate that the earlier reviews were prompted by a desire to be "wickedly" good humored after the manner of Christopher North. In this case, however, Poe's ire had been aroused, and the review is more vindictive than humorous. Most of the space is given to a plot summary with quotations designed to show the book at its worst. Very sensitive to harsh criticism of his own work, Poe's retaliation to such criticism was often equally ill tempered and made him a target for violent abuse.

Poe's book reviews in the June number, though generally undistinguished, should not be dismissed completely. A brief notice of Dickens' *Watkins Tottle and Other Sketches* proves that Poe was developing his theory of the short tale.[10] A novel, he said, certainly requires a sustained effort, but this effort is merely perseverance and has only a "collateral relation to talent." The short tale, however, must have unity of effect, a quality which is "not easily appreciated or indeed comprehended by an ordinary mind." It is a quality difficult to attain, "even by those who can conceive it." [11]

[9] *Ibid.*, 33.   [10] *Ibid.*, 45–48.
[11] Poe's concept of the unity of effect was not given in this particular review, but, as previously indicated, it was similar to Alison's unity of impression. A more immediate source was A. W. Schlegel. See Lubell, "Poe and A. W. Schlegel," 7. George Kelly's interpretation of Poe's concept of unity is substantially the same as my own as far as the short tale is concerned, but he is overly ingenious in trying to make a case for unity of impression in a

We have already noticed that Poe did not apply the criterion of a unified effect to the poems of Drake and Halleck, no doubt because he was more interested in being "philosophical" than in analyzing technique. Unity to Poe, insofar as it could be prescribed, was a question of technique, a logical and psychological strategy of adapting means to the proposed end. Because his reductionism was not so stringent for prose as for poetry, he was able to make a more satisfactory application of the principle to the short tale than he ever did to the poem. Poe did not explain here what he meant by unity of effect, but, remembering his use of Schlegel in the review of Mrs. Sigourney, we may assume that he meant total effect, or that correlation of feeling and thought that would be a unified response. If so, and it seems likely, he was demanding an interdependence among the various elements of form which would enable the objective structural unity, the relationship of part to part and part to whole, to be the vehicle of a subjective unity of impression. This interpretation is supported by his analysis of one of Dickens' tales. Poe offered "The Pawnbroker's Shop" as an illustration of the unity of effect, making the claim that each sentence gives a fuller view of the picture the artist is painting. A novel, Poe asserted, does not lend itself to such a technique; it is admired for its "detached passages, without reference to the work as a whole." As usual, Poe seized every opportunity to explain that the novel was not an art form, but in examining the short tale by the principle of unity of impression he elevated it to the traditional status of a fine art.

Poe's analogy between the short tale and a painting is significant, for it explains his concept of unity more clearly than any of his ab-

---

long work, such as a novel. See George Kelly, "Poe's Theory of Unity," *Philological Quarterly,* XXXVII (1958), 34–44. Poe categorically denied that a novel could transmit a unity of impression, and Mr. Kelly's argument that the denouement works psychologically to bring about the effect of the single impression is alien to Poe's concept. Although Poe was capable of admiring a well-plotted novel as evidence of skill, he thought that unity of effect was impossible in a novel and that unity of plot was not essential. The chief value of a novel, he said a number of times, was the author's thought.

stract definitions: "the *Pawnbroker's Shop* engages and enchains our attention—we are enveloped in its atmosphere of wretchedness and extortion—we pause at every sentence, not to dwell upon the sentence, but to obtain a fuller view of the gradually perfecting picture—which is never at any moment any other matter than the *Pawnbroker's Shop*. To the illustration of this one end all the *groupings* and *fillings in* of the painting are rendered subservient— and when our eyes are taken from the canvas, we remember the personages of the sketch not at all as independent existences, but as essentials of the one subject we have witnessed—as a part and portion of the *Pawnbroker's Shop*." If a narrative is regarded as a picture, it is a design extended in space, not a movement in time, and if characters are regarded as static groupings used as elements of a composition, there is little or no dramatic effect. It is the thematic design which is important, and character and setting are equivalent means by which the design is fulfilled. By Poe's theory one should not attempt to write a "character story" or an "action story," because undue emphasis on person or event would cause an imbalance in the composition. An "atmospheric story" would be allowable, however, for a symbolic rendition of scene would be as adequate for thematic purpose as it would be in a painting.

It would be tempting at this point to analyze one of Poe's own tales to see how well he followed his own theory. "The Fall of the House of Usher," published three years later, would be the obvious choice, for an interpretation of scene is just as necessary for apprehending the import of the tale as is the analysis of character. Yet this story has been competently analyzed many times,[12] and it should be enough to say that Poe's theory of unity works in "Usher," but it works at the expense of certain qualities which many of us today have been taught to expect in fiction. Roderick Usher, for instance, is not so much a convincing character as he is the pictorialization of theme. He is a "symbolic" character, according to some interpretations. Since Usher's fears are revealed more

---

[12] A recent analysis of the tale according to the approach I am suggesting is that of E. Arthur Robinson, "Order and Sentience in 'The Fall of the House of Usher,'" *PMLA*, LXXVI (1961), 66–81.

by description than by dramatic action, there is little conflict and almost no tension or suspense. The story can be regarded as mechanical—utterly contrived. For such a reason Cleanth Brooks and Robert Penn Warren criticized it harshly in the first edition of their textbook, *Understanding Fiction*. This textbook divides stories into three types—plot, character, and theme—although the authors are careful to emphasize that the quality of a particular story "may depend upon the organic relation existing among these elements." Thus, although Brooks and Warren, like Poe, would not approve of the isolation of any particular element in a story, their categories do permit the emphasis of one element over the other, which is pragmatically sound. Poe, however, a pioneer in the genre, was not *describing* the tale as it has come to be; he was *prescribing* the tale as he thought it ought to be, the ideal form as he conceived it.

"Usher" is a tableau, the illustration of an idea, in which the symbolic significance of scene is just as important as the sequence of events. In fact, it is more important, for temporal movement is relatively subordinate. The collapse and death motif is foreshadowed in the opening description, and significant change or development does not occur. Poe's own term for this type of tale, the "arabesque," is appropriate. This term, used to describe a graphic design, signifies an ordering of space, not a chronological development.[13]

[13] In a recent article Cecil L. Moffitt contended that Poe used the term "arabesque" to suggest that the important influence on his work was not Germany but the East. See Moffitt, "Poe's Arabesque," *Comparative Literature*, XVIII (1966), 55–70. This contention is questionable. Arthur Hobson Quinn was probably correct in pointing to an essay by Sir Walter Scott, published in 1827, as Poe's source for the terms "arabesque" and "grotesque." Scott's essay describes the tales of E. T. W. Hoffman as being grotesque, saying that they resemble the arabesque in painting, in which "strange and complicated monsters are introduced." Sir Walter Scott, "On the Supernatural in Fictitious Composition," *Foreign Quarterly Review*, I, (1827), 81–82. If Poe intended to deny German influence, it is unlikely that he would have used terms that suggested it. An essay by Scott would be well known, and the *Foreign Quarterly* no doubt had a good American subscription list.

We should take Poe at his word in his preface to the book publication of

2

The review of Dickens was the only real effort at criticism Poe was to make for some time. The other reviews in the June issue and all of those in July were perfunctory notices of nonliterary or subliterary material, although among them Poe did insert a tribute to Coleridge in the form of an announcement of the American publication of the *Letters, Conversations, and Recollections of S. T. Coleridge.* Poe wrote:

Tales of the Grotesque and Arabesque, in which he declared without explanation that the terms indicated the "prevalent tenor" of his stories. Apparently he assumed his readers would know the technical meaning of the terms. An "arabesque" is a surface decoration, painted or in low relief, in which fantastic figures are intertwined with flowers, leaves, branches, and scroll work. The entire design is called an "arabesque," while the term "grotesque," deriving from the *grotta* or excavations in which such decorations are found on ancient ruins, applies chiefly to the figures. In other words, the terms represent different aspects of a unified design, which was probably what Poe intended in his arrangement of the tales in his book, leaving the reader to understand that individual tales suggested the grotesque, while others, not monstrous, exhibited the beauty of the design itself. If Poe borrowed from Scott, he would hardly have overlooked the great novelist's remark that the public was surfeited by an overdose of oriental tales and by the "wild and fantastic tone." In all of English literature, Scott could find only Mary Shelley's *Frankenstein* and Washington Irving's "The Bold Dragoon" to illustrate a successful use of the "supernatural grotesque."

Poe denied German influence only by saying that he had avoided the "pseudo-horror" employed by second-rate German authors, and that when he had depicted terror, it was "not of Germany, but of the soul." This, of course, meant psychological terror, and Poe claimed to have deduced it "only from its legitimate sources," which meant human nature. This, too, he could have derived from Scott, for Scott had declared that the only interest in fantastic creatures came from their expression of feelings and sentiments that would be natural to them under the circumstances in which they existed.

Poe's use of the term "grotesque" offers more possibilities for interpretation than this extended note can suggest. For one interpretation see Lewis A. Lawson, "Poe's Conception of the Grotesque," *Mississippi Quarterly,* XIX (1966), 200–205. For Poe's use of the term in various contexts, his possible sources, and other interpretations, see Lawson, "Poe and the Grotesque: A Bibliography, 1695–1965," *Poe Newsletter,* I (1968), 9–10.

. . . with us (we are not ashamed to confess it) the most trivial memorial of Coleridge is a treasure of inestimable price. He was indeed a "myriad-minded man," and ah, how little understood, and how pitifully vilified! How merely nominal was the difference (and this too in his own land) between what he himself calls the "broad, predetermined abuse" of the Edinburgh Review, and the cold and brief compliments with the warm *regrets* of the Quarterly. If there be any one thing more than another which stirs within us a deep spirit of indignation and disgust, it is that damnation with faint praise which so many of the Narcissi of critical literature have had the infinite presumption to breathe against the majesty of Coleridge—of Coleridge—the man to whose gigantic mind the proudest intellects of Europe found it impossible not to succumb.[14]

This was the most unqualified praise that Poe ever gave to the critic whose work helped form his own critical theory and practice. Later he was to rebel consciously against Coleridge's influence and to complain somewhat petulantly about the British critic's "overprofundity" and "metaphysicianism," as did other American critics who professed to be baffled by Coleridge's obscurities.[15] At the moment, however, he was an ardent admirer. If the *Biographia Literaria* were published in America, Poe concluded, the publishers "would be rendering an important service to the cause of psychological science in America, by introducing a work of great scope and power in itself, and well calculated to do away with the generally

[14] *Works*, IX, 51.

[15] See Charvat, *American Critical Thought*, 78–81, 113, for an account of the reception of Coleridge prior to 1835. By 1835 a mixed reaction is evident that may be illustrated by two articles from the same journal. In April of 1835, G. B. Cheever, reviewing Coleridge's *The Friend* in one of those lengthy essays in the *North American Review*, had exhausted his vocabulary of praise on the British critic. See *North American Review*, XL (1835), 299–351. In October, however, A. H. Everett, an admirer of Dugald Stewart, had complained of Coleridge's "almost total want of clearness and precision of thought." *North American Review*, XLI (1835), 371. This charge was made in Everett's review of a lecture by William Ellery Channing, a review which had aroused Poe's ire for its uncritical praise of a New England author as well as for the censure of Coleridge.

received impression here entertained of the *mysticism* of the writer."

Mysticism, which in Poe's time could mean almost anything difficult to understand, was no bugaboo to him as yet; but in subsequent years, as he reacted against the New England transcendentalists, he began to display the usual American reverence for common sense and plain speaking and deprecated the "cloudland of metaphysics." This tendency became pronounced during his second attempt to make a place for himself in New York journalism and must be regarded, at least in part, as his contribution to the journalistic rivalry between New York and Boston.[16] At the moment, however, he was relatively isolated and could speak his mind with no further inhibition than that imposed by his apprehensive employer. Praising Coleridge and damning two British journals would have disturbed White far less than incurring the risk of a lawsuit by abusing Theodore Fay and William L. Stone.

In August, Poe was able to return to literary criticism with a review of *The Book of Gems*,[17] an anthology of British poets from Chaucer to Prior. This review added nothing to Poe's stature as a critic, for he revealed a narrowly contemporaneous taste. At least a third of our affection for the "old" poets, he claimed, is "simple love of the antique." Even when we do feel something like the "proper poetic sentiment" in reading their poems, he continued, the feeling comes in part from the quaint phraseology and grotesque rhythms, which are not the result of artistry but only the accident of time and place. The "old" English muse was without art, Poe declared, even though her devotees, such as John Donne and Abraham Cowley, might have been very learned in their own

[16] Like the South, New York was hostile toward Transcendentalism, but Poe showed relatively little concern about the New England *isms* until he moved to New York in 1844 and became more conspicuously involved in journalistic controversies. Not much disturbed by the political implications of transcendental thought, he had opposed it only as it manifested the idea of progress; and he was capable of referring to transcendental idealism as a "profound and ennobling philosophy." *Works*, XI, 253. It was dishonored only by some of the "muddle-pates" who called themselves transcendentalists.

[17] *Ibid.*, IX, 91–103.

way. These so-called metaphysical poets were far from metaphysical in the proper sense, because with them ethics or moral truth was the end of the poem, which to Poe was inadmissible. Wordsworth and Coleridge used metaphysical knowledge properly, because with them the end of a poem was quite properly the stimulation of poetic feeling "through channels suggested by mental analysis." [18] Donne and Cowley had failed where Coleridge, in particular, had succeeded brilliantly, because Coleridge knew what poetry was supposed to do and he knew how to accomplish his purpose. In contrast, Cowley and all the metaphysical poets of the seventeenth century were "simple and single-hearted men" who wrote directly from the "soul" with complete "abandon"—i.e., without art.

With the revival of interest in metaphysical poetry in the twentieth century, we may be disposed to dismiss Poe's strictures as incredibly naïve; but to do so would be to betray our own lack of perspective. From the age of Pope to Poe's own time, most critics had been inclined to think of seventeenth-century poetry, with the one exception of Milton, as an artless exhibition of mental gymnastics, "One glaring chaos and wild heap of wit," as Pope had described it. Without attempting to designate specific sources, we may be sure that Poe's attitude, though not the exact terms of his argument, was formed by such works as Dr. Johnson's *Life of Cowley*, Blair's *Lectures*, which denigrate Cowley (using Johnson as authority), and perhaps even Sir Francis Jeffrey's review of John Ford, who, though a dramatist, was contemporary with Cowley and in Jeffrey's opinion displayed the lack of taste characteristic of his period. From reading Kames and Blair, one would conclude that nothing happened in English literature prior to Shakespeare and that between Shakespeare and Dryden the only poet worth mentioning was Milton. *The Book of Gems* was an unusual anthology because it did contain the "early English poets." It was not uncommon to

[18] Poe's praise of Wordsworth represents a reversal of attitude. See Chapter II of this book. By the 1830's Wordsworth had won wide acceptance in America, and Poe, maturing as a critic, found it necessary to revise his position.

find Milton in an anthology—along with such late eighteenth-century favorites as Young, Beattie, Gray, and Collins.

It is not surprising, then, that Poe considered Donne and Cowley as primitive in respect to art, for to him art began with the recent application of psychological aesthetics. To compare Poe's opinion of seventeenth-century writers with that of Jeffrey is instructive. Poe writes: "To elevate immeasurably all the energies of the mind—but again—so to mingle the greatest possible fire, force, delicacy, and all good things, with the lowest possible bathos, baldness, and utter imbecility, as to render it not a matter of doubt, but of certainty, that the average results of mind in such a school, will be found inferior to those results in one (ceteris paribus) more artificial [i.e., more conscious of art]: Such, we think, is the view of the older English Poetry, in which a very calm examination will bear us out." Next, Jeffrey: "Unaccountable, however, as it is, the fact is certain, that almost all the dramatic writers of this age appear to be alternately inspired, and bereft of understanding; and pass, apparently without being conscious of the change, from the most beautiful displays of genius to the most melancholy exemplification of stupidity. . . . there is an inequality and a capricious uncertainty in the taste and judgment of these good old writers, which excites at once our amazement and compassion." [19]

Historically, then, Poe was exhibiting a stock opinion. More to the point of his development as a critic, however, he was basing his concept of artistry upon the artist's grasp of the psychology of response, his knowledge of emotional reactions and effective stimuli. The complexity of tone of the metaphysical poets, the yoking of intellect with emotion, the ironic indirection of the better metaphysical poems, were all lost on Poe, who considered the unity of emotional effect the prime desideratum of a poem. Poe's constriction of the limits of poetry had previously appeared in his review of Drake and Halleck, but this review is an even more obvious demonstration of his reductionism in practice. The only poem of

[19] *Contributions to the Edinburgh Review*, 304. The first printing of this review was in August, 1811.

The Book of Gems he was able to praise without qualification was Marvell's "Maiden Lamenting for her Fawn," [20] which contained none of the wit that would have offended the sensibilities of Poe's generation. His rhapsody about the poem reveals how completely his taste was that of sentimental romanticism: "How truthful an air of deep lamentation hangs here upon every gentle syllable! It pervades all. It comes over the half-playful, half-petulant air with which she lingers on the beauties and good qualities of her favorite. . . . The whole thing is redolent with poetry of the *very loftiest order*. It is positively crowded with *nature* and with *pathos*."

Scarcely a line of the poem is analyzed, and Poe's rapturous language seems hardly appropriate for the Zoilus of the *Messenger*. He was much more forceful in analyzing the defects of what he did not like than in demonstrating the quality of the works his taste approved.

The readers of the *Messenger* might have thought that Poe's hatchet had lost its edge if he had not included one harsh condemnation among the generally bland reviews of the August number. Nathaniel Parker Willis, although only three years older than Poe, was already an established writer in America. He was an editor of the New York *Mirror*, the journal that had attempted to "puff" *Norman Leslie* into success. Willis had published three books of poems and three volumes of literary "letters" called *Pencillings by the Way* before Poe reviewed his book of sketches, *Inklings of Adventure*.

Willis was an aesthete, a literary fop about New York whose mannerisms irritated some of the critics who reviewed his work; but Poe, fresh from having announced in his review of Drake and Halleck that a work should be criticized by principle and not by prejudice, denounced the practice of attacking a book on the basis of the author's personality: "We cannot sufficiently express our disgust at that unscrupulous indelicacy which is in the habit of de-

[20] Poe's title; the exact title is "The Nymph Complaining for the Death of Her Faun."

ciding upon the literary merits of this gentleman by a reference to his private character and manners. . . ." [21] Willis probably appreciated this attitude, for he had been subjected to a number of personal attacks, including two by Poe's enemies, Willis Gaylord Clark and Colonel William L. Stone. This in spite of the fact that the *Mirror* had "puffed" Colonel Stone's writings.[22]

Unfortunately for Willis, Poe found sufficient reason to demolish the book without reference to the author's character. The whole narrative was "disfigured and indeed utterly ruined by the grievous sin of affectation." This charge has been examined in a previous chapter in reference to the romantic requirement of sincerity, but it also represented a stylistic fault. Blair had devoted an entire lecture to the definition of simplicity and its opposite, affectation. Simplicity of composition, he explained, was virtually the same thing as unity, for it represented a design distinguished by a relatively small number of parts, as could be illustrated by Greek tragedy and Greek architecture, in contrast to the Gothic modes. Simplicity of style "stands opposed to too much ornament, or pomp of Language," whereas an affected style was overly ornate, or florid. Another way in which simplicity was manifested was in an easy and natural manner of expressing thought, "in such a manner, that every one thinks he could have written in the same way." [23] Affectation, on the other hand, was not simply ornament, but the labored effort to achieve rhetorical effects.

Poe's charge of affectation was properly applied to Willis' style. His striving for effect, his attempts at cleverness, elegance, and wit were the New Yorker's tokens of a sophistication that was unappreciated in the provinces; [24] but Poe judged Willis' frivolity by a stylistic principle considered sound in his day. Furthermore, in terms of unity of effect, Willis' mannerisms were productive of a

---

[21] *Southern Literary Messenger*, II (1836), 597.
[22] Moss, *Poe's Literary Battles*, 73–74.   [23] Blair, *Lectures*, II, 387–90.
[24] See Branch, *The Sentimental Years*, 141, for a lively description of Willis' sophistication. For a more detailed account of Willis' subject matter and Poe's reviews of Willis, see Richard P. Benton, "The Works of N. P. Willis as a Catalyst of Poe's Criticism," *American Literature*, XXXIX (1967), 315–25.

greater flaw. There was an "utter want of keeping" in the book, for the "absurd fripperies and frivolities" prevented the reader from appreciating his more serious subjects, such as the grandeur of Niagara Falls. The trivial could not be mixed with the sublime, according to the Allisonian principle of the single emotion.[25]

In later years Poe was to make amends to Willis and was even to become his friend. Willis employed Poe to write for the New York *Evening Mirror* in 1844 and defended him from his enemies in 1846 and after his death; but Poe never had a high regard for Willis as a writer. He judged Willis as a man of fancy rather than of imagination. Few would question his verdict.

3

In September, Poe reviewed a novel which interested him, *Sheppard Lee*, by Robert Montgomery Bird, author of *Calavar* and *The Infidel*.[26] *Sheppard Lee* was a humorous fantasy, an "original," Poe thought. Much of the book was social satire, but this element Poe ignored in favor of Bird's exploitation of the occult. The chief character experiences metempsychosis, his psyche inhabiting some seven different bodies (of persons who had recently died) in its transmigration. Poe himself had used metempsychosis in his tale "Morella," and he was to use it again in "Ligeia" and in "A Tale of the Ragged Mountains." Consequently he was intrigued by Bird's strategy in using the occult. Yet Poe was disturbed, as we might expect, by the humor of *Sheppard Lee*. The journey of the soul should be treated seriously, and the author should have made an effort to secure the reader's assent to the supernatural elements. Instead Bird violated the tone of the novel with incongruities until the final page and then ruthlessly disposed of the problem by alleging that the whole thing was only a dream, thus depriving the reader of the emotional effect he had secured through identifica-

---

[25] Alison provided illustrations of the way in which the introduction of "trifling circumstances" destroys the effect of beauty or sublimity. *Essays on Taste*, 91–102.

[26] *Works*, IX, 126–39.

tion with the character. Any use of the supernatural, Poe claimed, should be carefully planned. It should not be a mere structural device for stringing together six separate narratives. If Bird had caused his hero to preserve his identity through each successive existence, and if the events themselves had been contrasted in their effect upon an unchanging character, the book would have had a legitimate interest.

Such a method would be satisfactory, Poe asserted, but there was a superior stratagem:

> It consists in a variety of points—principally in avoiding, as may easily be done, that *directness* of expression which we have noticed in Sheppard Lee, and thus leaving much to the imagination—in writing as if the author were firmly impressed with the truth, yet astonished at the immensity, of the wonders he relates, and for which, professedly, he neither claims nor anticipates credence—in minuteness of detail, especially upon points which have no immediate bearing upon the general story—this minuteness not being at variance with indirectness of expression—in short, by making use of the infinity of arts which give verisimilitude to a narration—and by leaving the result as a wonder not to be accounted for. It will be found that *bizarreries* thus conducted, are usually far more effective than those otherwise managed. The attention of the author, who does not depend upon explaining away his incredibilities, is directed to giving them the character and the luminousness of truth, and thus are brought about, unwittingly, some of the most vivid creations of human intellect. The reader, too, readily perceives and falls in with the writer's humor, and suffers himself to be borne on thereby. On the other hand what difficulty, or inconvenience, or danger can there be in leaving us uninformed of the important facts that a certain hero *did not* actually discover the elixir vitae, *could not* really make himself invisible, and *was not* either a ghost in good earnest, or a bona fide Wandering Jew?

Poe wins our respect here by constructing a rationale for the supernatural in fiction. Lame endings that revealed the author's subservience to common sense were frequent in popular fiction. The highly respected Washington Irving had provided natural explanations for the supernatural events of some of his tales, as had

Charles Brockden Brown and Mrs. Ann Radcliffe before him. No such apology to reason and science is present in Poe's own tales of the supernatural. Morella's soul invades the body of her daughter, but the mystery is unexplained, as is the more startling transformation of the blonde Rowena into the brunette Ligeia. Poe's theory of unity of effect forbade the intrusion of materials that would dispel the illusion which all good fiction creates. He knew that readers give willing assent to the virtual existence which is the "life" of fiction, however incredible that existence may be when measured by ordinary experience.

Concerned, as always, with questions of technique, Poe explained how to secure the reader's acceptance of the occult by using the "arts" of verisimilitude. No longer did he generalize by referring to the power of identification, as he had in his review of *Robinson Crusoe*. Instead, he indicated that the illusion of reality could be achieved by the multiplication of minute details, even though these details were not directly relevant to the plot. *The Narrative of A. Gordon Pym*, on which he may have been working at this time (the first installment was published in the *Messenger* only four months later) makes use of such details. The technique itself was not new. The "sensation" stories of *Blackwood's*, from which he had learned part of his craft, had given minute details of bizarre experiences and the consequent emotional reactions; but Poe could not be content with a technique unless he could support it in theory.

The achievement of verisimilitude in action and setting, Poe had perceived, was possible through the multiplication of detail. How to achieve it in characterization was a problem he did not examine in this review but to which he addressed himself in a review published four months later. His own tales, however, furnish evidence that he was aware that the reader's assent to the incredible could be achieved, in part, by the plausibility of the narrator. Most of the sensation stories, including Poe's, made use of first-person narrators. If the character telling the story is obviously psychotic, the bizarre experience may be taken as hallucination, and verisimilitude is destroyed. This credibility-destroying device had been used by Irving in *Tales of a Traveller*, in which the "Adventure of the German Student" is narrated by a "nervous gentleman" who claims to have heard it from the student himself in a madhouse! Poe used the gambit in "The Tell-Tale Heart," with its opening sentence that testifies to the madness of the narrator. There is nothing wrong with such a device if the author has no intention of securing verisimilitude on external terms and wishes only to record the experience of a deranged mind. If, however, the purpose is to describe a strange adventure in an incredible setting, the author must in some way vouch for the sanity of the narrator. Poe went to extreme lengths to accomplish this in *The Narrative of A. Gordon Pym*, even writing a preface in which Pym, the *character*, makes the claim that Poe, the *author*, fictionalized the facts presented straightforwardly by Pym himself; then Poe added a postscript, claiming that Pym and his companion were still alive.

Such tactics are crude and indefensible. More to Poe's credit is his effort to establish Pym's plausibility by distinguishing the character's periods of near insanity from his periods of self-possession. In other words, the reader is informed of the times at which the character is subject to hallucination. In an earlier tale, "Ms. Found in a Bottle," Poe had endeavored to accomplish the same object by making his narrator unimaginative and skeptical. Pym does have imagination, but he insists that he retains his "powers of mind" at a time when his companions have been reduced to "a species of second childhood." Even when he encounters the wonders of the South Sea region, Pym merely records details instead of trying to explain the marvels. This technique is that of writing "as if the author were firmly impressed with the truth," the requirement Poe had proposed in his review of *Sheppard Lee*.

Poe's devices worked in a way that he did not expect. *Pym* was reviewed as an attempt at a realistic travel story that neglected probability,[27] surely an indication that his clumsier tactics an-

[27] It was reviewed in this way in *Burton's Gentleman's Magazine*, III (1838), 210–11. Walter E. Bezanson has described Burton's reaction to *Pym* and discussed the clumsier devices Poe used to achieve verisimilitude,

noyed his reviewer. For all of his theorizing, Poe had no gift for realism and the super-rationality of some of his narrators strikes most readers in a way quite opposite to what was evidently intended. James W. Cox furnishes this explanation: "He [Pym] is not the observer but forever the *actor*, and his experiences come more and more to seem the hallucinations of a madman." [28] To read *Pym* in terms of the Crusoe-like verisimilitude Poe invokes is unrewarding, to say the least. The novel assumes interest only if we interpret it as Patrick Quinn has done, as a symbolic journey of the mind.[29] Surely, however, it deserves better than Mr. Cox's comment that it is something between "a practical joke at the expense of the reader on one hand and a parody of the sensational adventure tale on the other." [30] Poe undoubtedly wrote the novel to sell and exploited relatively crude effects, but in this case his unconscious is better than his conscious art.[31] It may be taken as a crude thriller with a technique which foreshadows that of the modern science fiction adventure, such as A. E. Van Vogt's *The War Against the Rull*, but a search for symbolic meaning in Van Vogt's work yields no return, whereas both Patrick Quinn and Edward

---

at the same time giving him credit for a superficial credibility which "at its best . . . gives much of his work what might be called a secondary charm." Mr. Bezanson is correct in saying that we cannot take Poe's contrivances very seriously today. See Walter E. Bezanson, "The Troubled Sleep of Arthur Gordon Pym," in Rudolph Kirk and C. F. Main (eds.), *Essays in Literary History* (New Brunswick, 1960), 149–52. Another provocative study, together with a survey of critical opinion, is Sidney Kaplan's introduction to a modern reprint of the novel, *The Narrative of Arthur Gordon Pym* (New York, 1960).

[28] "Edgar Poe: Style as Pose," *Virginia Quarterly Review*, XLIV (1968), 73.

[29] *The French Face of Edgar Poe* (Carbondale, Ill., 1957), 169–215.

[30] "Edgar Poe: Style as Pose," 74.

[31] A recent article by Joseph V. Ridgely and Iola S. Haverstick casts light on the difficulties Poe had with the narrative structure of *Pym*. The novel was certainly not worked out with the "rigid consequence" of a mathematical demonstration, as Poe would have preferred. See Ridgely and Haverstick, "Chartless Voyage: The Many Narratives of Arthur Gordon Pym," *Texas Studies in Literature and Language*, VIII (1966), 63–80.

Davidson have found the "sensations" of *Pym* richly joined in implication.

4

In spite of the relatively inoffensive reviews that Poe had written for the July and August numbers of the *Messenger*, there was trouble in the office. On August 5, 1836, White had written to a contributor, William Cowper Scott, proprietor of the New York *Weekly Messenger*, that the next issue of his journal would be delayed because of illness. Again on August 25 he wrote that the November number was not ready because of "sickness among my most material hands," [32] which evidently meant Poe. In September, White himself was ill. An editorial note in the September issue stated that since both editor and publisher had been ill, there would be no notices of new books. In a letter to Sarah J. Hale, dated October 20, Poe admitted that he had been "sadly thrown back by late illness" [33] and would be unable to contribute anything to the *Ladies Magazine*, which she edited in Boston. About this time White was on the verge of discharging Poe and retained him only on the fulfillment of "certain conditions." [34] What these conditions were, we do not know. Perhaps they had to do with Poe's drinking. At any rate, with a slowly dying wife, financial difficulties, and illness of his own, White was evidently finding the vagaries of his brilliant editor too much to bear. Poe did recover from his indisposition in time to prepare the reviews for the October number—a full seventeen pages, though all of them may not have been Poe's—but in November there were further difficulties. White made a trip to New York about the middle of October, but on his return found his wife very low and his office in a state of

[32] Both these letters are quoted in Hull, "A Canon," 63.

[33] In *Letters*, I, 105.

[34] On December 27, 1836, White wrote to Beverley Tucker claiming that three months earlier (September?) he had given Poe notice, but that afterwards he was "overpersuaded" to retain him on the basis of these conditions, conditions which Poe had "again forfeited." Jackson, *Poe and the Southern Literary Messenger*, 110.

confusion.[35] If, as seems certain, he had left Poe in charge, Poe had violated the conditions White had imposed.

The November number was not ready for the press. It did not appear until December, and even then there was an apologetic note in the book review section: "A press of business connected with some necessary arrangements for Volume the third, has prevented us from paying, in this Messenger, the usual attention to our Critical Department. We have many books now lying by us which we propose to notice fully in our next. With this number we close Volume the Second."

The charitable conclusion is that Poe could not manage all of the work in White's absence—write the critical notices, handle the correspondence, pass judgment on contributions, prepare the magazine for the press, and read proof. His normal duties, if we can take White's letters to Lucian Minor as evidence of what he expected from his editor, would have been to handle book reviews and notices and furnish from fifteen to twenty pages of original material a month. But White had expected Minor to work only twenty-four to thirty hours a week,[36] and it is likely that Poe did much more than this. Normally he handled much of White's correspondence and read proof. Though he could be overruled by White, he passed judgment on contributions and wrote letters of acceptance and rejection. Probably Poe's work week was far in excess of thirty hours. When we add the time necessary for his own creative work and for the careful analysis he preferred to give the books he reviewed, it is no wonder that occasionally he took refuge in a bottle and got the reputation of having "bad habits." R. M. T. Hunter, a contemporary observer, gave his impression of the situation, and although we cannot always trust a memory of forty years, Hunter's account in 1875 squares with the impression we get from White's letters to his confidants. Hunter wrote,

---

[35] See White to Scott, November 24, 1836, in Hull, "A Canon," 63.

[36] See letters to Minor, February 17 and March 2, 1835, in Hull, "A Canon," 55. The letter of February 17 is quoted in full in Jackson, *Poe and the Southern Literary Messenger*, 93–94, but the March letter is omitted.

Here his [Poe's] habits were bad and as White did not appreciate his literary excellences I had hard work to save him from dismissal before it actually occurred. During a part of the time I was in Richmond, a member of the Legislature, and frequently volunteered to correct the press when pieces were being published with classical quotations. Poe was the only man on White's staff capable of doing this and when occasionally drinking (the habit was not constant) he was incapacitated for work. On such occasions I have done the work more than once to prevent a rupture between his employer and himself. He was reckless about money and subject to intoxication, but I was not aware of any other bad habit that he had.[37]

Considering the state of affairs in the *Messenger* office during November, it is not surprising that the November number, when it finally appeared in December, contained only four pages of criticism, of which the only point of interest was another expression of Poe's admiration for Dickens in a review of *The Posthumous Papers of the Pickwick Club*—and this review was chiefly quotation. By January, White had made good his threat to discharge Poe, and among the critical notices in the first number of Volume III was the announcement: "Mr. Poe's attention being called in another direction, he will decline, with the present number, the Editorial duties of the Messenger." [38]

[37] R. M. T. Hunter to Henry Tutwiler, May 20, 1875, in Hull, "A Canon," 49–50. Hunter may have been the person who "overpersuaded" White to retain Poe in September.

[38] *Southern Literary Messenger*, III (1837) 72. See *ibid.*, 96, for an announcement, apparently written by White, stating that Poe had "retired" on January 3 and that "the entire management of the work devolves upon myself alone." White then identified Poe's reviews in the January number. As late as January 9, however, Poe felt entitled to write a contributor, Allan B. Magruder, that his manuscript had been accepted. *Letters*, I, 106–107. White reacted indignantly and wrote Poe on January 17 (?) that Magruder's article was worthless and would not be printed, even though it had been set in type. Hull, "A Canon," 58.

In a letter to Beverley Tucker late in January, White charged that Poe had injured the *Messenger* through poor management. Hull, "A Canon," 61. The letter of January 24, printed in Jackson, *Poe and the Southern Literary Messenger*, 112–13, does not contain this particular charge, but in it White deprecated Poe by alleging that a certain contributor would no doubt

5

This account of Poe's difficulties between August and December of 1836 has been given in order to illustrate the problems he faced being a critic instead of a journalistic book-reviewer. Poe wanted to be a critic, to analyze the books that crossed his desk thoughtfully and at length; [39] but the exigencies of his routine tasks were a

stick by him now that Poe was no longer editor. In another January letter to Tucker, White wrote that more contributions were coming in than ever before, "since the fact has eked [sic] out that Poe is not to act as Judge or Judge Advocate." Hull, "A Canon," 65. A last letter, dated January 31, contains sarcastic references to Poe: "Poe pesters me no little—he is trying every manouvre [sic] to foist himself on some one at the North—at least I believe so.—He is continually after me for money. . . . Tell me candidly what you think of his Pym Maryatt's [sic] style I suppose and his Poetry. Treat all of this as private which you think ought to be private. Let all be private about Poe." Hull, "A Canon," 65.

Both Jackson and Hull have interpreted Poe's relationship with White partly on the basis of White's letters—a valuable corrective to some of the overly sympathetic biographers who have relied upon Poe's famous defense of his conduct in his letter to William Poe, August 15, 1840, in *Letters*, I, 141. Poe implied that he deliberately resigned, but White's letters indicate that he was discharged. The only original contribution I have made to this essentially biographical question has been my estimate of the taboos Poe violated both with his fiction and with his reviews and the effect on White, whom Poe called "an illiterate and vulgar, although well-meaning man." By Poe's standards, this is a correct description; but in a letter to Heath, which has unfortunately been lost, he evidently charged White with malice. In his reply Heath denied the charge and asserted that few men were "more disposed to cherish kindly and benevolent feelings" than White. Heath to Poe, September 12, 1839, in *Works*, XVII, 47–48. A reasonable interpretation is that White, plagued by personal misfortune and financial difficulties between August and December, 1836, was driven beyond endurance by Poe's erratic behavior and in a temporary mood of hostility made certain charges that were only partly justifiable. There is no reason to doubt Heath's statement in 1839 that White had no ill will toward Poe. The hostility evident in White's letters of January, 1837, had been forgotten.

[39] It must be remembered that Poe wrote reviews for a monthly instead of a quarterly. The essay-reviews of the *North American Review* often ran fifty pages or more. Poe rejected this kind of review because it amounted to a monograph-length study of the author and related topics; but rarely did he have space in the monthlies for which he wrote to examine more than one or two aspects of a work thoroughly, with ample quotations to illustrate

formidable obstacle. It is to his credit that during these exasperating months he still managed to write reviews, a few of them good ones. In the October number, among notices of nonliterary publications such as Dr. Haxall's *Dissertation on Diseases of the Abdomen*, Hall's *Latin Grammar*, and S. A. Roszel's *Address Delivered at the Annual Commencement of Dickinson College*, there is a review of a book of short stories, *Peter Snook . . . and Other Strange Tales*.[40] If we remember that collections of tales were not customarily honored with serious reviews during Poe's time, we can see that this review not only reveals the progress of Poe's ideas concerning the short story as a literary form but also indicates his efforts to establish the genre as worthy of criticism. For once he thought he had found a perfect example of the form: "The incidents of this story are forcibly conceived and even in the hands of an ordinary writer would scarcely fail of effect. But in the present instance so unusual a tact is developed in narration, that we are inclined to rank 'Peter Snook' among the few tales which, each in their own way, are absolutely faultless."

Reviewing Dickens' *Watkins Tottle* in June, Poe had compared the short story to a painting. Now he developed the analogy in detail:

"Peter Snook" is . . . a Flemish *home-piece*, and entitled to the very species of praise which should be awarded to the best of such pieces. The merit lies in the *chiaro 'scuro*—in that blending of light and shadow where nothing is *too distinct*, yet where the idea is fully conveyed—in the absence of all rigid outlines and all miniature painting—in the not undue warmth of the coloring—and in the slight tone of exaggeration prevalent, yet not amounting to

his points. His longest reviews ran from 10,000 to 12,000 words, less than a third the length of those in the *North American*; but most of his reviews were as brief as those of our modern journals, an inadequate space for Poe's method.

[40] *Southern Literary Messenger*, II (1836), 727–30. This review was printed in *Works*, XIV, 73–89, as an essay, but the text used was that of the *Broadway Journal* (1845). Poe added a long introduction on reviewing as an art and made minor revisions of the *Messenger* version. The text used here is that of the *Messenger* review.

caricature. We will venture to assert that no painter, who deserves to be called so, will read "Peter Snook" without assenting to what we have to say, and without a perfect consciousness that the principal rules of the plastic arts, founded as they are in a true perception of the beautiful, will apply in their fullest force to every species of literary composition.

To anyone familiar with Poe's aesthetic principles the statement above is astonishing. Usually vehement in his opposition to mimetic realism, he compared "Peter Snook" approvingly with a "Flemish home-piece," in spite of the fact that the Flemish school of painters was normally censured in his time for uncritical literalness and a delight in the commonplace. Their work was marked by accuracy and precision of outline, a result of a tradition of miniature painting, yet these are precisely the qualities that Poe denied to the best of the Flemish work. His use of the term chiaroscuro, however, suggests that he was referring not to the distinctive Flemish paintings of the fifteenth century but to the genre painting of the seventeenth century, after the influence of the Italian artist Caravaggio had made itself felt, particularly in the thematic use of light and shadow. That Poe was making an accurate comparison is indicated by his description of "the slight tone of exaggeration prevalent, yet not amounting to caricature." The Flemish genre painters had retained enough of Pieter Bruegel's passion for the details of homely life, invested with a certain amount of humor, to justify Poe's comparison. The author of "Peter Snook," Poe noted, "has some of the happiest peculiarities of Dickens"; then he quoted enough of the tale to show that these peculiarities had to do with a humorous presentation of a London clerk and his financial and amatory misadventures. The story is a "home-piece" in its exaggeration of low life and uses the technique of chiaroscuro to emphasize elements of character.

Obviously Poe did not object to Dickensian realism in a short tale, provided that details were organized into a total design—a composition that would convey a unity of impression. More surprising is the last sentence of his quotation, that "the principal rules of the plastic arts, founded as they are in a true perception of the beautiful, will apply in their fullest force to *every species of literary composition*" (italics mine). After 1831 he customarily denied, along with most other romantic critics, that poetry resembled painting, for painting was a mimetic art and poetry was not. However, when Poe referred to "principal rules," he was thinking in terms of the psychology of effect. The unity of effect was a first principle, to be observed in all arts. As he was to explain in a later review, effects differed according to genre, but the principle was always the same.

Poe continued to describe the short tale as a design or a composition rather than as a narrative characterized by action and drama. The pleasure to be derived from it was similar to the response to a painting—say by a master of the picturesque such as Salvator Rosa —in which the management of light and shadow is thematically significant. Details that call attention to themselves are to be avoided because they get in the way of the apprehension of the design, the idea of the story. We do not know whether at this time Poe had read any of Hawthorne's tales which S. B. Goodrich had published in *The Token*, but, whether he had read them or not, he described with precision what has been accepted as a chief characteristic of Hawthorne's symbolic art—the blending of light and shadow so that object, character, and event are never seen in insulated detail but only in a kind of relatedness that, taken as a whole, intimates the idea. The review of *Peter Snook* reveals that six years before Poe was to review Hawthorne's *Twice-Told Tales* he was prepared to do them justice. Hawthorne was practicing the technique for which Poe was attempting to formulate a theory. Where Poe's theory and Hawthorne's practice came to terms was in the picturesque tradition, which valued natural objects selectively for their picturesque qualities and their capability of being combined into compositions that would create a unified impression.[41] It is

[41] See Leo B. Levy, "Hawthorne and the Sublime," *American Literature*, XXXVII (1966), 391–402, for Hawthorne's use of the conventions of the picturesque and the sublime. The topic has not been thoroughly investigated, but Mr. Levy's notes list other references. It is interesting in this context that Henry James applied the term chiaroscuro to Hawthorne's tales and connected it with the picturesque. A valuable study of the vogue of

not at all surprising that in the few remarks Poe made about painters he showed preference for Claude Lorraine and Salvator Rosa,
whose paintings had helped establish the vogue of the picturesque
in the eighteenth century.

6

Since the November number of the *Messenger* did not appear
until December and even then contained only four pages of perfunctory notices, the last work of any significance that Poe accomplished as editor of the *Messenger* appeared in January, 1837. The
first five reviews in this issue are his; the others are by Judge Abel
P. Upshur and Beverley Tucker. Of Poe's five reviews, two merit
examination.

Poe gave *George Balcombe*, a novel published anonymously by
his friend Beverley Tucker, a full measure of attention. Some
months later White wrote to Tucker alleging that the "eulogistic
review" was written only because Poe suspected that Tucker was
the author of the novel. "Poe seldom or ever done [*sic*] what he
knew was just to any books," [42] White charged. Since this charge
was made in retrospect, after White should have had time to cool
off from whatever heat the immediate friction with Poe had
caused, it may have been a firm conviction. As has been shown, Poe
did write some caustic reviews, flippant in tone, of what White
called "some trashy novels." But White went on to say that Poe
rarely read through the books that he reviewed, and this accusation
is quite unfair in view of the circumstances. Poe's reviews demonstrated that he read very carefully the books that he thought merited attention. Even when he resorted to plot summary instead of
analysis, he appears to have read the books concerned, unless he
lifted the summaries from other magazines. When Poe did borrow
from other reviewers, which he did infrequently, he was more
scrupulous than many of his contemporaries in mentioning his

---

the picturesque in England is Elizabeth W. Manwaring, *Italian Landscape
in Eighteenth Century England* (New York, 1925).

[42] In Jackson, *Poe and the Southern Literary Messenger*, 115.

sources. Considering his duties at the *Messenger* office, however, and the number of books he had to review, it is unlikely that he was able to read them all. Any professional reviewer is likely to compile a review of an unimportant work from publisher's notices or previous reviews if he has a deadline to meet. Whenever Poe concentrated on peripheral matters such as dedications, footnotes, or slips in grammar (which could be culled by skimming), he was unjust, in White's sense, to the book reviewed. Otherwise White's charges have to be based on the five books that Poe reviewed harshly: *Confessions of a Poet, Paul Ulric, Norman Leslie, Ups and Downs,* and *The Partisan.* Poe himself had stated in September that he had reviewed ninety-four books for the *Messenger* and that in only five reviews had censure been "greatly predominant." In seventy-nine cases he had praised more than he had blamed.

This was Poe's reaction to the charge of "regular cutting and slashing" which had been made by the Richmond *Courier and Daily Compiler* in August of 1836.[43] Poe had answered the editor of the *Compiler* by supplying the facts, as he interpreted them, but from White's letter to Tucker we must assume that White was not convinced by Poe's facts. Either his troubles with Poe had made him incapable of being fair or Poe's reviewing standards were so strange to White that the publisher had no real basis for judgment. Since Poe judged on literary grounds and White on moral, they were obviously at cross-purposes much of the time.

The review of *George Balcombe* [44] was not blatantly eulogistic. Poe did call Tucker's work the "best American novel," an opinion time has not sustained; and he claimed that no other American novelist had succeeded as well as Tucker in creating female characters. This last was only relative praise. The inability to portray women realistically had been characteristic of the best of the novelists of Poe's time—Cooper, Simms, and Bird. Women thought worthy of portrayal in a novel were usually ladies, paper-and-paste specimens of sensibility. Poe quite rightly took exception to "Eliz-

[43] Poe's letter and the charge which provoked it are both in *Letters,* I, 100–102.
[44] *Works,* IX, 243–65.

abeth, the shrinking and matronly wife of Balcombe," who rises "suddenly into the heroine in the hour of her husband's peril." As Poe said, "She is an exquisite specimen of her class, but her class is somewhat hackneyed." The character of Mary Scott, who has the chief female role in the novel, was better, but "her nature is barely sketched." Even in the sketch, however, the novelist showed an unusual "creative vigor."

Unless we are aware that the American critics of Poe's time demanded a measure of realism in the portrayal of character, we would be disposed to grant Poe more credit than he deserves for seeing the defects of the female characters in the American novel. Actually, a number of critics had objected to Cooper's females, and the charge made recently by Leslie Fiedler—that American novelists were unable to present "full-fledged, mature women" [45]—was first intimated in the 1830's. This is not to say that the critics of the period would have accepted Fiedler's definition of a mature woman, but they were aware that American novelists were deficient in the characterization of women. The claim that Poe made for Tucker was that no other American novelist had depicted female character "even nearly so well," and this praise, considering the competition, must be regarded as qualified. Other characters in the novel were less effective:

> Napier himself is, as usual with most professed heroes, a mere non-entity. James is sufficiently natural. Major Swann, although only done in outline, gives a fine idea of a decayed Virginia gentleman. Charles, a negro, . . . is drawn roughly, but to the life. Balcombe, frank, ardent, philosophical, chivalrous, sagacious—and, above all, glorying in the exercise of his sagacity—is a conception which might possibly have been entertained, but certainly could not have been executed, by a mind many degrees dissimilar from that of Balcombe himself, as depicted. Of Keizer, a character evidently much dwelt upon, and greatly labored out by the author, we have but one observation to make. It will strike every reader, not at first, but upon reflection, that George Balcombe, in John Keizer's

[45] *Love and Death in the American Novel* (Meridian ed.; New York, 1960), xix.

circumstances, would have been precisely John Keizer. We find the same traits modified throughout—yet the *worldly difference* forms a distinction sufficiently marked for the purpose of the novelist. Lastly, Montague, with his low cunning, his arch-hypocrisy, his malignancy, his quibbling superstition, his moral courage and physical pusillanimity, is a character to be met with every day, and to be recognized at a glance. Nothing was ever more minutely, more forcibly, or more thoroughly painted. He is not original of course; nor must we forget that were he so, he would, necessarily, be untrue, in some measure, to nature. But we mean to say that the merit here is solely that of observation and fidelity.

To anyone familiar with Poe's theories of art, it is apparent that the quotation above is a subtle compliment to the author of the novel as a person but by no means a tribute to his ability as a novelist. Three characters are described as types. Two are said to be indistinguishable except for circumstances. Three are said to be natural, but that this represents limited approval is revealed by Poe's last sentence. Originality in characterization displayed the imagination at work, not mere observation. The question that had been occupying Poe's mind for several months was how to achieve verisimilitude in highly imaginative prose fiction. As we have seen, it was to be secured in terms of setting by the multiplication of detail. What about character? The unimaginative, skeptical type who narrated "Ms. Found in a Bottle" would have been to Poe's mind a nonentity, a species of Everyman. How, then, could an author win the reader's assent to a tale that presented a character so unusual as to be called an original? Although Poe's solution was irrelevant to the novel under consideration, he proposed it, following his customary practice of using the particular issue at hand as a point of departure to advance his own theory.

Original characters, so called, can only be critically praised as such, either when presenting qualities known in real life, but never before depicted, (a combination nearly impossible) or when presenting qualities (moral, or physical, or both) which although unknown, or even known to be hypothetical, are so skilfully adapted to the circumstances which surround them, that our sense of fitness is not offended, and we find ourselves seeking a reason why these things *might not have been,* which we are still satisfied *are not.* The latter species of originality appertains to the loftier regions of the *Ideal.*

This "latter species of originality" began to appear in Poe's own tales, particularly in "The Fall of the House of Usher." In "Berenice" he had made a rudimentary effort to prepare the reader for the unusual character of Egaeus by summarizing his long isolation in the "gloomy, grey, hereditary halls" of his fathers, but few details were given, and Poe himself admitted that "Berenice" was not successful.[46] In the character of Roderick Usher, however, Poe presented hypothetical qualities—neurotic sensitivity and fear exaggerated beyond the probable—but created in Usher's house a microcosm in which such a being could be expected to live, "skilfully" adapting Usher's qualities "to the circumstances which surround them." Such a technique, to Poe, was genuinely creative. An original character was "ideal" in the sense that the concept sprang from the mind of the author, instead of being copied from life like the characters of *George Balcombe.* Yet to secure verisimilitude (this quality was required in prose, but not in poetry), an environment must be invented in which the character would *seem* natural.[47] To increase plausibility, Poe made the narrator of "Usher" a commonplace Everyman much like the narrator of "Ms. Found in a Bottle."

It will be seen by the above that Poe, quite tactfully, was arguing that the author of *George Balcombe* had displayed little imagination. The characters were true to life, but hackneyed. Other aspects of the novel were less objectionable. The style was "bold, vigorous, and rich," and there were few faults of grammar. The *thought* of the novel was not impeccable, but since it was voiced by the main character, the author should not be held responsible. Poe understood quite well that it was possible for a fictional character to be

---

[46] Poe to White, April 30, 1835, in *Letters,* I, 57.
[47] Poe's use of contemporary theories of biological adaptation was pointed out by Leo Spitzer, "A Reinterpretation of 'The Fall of the House of Usher,'" *Comparative Literature,* IV (1952), 351–63.

an independent creation, not the author's voice. This does not mean that he was fully aware of the problem of identifying the "voice" of a novel, which is still a controversial issue. He customarily located the author voice in the commentary that appeared in the nineteenth-century novel as part of the privilege of the omniscient convention; and in a later review he attributed the chief value of a novel to just such comment.

Finally, Poe commended the plot of *George Balcombe*, but since he did not regard an ingenious plot as necessary or even desirable in longer works of fiction, this must not be taken as anything other than a tribute to the author's skill—his "ingenuity and finish in the adaptation of its component parts." Since a novel did not convey a unity of impression, Poe was to say in other reviews, such skill was only a secondary merit and usually went unappreciated.

Except for the unjustified claim that Tucker's was the best American novel, Poe accorded it no more praise than he had Bird's *The Infidel* and far less than he had given Bulwer. He concluded his review by stating that he did not wish to be understood as ranking *George Balcombe* with "the more brilliant fictions of some of the living novelists of Great Britain." White's accusation that Poe deliberately wrote a eulogistic review to gratify Tucker is unfair. Not that Poe never eulogized his friends. He did so more than once. In this particular instance, however, it is unlikely that White would have made the accusation had he not been making excuses to Tucker for his dismissal of an editor Tucker had praised; either this, or he failed to understand Poe's attempt to judge by literary principle. Remembering Poe's ridicule of Simms, White may have mistaken a tactful employment of standards for unqualified praise.

It is ironic that Poe's last review of a book of poems during his editorship of the *Messenger* was the one in which he most nearly approximated the standards he had announced in the review of Drake and Halleck. It may be, as has been suggested earlier, that Poe's criticism suffered because he rarely examined a book that possessed the qualities he demanded. Rigidly contemporaneous in his taste, he was unable to cope with the eccentricities of the metaphysical poets of *The Book of Gems*, but he could judge the merit of the poets of his own time with considerable accuracy. Yet until William Cullen Bryant's *Poems, Fourth Edition* appeared on his desk,[48] only Drake and Halleck had deserved serious attention. In reviewing Bryant, he had an opportunity to examine the work of the best American poet of the period, except for himself. Poe profited by the opportunity. As practical criticism, his review of Bryant is superior to anything else he had written for the *Messenger*, not excepting the critique of Drake and Halleck. It deserves a separate chapter, for it shows that Poe was capable of a more sophisticated method than he had demonstrated in his disposal of Mrs. Sigourney's mottoes and Drake's frogs and fireflies.

[48] The brief notice of Bryant's *Poems* that appeared in the *Messenger* for January, 1835, and was reprinted in *Works*, VIII, 1–2, was written by Heath.

VIII · *Standards Achieved: The Poet's Art*

THE *Poems* of William Cullen Bryant were worthy of extended analysis and invited the application of all the criteria by which Poe could evaluate poetry. With a distinguished reputation of some years' standing, Bryant could not be disposed of on the basis of a single glaring deficiency. He was known as a master of versification who showed exquisite appreciation of both physical and moral beauty; in fact, he was the best America had to offer for comparison with the great British romantic poets. Accordingly, it was incumbent on Poe to examine every aspect of Bryant's art. In so doing, he eliminated the critical generality that he had occasionally practiced by investigating theme, versification, diction, metaphor, grammatical construction, and the implied range of the poet's imagination. Except for a brief digression on metrics, Poe confined himself to the poems themselves. In its close adherence to the text, his review is anticipative of the "new" criticism of the twentieth century; but, ironically, his approach must have seemed antiquated to some of his readers. Twenty or thirty years earlier, American critics had focused their attention on diction and versification, but by 1837 the general essay was in vogue, and a review of a single book was likely to be a dissertation on the life and works of the author, or, if in a monthly magazine, an "appreciation" that attempted to catch the author's "spirit." [1]

Poe rarely explicated a complete poem in the modern manner, but a book review was no place for such a technique. The best he could do in specific analysis was to single out particular passages as illustrations of merits or defects, but the fact that he did analyze

---

[1] See Charvat, *American Critical Thought*, 86–110, for a description of American journalistic criticism of verse technique during the two decades preceding Poe's review. Poe's concern for diction was similar to that of the rhetoricians, but his metrical theory, sound or unsound, was a daring innovation.

192

some of these passages represented an improvement over the usual reviewing method of simply pointing out "beauties" and "faults." Considering the limitations of his medium, Poe's review of Bryant is quite detailed, remarkably so for his time and place.[2]

Poe began by examining one of Bryant's longer poems, "The Ages," first commenting on its theme. "It is, indeed, an essay on the perfectibility of man, wherein, among other better arguments, some in the very teeth of analogy are deduced from the eternal *cycles* of physical nature, to sustain a hope of progression in happiness." Had he been so inclined, Poe had an opportunity for a long digression on the subject of progress and perfectibility, ideas which he considered totally invalid.[3] Then too, he might have inserted a lecture on the fallacy of didacticism in poetry; but he announced that "it is only as a poem that we wish to examine *The Ages*," thus enforcing by example his precept that a review should not be an essay on the *subject* of the item reviewed.

Proceeding directly to metrical analysis, Poe conceded that there was melody and force in Bryant's versification, but, he said, there were also defects. As might be expected from a critic who emphasized the musical qualities of verse, Poe found a lack of fluency in Bryant's lines. For instance, "The line 'When o'er the buds of youth the death-wind blows' is impeded in its flow by the final *th* in youth, and especially in *death* where *w* follows. The word *tears* cannot readily be pronounced after the final *st* in bitterest; and its own final consonants, *rs*, in like manner render an effort necessary in the utterance of *stream* which commences the next line."

In Poe's phonetic discriminations liquids were preferred over other consonants, and all combinations difficult to pronounce were

---

[2] *Works*, IX, 268–305.

[3] Poe consistently denied belief in progress and perfectibility, apparently basing his opinion upon the old concept of a biological hierarchy of forms which exhibited what he called in "The Colloquy of Monos and Una" the "laws of gradation." This is nothing more than the Chain of Being in which each life form was supposed to have its fixed place. Poe appears to have been little affected by the early evolutionary ideas which in the 1830's transformed the chain into a kind of conveyor belt that moved onward and upward. See Arthur O. Lovejoy, *The Great Chain of Being* (Cambridge, 1936), for a definitive discussion of the concept.

considered flaws. Only combinations which were smooth, melodious, and harmonious were acceptable, since the harmony of sound was a primary consideration. It is obvious that Poe was completely sound-oriented and that he expected poetry to be read aloud.

Poe was equally concerned with the time of a poetic line; he thought of feet as being equivalent to measure in music.[4]

> In the verse "We think on what they were, with many fears" the word *many* is, from its nature, too rapidly pronounced for the fulfillment of the *time* necessary to give weight to the foot of two syllables. All words of two syllables do not necessarily constitute a foot (we speak now of the Pentameter here employed) even although the syllables be entirely distinct, as in *many, very, often,* and the like. Such as, without effort, cannot employ in their pronunciation the *time* demanded by each of the preceding and succeeding feet of the verse, and occasionally of a preceding verse, will never fail to offend.

To equalize the time of a given foot with others in the line, Poe continued, it may sometimes be necessary to add syllables not called for by a strict interpretation of the meter. The only stipulation is that the lines containing extra syllables must lend themselves to easy pronunciation in the same time as the metrically regular lines. For example, "Lo! to the smiling Arno's classic side / The emulous nations of the West repair!" is metrically sound even though the second line contains eleven syllables instead of the normal ten of iambic pentameter. Any variation such as the one above should be accommodated to the temporal requirement of the line, as a minimum, but a really superior poet would succeed in the *"balancing . . .* of time, *throughout an entire sentence."* The longer the sentence so balanced, the more skillful the poet!

Nathaniel Parker Willis had been censured by the *American Monthly* for using trisyllabic substitutions in iambic verse, but the

---

[4] Poe's metrical system will be discussed in a later chapter in connection with "The Rationale of Verse." A summary description is given here as an illustration of the criteria he used in the review. His minute discriminations among various phonetic qualities were unprecedented in American criticism.

reviewer had erred, Poe claimed, in scanning each line out of the context of the grammatical unit, the sentence. Poe was aware that scanning by sentences instead of by lines would be a startling innovation and immediately said so:

> This, we confess, is a novel idea, but, we think perfectly tenable. Any musician will understand us. Efforts for the relief of monotone will necessarily produce fluctuations in the time of any metre, which fluctuations, if not subsequently counter-balanced, affect the ear like unresolved discords in music. The deviations then of which we have been speaking, from the strict rules of prosodial art, are but improvements upon the rigor of those rules, and are a merit, not a fault. It is the nicety of this species of equalization more than any other metrical merit, which elevates Pope as a versifier above the mere couplet-maker of his day; and, on the other hand, it is the extension of the principle to *sentences of greater length* which elevates Milton above Pope.

Poe's theory of extended temporal balance throughout an entire sentence is well exemplified in his own verse. His grammatical units are frequently entire stanzas, though sometimes he used semicolons and dashes where others might consider the full stop more appropriate. Extended temporal balance is present in "Tamerlane" and "Al Aaraaf"; and in "Israfel" each stanza is a grammatical unit. Of his later verse, "The Raven" shows Poe experimenting with temporal balance in longer lines, although of the eighteen stanzas only nine may with some justification be considered as sentences. In "Ulalume" only four of the ten stanzas are grammatical units, but this poem, like "The Raven," is a dialogue. It would have been difficult for Poe to make each stanza into a grammatical unit unless he allotted each speaker a stanza in turn, and obviously he made no such attempt. When the poem employed only one speaker, however, Poe's tendency in the late verse as in the early was to extend the sentence throughout the entire stanza. The first four stanzas of "Annabel Lee" are grammatical units, and the last two stanzas together form a single sentence.

Poe's own substitution of trisyllabic feet to balance a temporally longer line of dissyllabic feet may be observed in the first two lines of "The Raven": "Once upon a midnight dreary, while I pondered, weak and weary, / Over many a quaint and curious volume of forgotten lore—." The first line is perfectly regular trochaic octameter; the second line is seven and *a half* feet, with the caesura represented by the dash at the end taking the place of the unstressed syllable in the final trochee. The second foot, however, contains three syllables. As Poe had said in his review of Bryant, words like "many," although dissyllabic, do not constitute a true iambic foot. Consequently he added another syllable, "many a," to compensate.[5] There are also three syllables in the fourth foot, "curious." Thus, in making trisyllabic substitutions, Poe chose words that might be rapidly pronounced so that he could achieve balance with preceding and succeeding feet. The effect is perfectly regular verse, as far as the ear is concerned, with the only variation in the rhythm being caused by the omission of the unstressed syllable in the final trochee of the second line. It is no wonder that Poe's "walloping rhythm" has offended such modern readers as Aldous Huxley, however much it may appeal to those who like pronounced rhythmic effects.

Poe's discussion of metrics and his digression on the poetry of Nathaniel Parker Willis represents his only departure in this review from the text of Bryant's poems. It was the only way he could introduce his theory into the review; and since he had announced that he was going to condemn or praise on principle, it was necessary for him to state the principle as he used it. Contemporary reviewers sometimes pointed out what they considered metrical flaws, but the discussion was rarely developed on a theoretical basis. The reviewer simply assumed that the reader knew the rules and exhibited the violation as an example of undue poetic license. To introduce a new system based upon extended temporal balance

[5] Poe seems to have been unaware that Bryant had argued for the substitution of trisyllabic feet in iambic verse in an article published in the *North American Review* nearly twenty years earlier (IX [September, 1819], 426–31). Bryant based his argument upon precedent and cited the practice of Shakespeare and Milton. Trisyllabic feet gave a more natural, livelier melody, Bryant contended, but he advanced no metrical "principle" in support.

instead of simply counting syllables or stresses was a daring act in a review.

After examining the metrics of Bryant's poems, Poe analyzed the figures of speech, applying some of the familiar rules of rhetoric but also making interpretations of import. When he merely pointed out an error, Poe's standards resembled Blair's rules for propriety of figure, but he went far beyond Blair when he examined metaphors for their extended implication. The old rhetorician had categorized figurative language as ornamentation, or "the dress of our sentiments"; [6] but Poe revealed an inclination to assess it in terms of concepts. He did not always explain the bases of his judgments, however, and we must reconstruct them on scanty evidence. For instance, he cited as an "unjust metonymy" a fragment of an extended personification from Bryant's "The Ages": "*Cradles*, in his soft *embrace*, a gay / Young group of grassy islands." Certainly the two words Poe italicized are not metonymic in the usual sense of the substitution of an attribute for an object. Blair, however, defined metonymy as a substitution of an effect for a cause,[7] and it is probably in this sense that Poe used the term. The islands are *in* the water of a bay as infants are *in a cradle*. Evidently Poe thought that the bay, which might *appear* something like a cradle for islands, should not be treated as an active agent, or cause, of the embrace. If this was his reasoning, he obscured it by quoting only part of the figure. The complete personification is as follows:

> And where his willing waves yon bright blue bay
> Sends up, to kiss his decorated brim,
> And cradles, in his soft embrace, the gay
> Young group of grassy islands born of him.

It would seem that Poe should have found fault with the inconsistent personification—a bay, masculine gender, being treated as the mother of islands—but he merely pointed out the error and did not explain it.

His objection to Bryant's personification of the Past is more un-

---

[6] Blair, *Lectures*, I, 300.   [7] *Ibid.*, 297.

derstandable. The lines singled out are, "And glorious ages gone /
lie deep within the shadow of thy womb." Here the reference was
"disagreeable" to Poe: "Such things are common, but at best, repulsive." Squeamish as any Victorian about matters of sex, he was
able to censure the line on principle according to Blair's dictum
that "an author should study never to be nauseous in his allusions." [8] He went beyond Blair, however, in examining the conceptual implication of the lines: "The womb, in any just imagery,
should be spoken of with a view to things future; here it is employed, in the sense of the tomb, and with a view to things past."
Such close reading was characteristic of Poe at his best. It shows
that he took into account the possibility of metaphorical extension
and required a coincidence between the import of the controlling
image and that of subsidiary comparisons. Bryant began his poem
by invoking the Past as a kind of personification of Death, monarch
of a "dark domain" where the dead are fettered. Then, in the second stanza, which Poe quoted, the image of the womb is not only
inconsistent with the original figure but introduces conflicting concepts by metaphoric extension.[9] In the fourth from the last stanza,

---

[8] *Ibid.*, 302.

[9] Blair's rules for perspicuity did provide a precedent for this charge. The
function of metaphor was "to make intellectual ideas, in some sort, visible
to the eye, by giving them colour, and substance, and sensible qualities."
Ibid., 297. The metaphorical "picture" must be accurately delineated, or
the idea could not be grasped. There are several other "Blair" rules which
Poe occasionally employed for the detection of "unjust comparisons": (1) All
figures should be suited to the nature of the subject. (2) Avoid using "such
allusions as raise in the mind disagreeable, mean, vulgar, or dirty ideas."
(3) The resemblance, "which is the foundation of the Metaphor," should
"be clear and perspicuous, not far-fetched, nor difficult to discover." (4)
Care should be taken "never to jumble metaphorical and plain language
together." (5) Avoid making "two different Metaphors meet on one object." (6) "Avoid crowding them together on the same object." (7) The
metaphor should not be "too far pursued," for if it is, it becomes an allegory, tires the reader, and makes the discourse "obscure." *Ibid.*, 300–314.
Blair's rule-of-thumb for testing metaphors was to try to visualize them
as pictures: "We should try to form a picture upon them, and consider how
the parts would agree, and what sort of figure the whole would present,
when delineated with a pencil. By this means, we should become sensible,
whether inconsistent circumstances were mixed, and a monstrous image

Bryant introduced the theme of resurrection by asserting that the Past would yield up its dead: "Thy gates shall yet give way, / Thy bolts shall fall, inexorable Past!" Then, trying to suggest the process of resurrection, he returned to the womb image to bring in the conventional idea of rebirth. Poe was being almost too kind when he concluded his discussion with the mild comment, "it seems that *The Past*, as an allegorical personification, is confounded with *Death*."

One of Bryant's poems aroused Poe's almost unqualified admiration. "Oh, Fairest of the Rural Maids" was commendable for its "rich simplicity" and its "ideal beauty," a quality which Poe admitted was not easy to analyze. He undertook to analyze it, nevertheless, and quoted the poem in full, italicizing the "ideal" passages. Bryant's "original conception," Poe affirmed, was highly imaginative:

A maiden is born in the forest. . . . She is not merely *modelled in character* by the associations of her childhood—this were the thought of an ordinary poet—an idea that we meet with every day in rhyme—but she imbibes, in her physical as well as moral being, the traits, the very features of the delicious scenery around her—*its loveliness becomes a portion of her own.* . . . It would have been a highly poetical idea to imagine the tints in the locks of the maiden deducing *a resemblance* to the "twilight of the trees and rocks," from the constancy of her associations—but the spirit of Ideality is immeasurably more apparent when the "twilight" is represented as becoming *identified* with the shadows of her hair.

When we remember Poe's praise of Shelley's Queen Mab in the review of Drake and Halleck, we are able to interpret his argument. *Physical* resemblances as such are unimaginative. However, if the qualities associated with or *expressed* by objects are identified with a subject, then both subject and object are "idealized." [10] The

___

thereby produced . . . ." *Ibid.*, 311. Poe used these rules too frequently to warrant drawing attention to each instance, but the pictorial test is obvious in the review of Bryant, as well as his use of rules 1, 2, 4, and 5.

[10] "Expressed" is Archibald Alison's term. According to his associationist theory, each object or scene expressed certain qualities. However, even the

phenomenal separateness of things is obliterated, and subject and object become one in a unity of effect. If Bryant's maiden—the subject—were merely influenced in character by the objects of her environment, then separateness would have been emphasized; but by a happy use of metaphor Bryant identified the qualities of her environment with the traits of the maiden herself.

Poe italicized only the metaphors of the poem. The similes, as he was careful to point out, were not italicized, and we are entitled to inquire into his reason. It appears that he considered metaphor a more appropriate vehicle of the ideal than simile because the two terms of the comparison are identified with each other. In a simile the use of the preposition—Poe italicized it to show the fault—weakens or qualifies the identification. Accordingly, the lines, "Thy step is *as* the wind that weaves / Its playful way among the leaves," were ineffective. Not only is the comparison hackneyed but also the separateness of the things compared is made obvious. Bryant's maiden walking in the woods trips here and there *like* a playful breeze stirring up the fallen leaves; but, in Poe's opinion, her step should actually have *been* the playful wind. To see one object entirely in terms of another is identification in Poe's sense, and the verbal structure should express this ideal conception. Yet even metaphors are limited in the expression of the ideal. "The image contained in the lines 'Thine eyes are springs in whose serene / And silent waters Heaven is seen—' is one which, we think, for ap-

---

"most beautiful scenes of real nature" exhibited a "confusion of expression." *Essays on Taste*, 84. It was the duty of the artist to select "only such circumstances as accord with the general expression of the scene to awaken an emotion more full, more simple, and more harmonious than any we can receive from the scenes of nature itself." *Ibid.*, 85. In painting or in landscape gardening the artist removed from his composition whatever was "hostile to its effects or unsuited to its character." Poe regularly employed variations of this aesthetic principle as a criterion of unity of effect, but he carried it one step farther than Alison in applying it to a poem. Alison did not require the "identification" Poe demanded as the absolute rhetorical expression of unity of idea. Elsewhere, however, Poe followed Alison by demanding the elimination of elements hostile to the proposed effect. Bryant was also a disciple of Alison in attempting to employ objects with congruent associations in a poem. Thus it is not surprising that Poe found many of Bryant's poems displaying a unity of effect.

propriateness, completeness, and every perfect beauty of which imagery is susceptible, has never been surpassed—but *imagery* is susceptible of *no* beauty like that we have designated . . . ." Again we are entitled to ask, why not? Poe was willing to concede a certain superiority to metaphors, but he was well aware that no comparison, whatever its rhetorical structure, could *force* identification upon the reader. No one would assume that the girl's eyes were actually springs, no matter how many resemblances Bryant's ingenuity discovered. In the remainder of the stanza, which Poe did not bother to quote, Bryant compared the girl's lashes with the herbs around the springs, thus, as Poe would have seen it, diminishing the ideality of the original concept by a fanciful yoking of physical details barren of suggestive import.

The lines of the poem that Poe italicized as imaginative, when they are figurative at all, employ general or even abstract terms that suggest a moral condition rather than a physical resemblance. Poe admired these pairs: "And all the beauty of the place / Is in thy heart and on thy face," followed by "The twilight of the trees and rocks / Is in the light shade of thy locks." Undoubtedly he interpreted these lines as expressing moral sentiment, even though the first pair is abstract statement and the second would have high associative value only to someone like Poe, who was capable of attaching considerable meaning to the various aspects of light and shade. He used an odd device to illustrate the quality he saw in the lines, printing them not as they appear in the poem, as the concluding and beginning lines of separate stanzas, but as if they were one stanza.

> The twilight of the trees and rocks
> Is in the light shade of *her* locks,
> And all the beauty of the place
> Is in *her* heart and on *her* face. (Italics mine.)

Whether Poe's substitution of *her* for Bryant's *thy* is a misprint, a careless error, or an intentional rewriting is impossible to determine without his manuscript; but the fact that he made a new stanza out of lines culled from two stanzas, and then printed the new stanza twice, is patently deliberate. Generally tactful in this review, he was demonstrating without comment how Bryant *should* have written the poem to achieve increased suggestiveness. The maiden's "twilight" hair in Poe's reordering of the lines becomes an aspect of the general beauty with which she has been identified.

For those who insist that Poe was the first American advocate of art for art's sake, it will be instructive to cite his opinion of Bryant's concluding stanza, which he offered as a specimen of "the most elevated species of poetical merit."

> The forest depths by foot impressed
> Are not more sinless than thy breast
> *The holy peace that fills the air*
> *Of those calm solitudes, is there.* (Italics Poe's.)

During this particular period Poe validated poetry by its expression of moral sentiment, which had been an essential quality of Ideality to the phrenologists and an aspect of taste to Archibald Alison. Poe was even willing to forgive Bryant's didacticism (elsewhere censured) when the message was an appropriate conclusion to the illustrative material which had preceded it. "To a Waterfowl" was not worthy of the admiration that had been accorded it, but "its rounded and didactic termination has done wonders."

It is fortunate that Poe explicated a few passages from Bryant's poems. Otherwise we would have to deduce his criteria for imaginative verse from the lines he italicized, a procedure of more value in illustrating his taste than in defining his principles. Since his principles were inevitably associated with his taste, however, the lines he chose for admiration are worth comment. Unless they are intended to illustrate technique, they invariably express what Poe considered to be appropriate poetic thought or concepts. By thought Poe did not mean philosophical import translatable into a prose paraphrase of theme. The lines he singled out as expressive of thought were usually pictorial renditions of the beautiful, the weird, the melancholy, or the spiritual. A few specimens will suffice (italics Poe's):

> The mountains that unfold
> In their wide sweep the colored landscape round,
> Seem *groups of giant kings in purple and gold*
> *That guard the enchanted ground.*
> > (From "Autumn Woods.")

> Pleasant shall be thy way, *where meekly bows*
> *The shutting flower, and darkling waters pass,*
> *And 'twixt the o'ershadowing branches and the*
> *grass* . . .
> > (From "To the Evening Wind.")

> *The innumerable caravan that moves*
> *To that mysterious realm where each shall take*
> *His chamber in the silent halls of death* . . .
> > (From "Thanatopsis.")

It is evident that by thought Poe meant pictorial concepts, ideas that could be depicted as "framed" compositions. The nearer Bryant's poems came to the landscape conventions of the picturesque,[11] the better Poe liked them; but there was one signal difference. As a rule, nature itself was the origin of Bryant's pictures, however he may have "improved" nature for compositional effect. Poe, with his concept of the ideal, preferred imaginary landscapes and shunned the representational. There is a deprecatory tone in his commendation of "The Prairies": "as a local painting, the work is, altogether, excellent. Here are, moreover, evidences of fine imagination." The lines that Poe italicized as imaginative are not at all characteristic of "local painting," however.

> The great heavens
> Seem to *stoop down upon the scene* in love—

> Breezes of the south!
> Who *toss the golden and the flame-like flowers* . . .

[11] For Bryant's poetic use of landscape conventions, see Donald A. Ringe, "Kindred Spirits: Bryant and Cole," *American Quarterly*, VI (1954), 233–44.

There were too many naturalistic details in the poem for Poe's taste, so he chose from it only conceptualized images, "figures of thought." [12]

We may dismiss Poe's hair-splitting discriminations in word choice and versification simply as evidence of his close reading and turn to his concluding evaluation of Bryant as an indication of his standards. Using Coleridge's approach, Poe made an estimate of Bryant's capacities. The poems reviewed gave tokens of an "ardent" appreciation of the beautiful and the ability to perceive and discriminate among the "legitimate items of the beautiful." Something more was needed, however, before Bryant could be placed in the highest rank of poets. This something was range of vision; "the relative extent of these peripheries of poetical vision must ever be a primary consideration in our classification of poets." Poe would not place Bryant with the "spiritual Shelleys, or Coleridges, or Wordsworth, or with Keats, or even Tennyson, or Wilson, or with some other burning lights of our own day, to be valued in a day to come." With this statement, if Wilson (Christopher North) were eliminated, we would have to agree. Poe's judgment is sound, but the judgment does not necessarily validate the criteria used in forming it. The test of poetic vision is appropriate for the use of a disciple of Coleridge, but did Poe equate vision with insight? Apparently not, at least not in the same way Coleridge did.

In *The Statesman's Manual* Coleridge had said that the imagination functioned in "incorporating the reason in images of the

---

[12] Blair's term. "Figures of words" are commonly called tropes and signify words used to mean something other than their strict denotation. A "figure of thought," however, employs words in their literal meaning, and the figure depends upon the concept or the "turn of the thought." *Lectures*, I, 275. A metaphor originates in a concept, an idea of resemblance between two apparently unlike things, and in this respect it is a figure of thought. However, since the actual words of a metaphor are not taken literally, it is a trope, or a figure of words, in its semantic aspect. *Ibid.*, 296. Trying to "idealize" poetry through conceptual images, Poe wanted as nearly as possible to obliterate any *obvious* difference between the literal and metaphorical meanings. The metaphorical meaning must be there, but, as he was to explain in later reviews, it must be submerged as an "undercurrent" of implication, not blatantly advertised as he thought was the case in most figures of speech.

sense." Such an incorporation resulted in symbols which suggested correspondences between isolated fact and universal significance, but the facts themselves remained as images. Poe, on the other hand, demanding conceptual images, found facts very troublesome. In Poe's view opposites were irreconcilable in the context of a poem, and poetic vision was manifested by the presence of pic-torialized ideas which were evocative of feelings that could be gen-erally classified as responses to the beautiful or the sublime in ob-jects or in thought. Poe demanded unity even more emphatically than did Coleridge, but, for all of his use of Schlegel, Poe's unity remained the old unity of impression which was achieved by a care-ful composition of objects or ideas that expressed a single emotion. Since by thought Poe meant a concept, mood, or attitude that could be depicted, it is not surprising that he commended Bryant's sonnet "November" for unity of thought. The poem is almost en-tirely pictorial, and the single thought that "pervades and gives unity to the piece" is the idea that the smile of the November sun enables man to bear the winter frost.

Poe is usually classified as a symbolist, but his review of Bryant reveals that his construction of symbolic meaning was different from that of Coleridge. Poe did not like clusters of symbols in the context of a single poem; instead, the whole poem should symbol-ize or be the expression of an idea, which, as we have seen, might well be a mood or an attitude, or even a suggestive image. The ele-ments of the poem did not have to be meaningful themselves, but they had to contribute to the compositional effect, the pictorializa-tion of the idea. This is why explications of Poe's more pictorial poems, such as "The City in the Sea," are usually unsatisfactory. We have been taught by the Coleridgean organic approach to ex-amine a poem line by line and image by image for a correlated de-velopment of meaning that can eventually be more or less ade-quately presented in a prose paraphrase. There is no more meaning in a pictorial poem than there is in a landscape by Salvator Rosa. The compositional theme is all. Poe's criteria, then, were perfectly valid for the judgment of a certain kind of poem, the kind that he admired and occasionally wrote. By the process of selection, he could find some that met his standards in nearly all of the great English romantics, but, as we shall see his choices revealed in subsequent reviews, relatively few of them are taken today as the most representative poems of the respective authors. Poe's final estimate of an author, then, is generally more acceptable today than are his evaluative procedures. For all of his borrowing from Coleridge, his test remained the test of effect, and in his practical criticism he tended to examine the rhetorical means by which the effect was stimulated. The organic approach, at least as it is used today, tends to eliminate the distinction between tenor and vehicle, the import of a figure and the image by which the import is rendered, but Poe maintained the distinction. He felt himself capable of judging an idea as imaginative even though the symbolic expression of the idea gave little evidence of imaginative power. To Poe a bad poem did not necessarily signify an absence of imagination in the author; it might well indicate a lack of skill that could be demonstrated by rhetorical analysis. This approach was both Poe's weakness and his strength. The weakness stemmed from his employment of rules that prescribed an elevated poetic diction; the strength was manifested by close analysis that offset the tendency, current in his time, to resort to vaporous "appreciations" of the beauties and sublimities of a work of art. The Coleridgean test, as Poe understood it, would have led him only to an evaluation of the ideas of a poet. A book reviewer, however, had to demonstrate the validity of his judgments if his criticism was to be taken as something other than mere opinion. Accordingly, Poe had to appropriate or invent rules for the detection of imaginative power which could be more easily understood than Coleridge's perplexing statement that the imagination was revealed by "the balance or reconciliation of opposites or discordant qualities," a test alien to Poe's concept of unity of impression.

One of his first attempts to devise a test for imaginative expression is evident in his review of Bryant. To Poe, opposites could be reconciled in idea alone. The phenomenal separateness of things was always apparent in expression, particularly in the figures of comparison, the metaphor and the simile. However, if one object were described entirely in terms of another—Bryant's maiden as a forest—then separateness would be disguised and unity of impression would be achieved. Such imaginative identification was present in Bryant's "original conception," Poe claimed, but the poet was not completely successful in expressing his idea. Poe was to continue to wrestle with the problem of devising rules by which he could judge imaginative power in a poem, but he was able to do so to his satisfaction only by eventually dispensing with Coleridge. Four years after his review of Bryant, Poe refuted Coleridge's definition of the imagination on the basis of an interpretation that diverts our attention from his real problem—the enormous difficulty, as it seemed, of reconciling opposites in a composition that was to convey a unified impression.

Poe's review of Bryant was the last important one he wrote as editor of the *Messenger,* and it was to be three years before he had an opportunity to evaluate by his newly achieved standards in the context of a review. In the meantime he had to support himself as well as he could by free-lance writing. Since there were no other opportunities for an editorial position in Richmond, he left in February of 1837 for New York, then as now the publishing center of the nation. On the face of it, his prospects should have been good, for his name was known throughout the East, and he had even received commendation from some of the New York journals. Yet he had made formidable enemies with his reviews of Theodore Fay and Colonel William L. Stone. Whether these enemies were influential enough to shut editorial doors against him is hard to say,[13] but he did not find work. Probably the panic of 1837 had something to do with his lack of success. Most of the journals had precarious financial backing and ofen failed when money was tight. Poe had had some hope of being employed on a religious quarterly, the New York *Review,* but he wrote only one review for the journal, a nonliterary critique of a travel book.

Besides this review Poe published little in 1837, only the tales "Von Jung, the Mystic" in the *American Monthly Magazine* and "Siope—A Fable" in a gift book. Two installments of *The Narra-*

[13] For a discussion of this possibility, see Moss, *Poe's Literary Battles,* 61.

tive of Arthur Gordon Pym had been printed in the January and February numbers of the *Messenger*, but White, financially hard pressed and still full of hostility toward Poe,[14] had refused to publish the remainder of the novel. Poe's income was meager. Mrs. Clemm, his mother-in-law, was taking in boarders, and from one of them, William Gowans, we learn that Poe was working very hard to complete *Pym*.[15] But unpublished manuscripts bring in no cash, and finally Poe was forced to leave New York. In the summer of 1838 he took his family to Philadelphia, probably hoping that the City of Brotherly Love would prove more hospitable than Manhattan.

[14] On January 31, White wrote to Beverley Tucker, "I am as sick of his writings, as I am of him . . . and am rather more than half inclined to send him up another dozen dollars in the morning, and along with it all his unpublished manuscripts." Hull, "A Canon," 173.

[15] Quinn, *Edgar Allan Poe*, 267.

IX · *Interlude with Billy Burton*
The Artistic Conscience

POE had reason to hope that things might be better in Philadelphia than in New York. His first tales had been printed in the Philadelphia *Saturday Courier,* and nearly ten years earlier he had gone there to meet Robert Walsh, then editor of the *American Quarterly Review.* Back in 1829 Poe had taken his poem "Al Aaraaf" to William Wirt, a Virginia writer and orator. Wirt could not understand the poem and advised Poe to go to see Robert Walsh, one of the best-known critics in the country at that time. Poe had craftily dropped Walsh's name in a letter to Isaac Lea,[1] of Carey, Lea, and Carey, and apparently it had carried enough weight to make the publisher read Poe's manuscript, *Al Aaraaf and Other Poems,* although he had refused to publish it without a guarantee.

Perhaps in Poe's mind Philadelphia was a city that was not hostile to unbiased criticism. Robert Walsh had not written the milk-and-water critiques favored by White and Heath on the *Messenger,* and he had often aroused the ire of sensitive authors, including William Wirt, for his forthright reviews. In fact Walsh was something of an analytic critic, which was rare in America, and Poe had praised him in 1836 as one of the "finest writers," "most accomplished scholars," and "most accurate thinkers" in the country.[2] So to the city of Robert Walsh came Edgar Poe, but the *American Quarterly Review* had been defunct for a year, and its editor, in search of health, had taken up permanent residence in Paris. There were other journals, of course, but none of them immediately made an editorial chair vacant for the former hatchet man of the *Messenger.*

Even Philadelphia was not completely free of enemies. Willis Gaylord Clark, who had attacked Poe in his Philadelphia *Gazette,*

[1] Before May 27, 1829, in *Letters,* I, 18–19.
[2] Review of Walsh's *Didactics,* in *Works,* VIII, 321.

was still alive, although he was to die in 1841, and it was his twin brother, Lewis Gaylord Clark of the New York *Knickerbocker*, who began harassing Poe in 1838. Whether Morris Mattson, the gentleman from Philadelphia whose *Paul Ulric* Poe had destroyed in a *Messenger* review, was able to cause difficulties, we do not know; but Poe's reputation had preceded him, and the Philadelphia magazines were cautious.

The first opportunity for publication came not from Philadelphia but from a new Baltimore journal edited by Nathan C. Brooks and Joseph Evans Snodgrass. Dr. Snodgrass thought well of Poe and gave him assistance in later years. It was in Snodgrass' magazine, *The American Museum*, that Poe published "Ligeia" in September, 1838. Poe considered this his finest tale, and in it he concentrated all that he had developed as the principles of the short story. Like Bird's *Sheppard Lee*, the novel that Poe had reviewed in 1836, "Ligeia" was based upon metempsychosis; but, following his dictum in the review, Poe preserved the identity of his heroine through the change of bodies. Rowena's body as well as her spirit becomes that of Ligeia. Nor did Poe use the common device of explaining the supernatural event as a dream or hallucination. The theme of the tale is personal victory over death through the instrumentality of a powerful will, a will subservient to neither disease nor mortality. Chiaroscuro, the quality Poe had found so attractive in *Peter Snook*, is also a characteristic of his own tale. It has "that blending of light and shadow where nothing is too distinct, yet where the idea is fully conveyed." Meaning is conveyed indirectly, either through symbols or through suggestive description. Thus the narrator of the tale, instead of naming the strange feeling he experiences when looking into Ligeia's eyes, uses analogies to convey his import, mentioning other objects that arouse the same feeling—a rapidly growing vine, a moth, a butterfly, a chrysalis, a stream of running water, the ocean, the falling of a meteor, glances of unusually aged people, and a changeable double star in the constellation of Lyra. Though Poe's analogies may not be rigidly confined to a single interpretation, they have one aspect in common, the preservation of identity through apparent physical change. The changeful ocean is still the same body of water; the chrysalis, becoming a butterfly, is still the same insect. Only the falling meteor does not seem to be appropriate to the theme, because it is destroyed in the process of becoming visible. Most of Poe's correspondences are apt, however; and, suggesting the ancient belief that the eyes are the window of the soul, Poe made the expression of Ligeia's eyes illuminate the theme of his story.

We have already seen that Poe considered the short story as a painting—an arrangement of details in space to convey an idea. The effects of this concept are illustrated by "Ligeia." There is little temporal movement in the story action. Time passes, but events are summarized rather than given in detail. Only two events are brought into the foreground, the death of Ligeia and the subsequent death of Rowena and her resurrection as Ligeia. The tale is heavy with description focusing upon the appearance of Ligeia and the furnishings of the chamber to which the narrator brings his second wife, "the fair-haired and blue-eyed Lady Rowena Trevanion." No other details are given of Rowena's appearance, since Poe needed only to distinguish her from Ligeia.

The home to which the narrator brings Rowena is a bedlam of decorative styles, particularly in the bridal chamber. Poe, whose interest in such matters was fairly keen, always prescribed absolute harmony or "keeping" in interior decoration, but in this bridal chamber "there was no system, no keeping, in the fantastic display, to take hold on the memory." In his detailed inventory of house and chamber Poe was suggesting two things: first, that the narrator did not *want* to remember, and second, that he was mad. In both "Usher" and "Ligeia" the qualities of the houses are identified with those of the owners, so the grotesquerie of the bridal chamber signifies a disordered mind. The ceiling is ornamented by medieval carvings. It is luridly lighted by a "Saracenic" censer that supplies a "continual succession of parti-colored fires." The chamber itself is rude—early Gothic—whereas its furnishings are Byzantine. To complete the confusion of styles, in each corner of the room stands a gigantic Egyptian sarcophagus of black granite, suggesting the preservation of the body against the ruin of time. However, the most significant feature of the room is the draperies, which are "spotted all over, at irregular intervals, with arabesque figures." These figures are arabesque from only one point of view. From other vantage points they are changeable, implying the theme already introduced in the expression of Ligeia's eyes. Upon entering the room, the visitor sees in the draperies only "simple monstrosities," but upon closer examination he finds himself "surrounded by an endless succession of the ghastly forms which belong to the superstition of the Norman, or arise in the guilty slumbers of the monk."

The Gothic decor of this tale functions as more than an atmosphere in which something terrible happens. It suggests not only the madness of the narrator, but also medieval superstition, Egyptian mysteries, and esoteric learning devoted to the service of evil. These Gothic trappings are conventional, but they are not used simply to explain what happens. They suggest a Faustian theme of the evil associated with the human will in its aspiration to surpass the limits of mortality. The story is heavy with the sense of guilt and evil. The narrator loathes his new bride and feels that the hours they spend together are "unhallowed," but even more unhallowed is the narrator's morbid brooding on his dead wife. The suggestions of black magic and mysterious ritual imply that the narrator would be quite willing to use such means to repossess Ligeia; and it is through his active psychic cooperation that Ligeia accomplishes her purpose. Rowena's illness is caused by the ghastly surroundings of the bridal chamber and the undisguised loathing of her husband.

Though the story is marred by Poe's overt use of magic (ruby-colored drops that fall into the glass of wine Rowena drinks) to bring about the possession of Rowena by Ligeia, it is a tale of psychological horror with the Gothic trappings used to give us an insight into the narrator's mind rather than a simple Gothic tale designed to create the effect of terror with ghosts and witchcraft. The moral implication is that Ligeia's idolatry of the narrator, her will to live, and the narrator's neurotic obsession with her are essentially evil passions, and what they accomplish is murder. It is appropriate that the story should end not with a cry of joy at the recovery of the dead wife but with a shriek, as the grave wrappings of Rowena fall away and the narrator sees the wild, black eyes of the ghastly revenant, Ligeia.[3]

[3] I have not attempted a full explication of "Ligeia" since this reading is intended to serve only as an example of Poe's application of his theories. Essentially, my interpretation agrees with that of Roy P. Basler except for one point. Mr. Basler has argued convincingly that the drops of red liquid which fall into Rowena's goblet of wine are actual poison, administered by her psychotic husband. Not having read Mr. Basler's essay in advance, and interpreting Poe's tale only in the light of the reviews he had written up to this point, I have considered this seemingly supernatural event as a failure of technique caused by the necessity of bringing the tale to a rapid conclusion. This interpretation is supported by Poe's exchange of letters with Philip Pendleton Cooke, which Mr. Basler cited but discounted. Poe acknowledged what Cooke called a "violation of the ghostly proprieties" and agreed with Cooke that the possession of Rowena's body should have been a gradual and intermittent affair, not completely successful. See Cooke to Poe, in Works, XVII, 49–51; and Poe's reply, in Letters, I, 117–19.

In the light of Poe's theory, he would be endeavoring to make the supernatural credible by letting the narrator doubt the reality of the event and attribute it to imagination stimulated by opium. This was a conventional gambit, and Mr. Basler's argument that Poe's conclusion is perfect as a "revelation of obsessional psychology" makes Poe a better artist than he himself realized. See Basler, "Poe's Ligeia," Sex, Symbol, and Psychology in Literature (New Brunswick, 1948), 143–59.

Whatever may be valid in the interpretation of this particular event, Mr. Basler's reading of the tale is close to Poe's concept of the proper use of terror in fiction, whereas Richard Wilbur's recent symbolic interpretation is not. Mr. Wilbur has interpreted Ligeia herself as a personification of the sentiment of beauty, which, when lost, must be regained at all costs. The grotesque bridal chamber is seen, not as a revelation of insanity, but as a "dream room" which scorns the proprieties of interior decoration. To accept this view, one must ignore Poe's "The Philosophy of Furniture" and "Landor's Cottage," in which he actually described "dream rooms" decorated in a florid but not outlandish taste. To accept Mr. Wilbur's interpretation in general, one must also ignore the tone of Poe's denouement. The narrator greets his resurrected Ligeia, his lost sentiment of beauty, with a shriek of terror instead of with the joy that should attend the "reunion of a divided soul." Poe demanded a unity of tone in his tales, and usually achieved it. This is not to argue that Mr. Wilbur's interpretation is necessarily invalid. If his reading is accepted, however, it indicates that Poe was far more of an unconscious artist than a conscious one and that his obsessional devotion to "poetic sentiment" furnished the symbolic import of what the author himself thought of as a tale of psychological terror. It

Poe's art in what he called the "arabesque tale," which may as well have been called the picturesque tale, since it represents a design in space rather than a dramatized action, reached maturity in "Ligeia" and "The Fall of the House of Usher"; but he had not yet managed to present his theory of short fiction fully in his reviews, probably because there was little opportunity to review short stories for the journals. He did have a chance to criticize the writings of Washington Irving for the *Museum*, but he declined on the grounds that he could not do the review on short notice since he had read nothing of Irving's since he was a boy.[4] This is not quite the truth, for he had reviewed *The Crayon Miscellany* and *Astoria* for the *Messenger*; but we may suppose that he excused himself because he would not have had time to do justice to a collected edition of a famous author, which was true.

Poe contributed two other short tales to the *Museum*, both of which were published in November; but his poverty must have been extreme, in spite of his claim to Nathan Brooks that he had "gotten nearly out of . . . late embarrassments."[5] He received only ten dollars for" Ligeia," and *The Narrative of Arthur Gordon Pym*, which had been published by Harper's in July, was not selling well. So during the winter of 1838–39 Poe did some hackwork, *The Conchologist's First Book: or, A System of Testaceous Malacology Arranged Expressly for the Use of Schools*. The textbook was a job of wholesale cribbing, agreed to by the publisher, with Poe listed as the editor simply because he was well known. When a charge of plagiarism was brought against Poe, he defended

---

would also indicate that Poe's technique, as consciously developed, was slipshod indeed. The psychotic condition of the narrator is stressed in the tale, not only by direct statement but also by his taste. To Poe, the taste of the *sane* artist was characterized by its recognition of harmony and beauty, and if Ligeia is indeed the sentiment of beauty, the tale is a prose rendition of the theme of "The Haunted Palace," in which the supervention of insanity changes the beautiful to the grotesque. This is a defensible interpretation, but it makes Poe's conclusion faulty. See Richard Wilbur, "Edgar Allan Poe," in Perry Miller (ed.), *Major Writers of America* (New York, 1962), I, 374–79.

[4] Poe to Nathan C. Brooks, September 4, 1838, in *Letters*, I, 111–12.
[5] *Ibid.*

himself by saying that all textbooks were done that way. This slave labor perhaps kept him from starving during the winter, and by May of 1839 he was negotiating with William E. Burton, an actor turned publisher who had just acquired a magazine.[6]

2

Billy Burton, a transplanted Englishman, had been successful as an actor in England before he came to America, where he made his first stage appearance in Philadelphia in 1834, as Dr. Ollapod in *The Poor Gentleman.*[7] A popular comedian, he was also a good stage manager and leased theaters in Philadelphia, in Baltimore, and finally in New York, where in 1848 he leased Palmo's Opera House, a theater Poe attended several times in 1845. Burton renamed it Burton's Theater, and under his management it became one of the most successful theaters in America. Although the theater was Burton's profession, he tried his hand at journalism, for pleasure and profit. In 1837 he founded the *Gentleman's Magazine*, which was designed to appeal to men-about-town. It focused upon sports, art, literature, and the theater. Poe was to write for it an article entitled "A Chapter on Field Sports and Manly Pastimes." Other articles were written by Burton himself, and he also prepared a miscellaneous column "consisting of unconnected paragraphs on morals, wines, conversation, manners, food." [8]

It would have been easy to predict that Poe, who was ambitious to found a superior literary journal, would be contemptuous of the *Gentleman's Magazine* and its editor. Poe was dedicated to journalism as a literary profession, whereas for Burton it was an avoca-

[6] According to Ostrom's check list (*Letters*, II, 577), Poe first wrote Burton between May 1 and May 10, 1839. Burton replied on May 11, making Poe an offer. See *Works*, XVII, 45–46. Poe wrote again between May 11 and May 30, and Burton answered on May 30.

[7] Poe evidently knew of this comic role, for he had cited the "graceful sermonic harangues of Dr. Ollapod" in his burlesque of a *Blackwood's* article, "A Predicament," published in the *American Museum* in November, 1838.

[8] Mott, *A History of American Magazines*, 674.

tion. Still Billy Burton was not as vulgar as Poe sought to make him out a year or so later.[9] At the time of his death in 1860, Burton's personal library was one of the largest in New York, and he had a fine collection of paintings in his home. In addition to his magazine writings and two plays, he published two collections of humor, one in 1848 and one in 1857.[10] Lacking the intense concern with literature that Poe demanded, however, Burton would inevitably clash with his assistant editor, who felt a continuous frustration at being unable to publish in the *Gentleman's Magazine* the kind of articles he wished to write.[11]

Poe met Burton early in 1839 and solicited a position on the staff of the magazine. Poe's proposal was rejected, but on May 11 Burton made a counterproposal, offering Poe ten dollars a week for the remainder of the year and stating that Poe's own proposition would be in effect for 1840 if mutual satisfaction were achieved. Two hours a day, Burton estimated, would be sufficient for Poe's editorial duties, plus any time he wished to spend on his own writing. It was Burton's presumption that Poe would not use his surplus time working for any of Burton's competitors. Poe did not accept this offer immediately but made another proposal which Burton answered on May 30. Unfortunately Poe's letter to Burton has been lost,[12] but Burton's reply reveals that Poe's temperament and his severe reviews were already known to the editor and that friction between the two began before Poe was actually employed. Burton's letter must be quoted in full because it shows the difficulties that Poe faced in accommodating himself to journalistic necessities.

> My dear Sir,
>   I am sorry that you thought necessary to send me such a letter as your last. The troubles of the world have given a morbid tone to

[9] In an angry letter to Joseph Evans Snodgrass, dated April 1, 1841, Poe called Burton a "buffoon and a felon." *Letters*, I, 155.

[10] *Dictionary of National Biography*, VIII, 20–21.

[11] Poe made this complaint in a letter to Burton, June 1, 1840. See *Letters*, I, 131–32.

[12] See *Letters*, II, 577.

your feelings which it is your duty to discourage. I cannot agree to entertain your proposition, either in justice to yourself or to my own interests. The worldly experience of which you speak has not taught me to conciliate authors of whom I know nothing and from whom I can expect nothing. Such a supposition is but a poor comment upon my honesty of opinion, or the principles of expediency which you would insinuate as actuating my conduct. I have been as severely handled in the world as you can possibly have been, but my sufferings have not tinged my mind with a melancholy hue, nor do I allow my views of my fellow creatures to be jaundiced by the fogs of my own creation. You must rouse your energies, and conquer the insidious attacks of the foul fiend, care. We shall agree very well, but you must get rid of your avowed ill-feelings towards your brother authors—you see that I speak plainly—indeed, I cannot speak otherwise. Several of my friends, hearing of our connexion, have warned me of your uncalled for severity in criticism—and I confess that your article on Dawes is not written with that spirit of fairness which, in a more healthy state of mind, you would undoubtedly have used. The independence of my book reviews has been noticed throughout the Union—my remarks on my friend Bird's last novel evince my freedom from the trammels of expediency, but there is no necessity for undue severity. I wish particularly to deal leniently with the faults of genius, and feeling satisfied that Dawes possesses a portion of the true fire, I regretted the word-catching tone of your critique.

Let us meet as if we had not exchanged letters. Use more exercise, write only when the feelings prompt, and be assured of my friendship. You will soon regain a wholesome activity of mind, and laugh at your past vagaries.[13]

From this letter it appears that Poe's reputation for "uncalled for severity" had indeed preceded him to Philadelphia. Burton was acute enough or kind enough to attribute the tone of Poe's letter to a state of depression and was willing to overlook Poe's imputations of critical expediency. It is evident that in the lost letter Poe was bitterly resentful of the attacks against him and that he thought that Burton himself was guilty of "puffing" his friends because he

[13] In Quinn, *Edgar Allan Poe*, 279–82.

had not liked Poe's review of Rufus Dawes. Although a brief review of Dawes's *Nix's Mate* was published in the December issue of the *Gentleman's Magazine*, it could not have been the one referred to in Burton's letter, because by any standard it was neither severe nor "word-catching." Probably it was not written by Poe.

The first review that Poe did for Burton appeared in the June, 1839, issue of the *Gentleman's Magazine*.[14] It was of Captain Marryat's *The Phantom Ship*, an adventure story evidently intended for young readers. Poe had no sympathy for limited aims, however, and condemned the novel without reservation. It displayed "a miserable mental inanity, a positive baldness of thought, an utter absence of all lofty imagination, an *inconsequence* of narration, and a feeble childishness of manner which would be unpardonable in any school boy of decent pretensions." The style was flat and exhibited a "deficiency of education."

Obviously Burton, as he had claimed, was not unduly disturbed by severity, or this review would not have been printed. As a matter of fact, some of the reviews in the *Gentleman's Magazine*, even before Poe was connected with it, were as abusive as anything Poe ever did. In the April number a critique of a book by Samuel F. Glenn, *Criticism: Its Use and Abuse*, outdid even Poe's review of *Norman Leslie* for sheer scurrility of attack. Burton's own review of *The Adventures of Robin Day*, by Robert Montgomery Bird, was a wholesale condemnation of the book, even though Bird was a Philadelphia physician and a personal friend.

Thus Burton was not guilty of "puffing" his friends, and he had no objection to severity in a review when the accepted general standards were applied. Poe, however, was prone to make detailed analyses of figures of speech and grammatical constructions, or he might devote an entire page to comment on a florid dedication or a misleading title. It was this concentration on minor details that was responsible for Burton's opinion that Poe's reviews were "word-catching."

[14] *Burton's Gentleman's Magazine*, IV, 359. This journal had a variable title during the three and a half years of its existence, but will here be referred to as *Burton's Gentleman's Magazine*.

It is clear that Poe's method, rather than his severity, was responsible for Burton's objections. In turn, it appears that Poe's criticism of the reviews in the *Gentleman's Magazine*—Burton's letter implies such criticism—would have been that they were mere "puffs," or uncritical praise of the publisher's friends. Poe could have criticized them for other reasons. They were impressionistic, padded with quotations and abstracts, and they levied praise or blame without analysis. Furthermore, Burton treated with condescension "the metaphysical subtleties and abstruse niceties of the German schools," and admired the "chaste and classical" style in poetry. He even advocated a "return to those purer models in the most elegant and difficult of the fine arts," while he castigated "that school whose characteristic is a morbid and turbulent excitement," [15] the romantic "school" that Poe liked.

Burton's taste was that of Heath and White. Once more Poe had to submit to the supervision of a publisher who abjured the extremes of romantic expression but who had acquired enough of the romantic attitude toward criticism to dislike close analysis. Burton, like the young Poe in 1831, thought that analysis was "deliberately pulling to pieces a beautiful moss rose in order to point out its botanical characteristics." [16] Yet in spite of the mutual misgivings of publisher and prospective employee, the July, 1839, number of the *Gentleman's Magazine* listed the name of Edgar Poe as editor, and he wrote all of the reviews for that issue.

As he admitted to Philip Pendleton Cooke, however, most of these reviews were merely paragraphs.[17] Only one, of Fenimore

---

[15] Review of *Stanley, or The Recollections of a Man of the World*, in *Burton's Gentleman's Magazine*, IV, 65; and review of *Indecision, A Tale of the Far West, and Other Poems*, ibid., 353. The poem Burton admired was in heroic couplets!

[16] *Ibid.*, 354.

[17] In the same letter in which he had discussed "Ligeia," Poe told Cooke "Do not think of subscribing [to the *Gentleman's Magazine*]. The criticisms are not worth your notice. Of course I pay no attention to them—for there are two of us. It is not pleasant to be taxed with the twaddle of other people, or to let other people be taxed with ours. Therefore for the present I remain upon my oars—merely penning an occasional paragraph, without care. The critiques, such as they are, are all mine in the July num-

Cooper's *History of the Navy*, requires comment. Poe had reviewed Cooper somewhat favorably in 1836 [18] and had applauded the New Yorker's criticism of the "bull-headed and prejudiced" American public, but in the *Gentleman's Magazine* review he echoed the hostility of the press toward the irritable novelist, saying that even Cooper's friends were "ashamed of the universality of his cynicism." In addition, Poe claimed, "a flashy succession of ill-conceived and miserably executed literary productions, each more silly than its predecessor, and wherein the only thing noticeable was the peevishness of the writer, the only amusing thing his self-conceit—had taught the public to suspect even a radical taint in the intellect, an absolute irreparable mental leprosy, rendering it a question whether he ever would or could again accomplish anything which should be worthy of the attention of people not positively rabid." [19]

Whether Poe's attitude had been changed by the publication in 1838 of Cooper's *Homeward Bound* and *Home as Found,* two novels of social criticism, or whether he was simply copying Burton's harsh line with Cooper, is not certain. In January, Burton had reviewed *Home as Found* in savage terms: "Considered as a novel it is flat, stale, and miserably dull; as a literary composition it is puerile and commonplace; as a national disquisition it is marked with undeniable stains of prejudice and ill-temper." [20] Burton went on to suggest, as Poe did, that Cooper might be mentally ill.

Ordinarily Poe did not feel bound by the editorial policy of the magazine on which he worked. He certainly had not with the *Messenger.* Why in this case he should have echoed Burton is difficult to understand. If Cooper's opinions about America were the reason for Poe's attack, it is not apparent in the review. The condescending moral tone does not even sound like Poe, and without his letter to Cooke claiming all of the reviews of the July issue we

---

ber and all mine in the August and September with the exception of the three first in each—which are by Burton." *Letters*, I, 118–19.

[18] Review of Cooper's *Sketches of Switzerland*, in *Works*, IX, 163.

[19] *Burton's Gentleman's Magazine*, V (July–December, 1839), 56.

[20] *Burton's Gentleman's Magazine*, IV, 66.

would have grounds for attributing the review to someone else. Perhaps it was only part of the "twaddle" he described in his letter to Cooke as characterizing the reviews of the *Gentleman's Magazine*, or perhaps he was only trying to win the good graces of Burton.

Poe also wrote all of the criticism for the August number, but it was not much more impressive than that for July. He did manage a fairly long review of *Tortesa, the Usurer*, a play by Nathaniel Parker Willis.[21] In August of 1836 Poe had handled Willis' *Inklings of Adventure* severely in the *Messenger*, but he was able to find certain merits in the play: "These merits are naturalness, truthfulness, and appropriateness, upon all occasions, of sentiment and language; a manly vigour and breadth in the conception of character; and a fine ideal elevation or exaggeration throughout—a matter forgotten or avoided by those who, with true Flemish perception of truth, wish to copy her peculiarities in disarray. Mr. Willis has not lost sight of the important consideration that the perfection of dramatic, as of plastic skill, is found not in the imitation of Nature, but in the artistical adjustment and amplification of her features."

In this, Poe's first review of the drama, there is nothing distinctive. The merits he praised would have been recognized by the critics of the eighteenth century, and, in contrast to the opinion he was to express in 1845, he saw the drama as an imitative art only in its imitation of the ideal. The truth of the drama did not consist in copying nature's peculiarities but in the elevation of character, event, and language in the direction of what we may presume to be the rational ideal, at the same time preserving the probabilities. The Flemish painting which he had praised in his *Messenger* reviews in reference to the short tale he now disparaged; and his standards would have appeared familiar to Joseph Addison or to Dr. Johnson.

Poe's conception of the plot of drama was Aristotelian, and he found Willis' play defective because of incidents that were not connected with the main action:

[21] *Works*, X, 27–30.

The plot is miserably inconsequential. A simple prose digest, or compendium, of the narrative, would be scarcely intelligible, so much is the whole overloaded with incidents that have no bearing upon the ultimate result. Three-fourths of the play might be blotted out without injury to the plot properly so called. This would be less objectionable, if it were not that the attention of the reader is repeatedly challenged to these irrelevant incidents, as if they were actually pertinent to the main business of the drama. We are not allowed to pass them by, in perusal, as obviously episodical. We fatigue ourselves with an attempt to identify them with the leading interests, and grow at length wearied in the fruitless effort.

All in all, Poe's criticism of Willis' play was perfectly conventional. He applied principles that he could have learned from Dr. Johnson, from Aristotle, or from Hugh Blair's redaction of Aristotle in number forty-five of his famous *Lectures*. That he had as yet developed nothing original in dramatic criticism is scarcely surprising. Critics in America had paid little attention to the drama, and when they did they failed to analyze form and technique.[22] In 1836 Poe had recognized the need in America for dramatic criticism and had stated that it should be rescued "from the hands of illiterate mountebanks" and placed "in the hands of gentlemen and scholars,"[23] but heretofore he had had no opportunity to show what a gentleman and a scholar could do. Apparently a gentleman and a scholar would simply apply the principles he had derived from classical and neoclassical sources. It was admitted by most critics that American drama was inferior and derivative. Willis' play, as Poe pointed out, borrowed liberally from *Romeo and Juliet* and *The Winter's Tale*, but he still considered it the best American play in spite of all its blemishes. Considering the competition, this was not an extravagant claim.

3

Although Poe deprecated his own reviews in the July and August numbers of the *Gentleman's Magazine*, he came up with some-

[22] See Charvat, *American Critical Thought*, 130–31.
[23] Review of Walsh's *Didactics*, in *Works*, VIII, 322.

thing better in September. All of the reviews except the first three are his. Most of them were short notices of ten or fifteen lines, but he was granted enough space for one review of considerable length [24]—of a work that he admired. This was the prose romance *Undine,* by Baron De La Motte Fouqué, a book James E. Heath would have called a mere fairy tale.

In the "Letter to Mr.—— ——" Poe had distinguished the romance from the poem by saying that the former aimed at a definite pleasure instead of the indefinite pleasure of poetry, but the review of *Undine* was the first opportunity he had had to review a pure romance instead of the mixed genre, the historical romance, which combined fiction and fact. Accordingly, if he still retained the early distinction, it would be necessary for him to explain the definite sensations which could be derived from this prose romance, while at the same time he would have to account for its effect upon the imagination, wherein it would resemble poetry. The criteria for the novel or the realistic Dickensian tale, which he had used previously, would not apply to *Undine,* and he was faced with the proposition of having to define its import both as prose and as poetry. As we shall see, this task involved him in obscurities and contradictions, but his general purpose may be discerned.

Poe revealed in the opening sentence of his review that he was engaging in literary polemics instead of simply analyzing *Undine* as a work of fiction: [25] "The republication of such a work . . . in the

[24] *Ibid.,* X, 30–39.

[25] Poe's chief object in this review was to defend the romance against its American detractors. He even sent a copy of the number containing his review to Heath, whom he knew disliked "fairy tales" such as *Undine.* The issue also contained Poe's "The Fall of the House of Usher." Heath reacted in a predictable way. In his letter of acknowledgment to Poe (*Works,* XVII, 47–48) he admitted that "Usher" showed great imagination, but it had no tendency to "improve the heart." Heath did not mention the review of *Undine,* but he may have referred to it obliquely in advising Poe to use his "dissecting knife" vigorously to rid the country of the "silly trash and silly sentimentality" that poisoned the "intellectual food" which literature should provide. Poe's letter of September 5 to Heath has been lost, but apparently he had requested Heath to see if White would not reprint "Usher" in the *Messenger.* Heath replied that White had no space and doubted that his readers had "much relish for tales of the German School."

very teeth of our anti-romantic national character, is an experiment well adapted to excite interest . . . ." It was the duty of lovers of literature, Poe went on, to speak out against the prejudices in America which had kept the romance from receiving full appreciation. Aware that *Undine* had an excellent "foreign reputation," [26] Poe insisted that the tale should be defended against the "evil genius of mere matter-of-fact" that haunted America. Americans were prone to ask questions about the utility of literature, irrelevant queries as far as Poe was concerned; therefore it was his duty to impress "upon the public mind . . . the exalted and extraordinary character" of this romance.

Poe knew quite well the strength of the opposition.[27] Romance dealt with the passions; it created admiration for outlaws and pirates and the manners of the "superstitious" ages. In *Graham's Magazine*, as late as 1851, one writer attacked the "Satanic and sensual school of romance" as being "a compound mass of passionate nonsense, immorality, and irreligion passing under the nickname of popular literature." Knowing that American critics were likely to claim that romance was immoral, Poe based his strategy of defense accordingly. He set out to prove that this particular romance had a utilitarian moral value. In its allegorical meaning, Poe asserted, *Undine* was a sort of treatise on conjugal relations. From internal evidence he deduced that the author had suffered greatly from a bad marriage, from the "interference of relations," and from public quarrels with his wife. Thus in its definite aspect, or its prose import, the fairy tale became a dramatization of the causes of marital unhappiness!

Having appeased the hunt-the-moral critics by asserting that *Un-*

Without Poe, the *Messenger* could maintain its policy of moral improvement.

[26] *Undine* had been published in German in 1811. Poe's review was of a translation by Grenville Mellen. The tale had been praised by Goethe, Heine, and Coleridge, among others.

[27] For a summary of the antiromantic attitude of many American critics, see G. Harrison Orians, "The Rise of Romanticism, 1805–1855," in Harry Hayden Clark (ed.), *Transitions in American Literary History* (Durham, 1953), 171–78.

dine did have moral utility, Poe turned the tables on the opposition by claiming that this, the "allegorical" meaning, was the only radical defect of the romance. If it were to succeed as high art—like poetry—it should not be allegorical, for allegory was the "most indefensible species of writing." The "under-current of meaning" in this case did not "appertain to the higher regions of ideality." Poe then concluded his review by describing the poetic or imaginative aspect of the tale to demonstrate that the pictorialization of moral beauty subserved a purpose infinitely higher than that of mere domestic advice:

> What can be more divine than the character of the soulless Undine?—What more august than her transition into the soul-possessing wife? What can be more intensely beautiful than the whole book? We calmly think—yet cannot help asserting with enthusiasm—that the whole wide range of fictitious literature embraces nothing comparable in loftiness of conception, or in felicity of execution, to those final passages of the volume before us which embody the uplifting of the stone from the fount by the order of Bertalda, the sorrowful and silent readvent of Undine, and the rapturous death of Sir Huldbrand in the embraces of his spiritual wife.

Thus to Poe whatever was spiritual, whatever exalted the soul, was morally formative by its beauty, even though it violated the local ground rules of moral behavior. Such a concept, of course, was patently un-American, though it was as readily derivable from the Scottish Platonistic aesthetic as was the more characteristically American requirement of sententious moral statement or moral action that could be emulated. How, Poe was asking his audience, can a romance such as *Undine* be condemned when it enacts the highest moral ideals—the development of a soul through the power of love, fidelity even when it was not deserved, grief, and finally sincere repentance? This romance, then, depicted the sublimest moral concepts under the aspect of beauty; it failed only when its "allegorical" import lowered it into the category of the patently didactic.

Poe's disparagement of the allegory, distinctive in this review, needs to be noted. The Reverend Hugh Blair had had no objection to such a morally useful form, but he had proclaimed that the meaning should not "be too dark." The moral, Blair had said, was the "unfigured sense or meaning," although the form was only a "continued Metaphor." However simple in form, an allegory was not easy to compose, for "the proper mixture of light and shade, . . . the exact adjustment of all the figurative circumstances with the literal sense, so as neither to lay the meaning too bare and open, nor to cover and wrap it up too much, has ever been found an affair of great nicety; and there are few species of composition in which it is more difficult to write so as to please and command attention, than in Allegories."

It is easy to see why romantic critics, including Poe, objected to the form. The contrived point-by-point equivalence between the objects, characters, and events of the fable and the system of ideas they were intended to illustrate left little room for suggestiveness. If the meaning were left "too dark," the composition failed in purpose; on the other hand, if the meaning were too obvious, it was an unimaginative exposition of ideas inhibited by the metaphorical form. Poe reserved his discussion of the problem of meaning in a poem for a later review, and even then he was unable to solve it satisfactorily. As a romantic poet he could not resort to Blair's requirement of perspicuity as a test for figurative language; and he had learned from Coleridge and Schlegel that the imagination of a poet was somehow revealed by the import of his poems. Poe had to answer the question, How can imaginative import be properly rendered? Figures of speech had to obey the rules; "unfigured meaning" was mere prose. The meaning of a poem, like the feelings it inspired, must be indefinite, yet clear enough to be understood. Poe attempted to answer this question four months later, but in the interim other books raised other questions, and the discussion of meaning had to be delayed until an appropriate occasion arose.

4

The criticism in the October issue of the journal was less interesting than that in September. The notices were brief, and, with one exception, the books reviewed were nonliterary. Poe did take an opportunity to reprove Longfellow for his prose romance *Hyperion*, not because it was a romance but because it was a careless performance. It was a sad fact, Poe admitted, that men of talent were sometimes irresponsible; actually they tended to be "indolent," but this temperamental bent did not relieve them of their duty to the public and to their art:

> A man of true talent who would demur at the great labour requisite for the stern demands of high art—at the unremitting toil and patient elaboration which, when soul-guided, result in the beauty of Unity, Totality, Truth—men, we say, who would demur at such labour, make no scruple of scattering at random a profusion of rich thought in the pages of such farragos as "Hyperion." Here, indeed, there is little trouble—but even that little is most unprofitably lost. To the writers of these things we say—all Ethics lie, and all History lies, or the world shall forget ye and your *works*.[28]

Poe was beginning to assume a more responsible attitude as a literary critic. When he first joined the *Messenger* he could glibly defend his horror stories by claiming that people would read them and that they would make the magazine successful. And he could defend his satirical reviews by citing the example of *Blackwood's*. Now, however, he assumed that it was the duty of the critic to educate the public taste and to refuse to tolerate mediocrity or self-serving. Therefore he claimed that works like *Hyperion* were the "grief of all true criticism," for they undermined the popular "faith in Art," which needed the support of all men of letters.

Of equal interest is Poe's argument that "genius" must submit to the necessity of "unremitting toil and patient elaboration." Though he was to object to the kind of criticism that validated a work of art by the sustained effort it manifested, as if the value could be estimated by the pound, he was consistent in his concept of the duty of the artist.

Coleridge had qualified the concept of purely inspirational composition with his description of the secondary imagination, which coexisted with the conscious will and the judgment; but others

[28] *Works*, X, 40.

considered genius in the light of Shelley's skylark, who sang in "profuse strains of *unpremeditated* art." Poe had seen examples enough of unpremeditated art submitted to the *Messenger*, and perhaps for this reason he concluded that no artist, however talented, could produce a *work* of art without "unremitting toil and patient elaboration." A year later he was to explain that a work of genius would appear to have been composed without effort, but he was fairly consistent in demanding that innate ability be controlled by the artistic conscience. In the South of Poe's youth some essayists, like William Wirt and Francis Walker Gilmer, had considered the development of compositional skills as a public duty, invoking the Ciceronian ideal of character plus art; but these essayists were concerned with oratory. It remained for Poe to transfer the ideal to literary composition.[29] It was the ethical duty of the writer, he maintained, to pledge himself to the highest standards and to refuse to betray his public trust by "scattering . . . rich thought" in a formless book.

Those writers who committed themselves to the idea that message was all—that the poem would find its own shape to express the intuitive insight of the poet—were less likely to recognize the obligation to maintain artistic standards. To Emerson, for all of his ethical concern, artistic craft was not a duty because the form was given, not made. Whitman, of course, exploited this attitude to the limit. He pretended to be one of the "roughs," an uneducated bard uttering his "joyous leaves" as naturally as a tree; and only the scholarship of later years has revealed that Whitman projected a spurious image. In contrast to the romantic emphasis on inspiration, Poe's attitude was distinctly Horatian. A poem or a novel was a *made* thing, not simply something *given*. Burton's notion that the faults of genius must be forgiven earned Poe's contempt.

Correlated with the concept of natural genius in romantic criticism was the value of originality. Originality was one of the tests of inspiration. What was inspired could not have been imitated from someone else, so a high premium was placed upon originality as the

[29] On this point see Herbert M. McLuhan, "Edgar Poe's Tradition," *Sewanee Review*, LII (1944), 24–33.

hallmark of genius. Poe, too, saw value in originality but, as one might expect from his demand that a genius observe high artistic standards, his definition of originality placed the burden upon the artist's knowledge, skill, and ethical standards rather than upon his inspiration. Eventually Poe was to claim that true originality was not a matter of "impulse or inspiration" as was commonly supposed. Instead, it was "carefully, patiently, and understandingly to combine." [30] This remark, buried in a discussion of journalistic practices, is a key to the attitude Poe frequently displayed in his reviews. Since originality was not *necessarily* an innate quality of the mind, since it could be achieved by patient skill, the artist who tamely imitated someone else was guilty of self-indulgence or laziness and shirked "the stern demands of high art." This, to Poe, was unforgivable and merited the reproof of the critic.

In November, Poe brought up this failure of duty in a review of a novel by William Gilmore Simms.[31] In 1836 he had reviewed Simms's *The Partisan* quite unfairly. Now he was more nearly prepared to acknowledge Simms's achievement. His first novel, *Martin Faber*, deserved a permanent success, Poe thought. However, the novel at hand, *The Damsel of Darien*, suffered from imitativeness. Every sentence reminded Poe of something he had read before. The chapter headings were "Bulwerized," and the characters were reminiscent of Scott. Although the defects of the novel "were few and seldom radical," Poe could not bring himself to praise an author who let other authors supply his ideas. Poe had his own views of how to achieve originality in characterization, and he had expressed them in his review of *George Balcombe* two years earlier. A writer of fiction could create original characters by the presentation of "qualities known in real life but never before depicted," but this was very nearly impossible. More practicable would be the presentation of hypothetical qualities which were "so skilfully adapted

[30] This remark appears in Poe's revision of his review of *Peter Snook* for the *Broadway Journal*. See *Works*, XIV, 73. He had implied much the same thing, however, when in the review of Drake and Halleck he argued that even without a high degree of imagination, a poet could create the proper effect by using psychology.

[31] *Ibid.*, X, 49–56.

to the circumstances which surround them, that our sense of fitness is not offended . . . ." Thus, in Poe's opinion, a novelist *could* develop original characters, and it was his duty to do so.

The remainder of Poe's review is conventional. He found Simms guilty of grossness of language and applied the rules of rhetoric accordingly. Like Blair, Poe objected to images "which repel and disgust," such as, " 'The Sabueso has no keener scent for his victim, and loves not better to snuff up the thick blood with his nostrils,' " or, " 'I will advance to the short banyan that stands within the path, and my dagger shall pick his teeth, ere he gets round it.' "

Simms was also guilty of bad taste in a more strictly literary sense. Poe quoted a passage in which the novelist professed to find something "true and poetical" in lips painted upon partly opened oysters, as if the pearls inside were teeth. "Now we can have no doubt in the world that the artist was a clever fellow in his way," Poe wrote, "but it is really difficult to conceive what kind of *poetical beauty* that can be which Mr. Simms is so happy as to discover in the countenance of a gaping oyster." On this jocular note Simms was disposed of again, and he could hardly have derived much more satisfaction from this review than he had from Poe's previous notice of *The Partisan*.

5

In spite of the fact that the *Gentleman's Magazine* was by no means a literary journal, Poe managed to introduce some of his theories into his reviews. Each issue during the fall and winter of 1839 contained at least one fairly lengthy review in addition to the customary short notices. In December, among a dozen or so brief reviews, was an analysis of the song poem as genre, [32] occasioned by George P. Morris' *National Melodies of America*. Morris, who is remembered today, if at all, only as the author of the sentimental appeal "Woodman, Spare That Tree," was in Poe's opinion America's best writer of songs. This meant that he ranked high as a poet.

[32] *Ibid.*, 41–45.

Yet in Poe's review Morris' poems were scarcely mentioned. Poe used the review to explore the relatedness of music and poetry, a topic on which he had strong opinions. He had not really had an occasion to go into the matter since his republication of the "Letter to Mr.—— ——" in the *Southern Literary Messenger,* and now he made the most of his opportunity.

Songs, Poe asserted, should be examined by different criteria from those used for ordinary poetry. The conceits that Dr. Johnson had found objectionable in poetry and that were still condemned by most critics, including Poe, were at home in the song: "These views properly understood, it will be seen how baseless are the ordinary objections to songs proper, on the score of 'conceit' (to use Johnson's word), or of hyperbole, or on various other grounds tenable enough in respect to poetry not designed for music." The emotional pleasure derived from music, Poe claimed, was "nearly in the ratio of its indefinitiveness." This much he had said in 1831, but now he explained more fully: "Give to music any undue *decision*—imbue it with any very *determinate* tone—and you deprive it, at once, of its ethereal, its ideal, and, I sincerely believe, of its intrinsic and essential character." Again we are confronted with a problem of jargon. In the "Letter to Mr.—— ——" Poe had denied *ideas* to music; here he claimed that the *ideal* was characteristic of music. We must remember, before we can make sense of his statement, that he had acquired the idiom of phrenology, and that the "ideal" was now a sentiment, or an idea of emotion, properly expressed even by instrumental music. That he was thinking of instrumental music is indicated by his illustration, "The Battle of Prague," in which imitations of battle noises were provided. Such imitation, Poe argued, deprived music of its true character and eliminated its proper effect. Music had no reference to objects and events in the external world.[33]

Music was, or should be, purely expressive. Consequently a song, even though in words, would be as close as language could come to

[33] See Chapter II of this book for a discussion of the background of this idea in British aesthetics.

the nonreferential quality of music. A songwriter would be relieved of the rhetorical requirements of perspicuity and consistency in his figures because the feeling was all, and if he chose to compare his breaking heart with the breaking dawn he should be permitted to do so, because he felt that way. Thus the conceit which certain critics had objected to by the rules, "Her heart and morning broke together / In the storm . . . ," was "merely in keeping with the essential spirit of the song proper."

This review enables us to understand how strictly Poe made his discriminations in terms of genre. Although he declared many times that the same general principles applied to all the arts, these principles had to do with the artist's purpose and with the psychology of effect; they did not prescribe all details of execution, which differed with each form. That a lyric poem was not to be confined by the rules was a commonplace of neoclassical criticism—except that Dr. Johnson had opposed this kind of license in one of the numbers of *The Rambler*.[34] Poe, we see, accepted the old commonplace in regard to the song, but he validated it by the new expressivist aesthetic that was emphasized by the German romantic critics far more than by the British. Yet in criticizing lyric poems other than songs, Poe objected to conceits and hyperbolic expression just as strenuously as Dr. Johnson or Hugh Blair. In his review of *The Book of Gems* he had deplored the wit of the metaphysical poets, claiming that Donne and Cowley had lacked art; but now, seemingly reversing his opinion, he commended the "fervid, hearty, free-spoken songs of Cowley and Donne." This is only an apparent reversal, however, for a genuine song, such as Donne's "Sweetest Love, I Do Not Go," would fit Poe's criteria, as would some of Cowley's imitations of Anacreon.

That Poe mitigated the rigor of his rules in criticizing the song does not imply that he deprecated the genre. On the contrary he

[34] In *Rambler* No. 158, Dr. Johnson explained the license granted lyric poets on historical grounds and complained that critics had set lyric poems "free from the laws by which other compositions are confined," allowing them to neglect transition, to enter into "remote digressions," and to move from one pattern of imagery into another.

wrote, perhaps unconsciously echoing Addison,[35] that he "would much rather have written the best *song* of a nation than its noblest *epic*." This is not saying too much, for he disliked epics, and, as a subsequent explanation reveals, he did not consider the song as representing the highest poetic art, whatever its evocative capacity.

When verse is "most strictly married to music," Poe went on to say, it was characterized by *abandonnement* (a term he was to use pejoratively in reference to Shelley's habits of composition). In other words, the lyricist was directed by emotion instead of by conscious artistry. Ordinarily such a practice would have to be condemned, but since the lyricist had no object but the expression of feeling, his figures should be "independent of merely ordinary proprieties" and should be considered chiefly for the evocative capacity of "sweet sound." Music, whether instrumental or vocal, evoked sentiments beyond the "reach of analysis," and to analyze these sentiments, if it were possible, would be to destroy their effect, which was to bewilder and enthrall. If Morris' songs were judged as poems, Poe concluded, there would be two or three which might be considered superior to the two songs he had selected for illustration, but it was for these latter that Morris was "immortal."

The question might be asked, if the answer is not already too obvious, just how did Poe distinguish the song from the ordinary lyric poem? The song is vocal music, usually accompanied by instrumental music. Old English ballads and carols, the verse of Anacreon, Homer, Aeschylus, the French lyricist Béranger, Cunningham, Harrington, Carew, and especially the Irish "Anacreon," [36] Thomas Moore, exhibited the essence of song. In America there was only George P. Morris! Poe's list might seem a little puzzling in its inclusion of Homer if we did not remember that Poe, like his predecessors, cherished an image of the blind bard of Nature, chanting his poems to the accompaniment of a lyre; and in select-

---

[35] Addison, in reference to the "Old Song of Chevy-Chase," had quoted Ben Jonson as saying that he would rather have written it than all of his own works. *Spectator*, LXXX (May 21, 1711).

[36] Byron had dubbed Thomas Moore "Anacreon" Moore.

ing Aeschylus he obviously had in mind the singing of the Greek chorus. Of the limitations that the "marriage" of verse to music places on the poet, Poe said nothing, nor did he attempt to account for the fact that songs are frequently inferior on grounds other than the "wild license" he considered characteristic of the genre; but, as always, we must take into consideration his medium. He had expended his space to make one point, that the song was worthy of esteem. He had room for no further discussion.

6

The beginning of the new year, 1840, found Poe restless and irritable, but occasionally he wrote a good review. His review of *Alciphron*,[37] a verse romance by Thomas Moore, appeared in the January number and must be considered the most important criticism that he wrote for Burton's magazine. His method of using a critique as a vehicle for theory is well illustrated by this review, in which he renewed his discussion of the psychology of creativity which he had initiated in his earlier review of Drake and Halleck. He was now prepared to dispute Coleridge's definition of the imagination, which he had cited in a footnote to the Drake-Halleck critique.

> "The fancy," says the author of the "Ancient Mariner," in his *Biographia Literaria,* "the fancy combines, the imagination creates." And this was intended, and has been received, as a distinction. If so at all, it is one without a difference; without even a difference of *degree*. The fancy as nearly creates as the imagination; and neither creates in any respect. All novel conceptions are merely unusual combinations. The mind of man can imagine nothing which has not really existed; and this point is susceptible of the most positive demonstration—see the Baron de Bielfeld, in his "*Premiers Traits de L'Erudition Universelle,*" 1767. It will be said, perhaps, that we can imagine a *griffin* and that a griffin does not exist. Not the griffin certainly, but its component parts. It is a mere compendium of known limbs and features—of known qualities.

[37] *Works*, X, 60–71.

Thus with all which seems to be *new*—which appears to be a *creation* of intellect. It is resoluble into the old. The wildest and most vigorous effort of mind cannot stand the test of this analysis.

Whether Poe failed to comprehend Coleridge's extended definition or whether he simply reduced it in order to set up a straw man for easy destruction is impossible to say. From what we have seen of his work, he was capable of either. Considering his admiration for Coleridge, however, it is more likely that he made a superficial reading and fixed upon Coleridge's explanation of the primary imagination ("the living Power and prime Agent of all human Perception, and . . . a repetition in the finite mind of the eternal act of creation in the infinite I AM") as affirming the power of the human being to create an image of elements alien to human experience. In this respect, of course, Poe was right. All imaginary images are made up of the elements of experience, however distorted these elements may be. Yet to refute Coleridge, he had to misinterpret him. Coleridge never claimed that the imagination created substantially. Instead it was "that reconciling and mediatory power, which incorporating the reason in images of the sense, and organizing (as it were) the flux of the sense by the permanence and self-circling energies of the reason, gives birth to a system of symbols, harmonious in themselves, and consubstantial with the truths of which they are the conductors." [38]

It is possible, of course, that Poe had never seen this passage from *The Statesman's Manual* (1816), which is much less obscure than the definition from the *Biographia Literaria* which Poe refuted; but it is still necessary to examine Poe's own attempts to define the imagination for the light these attempts shed on his criticism. Coleridge saw nature as process; for him, the creative activity that is art imitates the creative activity that is nature.[39] Poe, on

[38] "The Statesman's Manual," in W. G. J. Shedd (ed.), *Complete Works of Samuel Taylor Coleridge* (New York, 1853), I, 437.

[39] An essay on Poe is not the place to discuss Coleridge's theory of the imagination, an enterprise which has demanded and received the full attention of critics and scholars. I have been guided in my interpretation of Coleridge by Walter Jackson Bate, "Coleridge on the Function of Art," in

the other hand, still saw nature as an aggregation of fixed elements which are known to man only through his senses. He was attempting to refute Coleridge on eighteenth-century premises.

In the eighteenth century the imagination had often been equated with invention, and in this sense demons, witches, chimeras—creatures that did not exist—were regarded as evidences of the imagination. Thus this power, as Addison affirmed in *Spectator* No. 419, could make "new worlds of its own." Joseph Warton, writing of Shakespeare, had praised his creative imagination in the depiction of such a monster as Caliban. It was undoubtedly this idea of creativity which Poe thought he had found in Coleridge and which he undertook to refute on the basis of Lockean psychology. Since, according to Locke, all ideas originated in experience, the mind could contain nothing outside of experience. A creature like Caliban would be a combination of empirical elements. Bielfeld, whom Poe quoted, was in the Lockean tradition, but Poe's example of the griffin, like the more familiar one of the chimera, goes back to Hobbes. It was customary in the eighteenth century to distinguish the imagination from the memory, for the memory was bound to a certain extent to the order of perception, whereas the imagination could transpose, recombine, or totally re-order prior sensations by making obscure associative linkages. But so could the fancy, and in many eighteenth-century discussions of the power the terms were interchangeable. According to Gordon McKenzie, James Beattie's definition of the imagination was typical: "In the language of modern philosophy, the word 'imagination' seems to denote: first, the power of apprehending or conceiving ideas, simply as they are in themselves without any view to their reality; and secondly, the power of combining into new forms or assemblages, those thoughts, ideas, or notions, which we have derived from experience or from information." [40]

Harry Levin (ed.), *Perspectives of Criticism* (Cambridge, Mass., 1950), 125–59; I. A. Richards, *Coleridge on Imagination* (New York, 1935); and Gordon McKenzie, *Organic Unity in Coleridge* (Berkeley, 1939). The interpretation to which this particular note is appended is derived most specifically from Bate.

[40] Quoted by McKenzie in *Critical Responsiveness*, 195.

Thus in the old view the imagination, like the fancy, simply combined the elements of experience or information. Poe was not the only romantic writer who clung to Locke's psychology. Even Wordsworth, qualifying Coleridge's definition, had said in his Preface to the 1815 edition of his poems that "to aggregate and to associate, to evoke and to combine, belong as well to the Imagination as to the Fancy," and he then went on to make his personal distinction between the two as did Poe.

Poe did think that there was a difference between the two faculties, even though he was unable to accept either Coleridge's distinction or the more familiar one—that the imagination is more "loftily employed" than the fancy. In Poe's opinion the fancy would remain the fancy no matter how elevated the theme with which it engaged. To illustrate, he reverted to *The Culprit Fay*, the allegedly imaginative poem of Joseph Rodman Drake, and quoted pertinent passages from his review of 1836. He then went on to make his own distinction, which is not so different from that of Coleridge as his refutation would lead us to believe.

> The truth is that the just distinction between the fancy and the imagination (and which is still but a distinction *of degree*) is involved in the consideration of the *mystic*. We give this as an idea of our own, altogether. We have no authority for our opinion—but do not the less firmly hold it. The term *mystic* is here employed in the sense of Augustus William Schlegel, and of most other German critics. It is applied by them to that class of composition in which there lies beneath the transparent upper current of meaning an under or *suggestive* one. What we vaguely term the *moral* of any sentiment is its mystic or secondary expression. It has the vast force of an accompaniment in music. This vivifies the air; that spiritualizes the *fanciful* conception, and lifts it into the *ideal*.[41]

[41] Poe's parenthetical allusion in the first sentence of this statement is probably to Chapter IV of the *Biographia Literaria*, in which Coleridge described the way in which he came to doubt that the fancy and the imagination were the "lower and higher degree of one and the same power" (I, 61). Poe was attempting to refute Coleridge's views in two ways, first by denying that the imagination could create, and next by affirming what Coleridge denied, that the distinction was one of degree. Poe was simply saying that the imagination and the fancy worked the same way, but that the *result*

Though Poe's use of the term "mystic" may be misleading, it is obvious that he considered the presence of suggestive or symbolic meaning as the distinction between an imaginative and a fanciful poem, a conclusion not essentially different from Coleridge's. Poe had intimated as much in his review of Drake and Halleck, but he had confused the issue by declaring in his review of *Undine* that an "under-current of meaning" in a romance was to be deplored—it was too much like allegory. Does this mean that symbolic meaning was appropriate for a poem but not for a prose romance? Apparently not, for Poe continued, "If we carefully examine those poems, or portions of poems, or those prose romances, which mankind have been accustomed to designate as *imaginative* . . . , it will be seen that all so designated are remarkable for the *suggestive* character which we have discussed. They are strongly *mystic*, in the proper sense of the word." Then he gave the list of imaginative works he had previously cited in the review of Drake and Halleck

---

of the imagination at work was evidenced by a second level of meaning. In a fanciful poem the surface was all.

His reference to Schlegel may be very general, for the German critic discoursed at length on the way the advent of Christianity had caused men to lose what was "finite and mortal" in the "contemplation of infinity." Modern poetry expressed the Christian's yearning for his immortal home, and Poe's "mystic" undoubtedly refers to the suggestion of a more perfect beauty beyond the grave. Schlegel did distinguish symbolism from allegory, and yet his distinction required symbolic poetry to have that reference to reality that Poe deplored. In fact, Schlegel's definition of allegory is a fair description of what Poe considered the proper way to enact a poetic idea: "Allegory is the personification of an idea, a poetic story invented with such a view; but that is symbolical which, created by the imagination for other purposes, or possessing an *independent reality of its own* [italics mine], is at the same time easily susceptible of an emblematical explanation; and even of itself suggests it." Schlegel, *Lectures*, 88. Poe's confusion, as exhibited in his condemnation of the allegorical meaning in *Undine* and his subsequent praise of its undercurrent of meaning, may have derived from his interpretation of Schlegel. It is strange that Poe did not oppose symbolism to allegory, as did Schlegel; but if he had, it would have involved him in a reversal of all his convictions about the "indefinite" nature of poetry, because a symbol possessed an *independent reality*. Poe used the term "symbol" only a few times in the entire corpus of his criticism, but he did use "emblem" as an explanation of his infusion of meaning into "The Raven" (in "The Philosophy of Composition").

and added to it the recently reviewed *Undine,* classifying it with Shelley's "Sensitive Plant" as an example of the purely ideal.

At this point one is tempted to abandon Poe's criticism and leave him with the obscurantists, where Yvor Winters located him.[42] In one review he deprecated an "under-current of meaning" as being too like allegory, and only four months later, using the same phrase, he demanded it. Giving him the benefit of the doubt, however, we may explore to see whether he was describing the same phenomenon in the different reviews. The fault may lie in Poe's idiom instead of in his thought.

In the review of *Alciphron* Poe attempted to explain his terminology: "With each note of the lyre is heard a ghostly, and not always a distinct, but an august and soul-exalting *echo*. In every glimpse of beauty presented, we catch, through long and wild vistas, dim bewildering visions of a far more ethereal beauty *beyond*. But not so in poems which the world has always persisted in terming *fanciful*. Here the upper current is often exceedingly brilliant and beautiful; but then men *feel* that this upper current *is all*. No Naiad voice addresses them *from below*."

In the review of *Undine* Poe had used the phrase "under-current of meaning" in reference to the domestic situation of an unfaithful husband and interfering relatives. This was, in his interpretation, the "unfigured sense" or moral of the romance and as such was to be deprecated—it had no business in an imaginative work. In the review of *Alciphron*, however, his "under-current" must be translated as symbolic rather than allegorical import, since it is not limited to a specific idea or a particular situation. Poe's rhapsodical language in the quotation above intimates some kind of Platonic beauty beyond appearances that could be communicated by symbolic suggestion; and since such suggestion could be achieved only by the ability to imagine the beauty beyond, its presence denoted imaginative power in the poet. Thus, in refuting Coleridge, Poe actually made his closest approach to interpreting the imagination as Coleridge had defined it—as a symbol-making power. The only

[42] See Winters, "Edgar Allan Poe: A Crisis in the History of American Obscurantism," *In Defense of Reason* (New York, 1947), 234–61.

difference is this: Coleridge saw the imagination at work in symbolizing truth; Poe recognized its activity in symbolizing a beauty
beyond appearances. A small difference, if truth and beauty were
one, but Poe would not have it so. Truth, to Poe, meant logical deduction, useful information, or accurate representation; or it meant
didactic precepts such as those that could have been derived from
reading *Undine* as an allegory. Reading it as a poem, however, one
obtained suggestions of moral beauty more "divine" and "soul-
exalting" than any examples of rectitude ever observed in the real
world. This was the beauty beyond; this was the ideal.

Poe, then, had not reversed his position; he had simply used a
phrase carelessly to signify one thing in one review and something
different in another, a signal fault in a critic but one which can be
explained in Poe's case. Like Coleridge, Poe had to devise a vocabulary to describe the values he sought in a poem.[43] There was no
idiom which adequately described symbolic value, and Coleridge's
coinages were incomprehensible to Poe's public and perhaps to Poe
himself. Poe showed a certain amount of daring in appropriating
the term "mystic" (allegedly from German criticism), for this
term was used pejoratively by American critics and occasionally by
Poe to mean the obscure and the unintelligible. Struggling to rescue the word from its unfortunate associations, he attributed the

---

[43] Attempting to defend himself against the expected charge of pedantry,
Coleridge explained why he constructed the word "esemplastic" from Greek
roots to describe the power of the imagination to shape the many into one.
Biographia Literaria, I, 107. Poe, as a journalist, had to use words a general
audience could comprehend. Even if he had had the scholarship to invent a
precise new terminology, it is doubtful that he would have employed it, for
to do so would have brought against him the same charges that were levied
against Coleridge. Terms like "ideality" and "taste" could be understood
by Poe's audience, for they came from the popular phrenological texts and
the rhetorics, but there was no common idiom to describe symbolic import
without confusing it with allegorical meaning on the one hand or the required perspicuity of figurative language on the other. Like Coleridge, Poe
did not want poetry to be clearly and perfectly understood, and he may have
derived his "under-current" metaphor from Coleridge's requirement of
"depth". Coleridge described Shakespeare's "creative power" and "intellectual energy" as being like two streams which eventually meet and "flow
on in one current and with one voice." *Biographia Literaria*, II, 19.

usage to Schlegel and then proceeded to define it as an "undercurrent of meaning," perhaps forgetting for the moment that he had used the phrase for a different kind of meaning in a previous review.

It is easy enough to determine what Poe considered to be an imaginative "under-current of meaning" by examining the passages he quoted from Moore's poem. The sense of these passages is either commonplace or hackneyed. Moore intimated (1) that guardian angels communicate with the soul, (2) that at the end of the world Time (personified) will take his last look from the pyramids of Egypt, and (3) that man, redeemed, is immortal. Actually these ideas are presented with minimal suggestiveness. Only one of the quoted passages lends itself to symbolic interpretation:

> The pyramid shadows, stretching from the light
> Look like the first colossal steps of night,
> Stalking across the valley to invade
> The distant hills of porphyry with their shade!

Poe did not explain what meaning he found in these lines, but one may presume that since the pyramids are an apt symbol of human time, having endured for ages, their shadows invading the eternal hills suggest the fall of night, or the end of time. Poe, like his romantic peers, found full associative value in the play of light and shade.

If we were to credit Poe with an anticipation, in theory at least, of richly meaningful symbolic verse, we would be in error. His examples of imagination from *Alciphron* contain no treasures of symbolic implication but merely conventional poetic associations; yet the affective content was enough for Poe and validated certain portions of the poem as imaginative. "In truth, the exceeding beauty of 'Alciphron' has bewildered and detained us. We could not point out a poem in any language which, as a whole, greatly excels it. . . . While Moore does not reach, except in rare snatches, the height of the loftiest qualities of some whom we have named, yet he has written finer poems than any, of equal length, of the greatest of his rivals." Yet, in spite of these superlatives, Poe's general opinion of Moore is defensible. "A vivid fancy, an epigrammatic spirit, a fine taste, vivacity, dexterity, and a musical ear have made him very easily what he is, the most popular poet now living—if not the most popular that ever lived—and, perhaps, a slight modification at birth of that which phrenologists have agreed to term *temperament*, might have made him the truest and noblest votary of the muse of any age or clime. As it is, we have only casual glimpses of that *mens divinior* which is assuredly enshrined within him." [44] Even today few would object to a description of Moore as a popular poet who now and then achieved a felicity of expression which suggested abilities that were never developed, and really this is about all that Poe was saying. Imagination could be estimated only by expression, and occasionally Moore produced lines that compared favorably with those of greater poets.

One other point in the review of *Alciphron* requires discussion. In his criticism of Bryant in 1837, Poe had deprecated figures of speech that adduced "mere resemblance" between the objects compared and had praised the metaphorical identification of one object or quality with another. In the review of Moore he continued his argument:

> Similes (so much insisted upon by the critics of the reign of Queen Anne) are never, in our opinion, strictly in good taste, whatever may be said to the contrary, and certainly can never be made to accord with other high qualities, except when naturally arising from the subject in the way of illustration—and, when thus arising, they have seldom the merit of novelty. To be novel, they must fail in essential particulars. The higher minds will avoid their frequent use. They form no portion of the ideal, and appertain to the fancy alone.

Since Poe had claimed that the imagination, like the fancy, only combined the elements of experience, it is hard to see why he

[44] Spurzheim used the word "temperament" to refer to "mixtures of the constituent elements of the body" and used these alleged mixtures to estimate character traits much as some modern theorists have used somatic types. See Spurzheim, *Phrenology*, 191–93. This was not much more than an updating of the old theory of the "humours."

claimed that all similes were merely fanciful. If we understand that the meaning he attributed to the imagination was a kind of generalized symbolic import, however, his denigration of figures of speech is understandable. A figure of speech, insofar as it specifies resemblance between objects, belongs to the real world, the phenomenal world that can be perceived by the senses. A novel figure of speech, to Poe, was merely an effort of the wit to put together combinations that had not been put together before—say by comparing an inconstant lover to an abacus. Such a novelty "must fail in essential particulars" because it would be a logical absurdity. Whatever was put together by intellectual effort had to be examined logically. If it did not make sense, then by the rhetorical rules it would have to be declared faulty. The only escape from this dilemma was to refrain from using sense metaphors altogether and instead to use evocative language that would arouse the desired emotional response without yielding to logical analysis. This was the basis for Poe's demand for the vague and the indefinitive in poetry. Logical meaning, he thought, was better communicated by prose. Figures, since they merely combined the elements of experience, were likely to be hackneyed. The meaning of a poem, on the other hand, should be something like the meaning of music, felt but untranslatable, a "soul-exalting echo." Poe would have had the imagination soar completely beyond actuality and give us emotional experience that by its very nature was inimitable and untranslatable, experience that could be gained by the unimaginative only through art. To supply this experience in some measure was the high purpose of the true artist.

7

A work of art, for Poe, originated either in a state of feeling or in an idea. The feeling or the idea was to be patiently elaborated into artistic form by the combination of various elements in accordance with a controlling purpose; and this purpose was to produce an appropriate effect. The idea preceded the design, the design preceded the execution; and of these three only the idea or the emotive meaning could be said to spring from the unconscious mind by inspiration, intuition, or whatever agency. Thus the idea of a poem was its imaginative element. Given the idea, Poe thought, any skillful artist could work out an appropriate design and carry it into execution.

This concept of the way a work of art comes into being is responsible for Poe's seemingly ill-tempered attack on Longfellow for plagiarism in his review of *Voices of the Night* in the February, 1840, issue of the *Gentleman's Magazine*.[45] Longfellow's "Midnight Mass for the Dying Year," Poe claimed, was plagiarized from Tennyson's "The Death of the Old Year," although scarcely a word or image is identical:

> We have no idea of commenting, at any length, upon this plagiarism, which is too palpable to be mistaken, and which belongs to the most barbarous class of literary robbery: that class in which, while the words of the wronged author are avoided, his most intangible, and therefore his least defensible and least reclaimable property is purloined. Here, with the exception of lapses, which, however, speak volumes (such for instance as the use of the capitalized "Old Year," the general peculiarity of the rhythm, and the absence of rhyme at the end of each stanza), there is nothing of a visible or palpable nature by which the source of the American poem can be established. But then nearly all that is valuable in the piece of Tennyson is the first conception of personifying the Old Year as a dying old man, with the singularly wild and fantastic *manner* in which that conception is carried out. Of this conception and of this manner he is robbed. Could he peruse to-day the "Midnight Mass" of Professor Longfellow, would he peruse it with more of indignation or of grief?

There is little evidence that Poe thought of "form as proceeding"—a process of evolution in the mind of the poet. Coleridge had said that form as proceeding "is its self-witnessing and self-effected sphere of agency." To Poe, however, form was imposed, which to Coleridge was the "death or imprisonment of the thing." [46] Longfellow, according to Poe, had stolen the idea of the controlling image and the manner of the execution. Since form was an arbitrary shape imposed on the material by the poet's will, another poet, borrowing the idea and the tone, could be expected to execute the design. In later years Poe was to state that an artist could impose any design he wished upon a given material.[47] It is enough to say here that this concept was at least partly responsible for his vehemence in condemning the "theft" of a poetic idea.

Also revealed in Poe's review of Longfellow is his concept of unity, and again it will be instructive to compare him with Coleridge. To Coleridge, unity was indwelling, organic. The poet saw beneath surface identities and was able to "imitate that which is within the thing. . . . The idea which puts the form together cannot itself be the form. It is above form, and is its essence, the universal in the individual, or the individuality itself,—the glance and the exponent of the indwelling power." To Coleridge unity was not imposed; it sprang from the perception of the oneness beneath diverse appearances, the "coalescence of the diverse." The artist did not merely achieve a rhetorical unity but communicated an intuition of the essence, "the *natura naturans*, which presupposes a bond between nature in the higher sense and the soul of man."

Unlike Coleridge, Poe did not conceive of an indwelling organic unity. His criterion of unity tended to vary depending upon the nature of the work he was reviewing. In a true poem, which had to be tested by emotional response, it was the unity of effect that he emphasized. In a short narrative he required an Aristotelian formal unity, in which no part might be removed or transposed without dislocation of the whole. In a poem which had a cognitive import, a logical meaning, Poe looked for conceptual unity, the unity of idea. He did not care for such poems, but when he examined them he employed rational analysis. Longfellow's poems, usually equipped with a paraphrasable moral, fell into this last category and were judged accordingly.

[46] All quotations from Coleridge given in this context are from "On Poesy or Art," *Biographia Literaria*, II, 257–62.
[47] "Marginalia," *Works*, XVI, 99.

Poe found a violation of the unity of idea in Longfellow's "Hymn to the Night." The sensitive reader, Poe claimed, would find that in the poem he would waver "disagreeably between two ideas which would have been merged by the skilful artist into one." Longfellow had personified the night as a woman in his poem:

> I heard the trailing garments of the Night
> Sweep through her marble halls!
> I saw her sable skirts all fringed with light
> From the celestial walls!

First, Poe stated, we are conveyed to a palace "tenanted by the sable-draperied, by the Corporate Night." But the "single epithet *celestial*" refers us "to the natural and absolute quality or condition, the incorporate darkness." Had Longfellow substituted for "marble halls" something like "azure halls" or "heavenly halls," unity of idea would not have been violated. The personification would have remained intact.

Another flaw Poe found in the poem was that the last stanza was not readily intelligible. This quibbling seems odd in the light of his demand for vagueness and indefinitiveness in poetry. However, the poem under consideration employed a conventional strategy of personification, and, whenever imagery was used, Poe examined the poem rhetorically and demanded precision of reference. Thus he found ambiguity in the following lines:

> Peace! Peace! Orestes-like I breathe this prayer!
> Descend with broad-winged flight,
> The welcome, the thrice-prayed for, the most fair,
> The best-beloved Night.

Poe interpreted the stanza to mean that "Peace is invoked to descend the Night—as we say descend the stair," but that on a first reading one is likely to take the passage as containing "a double invocation,—to Peace and to Night."

Thus it is clear that Poe used different approaches to different poems. The quality of suggestiveness, as he had explained in his review of *Alciphron*, was imaginative or ideal because it did not yield itself to logical analysis but simply enhanced the emotional effect of the poem as an accompaniment enhances a song. When the poem, by employing imagery, did open itself to analysis, however, Poe demanded precision, clarity, and unity of idea as firmly as would an eighteenth-century rhetorician. The poet who operates on this lower level must not neglect the conventions that make his work intelligible to an audience. Poe's objections to Longfellow were based on minor defects, he admitted, but he considered them representative of the "prevalent deficiencies of the writer." Longfellow's poem could have been "richly ideal," but he neglected the minor graces of composition. Thus, in spite of Billy Burton's advice to deal "leniently with the faults of genius," Poe maintained his standard of criticism. Within two years he was to assert firmly that pointing out such minor faults was one of the inescapable duties of the critic.

8

The review of Longfellow's *Voices of the Night* was Poe's last for the *Gentleman's Magazine* that had any intrinsic critical interest. In the spring of 1840 the difficulties between Burton and Poe were coming to a head. Our information about Poe's activities during these months is scanty. We know that he was away from Philadelphia for a fortnight early in April [48] and that there were no criticisms from his pen in the April number, only a short paragraph on the copyright question. In May his contributions reappeared, among them a notice of the poems of William Cullen Bryant. This was one of the few he actually signed, but it contained nothing new. Poe merely summarized Bryant's career and then cribbed from his earlier *Messenger* review his analysis of "Oh, Fairest of the Rural Maids."

Poe's final break with Burton occurred late in May of 1840. The actor-editor wrote to Poe on May 30 in a tone Poe bitterly resented, stating, among other things, that Poe owed him a hundred dollars. In a furious reply, dated June 1, Poe attempted to prove that the debt was considerably less and went into his grievances against Burton: the actor had attempted to "bully" him; the long critical articles he had written when he first joined the magazine had been

[48] See Poe to Hiram Haines, April 24, 1840, in *Letters*, I, 128.

rejected; Burton had enforced a deduction from his salary to pay the debt; the actor had spoken disrespectfully of Poe behind his back; and, lastly, Burton had advertised his magazine for sale without consulting Poe. This act, Poe said, was responsible for his own attempt to found a journal, which Burton had resented.[49] Seventeen days later Poe wrote to his friend Snodgrass that Burton was a liar, a scoundrel, and a villain.[50]

Poe's formal letter of resignation was submitted in June, and thereupon Burton turned down some six or seven critiques Poe had prepared for the journal.[51] Thus with mutual recriminations the two parted company, Billy Burton on his way to theatrical triumphs in New York, Poe to attempt to found a magazine of his own. But Poe was not yet through with the *Gentleman's Magazine*. In November, 1840, Burton had sold the magazine with its list of subscribers to George R. Graham, editor and owner of another magazine called the *Casket*, with which the *Gentleman's Magazine* was to be combined. Thus the last number of the *Gentleman's Magazine*—December, 1840—was also the first number of *Graham's*. It contained Poe's story "The Man of the Crowd," but the reviews were not his. It was not until April of 1841, after the combined *Gentleman's* and *Casket* had been titled *Graham's Lady's and Gentleman's Magazine*, that Poe's reviews reappeared. He had found a position with the new owner. In the meantime he had worked energetically to establish his own journal, which he planned to call the *Penn*.

[49] Burton's letter is unavailable, but its content may be deduced in part from Poe's reply. *Ibid.*, 129–32.

[50] Poe to J. E. Snodgrass, June 17, 1840, *ibid.*, 137–38.

[51] This information is given in Poe's letter to Snodgrass, cited above. See also Ostrom's notes to this letter and Poe's June 1 letter to Burton, *ibid.*, 133, 139. Poe's ill-feeling toward Burton was intensified later when Snodgrass told him that a report had been circulated, allegedly from Burton, that Poe had frequently been drunk while working on the *Gentleman's Magazine*. Furious, Poe wrote to Snodgrass on April 1, 1841, that he could not call Burton out as gentleman to gentleman because Burton was a "buffoon and a felon," and that his only recourse was the law, but that Burton would enter a countersuit. Poe claimed that he could prove that he was never drunk while working for Burton, although he admitted drinking while he was employed on the *Messenger*. See *Letters*, I, 155–57.

X · Graham's: Honest and Fearless Opinion

ALTHOUGH Poe was employing every stratagem to found his own journal, the *Penn*, he did not fail to give George R. Graham a full measure of service. For the first time he was comparatively unrestricted as to the length of his reviews and the level of severity he could display, and he was able to use the magazine as for a time he had used the *Messenger*: to gibbet dunces and to call for higher standards in American letters. By higher standards Poe meant first of all a criticism without fear or favor, uncommitted to increasing the profits of publishing houses, magazines, or individuals at the expense of quality. Scarcely less important, he wanted an improvement in the quality of the magazines themselves. It must be emphasized, however, that Poe was by no means a solitary Jeremiah. James Russell Lowell, also a magazinist for a time, made the same complaints and called for the same reforms, as did other responsible journalists. In fact many fledgling magazines, in the tall talk of their prospectuses, claimed that they would be just and impartial in their reviews and that they would employ writers only of the highest quality.[1] Poe's distinction lay in the fact that while others were talking of higher standards he was doing his best as a critic to enforce them, subject, of course, to the limitations of his temperament and taste. His first reviews for *Graham's* reveal considerable asperity, and he showed an increasing tendency to make judgments on the basis of rhetorical rules, either the conventional ones or those he made up for his own purposes. Occasionally he still launched into a rhapsody of appreciation for ideality, which he treasured both on a theoretical and on an emotional basis, but in general during the period with Graham his reviews were tough-minded critiques based upon traditional criteria.

The first review in *Graham's* that can be considered secure in the

[1] For a description of the practices that would-be publishers promised to reform, see Mott, *A History of American Magazines*, 405–408.

Poe canon was that of Bulwer's *Night and Morning,* in the April, 1841, number.[2] As has been brought out earlier in this study, it was customary for American critics to deplore the tendency toward immorality in Bulwer's novels, but Poe, limiting critical inquiry chiefly to questions of literary value, was prone to ignore any infringements on American prudery. He was opposed to vulgarity and coarseness of language, but in Poe's schemata of faults this offense came under the heading of bad taste. Accordingly, it is no surprise that instead of taking Bulwer to task for his alleged voluptuousness Poe proceeded immediately to discuss the plot of the novel and, as was his custom, he outlined his theory of what a plot should be and then measured the novel against it.

> The word *plot,* as commonly accepted, conveys but an indefinite meaning. Most persons think of it as a simple *complexity;* and into this error even so fine a critic as Augustus William Schlegel has obviously fallen, when he confounds its idea with that of the mere *intrigue* in which the Spanish dramas of Cervantes and Calderón abound. But the greatest involution of incident will not result in plot; which, properly defined, is *that in which no part can be displaced without ruin to the whole.* It may be described as a building so dependently constructed, that to change the position of a single brick is to overthrow the entire fabric. In this definition and description, we of course refer only to that infinite perfection which the true artist bears ever in mind—that unattainable goal to which his eyes are always directed, but of the possibility of attaining which he still endeavours, if wise, to cheat himself into the belief. The reading world, however, is satisfied with a less rigid construction of the term. It is content to think that plot a good one, in which none of the *leading* incidents can be *removed* without *detriment* to the mass. Here indeed is a material difference; and in this view of the case the plot of "Night and Morning" is decidedly excellent.

This definition of plot, which prefigures the much more familiar one Poe made in his review of Hawthorne's *Twice-Told Tales* a year later, suggests a development not only in Poe's critical theory but also in his self-assurance. In his *Messenger* days he had leaned

[2] *Works,* X, 114–33.

on the authority of Coleridge and Schlegel. With Burton he had dared to "correct" Coleridge, and now he undertook not only to point out an error by Schlegel but to make an improvement on Aristotle's description of excellence of plot. Not too much should be made of Poe's finding fault with Schlegel. He had learned the trick of finding some point, however minor, that he could challenge in the work of an acknowledged authority in order to draw attention to his own brilliance. Actually Schlegel did not commend the plots of the Spanish dramatists, as Poe implied. He simply stated that "ingenious boldness, joined to easy clearness of intrigue," was "exclusively peculiar" to the Spanish drama.[3] Apparently Poe consciously or unconsciously was misconstruing Schlegel in order to dispute an authority.

More important than the pointless refutation of Schlegel are the implications of Poe's improvement on Aristotle. Aristotle had described the requirements of a good plot as follows: "the plot, being an imitation of an action, must imitate one action and that a whole, the structural union of the parts being such that, if any one of them is displaced or removed, the whole will be disjointed and disturbed. For a thing whose presence or absence makes no visible difference is not an organic part of the whole" (Butcher's translation). Poe simply exaggerated this requirement by saying that in a perfect plot no part could be displaced without *ruin* to the whole. It is the metaphor of the building that can be overthrown by the removal of a single brick that is important. Poe thought an artist who worked from a preconceived design was like an architect who drew up a blueprint before construction was actually begun. This is analogous to the usual eighteenth-century concept of the universe as planned by God, and eventually, in *Eureka*, Poe was to describe God as the perfect plotter. Poe's concept of the work of art was mechanistic, like the Newtonian cosmology. Perfection of plot was unattainable on any level except the divine, but the human artist should keep this goal before him as a conscious ideal. By implication the critic, too, should keep in mind this unattainable perfection and should measure all actual plots by the ideal plot.

[3] Schlegel, *Lectures*, 488.

If Poe had considered the work of art as a living organism, as did Coleridge, Emerson, and Whitman, he might have maintained his early attitude toward close examination—to analyze is to destroy. Now, however, looking upon the work of art as a construction, he would analyze it, part by part, in order to arrive at a judgment of the quality of the artist's design. This he proceeded to do with Bulwer's novel, pointing out incidents that did not develop the main events, actions that pointed to later developments that the author had "forgotten," and "interposed afterthoughts" that were not elements of the original plan. Then, surprisingly, he claimed that Bulwer's obvious intention of achieving a perfect plot was "conceived and executed in error." The pleasure derived from appreciation of a perfect design, Poe stated, was confined to the few readers who were capable of perceiving it. The mass audience was not. And even at best, plot was "but a secondary and rigidly artistical merit, for which no merit of a higher class—no merit founded in nature—should be sacrificed."

Here we would be justified in leaping to the conclusion that Poe was contradicting himself. After announcing that the artist should keep perfection of plot in mind, he claimed that Bulwer erred in doing just that. The paradox lies in the fact that Poe, however he might invoke the ideal in *theory*, was nothing but practical in many of his book reviews. He was a journalist writing to a mass audience. He knew that many successful novels (he cited *Gil Blas* and *Robinson Crusoe*) neglected plot. The novel, like the drama, was an imitation of life, and in Poe's opinion it could proceed with the inconsequent and haphazard motion of life itself. The novelist need not even consider perfection of plot, that "rigidly artistical merit," and if he did he would be wasting his ingenuity, for the novel was too long for most readers to take in the design as a whole. The novel was "essentially inadapted to that nice and complex adjustment of incident" which was required for perfection of plot.

> In the wire-drawn romances which have been so long fashionable (God only knows how or why) the pleasure we derive (if any) is a composite one, and made up of the respective sums of the various pleasurable sentiments experienced in perusal. Without excessive

and fatiguing exertion, inconsistent with legitimate interest, the mind cannot comprehend at one time and one survey the numerous items which go to establish the whole. Thus the high ideal sense of the *unique* is sure to be wanting; for, however absolute in itself be the unity of the novel, it must inevitably fail of appreciation. We speak now of that species of unity which is alone worth the attention of the critic—the unity or totality of effect.

If we remember Poe's review of Mrs. Sigourney, the premises underlying his argument are immediately clear. He saw little value in structural unity unless it contributed to that total impression on the reader wherein the sentiments or "ideas of emotion" stimulated by a work proceeded in a uniform train of association toward a single effect. Lord Kames had defined sentiments as thoughts prompted by strong feeling,[4] and Poe insisted that the feelings be pleasurable. In his calculus of pleasure he assumed that an easy apprehension and retention of *all* the sentiments inspired by reading were necessary for the unity of effect. If the sentiments were experienced singly the result would be a dissipation of effect, like looking at a landscape detail by detail without ever comprehending the whole as a composition. No matter how well a painter has composed his scene, the effect must be apprehended as a whole. In a composition ordered in time instead of space the same principle must be observed, except that the limits of attention and recall are invoked, instead of the limits of perception. In Poe's view the mind, in this case the memory, could not retain the details of a novel as a composition, no matter how carefully the writer had worked out his plot. He had said as much in reference to the long poem in his review of Mrs. Sigourney, but now he applied the principle to a different genre. In a long composition it is better to be natural than it is to be artistic.[5] In his practical, journalistic way Poe was making a sound point. "Art" novels have never reached a mass audience. James Joyce, following art instead of nature in

---

[4] *Elements of Criticism*, 483.

[5] Since the novel was not an art form but a representation of the observations and ideas of the author, it should not aim at unity of effect, the first principle of all the arts to Poe. Instead, it should appear to be true and should exhibit the author's thought.

Finnegans Wake, produced a design that can be comprehended only after intensive study, but his short tales reach a wide audience.

Poe assumed that Bulwer, were he to read Poe's comments, would defend his carefully constructed plot on the basis that the novel was essentially dramatic and, like the play, should present structural unity. Not so, Poe said. The novel is dramatic chiefly as it exhibits the deficiencies of the drama, the "continual and vexatious shifting of scene." Dialogue is suitable to the narrative form, but the "drama of action and passion will always prove, when employed beyond due limits, a source of embarrassment to the narrator, and it can afford him, at best, nothing which he does not already possess in full force." By the drama of "action and passion" Poe meant a verbal representation of exciting events and the expression of strong feeling either in soliloquy or in the passionate speeches which characters in the nineteenth-century novel frequently made to each other. These, to Poe, were conventional in the drama but should be used with extreme care by the novelist. The novel had a flexibility that the drama had yet to exhibit. Not such a strictly imitative form, the novel could exhibit the "combining, arranging and especially . . . the commenting power." These techniques should be used to develop a smooth narrative pattern without the hiatuses (shifts of scene, divisions between acts) inevitable in the drama.

Poe's use of the term "commenting power" represents a development of his ideas about the nature of the novel which certainly would not be regarded as an improvement by critics since Henry James. In previous reviews of novels he had been content to use the standard criteria, but from this time on he demanded authorial comment, an element which in his opinion lifted a narrative from a barren imitation of action into a vehicle of the author's thought. Apparently it never occurred to Poe that the characters themselves might be the vehicle of the author's thought; the author had to enter the novel in person to express his ideas.[6]

[6] For a convincing argument that authorial intrusion is not necessarily damaging to the illusion of reality given by a novel, see Louis D. Rubin, Jr., *The Teller in the Tale* (Seattle, 1967), 7–14.

It is clear that Poe never thought deeply about the novel, although he reviewed many; and the criteria he added to the standard list have been disallowed by the subsequent development of the novel form. The virtual disappearance of authorial comment in the modern novel, along with the increasing use of dramatic techniques in fiction, were not only unforeseen by Poe, he firmly opposed both tendencies. The "deficiencies of the drama," he insisted, should not be imposed upon the novel, although the "drama of colloquy, vivacious and breathing of life, is well adapted to narration."

2

Poe's other reviews in the April number of *Graham's* require no comment, since the books he reviewed did not inspire him to an effort. In May, however, he reviewed the collected *Writings of Charles Sprague*.[7] This gentleman, now forgotten, was in Poe's time a frequent contributor to magazines and appeared in lists of the best American poets, along with Longfellow, Bryant, and Halleck. Thus Poe demonstrated his independence as a critic when with deft irony he characterized Sprague as a poet of negative merit. Sprague's "Curiosity" was a fine thing in its way: "Its versification is superb—nothing could be better. Its thoughts are tersely put forth. The style is pungently epigrammatic. Upon the whole, it is fully as good a poem as Pope could have written, upon the same subject, in his finest hour of inspiration. We must bear in mind one important distinction, however. With Pope the ideas and management of the piece would have been original; with Mr. Sprague they are Pope's."

More to Poe's taste than Mr. Sprague's poems was Dickens' *The Old Curiosity Shop*, which he also reviewed in the May number.[8]

[7] *Works*, X, 139–42.

[8] *Ibid.*, 142–45. Any investigator of Poe's reviews of Dickens will find a series of articles by Gerald Grubb indispensable. This particular review was discussed by Mr. Grubb in Part One of "The Personal and Literary Relationships of Dickens and Poe," *Nineteenth Century Fiction*, V (1950–51), 1–22. He found Poe's review generally excellent, marred only by an-

Dickens, to Poe, was an authentic genius. In the *Messenger* period he had taken Dickens' "The Pawnbroker's Shop" as a perfect illustration of the principle of unity of effect. Now he considered *The Old Curiosity Shop* as an illustration of excellence in plot. Its conception was beautiful, "simply and severely grand," with none of the "involute complexity of incident" that marred the work of Bulwer. With *Night and Morning* still in mind, Poe then proceeded to make a comparison between the genius of Bulwer and that of Dickens which in thought and language harks back to eighteenth-century criticism, reminding us again of Poe's tendency to use traditional approaches during his tenure with *Graham's*:

> The Art of Mr. Dickens, although elaborate and great, seems only a happy modification of Nature. In this respect he differs remarkably from the author of "Night and Morning." The latter, by excessive care and patient reflection, aided by much rhetorical knowledge and general information, has arrived at the capability of producing books which might be mistaken by ninety-nine readers out of a hundred for the genuine inspiration of genius. The former, by the promptings of the truest genius itself, has been brought to compose, and evidently without effort, works which have effected a long-sought consummation, which have rendered him the idol of the people, while defying and enchanting the critics. Mr. Bulwer, through art, has almost created a genius. Mr. Dickens, through genius, has perfected a standard from which Art itself will derive its essence, its rules.

This passage, more obviously than any that we have seen thus far, illustrates Poe's tendency to rely upon the authority of the past in discussing questions he had not answered in terms of his own theory.

---

imadversions on the title page of the book. Since the work he reviewed was a "pirated" edition, Poe should not have blamed Dickens for the misleading "double title," which insinuated that the book was a whole instead of one of a series. "The Old Curiosity Shop" was the title story of one collection of tales, "Master Humphrey's Clock" the title story of the second collection under one cover. Poe thought the title should have been: "*Master Humphrey's Clock*. By Charles Dickens. Part I. Containing The Old Curiosity Shop, and Other Tales, with Numerous Illustrations, &c., &c."

In the passage above, Dickens is taken as an original genius, Bulwer as a man of talent whose rhetorical skill and habits of work could produce novels that seemed to be works of genius and so would impress most readers.

The distinction between the original genius and the mere craftsman was often made in the eighteenth century. We find it in Addison's *Spectator* No. 160. It is present in Pope's prefaces to his edition of Shakespeare and in his "Essay on Criticism." Homer, usually the illustration of natural genius in eighteenth-century criticism, was supposed to have learned directly from nature; and from his works, which were "Nature methodized" (Poe's "happy modification of Nature"), the rules of art were derived—which is precisely what Poe said about Dickens. The concept that original genius drew from nature instead of from art persisted throughout the eighteenth century in one form or another. It was presented at length in such works as Edward Young's *Conjectures on Original Composition* (1759), Alexander Gerard's *Essay on Genius* (1767), and, of course, in the Reverend Hugh Blair's *Lectures*. "A masterly genius," wrote Blair, "will of himself, untaught, compose in such a manner as shall be agreeable to the most material rules of criticism: for as these rules are founded in nature, nature will often suggest them in practice. Homer, it is more than probable, was acquainted with no systems of the art of poetry. Guided by genius alone, he composed in verse a regular story, which all posterity has admired." [9]

The romantic critics were as much interested in the psychology of genius as the neoclassic critics had been, but the emphasis had changed from an examination of the way genius revealed the laws or rules of art or general nature to an exploration of the mysterious, spontaneous, almost involuntary aspects of creativity. Poe wanted to have it both ways; as a critic he felt that he had to develop rules or principles drawn from nature as criteria for evaluation, and as a

[9] Blair, *Lectures*, I, 37–38. Such an opinion would appear to eliminate the necessity of criticism, but not according to Blair. Critics were still necessary to point out the faults of genius and direct it "into its proper channels." This is what Poe did with Dickens—pointed out his faults, at the same time acknowledging that his "art" came from nature.

poet he wanted to understand the nature of the creative act in order to bring it under the dominion of his conscious will. He did not
wish his visions or inspirations to come at random. Like Hart
Crane, who tried to compel poetic inspiration through jazz and
wine, Poe wanted to master the creative *élan* and make it function
on demand. He was well aware that rhetorical skill and a knowledge of audience psychology could very nearly create the *effect* of
genius, but he felt that a discriminating reader could detect the
difference between a work of genius and a work of talent. His problems were how to control inspiration and make it function steadily
instead of sporadically, and, above all, how to make a genuine work
of genius reveal itself as such to both the discriminating and the
mass audience. His solution was to emphasize the artistic will. He
had said as much in his review of Longfellow's *Hyperion* when he
had spoken of Longfellow's shirking "the great labour requisite for
the stern demands of high art . . . the unremitting toil and patient elaboration which, when soul-guided, result in the beauty of
Unity, Totality, Truth . . . ." [10]

True genius, operating from unconscious sources, made art look
easy, but Poe knew that it wasn't. Dickens' genius enabled him to
compose "evidently without effort," but, as Poe went on to say, his
art was "elaborate and great." This did not mean that Dickens' artistry was perfect. Perfection would be achieved, Poe thought—and
said some years later—only when the unconscious genius of a poet
like Shelley could be united with the conscious art of a poet like
Tennyson, and this combination did not yet exist. As far as
Dickens was concerned, Poe found minor defects in plotting and in
depiction of character; but the charge already being brought
against the novelist, that his characters were caricatures, Poe disallowed. Even in an artistic mode so imitative of nature as the novel,

[10] Nothing is more annoying than Poe's use of the term "truth." In his
review of Longfellow's *Hyperion* he was examining a prose narrative, and he
did not forbid prose to have the object of communicating truth. In this
case he was referring to "scattered" thought which was not organized into
an appropriate form. The unity invoked was the unity of thought and expression, not the unity of impression required of a poem.

Poe claimed, art is not a mirror image. The artist does not "paint an object to be true, but to appear true to the beholder. Were we to copy nature with accuracy, the object copied would seem unnatural." Thus Dickens' art was not nature itself but "a happy modification of Nature." Had his characters really been caricatures, "they would not live in public estimation beyond the hour of their first survey."

In spite of his often expressed contempt for the standards of the mob, Poe never quite relinquished the neoclassic notion that universality of appeal was one of the tests of art. The public could be fooled temporarily, he thought, but not for long. The fact that Dickens was the "idol of the people" was of undeniable importance to the critic who evaluated his work. To Poe as to the neoclassic critic, the first duty of the artist was not to express himself but to appeal to an audience. This was the reason for his emphasis, from the very beginning of his serious criticism, upon unity of effect, instead of the classical formal unity, or the transcendental unity invoked by Coleridge and Schlegel. Many critics, including M. H. Abrams, have taken Poe's statement in "The Poetic Principle," that a poem is written "solely for the poem's sake," to mean that art should be released from the burden of "external causes and ulterior ends." [11] This is true enough, but chiefly Poe wished to release the poem, as genre, from the burden of didactic statement. There was an end—pleasure—and this end might be called ulterior in that Poe conceived of the poem as stimulating a feeling more intense than the aesthetic response, although the appreciation of the poem *as* poem contributed to the delight of the connoisseur. Yet in his theoretical criticism Poe sought to develop a formula for pleasing everyone. Through psychology he would locate principles of composition that would allow the artist to please the uncultivated as well as the cultivated taste. Even in "The Poetic Principle," which is rhapsodic about the ideals of art, he stated that "it is

[11] Abrams, *The Mirror and the Lamp*, 27. Mr. Abrams has placed Poe historically with the advocates of "art for art's sake," but it is clear that Poe advocated art for the soul's sake.

to be hoped that common sense, in the time to come, will prefer deciding upon a work of art, rather by the impression it makes, by the effect it produces, than by the time it took to impress the effect, or by the amount of 'sustained effort' which had been found necessary in effecting the impression." Poe felt that works of genius produced an impression of apparent ease; works of talent seemed laboriously contrived. Neither the author's ease nor his effort should be used for evaluation, however. Audience reaction, the impression a work of art makes, should be its final test.

In Poe's opinion Dickens' characters had lived in the public estimation because they were not caricatures, but "*creations . . .* only not all of the highest order, because the elements employed are not always of the highest." The "highest order" of imagination made its combinations approach the ideal, whereas some of Dickens' characters, such as Quilp, with his "mouth like that of a panting dog," his cowardice and malevolence, were made up of low elements indeed. Nevertheless, "the great feature of the 'Curiosity Shop' is its chaste, vigorous, and glorious imagination."

By the statements above we can deduce Poe's concept of the role of the imagination in the construction of character. It combines the most admirable aspects of character to produce idealized portraits that represent a "happy modification of Nature." The concept is obviously neoclassic, but we should remember also that in his review of *George Balcombe* Poe had said that the only way a writer of fiction could achieve originality in characterization would be to present hypothetical qualities which were "so skilfully adapted to the circumstances which surround them, that our sense of fitness is not offended . . . ." [12] Thus, to Poe, fidelity to the actual was not necessary to achieve the "happy modification of Nature" which was art. The elements of character that made up the idealized portrait could be completely hypothetical so long as the character was adapted to his environment. Adaptation was a law of nature, and the character who was adapted to the circumstances in which he lived could be said to be natural so long as audience

[12] *Works*, IX, 261–62.

assent was secured. By emphasizing the law of nature instead of empirical observation, Poe was able to accommodate his theory of the ideal—something that happens in the mind—to the neoclassic criterion of propriety. The imaginary character would not offend our sense of fitness if he suited his world, which in Poe's opinion might be an invented world, not an actual one. Thus, Dickens' characters, though seemingly exaggerated when measured by the standards of experience, yet followed nature because they were adapted to the London which Dickens described. They were produced by a vigorous imagination that transcended mere observation and recording of facts by imitating not nature itself but natural law.[13]

[13] Poe's clearest exposition of adaptation is in an item from his "Marginalia" (*Works*, XVI, 9), but his first consideration of the subject may have been prompted by his reading of Roget's *Animal and Vegetable Physiology*, which he reviewed for the *Messenger* in 1836. *Works*, VIII, 206–10. This book was one of the "Bridgewater Treatises," sponsored by a bequest from the Earl of Bridgewater. As Poe noted in this review, the Bridgewater researchers were limited by the terms of the bequest, for they were required to use "natural philosophy" (science) to point out the wisdom and benevolence of God as "manifested in the Creation." Accordingly, they looked for evidence to prove that the laws of nature were framed for the benefit of man: nature was adapted to man, instead of the reverse. Poe perceived this error and in his "Marginalia" declared that God's work exhibited "reciprocity of adaptation" in which cause and effect could not be distinguished. In other words, we could not really tell whether man became adapted to his environment or whether the environment was planned in such a way as to permit the specific adaptation. Adaptation, then, should be observed as a complex interaction, not a simple cause and effect relationship. In human creations, however, such as that of character in a novel, the cause-effect relationship was easy to comprehend. Although in the review Poe did not explain *why* Dickens' characters were "original" yet true to nature, his concept of adaptation enables us to interpret his argument that caricature is rarely present when "the component parts" of the character are "in keeping." This would mean that the character traits, however exaggerated, were of a piece, and that, furthermore, they were "skillfully adapted to the circumstances which surround them." The despicable Quilp, for instance, has his haunts "among the wharf rats." Poe may have developed his concept of a prevailing disposition (all parts "in keeping") from the phrenological description of temperament, or observable somatic type. See Note 44, Chapter IX, of this book.

3

In the June number of *Graham's* the only review worth consideration is that of Thomas Babington Macaulay's *Critical and Miscellaneous Essays*.[14] Poe occasionally expressed admiration for
Macaulay's criticism. If he had read—and probably he had—
Macaulay's review of the poems of Robert Montgomery in the
April, 1830, issue of the *Edinburgh Review*,[15] he would have
found a method similar to his own as well as attitudes of which he
would have approved. Macaulay attacked "puffery," corrupt publishing practices, and the dishonesty of journalistic reviewers. Like
Poe, Macaulay began his review by announcing that he had to
render justice because the author's work had "received more enthu-
siastic praise and [had] deserved more unmixed contempt, than
any which . . . [had] appeared within the last three or four
years." Macaulay accused Montgomery of plagiarism in a manner
strikingly similar to Poe's and then proceeded to examine the
poet's imagery and his grammar, making satirical comments about
both, as Poe was to do many times. Of course this resemblance is
not surprising. Poe had learned his early reviewing method from
the British magazines. What is surprising is that instead of praising
the review of Montgomery's *Poems*, which was Macaulay's nearest
approach to criticism in Poe's sense, he chose to comment on
Macaulay's review of Leopold Ranke's *Ecclesiastical and Political
History of the Popes of Rome*, published in the October, 1840,
issue of the *Edinburgh Review*. Macaulay's article, Poe claimed,
was not a review at all. Instead, it was "nothing more than a beautifully written treatise on the main theme of Ranke himself, the
whole matter of the treatise being deduced from the History."
Poe's comment is perfectly accurate. The review was a long summary of the history of the period under consideration without a

[14] *Works*, X, 156–60.
[15] Since Macaulay began contributing to the *Edinburgh Review* in 1825,
it is probable that Poe was familiar with his reviews before the publication
of the collected edition.

single line of criticism. Macaulay, a historian, frequently wrote this kind of review, and, as far as Poe was concerned, it was typical of the reviews currently being published in the quarterlies—long essays designed to inform the reader of the content of a work rather than to criticize it.

Within a few months Poe was to state in full his opinion of what a review should be, and his remarks about Macaulay are anticipatory. If he actually read the review of Montgomery, which was included in the collected edition, he deliberately avoided mentioning it because it would have diluted his thesis, and, in addition, it was not really characteristic of the reviews in the collection.

In the July number Poe reverted to his satirical manner in a review of Seba Smith's *Powhatan: A Metrical Romance* (Smith was better known as the humorist Jack Downing).[16] Prefixed to the poem was one of those pretentious, self-congratulatory prefaces that always aroused Poe's anger, but the poem itself, he felt, was beneath contempt because it gave no evidence of artistry:

> The leading fault of "Powhatan," then, is precisely what its author supposes to be its principal merit. "It would be difficult," he says, in that pitiable preface, in which he has so exposed himself, "to find a poem that embodies more truly the spirit of history, or indeed that follows out more faithfully many of its details." The truth is, Mr. Downing has never dreamed of any artistic *arrangement* of his facts. He has gone straight forward like a blind horse, and turned neither to the one side nor to the other, for fear of stumbling. But he gets them all in, the facts, we mean. Powhatan never did anything in his life, we are sure, that Mr. Downing has not given in his poem.

Smith's attempt to make a poem into an accurate historical treatise showed that he had no conception of the proper function of art.

In August, Poe had the uneasy task of reviewing a work by a friend, Lambert A. Wilmer,[17] with whom he had hoped to

---

[16] *Works*, X, 162–67.

[17] Review of *The Quacks of Helicon: A Satire*, by Lambert A. Wilmer, *ibid.*, 182–96. Poe was careful to announce that Wilmer was a personal friend, thus attempting to avoid any imputation of the bias that could have easily been concealed behind his editorial anonymity.

launch a magazine in the Baltimore period before he joined the
Messenger. The work, called *The Quacks of Helicon,* had some
merit because it satirized some of the "prominent *literati*" and gave
them, Poe said, what they deserved. Yet not even for Wilmer,
whom he had once reviewed leniently, did he shirk the essential
function of a critic, an examination of the faults of the work.

> Its prevalent blemishes are referrible [*sic*] chiefly to the leading sin
> of *imitation.* Had the work been composed professedly in para-
> phrase of the whole manner of the sarcastic epistles of the times of
> Dryden and Pope, we should have pronounced it the most in-
> genious and truthful thing of the kind upon record. So close is the
> copy, that it extends to the most trivial points; for example, to the
> old forms of punctuation. The turns of phraseology, the tricks of
> rhythm, the arrangement of the paragraphs, the general conduct of
> the satire—everything—all—are Dryden's. . . . We have here the
> bold, vigorous, and sonorous verse, the biting sarcasm, the pungent
> epigrammatism, the unscrupulous directness, as of old. Yet it will
> not do to forget that Mr. Wilmer has been *shown how* to accom-
> plish these things. He is thus only entitled to the praise of a close
> observer, and of a thoughtful and skilful copyist.

Almost equally reprehensible was the coarseness of the satire,
and Poe managed to excuse what he considered "the gross ob-
scenity, the filth," only by alleging that it came not from the mind
of the author but from his indiscriminate imitation of the "Swift
and Rochester school." In Poe's opinion nothing vulgar should ever
be said, or even conceived.

Since Wilmer's satire did not qualify as a work of art, Poe was
free to comment upon the subject matter, a practice he usually abjured, but this particular subject enabled him to reopen the campaign he had begun in the *Southern Literary Messenger* against
corrupt publishing practices, sycophantic reviewers, and the manip-
ulations of the literary coteries. Poe's first satirical reviews had
probably been for the purpose of attracting attention; but now,
writing as an established critic known for his independence, he was
less open to the charge of self-serving, and his opinions carried
more weight. Perhaps he was not completely without guile, for his

own magazine project was in his mind throughout his tenure with *Graham's*, and he was able to use the journal to prove that Edgar Poe was the most fearless critic in America. To supply this proof beyond any doubt, in the review of Wilmer he exhumed the case of *Norman Leslie*, as if daring his old enemies, Lewis Gaylord Clark, the powerful editor of the *Knickerbocker*, Colonel William L. Stone, and Theodore Fay himself to renew the combat.[18] Poe wrote: "It is needless to call to mind the desperate case of Fay—a case where the pertinacity of the effort to gull, where the obviousness of the attempt at forestalling a judgment, where the wofully overdone be-Mirrorment of that man-of-straw, together with the pitiable platitude of his production, proved a dose somewhat too potent for even the well-prepared stomach of the mob. We say it is supererogatory to dwell upon 'Norman Leslie,' or other by-gone follies, when we have, before our eyes, hourly instances of the machinations in question."

Poe's admission is correct; it *was* supererogatory to bring up the *Norman Leslie* case, and it was inaccurate to say that the mob rejected the novel. It was quite popular, in spite of Poe's attacks. Poe, as he admitted in a letter to Snodgrass, was preaching a "fire-and-fury sermon," and the remainder of his review was a general castigation of the abuses he detested in journalistic criticism: vainglorious nationalism, uncritical praise of literary hacks, and the "ruthless" character assassination and "untraceable slanders" practiced against the few critics with courage to be severe and honest, by which he meant himself.

The "slanders" were already circulating. In April, Poe had writ-

[18] Poe's old opponents were much less in evidence by this time. Willis Gaylord Clark died this same year, and Theodore Fay was abroad serving as a diplomat (Fay had never retaliated directly). Colonel Stone, though only fifty years old, had but three years to live. Lewis Gaylord Clark was one year older than Poe and continued to be most obliging in responding to Poe's challenges, but now Poe was writing for an increasingly powerful journal, and evidently George R. Graham was an astute journalist who recognized Poe's commercial value as well as his literary ability. At any rate, Graham did not often try to make Poe temper his criticism, as had White and Burton. Graham continued to think highly of Poe, even after Poe's inevitable dissatisfaction with working for someone else had caused a break.

ten to Snodgrass accusing Burton of "erecting" slanders concerning his drinking; and within the next two years the slanders were being circulated not only in Philadelphia but elsewhere. About a year later, in 1843, even Wilmer, Poe's "personal friend," wrote to John Tomlin in Tennessee that Poe had become strange and was "going headlong to destruction." [19] Poe reacted with characteristic violence when Tomlin informed him of Wilmer's letter and responded that Wilmer was an "envious scoundrel," "a reprobate of the lowest class," and a "villain." Not only this, but Poe claimed that his review of *The Quacks of Helicon*, which he had used as an excuse to renew journalistic warfare, was really an attempt to befriend Wilmer out of pity.[20] It is obvious that Poe's sensitivity to criticism was the cause of much of his trouble. Whenever anyone, friend or foe, touched a sensitive spot, however lightly, Poe became vengefully furious. The rumors of his instability were based upon fact, but, like most rumors, they exaggerated the situation. Poe was obviously a capable man most of the time, and he knew that the alleged slanders endangered his cherished project of starting a magazine of his own, as well as his status as a critic. He had to find a backer, and men with money were unlikely to entrust it to an unstable editor who might be an alcoholic; so in his personal letters Poe raged against the slandermongers and rationalized by claiming that the slanders were a reaction to his severe and honest criticism.

Perhaps accurate in his general assessment of the journalistic criticism of the country, Poe was more reckless, to say the least, when he demonstrated his courage with satirical comments on some of the very authors whom he—and Graham—had been trying to cultivate. In June, 1841, he had solicited the support of Longfellow, Willis, and Bryant for his personal magazine project.[21] Now

[19] May 20, 1843, in Quinn, *Edgar Allan Poe*, 401. Wilmer's letter to Tomlin seems indicative more of concern than of groundless malice, as Poe interpreted it; but since in 1843 Poe was making every effort to establish a journal of his own, and since Tomlin was a supporter, he had to defend his character.

[20] Poe to John Tomlin, August 28, 1843, in *Letters*, I, 235–36.

[21] See Poe to Longfellow, June 22, 1841, *ibid.*, 166–68. If he actually wrote to Willis and Bryant, the letters are not available, but in a letter to Washington Irving on June 21, 1841 (*ibid.*, 161–63), he declared that he

in August, ostensibly to defend them against the "indiscriminate censure of Wilmer" in *The Quacks of Helicon*, he conducted the defense in ironic understatement probably less pleasing to the authors than Wilmer's attack: "Mr. Bryant is not *all* a fool. Mr. Willis is not *quite* an ass. Mr. Longfellow *will* steal, but, perhaps, he cannot help it, (for we have heard of such things), and then it must not be denied that *nil tetigit quod non ornavit*." Poe was fearless, no question about that; but his effrontery in making such statements about the very writers he was trying to attract is incredible. Tactics as irrational as these must be explained by psychiatry, not by a critical essay. Poe had his own axes to grind, and, as he admitted in his letter to Snodgrass, he used the review of Wilmer as a grindstone.

4

Although Poe wrote some two dozen reviews in the remainder of 1841, they may be summarized. He continued his campaign against what he considered illegitimate methods of gaining literary popularity and critical esteem, at the same time asserting his own opinion that literary merit, validated by comparison with ideal standards, was the only basis for approval of any work that pretended to be art.

Running the risk of alienating himself from an audience of sentimentalists on both sides of the Atlantic, Poe dared to suggest that those sweet and tragic sisters, Lucretia and Margaret Davidson, both of whom "perished of consumption" in their teens, were not quite the geniuses that their admiring biographers, Catherine Sedgwick and Washington Irving, had made them out to be. Lucretia had been elevated into public admiration by England's laureate, Robert Southey, and the "awe of the laureate's *ipse dixit*" had not yet disappeared. "We yield to no one," Poe wrote, "in warmth of

---

was sending similar letters requesting contributions to Cooper, Paulding, Kennedy, Bryant, Halleck, and Willis. The letters to Kennedy and Halleck, similar in content to those cited above, are printed in *Letters*, I, 163–65, 168–70. The letters of solicitation that are available are all dated between June 21 and June 24, 1841.

admiration for the personal character of these sweet sisters, as that character is depicted by the mother, by Miss Sedgwick, and by Mr. Irving. But it costs us no effort to distinguish that which, in our heart, is love of their worth, from that which, in our intellect, is appreciation of their poetic ability. With the former, as critic, we have nothing to do. The distinction is one too obvious for comment; and its observation would have spared us much twaddle on the part of the commentators . . . .[22]

If, as E. Douglas Branch has written, criticizing Mrs. Sigourney was like criticizing George Washington, daring to criticize the sweet sisters Davidson must have been like casting aspersions on the saints, yet Poe took his chances in order to make his point: personal worth had nothing to do with literary merit, and it was with literary merit alone that a critic should concern himself.

Poe's tone in his review of the Davidson sisters was appropriately tender, but he was much harsher in attempting to counteract the popularity of Captain Frederick Marryat. There was nothing in Marryat's novels, Poe thought, to arouse intelligent interest, not plot or style or thought. Written for the mob, *Joseph Rushbrook* had no semblance of originality and provided no incentive for thought. Incident was piled on incident in Marryat's work, and authorial comment—which Poe was beginning to demand to supply the intellectual content of a novel—was entirely absent. "The commenting force," Poe argued, "can never be safely disregarded. It is far better to have a dearth of incident, with skilful observation upon it, than the utmost variety of event. . . . The successful

[22] *Works*, X, 225–26. In this connection, one should also read Poe's review of Margaret Davidson's *Poetical Remains* (*ibid.*, 174–78). His review of Margaret Davidson was quite tactful and displayed admiration for the girl's precocity. Her longest poem "Lenore" (that ubiquitous "poetic" name also favored by Poe) was remarkable for a child of fifteen, but not so remarkable as other poems she wrote at the ages of eight and ten. In the review of Lucretia Davidson's poems, Poe avoided direct criticism by intimating that Southey had taken leave of his wits and that Miss Sedgwick had erred in quoting Southey. Miss Sedgwick's praise was at least honest, but "the cant of a kind heart when betraying into error a naturally sound judgment, is perhaps the only species of cant in the world not altogether contemptible." Poe did not censure the poetry of the Davidsons, but his opinion is clear in his remarks on their critics and biographers.

novelist must . . . be careful to bring into view his *private* interest, sympathy, and opinion in regard to his own creations." [23] Poe
could conceive of no way for a novelist to reveal his ideas except by
commentary; and yet we would have to agree with him that a narrative devoid of intelligence would be as dull as a ship's log. It is
hard to imagine a novel completely lacking in evidence of the author's opinions, but there is a relative dearth of thought and feeling
in purely commercial fiction, and in Poe's opinion that was what
Joseph Rushbrook was, a commercial novel designed only to produce excitement.

Equally obnoxious to Poe were publishing tricks designed to gull
the public into buying inferior works, and he hit hard at *The Pic
Nic Papers*,[24] "edited" by Charles Dickens. This book was a collection of articles from Dickens, G. P. R. James, W. H. Ainsworth,
and others; but the title, together with Dickens' name, Poe
claimed, would make the prospective buyer think of the currently
popular *The Pickwick Papers*. The similarity of titles was "a piece
of chicanery which not even the end in view can sanction." The
purpose in this case was to raise funds for the widow and orphans
of a young publisher who had died recently, but Poe, campaigning
for publishing honesty, would not allow the end to justify the
means. "No body of men are justified in making capital of the public's gullibility for purposes of charity, public or private—for any
purposes under the sun."

Poe's attitude was uncompromising. Traditionally critics in
America had assumed guardianship over the public morals. Poe,
not much concerned with morals, assumed guardianship over the
public taste in both a theoretical and a practical sense. A collection
such as the one he was reviewing, Poe affirmed, was invariably
made up of the miscellaneous scraps that the authors were unable
to dispose of to better advantage, the least valuable manuscripts
they happened to have about them. "The refuse labour of a man of
genius," Poe stated, "is usually inferior, and greatly so, to that of a
man of common-place talent . . . ." When a genius was con-
strained to write by external necessity, he would "occasionally

[23] *Works*, X, 201.   [24] *Ibid.*, 206–209.

grovel in platitudes of the most pitiable description." Consequently it did not surprise Poe to find that *The Pic Nic Papers* contained a great deal of "trash," and it was an imposition upon the public to sell such material by advertising the famous names of the contributors.

Poe's argument here was perhaps colored by his own predicament. Many times he protested that to be forced to compose at all hours, in whatever condition of health, was intolerable; yet he had been compelled to write in this way. He knew his own work was uneven, and it was comforting to him, no doubt, to revert to the traditional psychology of genius. Genius was wild and irregular, the eighteenth-century critics had proclaimed; and when it was subjected to restraints its products were likely to be inferior. Men of talent could compose well by the rules, but genius, writing from nature, made the rules. Poe did not hesitate to examine the products of genius in relation to ideal standards, but he was conventional in thinking that artistic genius was temperamental. We know that he published his own inferior work out of sheer necessity, and that he had allowed his name to be used for *The Conchologist's First Book*, but as guardian of the public taste he felt it necessary to oppose practices in which he sometimes engaged.

If the miscellaneous scraps of genius should not be foisted on the public, it was even worse for a critic to "puff" a piece of hackwork into fame. Poe saw the *Crichton* of William Harrison Ainsworth, the popular British novelist, in this light. A Philadelphia critic had proclaimed that *Crichton* was "unapproachable and alone" at the head of the list of English novels. Poe found it only "a somewhat ingenious admixture of pedantry, bombast, and rigmarole . . . one continued abortive effort at effect." [25] Ains-

---

[25] Poe's opinion of *Crichton* is expressed in a review of Ainsworth's *Guy Fawkes*. See *Works*, X, 214–20. In this review he violated his own principles by using most of his space to discuss a work other than the subject of his own review, justifying himself by declaring that *Guy Fawkes* was beneath contempt. It should be noted that here Poe used the term "effect" perjoratively. In this usage, it meant an unsuccessful effort to provide anticipation by letting the reader think that something remarkable was about to happen.

worth's *Jack Sheppard*, which American critics had condemned for "immoral tendencies," had some merit as a work of art. At least it was not disfigured by bombast of style, though it was completely lacking in authorial comment. The events were merely narrated instead of being "discussed" by the author.

For several months now, Poe had been stressing the virtue of comment in a novel, and gradually his point had been made clear. What he disliked was a completely barren ("naked") sequence of events, an objective account of action. *Robinson Crusoe* and Godwin's *Caleb Williams*, he thought, provided the best examples of a rich variety of incident colored by emotion and thought in such a way as to engage a reader's sympathetic attention. Poe's citation of these two works is revealing. In *Robinson Crusoe* it is the subjectivity of the character that counts. We experience what Crusoe experiences, what he thinks and feels. In Poe's opinion the novel showed Defoe's sympathetic imagination, his power of identifying with his character. *Caleb Williams*, on the other hand, is both a detective story and a thesis novel designed to convey Godwin's political views. Poe admired it as a novel that contained not only an ingenious plot and exciting action but also thought.

Poe wanted to be immersed in thought and feeling when he read fiction, to experience the mental and emotional life of the characters and of the author. The sympathetic imagination of the reader would be unaffected by a narrative that merely told what happened. Poe wanted a novel to be heavily subjective, and apparently it did not matter too much whether the subjectivity proceeded from the character or directly from the author. The pleasure derived from any kind of art, Poe always insisted, was in direct ratio to its effect. "Bald," "naked," and "barren" were the terms he usually applied to a narrative that did not reverberate with emotional and intellectual overtones.

Since, to Poe, Ainsworth's writings lacked thought and emotional intensity, he judged the author to be only a hack, writing a "stipulated number of pages" for a "certain sum of money." Ainsworth only wrote for the "lowest order of the lettered mob." Consequently, *Guy Fawkes* was beneath criticism, and the next work by Ainsworth that came to his desk, Poe promised, he would throw to the pigs, who had more "leisure for its examination" than he.

One other review during the closing months of 1841 has some interest. This was of Dr. Samuel Warren's *Ten Thousand a Year*.[26] Warren had gained some fame with his *Passages from the Diary of a Late Physician*, which had appeared serially in *Blackwood's* and may have influenced Poe in some of his early tales. *Ten Thousand a Year* became a very popular novel, but Poe, in his campaign to purify the public taste and to expose undeserved popularity, thought it "shamefully ill-written." It was full of the "grossest misusages of language," and the whole tone was "in the last degree mawkish and inflated." Some of the incidents were "wofully inadapted and improbable," and the "moralizing throughout" was extremely tedious.

The fact that Poe objected to Warren's moralizing indicates that the comment he had been demanding from a novelist had nothing to do with those long sermons of direct address too frequently present in the nineteenth-century novel. He did not demand moral instruction in author comment; in fact, it bored him. What he wanted was evidence that the writer was totally engaged with his subject, emotionally and intellectually.

5

We have seen that Poe, although still maneuvering to establish his own journal, was able to use *Graham's Magazine* as a medium through which he could publicize his ideas about the function of criticism and the corruption of American journalism. Furthermore, since he had the space for one long, analytical review in each number (with the exception of the October, 1841, issue to which he did not contribute), he was able to express certain aspects of his devel-

---

[26] *Works*, X, 210–12. An interesting sidelight on Poe and Warren is furnished by Ada B. Nisbet. Warren wrote a vitriolic *Blackwood's* review of Dickens' *American Notes* that was attributed to Poe by the biographer Mary E. Phillips. See Nisbet, "New Light on the Poe-Dickens Relationship," *Nineteenth Century Fiction*, V (1950–51), 295.

oping theories. He reviewed no books of poetry during 1841 which were important enough to serve as a springboard for theory, but he gave a definition of fictional plot that represented a refinement of his earlier statements. In addition, he showed himself more confident in expressing his own opinions; he was less prone to rely upon authority from abroad. His argument with Coleridge and Schlegel may seem to be more factitious than genuine to us, but to Poe the distinctions were important because they furnished a theoretical basis for his conviction that art was, or should be, a conscious, willed activity, not completely subservient to the vagaries of inspiration. At the same time, he was aware that these vagaries did exist and that the critic had to take them into account when examining the inferior work of a genius. His temporary solution, a pragmatic one, was that the lesser works of a genius should not be given to the public, because they were likely to be inferior to the work of a merely talented man who possessed skill and patience. And if the inferior work of genius were given to the public, it must be judged by ideal standards and not by the reputation of the author, which could always have been achieved by dishonest publishing practices. The true work of genius, on the other hand, could stand the test of analysis; it was the duty of the critic to examine the work as an autonomous construct.

The first nine months with *Graham's*, then, may be regarded as a period of preparation for Poe's most significant criticism. Relative freedom from restraint by his employer, sufficient space to make the extended analyses he preferred, a large and rapidly increasing audience, and letters of encouragement from certain of his friends gave Poe the reinforcement he needed to pronounce boldly the elements of his critical theory and his ideas of the function of the critic. This he was to do within the first six months of the coming year, 1842. This year was to be Poe's *annus mirabilis* as a critic; and he was to begin it by making his most forceful statement of what criticism should and should not be.

XI · The Province of the Critic

ALTHOUGH Poe's prospects for publishing his own magazine were not very promising in the fall of 1841, there were many reasons for him to feel confident about the future. The subscriptions to *Graham's* were coming in "at the most astounding rate," he wrote Frederick Thomas. In January of 1842, 25,000 copies would be printed. Poe had never had such an audience, and he had a relatively free hand in writing the kind of reviews he wanted to write.[1] Previously he had had to smuggle his demands for critical reform into his reviews, but in January he was able to publish his first, indeed his only, full-length essay on the function of criticism. The title of the essay, "Exordium," indicated that it was an explanatory preface which would define what Poe intended to do in criticism, and it was precisely that—Poe's definition of critical imperatives.

[1] Unlike Poe's previous employers White and Burton, Graham appears rarely to have pressured him to mitigate his tone. Even then, Poe became angry when Graham asked him to speak favorably of some local Philadelphians. Early in 1842, Poe wrote to Frederick Thomas that he had been "weak enough to permit Graham to modify my opinions . . . ." He had been asked to praise Judge Robert T. Conrad, an important political and minor literary figure of Philadelphia, and to "speak well" of Thomas G. Spear, Ezra Holden, and Charles J. Peterson. Since this requirement was in connection with Poe's "Autography" series which had been initiated in the *Messenger* and continued in *Graham's* for November, 1841, it was understandable. The series pretended to analyze each subject by his handwriting, and Poe's remarks, often satirical, could be taken as personal affronts. His comments on Conrad in the "Autography" do represent unenthusiastic praise, while those on the other three were perfunctory favors indeed, for in all items except the Conrad Poe inserted an uncomplimentary remark. Spear was a minor poet, Peterson a journalist who worked for Graham, and Holden the editor and publisher of the Philadelphia *Saturday Courier*, a literary weekly. As incautious as ever, Poe did not mind antagonizing those "ninnies" Holden, Spear and Peterson, but Graham was more careful. Fuming over this unimportant matter, Poe acted as if his reputation had been ruined and exclaimed to Thomas, "Let no man accuse me of leniency again." See *Letters*, I, 193. For Poe's uncharacteristic "leniency," see "Autography," *Works*, XV, 210–11, 212, 232–33, 235.

As was customary with him, Poe took his lead from an article in a contemporary journal, *Arcturus*, the organ of a politico-literary group in New York called "Young America." Since Perry Miller has given a lively account of this group and its relations with Poe and Melville,[2] it is sufficient to say here that Cornelius Mathews, one of the editors of *Arcturus*, was one of the most vociferous advocates of literary nationalism. This alone would have been enough to make him a tempting target for Poe's tomahawk; but when Mathews declared that "criticism . . . dismisses errors of grammar, and hands over an imperfect rhyme or a false quantity to the proof-reader," he was belittling Poe's method. To make things even worse, Mathews broadened criticism to include "every form of literature except perhaps the imaginative and the strictly dramatic." A criticism, he wrote, could be "an essay, a sermon, an oration, a chapter in history, a philosophical speculation, a prose-poem, an art-novel, a dialogue; it admits of humor, pathos, the personal feelings of autobiography, the broadest views of statesmanship."[3] If such views were accepted, then everything that Poe had advocated for the five years he had been a practicing critic would be disallowed. A rebuttal was necessary, and "Exordium" is a point-by-point refutation of Mathews, but it is more: it is a testament to the value of criticism and an account of the imperative duties of a critic.

The public, Poe asserted, was beginning to display an unusual interest in literary criticism. Periodicals were treating it as a "science" instead of an expression of opinion. Because of "subserviency" to British critical dicta, America had lagged behind in this science, but finally, in a "revulsion of feeling," American critics had gone to the other extreme of a perfervid nationalism, praising books merely because they were American. Our magazines had spoken of "tariffs" and "protection" for native genius as if "the

[2] Miller, *The Raven and the Whale*. See also John Stafford, *The Literary Criticism of "Young America,"* (Berkeley, 1952).

[3] The quotation from *Arcturus* is omitted in *Works*. I have used the text printed by Arthur Hobson Quinn and Edward H. O'Neill (eds.) in *The Complete Poems and Stories of Edgar Allan Poe* (New York, 1946), II, 929–33.

world at large were not the only proper stage for the literary *his-trio*." At the moment, however, this "anomalous state of feeling" was subsiding, and Americans had begun to "demand the use—to inquire into the offices and provinces of criticism—to regard it more as an art based immovably in nature, less as a mere system of fluctuating and conventional dogmas." This sounds like wishful thinking on Poe's part, but perhaps he believed it, for he was firmly convinced that a literary magazine, featuring his kind of criticism, would be a financial success.

Although they were beginning to recognize the danger of uncritical nationalism, American critics, Poe averred, were running into another danger, that of "a most despicable species of cant—the cant of generality." This had occurred because of their slavish imitation of the British quarterlies. Foreign quarterlies had originally reviewed books properly, by analyzing the contents of the book and passing judgment upon merits and defects. Now, however, because of the pernicious system of anonymous reviewing, the natural process had lost ground. The reviewer, being known only to a few, had no reputation to defend and sought only to turn out as many pages as he could "at so many guineas per sheet."

Poe's analysis of the reason for the popularity of the essay-review tells us more about him than it does about the history of criticism. Poe liked to sign his publications, though he was not always able to do so. He signed his poems in the *Messenger* in spite of the fetish of anonymity in the South, and he liked to see his name on the masthead as being responsible for the criticism of a magazine. He was angry when because of the system of anonymous reviewing someone else's "twaddle" was attributed to him. Poe wanted to build a reputation; he wanted recognition and was not always completely scrupulous in the ways he sought to gain it. This is one of the reasons he could barely tolerate being a subordinate editor of a book review section in which the anonymous reviews of others could be confused with his own. Whether the result were adulation or damnation, Poe wanted to be known as America's foremost critic, but for this he had to have a magazine of his own.

A second reason that uncritical reviews were proliferating, Poe asserted, was that critical analysis required much time and mental exertion. It was much easier to summarize the book under consideration and to generalize one's impressions, or to write a "diffuse essay on the subject matter of the publication." The essay-review, the most prevalent type, gave the appearance of learning and effort, but it was simply not criticism: "Now, while we do not mean to deny that a good essay is a good thing," wrote Poe, echoing by a curious feat of memory the words of a correspondent who had challenged him on the *Messenger*,[4] "we yet assert that these papers on general topics have nothing whatever to do with that *criticism* which their evil example has nevertheless infected *in se.*"

It was this kind of review—the general essay—that Cornelius Mathews had spoken of as the characteristic growth of the nineteenth century. Not so, said Poe, it was only a development of the last two or three decades in Great Britain. The French reviews, which preserved "the *unique* spirit of true criticism," did not generalize. Neither did the "magnificent *critiques raisonnées*" of the Germans—Winckelmann, Novalis, Schelling, Goethe, and the brothers August Wilhelm and Friedrich Schlegel. Their criticism did not differ in principle from that of the eighteenth-century British critics, Dr. Johnson, Lord Kames, and Hugh Blair, "for the principles of these artists will not fail until Nature herself expires." [5] The Germans, however, were more thorough and profound in the application of the principles than their British predecessors had been.

Taken out of its context and surveyed in the light of literary history, Poe's argument seems odd, to say the least. Why should the rationalist Johnson, the psychologist Kames, and the rhetorician Blair be linked with the German *Frühromantiker?* Yet if we think in terms of approach, as Poe was doing, his statement makes sense. A criticism in any age, Poe thought, should be a judgment of the

---

[4] The editor of the Washington *Telegraph* had criticized Poe's approach in these words, "Now he who gives a good essay, gives a good thing." Quoted in Supplement, *Southern Literary Messenger*, II (1836), 136.

[5] Although he had made an unacknowledged and perhaps even an unconscious use of eighteenth-century principles, this is the first time that Poe spoke well of the eighteenth-century critics.

278 · POE: *Journalist and Critic*

literary quality of the work criticized. Furthermore, he thought, any act of judgment must be based upon standards, and these standards could come only from an analysis of human nature. Art exists for the needs of an audience, and it is the critic's task to evaluate its success in meeting those needs. Therefore a criticism in one period of history should not be any different in principle from a criticism in any other period. To say that it should is to "insinuate a charge of variability in laws that cannot vary—the laws of man's heart and intellect—for these are the sole basis upon which the true critical art is established." Consequently, criticism in 1842, as well as in the time of the *Dunciad*, could not without neglecting its duty ignore such matters as bad grammar, imperfect rhymes, or mixed metaphors, those flaws which could keep a literary work from meeting the intellectual and emotional needs of the audience. The rules, if based, as they should be, upon the "laws of man's heart and intellect," should be observed by both author and critic; and the sole function of the critic was to criticize: "Criticism is *not*, we think, an essay, nor a sermon nor an oration, nor a chapter in history, nor a philosophical speculation, nor a prose-poem, nor an art-novel, nor a dialogue. In fact, it *can be* nothing in the world but—a criticism." Poe, then, would "limit literary criticism to comment upon *Art*." The critic should not be concerned with the opinions expressed in a book, for it is his function "simply to decide upon *the mode* in which these opinions are brought to bear." For evaluation of the concepts of a book, ideas which must be judged for their truth or falsity, "the work, divested of its pretensions as an *art-product*, is turned over for discussion to the world at large," particularly to the appropriate specialist in the subject, say the historian or the philosopher. Criticism is "the test or analysis of *Art*," and it is "only properly employed upon productions which have their basis in art itself . . . ."

The statement above is one of the most satisfactory generalizations that Poe ever made about the function of literary criticism, and he is to be applauded for adhering to his own principle except in the few reviews in which he objected to the idea of progress, to transcendental philosophy, and, in one case, to abolition sentiment. Needless to say, critics who have involved themselves in various causes would find fault with Poe's statement, but as a first principle for *literary* criticism it is faultless.

As for the critic himself, Poe appropriated a statement from the often maligned Bulwer to describe his qualities: "he must have courage to blame boldly, magnanimity to eschew envy, genius to appreciate, learning to compare, an eye for beauty, an ear for music, and a heart for feeling." To this Poe added, "a talent for analysis and a solemn indifference to abuse," no doubt speaking from his own experience.

2

Poe was never quite able to maintain the ideal standards he described, but in the forthcoming reviews in *Graham's* he was to make his best effort. One indication of a maturity of attitude appears in his review of the *Essays* of Christopher North (John Wilson),[6] whom he once had admired and defended. Having made a public commitment to responsible criticism, Poe perceived the errors of his former model. Although North displayed commendable wit, humor, imagination, sarcasm, and power of analysis, his tone was too often flippant and his scholarship was superficial (this in spite of the fact that Wilson was a university professor). Frequently, Poe continued, Wilson was betrayed into gross injustice by the strength of his personal feelings. Far from displaying the objectivity of a scientist, Professor Wilson allowed emotion to dominate his judgments.

Significantly, Poe criticized Wilson for some of the very faults that had marred his own first reviews; the implication is that this review represents at least a temporary repudiation of the satirical method. Ideally a critic should rise above the quagmires and fogs of personal controversy; he should soar to see the sun, Poe wrote a few years later in his "Marginalia."[7] The judgment of the critic should

[6] Review of Christopher North's *Critical and Miscellaneous Essays*, in *Graham's Magazine*, XX (1842), 72.
[7] *Works*, XVI, 81.

not be invalidated by personal feeling, political affiliation, or pro-vincial bias. His work should be as objective as science.

So much for the attitude of the critic. In actual practice the critic should be just as alert for faults as for virtues, Poe declared (soon he was to say that excellence speaks for itself). The undis-criminating mass of readers should be advised of the defects of a literary work. Since Poe had spoken well of Blair in "Exordium," it is not surprising that he should have mentioned this particular critical responsibility, which had been assigned by the old rhetori-cian. The final judgment on a work of art, Blair had written, must always be rendered by the public, but the "first applause" that greeted a new work was likely to originate in a superficial appeal to temporary passions and prejudices. It was sometimes the office of criticism to condemn while the public praised, but eventually the public would have to agree with the critic. Criticism was designed to correct the faults of genius, for no "human genius is perfect." True criticism, Blair had said, was "an art founded wholly on expe-rience," which meant that the rules or laws of criticism were derived from human nature, a constant that could be relied upon in any period of history, ancient or modern.[8] Poe reaffirmed this proposition in "Exordium."

Since the public could easily be misled by sensational material, it was the critic's responsibility to avoid the common error of estimat-ing the worth of a book by its popularity. This was the case with *Stanley Thorn*, a novel by Henry Cockton.[9] Such a work would al-most inevitably be popular with semiliterates, Poe wrote, because it appealed to the animal spirits. It required no thought, no reflec-tion; instead it repelled thought, as a "silver rattle" repels the "wrath of a child." In reading it, one experienced a "tingling physico-mental exhilaration, somewhat like that induced by a cold bath, or a flesh-brush," but this exhilaration had no bearing on literary merit. A lively account of exciting incidents was not a novel, of which the chief idiosyncrasy was thought, not deed.

The critic could not legitimately object to any work that gave pleasure—the end of art was pleasure, not instruction, in spite of

[8] Blair, *Lectures*, I, 36–43.   [9] *Works*, XI, 10–15.

the error of Wordsworth and the didactic Lake School. *Stanley Thorn* should not be condemned merely on the ground that it pleased the public, but it deserved censure because it was only a practical joke. It was beneath the level of literature, and Cockton had stolen the incidents and style from his betters—Smollett, Fielding, and Dickens.

Another error prevalent in American criticism was overpraise of native authors. Poe had a case in point, the reputation of the poet John G. C. Brainard: [10] "No poet among us has composed what would deserve the tithe of that amount of approbation so innocently lavished on Brainard." To prove the poet unworthy of his reputation, Poe chose to analyze one poem from Brainard's collection, "The Fall of Niagara," which was usually called the author's best poem and the best ever written on the subject. Poe's analysis is a specimen of his rhetorical criticism as distinguished from his philosophical. When Poe was Blair-ing it, as he was in this review, he looked for mixed metaphors, for bathos, for imperfect rhymes, bad grammar, and impropriety in diction. Obviously he had meant it when he said in "Exordium" that a modern critic should neglect such faults no more than a critic in the time of the *Dunciad,* for he used the neoclassic definition of the bathetic to condemn Brainard's attempt at sublimity in describing Niagara Falls. There was a sinking of effect when the poet wrote of the Falls as being poured from the hollow of God's hand. Even when we think of God in human form ("at best a low and most unideal conception"), we associate ordinary size with the image of a hand. Such a figure reduced the mighty torrent of Niagara to a "trifling quantity of water." The image was "contemptible." [11] The rest of the stanza was equally bad: "The handful of water becomes animate; for it has a front—

[10] *Ibid.,* 15–24.

[11] In a footnote Poe quoted a description of Niagara he considered appropriate to the sublime, italicizing the more striking lines: "When o'er the brink the tide is driven / *As if the vast and sheeted sky* / *In thunder fell from Heaven.*" Curiously, these "magnificent" lines are from Drake's *The Culprit Fay,* which Poe had reviewed adversely in 1836. According to the psychology of the sublime, Drake's figure would elevate the impression of grandeur rightly associated with the falls.

that is, a forehead, and upon this forehead the Deity proceeds to hang a bow, that is a rainbow. At the same time he 'speaks in that loud voice,' etc.; and here it is obvious that the ideas of the writer are in a sad state of fluctuation; for he transfers the idiosyncrasy of the fall itself (that is to say its sound) to the one who pours it from his hand." Thus the whole first stanza of the poem was composed of "the most jarring, inappropriate, mean, and in every way monstrous assemblages of false imagery." But in the second stanza, the poet recovered by following, no doubt unconsciously, a rule which Poe was pleased to state in full, italicized: *"subjects which surpass in grandeur all efforts of the human imagination are well depicted only in the simplest and least metaphorical language . . . ."* [12] Yet even at his best Brainard erred, for he did not immediately discard all imagery.

In his *Messenger* review of Bryant, Poe had claimed that metaphor was more imaginative than simile, but he had also suggested that an imaginative poet rarely used figurative language. It was not made clear in this early review *why* figurative language was relatively unimaginative, but now it appears that Poe felt that pure beauty or sublimity could not be evoked by comparisons, however apt. Beauty and sublimity in their most nearly absolute qualities could only be suggested because there was no basis for comparison with anything else. A sublime subject like Niagara Falls required language that evoked sublimity, something like Milton's mighty line, and Poe was able to say something good about Brainard only when the poet made a verbal gesture in Milton's direction:

[12] Even this rule, which appears to be of Poe's own devising, is implicit in Blair, who had taken exception to Longinus by declaring that figurative language was not effective in generating the emotion of the sublime. The sublime object, Blair wrote, should be described with "strength, with conciseness, and with simplicity." The least intrusion of an "ornamental" figure relaxed the "tension of the mind" and "emasculated" the feeling. A specific fault was the "frigid" style, characterized by "sinking" or bathos. Instead of heightening the enthusiasm of the reader, this style, as its label indicates, chilled it by degrading the sublime object or sentiment. In handling the sublime, a writer must avoid demeaning his subject by elaborate images, unworthy conceptions, or "low" descriptions. Blair, *Lectures*, I, 59–60, 66, 78.

Deep calleth unto deep. And what are we
That hear the question of that voice sublime?
O, what are all the notes that ever rung
From war's vain trumpet by thy thundering side?

These lines are too rhetorical for modern taste, perhaps even for
Poe's, but he found little enough in Brainard that he could admire,
and, for the moment at least, he was trying to be judicially impartial. The rules did not condemn elevated diction, so long as the obvious faults were avoided.

As if the poetry of Brainard did not provide a fitting illustration
of the havoc a critic could create on legitimate grounds, Poe found
another victim at hand in Cornelius Mathews, with whom he had
already clashed in "Exordium." Mathews was fair game. The trouble with the young man, as Perry Miller has described it, was that
he appointed himself the tutelary genius who would lead American
literature out of its wilderness by producing the great American
novel (*The Career of Puffer Hopkins*, published serially in
Arcturus), the great American literary journal (*Arcturus*), and the
great American epic (*Wakondah*). Mathews' brash ego put him at
odds with most of the journalistic writers in New York, and only
Evert Duyckinck's support kept him afloat. Mathews represented
nearly everything Poe held in contempt: a journalist who "puffed"
his own work in his own magazine; a member of a literary clique; a
proponent of literary nationalism; a critic who espoused the "cant
of generality"; and an inferior author. Within two years Poe was to
move to New York and associate himself with the Young America
group to which Mathews belonged, but this future alliance, always
an uneasy one, was necessary for Poe's survival. He had already an-
tagonized the powerful Whig journal, the *Knickerbocker*, edited by
his enemy Lewis Gaylord Clark; and although Poe was a Whig,[13]

[13] In 1841 Poe began to discover an interest in Whig politics, or at least
in what political influence could do. His friend Thomas secured what was
apparently a sinecure in Washington at a thousand dollars a year. Enviously,
Poe wrote to Thomas that *any* appointment, even a five-hundred-dollar one,
would be better than being an assistant editor: "To coin one's brain into
silver, at the nod of a master, is to my thinking, the hardest task in the
world." June 26, 1841, in *Letters*, I, 170–72. With Thomas' help Poe

he could gain support in 1844 only by joining Clark's opponents, the Democrats. But this was 1842 and he was still in Philadelphia. He could review the great American epic *Wakondah* with all the savagery he reserved for pretentious asses like Cornelius Mathews.

If the ideal critic displayed "calm breadth and massive delibera-tion," as Poe had written in his review of Christopher North, if he avoided being flippant and sarcastic, if he never let personal bias in-terfere with his judgment, then Poe fell considerably below his own standards in reviewing *Wakondah*.[14] First he informed the world that Mathews had published the poem in his own journal, *Arcturus*, "very much '*avec l'air d'un homme qui sauve sa patrie.*' " But, Poe continued ironically, the poem was not the leading article of the number. "It did not occupy that post of honor which, hith-erto, has been so modestly filled by 'Puffer Hopkins.' " Still Mathews had given his own work precedence over that of Longfel-low. This alone was enough to convince Poe that Mathews was placing himself above his betters.

Feigning regret, Poe claimed that out of courtesy to a fellow editor he had not wished to review the poem and would not have done so had it not appeared as a book. But now his hand was forced and he would have to do his duty. However specious Poe's regrets may appear to be in this case, he did his duty with all the *élan* of a crusader against vice. The cleverly managed apologies were soon discarded, and he began the direct assault. The pertinent

---

hoped to use the influence of Robert Tyler, the President's son, to secure an appointment to a Customs House, and he also hoped to interest the Whig administration in backing his magazine in return for political sup-port. Through no fault of his own, he failed to get the Customs appoint-ment, but he was at least partly responsible for the failure of his magazine project. He succumbed to wine at a Washington party and evidently be-haved in such a way as to preclude political favor. For Thomas' account of this affair, see *Works*, XVII, 137–38. The pertinent correspondence is also quoted in Quinn, *Edgar Allan Poe*, 377–81. For a detailed account of Poe's relations with Thomas and the Tylers, see my article, "Poe Among the Virginians," *Virginia Magazine of History and Biography*, LXVII (1959), 30–48.

[14] *Works*, XI, 25–38.

passage is worth quoting in full, for it shows that Poe's "tact" was sometimes as satirically destructive as his outright vilification:

> Now, upon our first perusal of the poem in question, we were both astonished and grieved that we could say, honestly, very little in its praise:—astonished, for by some means, not just now altogether intelligible to ourselves, we had become imbued with the idea of high poetical talent in Mr. Mathews:—grieved, because under the circumstances of his position as editor of one of the *very* best journals in the country, we had been sincerely anxious to think well of his abilities. Moreover, we felt that to *speak ill* of them, under any circumstances whatever, would be to subject ourselves to the charge of envy or jealousy, on the part of those who do not personally know us. We, therefore, rejoiced that "Wakondah" was not a topic we were called upon to discuss. But the poem is republished, and placed upon our table, and these very "circumstances of position," which restrained us in the first place, render it a positive duty that we speak distinctly in the second.
>
> And *very* distinctly shall we speak. In fact this effusion is a dilemma whose horns *goad* us into frankness and candor. . . . If we mention it at all, we are *forced* to employ the language of that region where, as Addison has it, "they sell the best fish and speak the plainest English." "Wakondah," then, from beginning to end, is trash. With the trivial exceptions which we shall designate, it has *no* merit whatever; while its faults, more numerous than the leaves of Vallombrosa, are of that rampant class which, if any schoolboy *could* be found so uninformed as to commit them, any schoolboy should be remorselessly flogged for committing.[15]

This was plain English indeed, and Poe's pretense at having been inhibited by editorial courtesy would have been amusing to the informed reader of the time who knew that in magazine reviewing both in England and in America there was little courtesy ex-

---

[15] Poe's remark that Mathews was connected with one of the best journals in the country was evidently sincere. William A. Jones, an excellent journalist and critic, did most of the editorial work. See Miller, *The Raven and the Whale*, 88–89. After Poe found it necessary to cultivate Mathews, he wrote what must be taken as a hypocritical letter of apology for this review. *Ibid.*, 116.

cept among editors of the same clique, or the same political party, or sometimes the same geographical region. A Philadelphia critic would have no compunction about attacking a New York editor, just as New York critics had no compunction about assailing editors in Boston. Mathews was a special case. Nearly everyone wanted to take some of the brashness out of the Centurion (as he was called) except his cohorts in the Young America group, which was publishing *Arcturus*. There was certainly no reason for Edgar Poe to be squeamish. Still, if he wished to live up to the standards of criticism he had recently announced, he should do more than make generalizations about Mathews' "epic."

In spite of his call for objectivity and fairness in the "Exordium," Poe reverted in this review to broad sarcasm and direct ridicule. The poem begins, he said, with an oration by Wakondah, the Master of Life, an oration which "to be plain, is scarcely equal to a second-rate Piankitank stump speech." Then there is a second oration, and the two, "taken altogether, are the queerest, and the most rhetorical, not to say the most miscellaneous orations we ever remember to have listened to outside of an Arkansas House of Delegates."

Then, making a show of fairness, he looked for something to commend in the poem and found it in a stanza that describes the great bulk of Wakondah as intercepting and blotting out the light of the moon

> With darkness nobler than the planet's fire,—
> A gloom and dreadful grandeur that aspire
> To match the cheerful Heaven's far-shining might.

Surprisingly, Poe ignored Mathews' obvious imitation of Milton's Satan in this description and asserted that the "general conception of the colossal figure on the mountain summit, relieved against the full moon, would be unquestionably *grand* were it not for the *bullish* phraseology by which the conception is rendered abortive." That Wakondah's bulk could continuously shut out the light of the rising moon is a denial of physical fact, Poe asserted, because however big he was the moon would soon soar over him. This was common sense with a vengeance. Poe could be very strict about adherence to physical fact whenever he chose to be.

In addition to his error in rendering a "grand" concept, Mathews violated most of the rules. Poe found mixed metaphors, flaws in rhythm, incomprehensible gibberish, redundancy, imitation (amounting to plagiarism), inconsistency in stanza form, faulty rhymes, misspelled words, and flaws in both grammar and logic. In fact, Poe said, with a final flourish of his hatchet, the best stanza in the poem is ridiculous because it compares Wakondah's head, falling in dejection to his knees ("the thing could not be done by an Indian juggler or a man of gum-caoutchouc"), to a high city being toppled by an earthquake. How can we compare a single descending head, Poe asked matter-of-factly, to "the innumerable pinnacles of a falling city"?

Poe's judgment of *Wakondah* is defensible, but his lack of fairness is not, for he would be content with nothing less than utter destruction. He exaggerated flaws by claiming certain lines incomprehensible which actually offer no more difficulty than most images. One such "incomprehensible" line, "Its feathers darker than a thousand fears," is inflated rhetoric, but its import is clear enough. A point of interest here is that Poe was examining the logic of metaphor as strictly as if each metaphor were a scientific proposition to be proved. Sometimes he did explain why a given metaphor was bad—as when he objected to the phrase, the "sea-blue sky." In this image the element of similarity was too great. There was no metaphorical extension in comparing the blue sea to the blue sky. More frequently, however, he simply quoted the faulty lines and claimed that they were meaningless. Examined for logical meaning, they are. "A sudden silence like a tempest fell" is a faulty comparison, as is "A sorrow mightier than the midnight skies." Had Poe gone on to correct the second figure as he sometimes did in a review, he might have indicated that Wakondah could have been overwhelmed by sorrow even more completely than the sky is overwhelmed by night, but his review was already lengthy and he closed it with a random selection of loose, "meaningless" comparisons.

Obviously Poe varied his approach according to his preliminary estimate of the book he was reviewing. A thoroughly bad work should be exposed by a close examination of its inanities, and all the devices of ridicule should be employed as well as the rules of rhetoric. One could not expect to find imagination in such a work as *Wakondah*, so the reviewer's tone and method had to be lowered in order to administer the proper chastisement. Mathews was a dull schoolboy in art who could learn only if he were subjected to a "remorseless flogging." Yet even by Poe's own standards the flogging was more merciless than necessary. Lockhart or Gifford could scarcely have improved on this:

> We should be delighted to proceed—but how? to applaud—but what? Surely not this trumpery declamation, this maudlin sentiment, this metaphor run-mad, this twaddling verbiage, this halting and doggrel rhythm, this unintelligible rant and cant! "Slid, if these be your passados and montantes, we'll have none of them." Mr. Mathews, you have clearly mistaken your vocation, and your effusion as little deserves the title of poem (Oh sacred name!) as did the rocks of the royal forest of Fontainebleau that of *"mes deserts"* bestowed upon them by Francis the First. In bidding you adieu we commend to your careful consideration the remark of M. Timon, *"que le Ministre de l'Instruction Publique doit lui-même savoir parler Français."*

After this review the Centurion should never have risked another line, but Mathews' skin was thicker than most; besides, he had the support of Evert Duyckinck and William A. Jones. The review is important chiefly as it demonstrates that Poe, whatever theoretical announcements he might make regarding the proper attitude and function of the critic, did not hesitate to punish literary offenders.

3

Next we find Poe at his most pragmatic level, attempting to demonstrate that a theory was only as good as its practice. If analysis could be used to show up a bad writer, it could also be used to show that even a writer of genius had flaws when his work was measured against an ideal standard. Poe opened his review of *Barn-aby Rudge* [16] by examining what he considered to be a popular fallacy: "We often hear it said, of this or of that proposition, that it may be good in theory, but will not answer in practice; and in such assertions we find the substance of all the sneers at Critical Art which so gracefully curl the upper lips of a tribe which is beneath it. We mean the small geniuses—the literary Tit Mice—animalculae which judge of merit solely by *result*, and boast of the solidity, tangibility and infallibility of the test they employ." By result Poe meant the test of popularity, for the "small geniuses" measure the value of a book by its sales.

In 1841, in his review of Dickens' *Old Curiosity Shop*, Poe himself had stated that popular esteem had some value as a test; Dickens' characters would not have "lived in the public estimation" for one hour had they been the caricatures that some critics had claimed. In the review of *Barnaby Rudge* Poe made the necessary discriminations. Popularity in itself was not a test of excellence, but popularity and literary excellence were not incompatible. He would give the literary titmice "the very kind of demonstration which they chiefly affect—*practical* demonstration—of the fallacy of one of their favorite dogmas . . . that no work of fiction can fully suit, at the same time, the critical and popular taste . . . ." By doing this he would also refute their contention that "the disre-

---

[16] *Works*, XI, 38–64. This was actually Poe's second review of *Barnaby Rudge*; the first was printed in the *Saturday Evening Post* of May 1, 1841. Gerald Grubb has described the misleading aspects of this second review and suggested that it was timed to appear while Dickens was visiting America. Poe's friend, John Tomlin, had written him on December 1, 1841, that Dickens was coming to America soon, and Poe published Dickens' letter to Tomlin in *Graham's*, XX (February, 1842), 83–84. Poe wrote to Dickens for an appointment and enclosed a copy of his review. Dickens granted the appointment in a letter dated March 6, 1842; in *Works*, XVII, 107. Evidently Poe was attempting to persuade Dickens to interest a British publisher in Poe's tales, but Dickens' attempt was unsuccessful. See Dickens to Poe, November 27, 1894, *ibid.*, 124–25. It is, of course, possible that Poe was attempting to curry favor with Dickens by a favorable review, but he had praised Dickens just as highly in previous reviews as in this one. See Grubb, "The Personal and Literary Relationships of Dickens and Poe," 1–22, 101–20, 209–21, for a detailed discussion of these questions.

garding or contravening of Critical Rule is absolutely essential to success beyond a very certain and limited extent, with the public at large." He would accomplish his practical demonstration by showing that the "vast popularity" of *Barnaby Rudge* should be regarded less as the "measure of its value than as the legitimate and inevitable result of certain well-understood critical propositions reduced by genius into practice."

The review of *Barnaby Rudge*, then, continued the argument which Poe had initiated in his review of *The Old Curiosity Shop* and continued in "Exordium." Genius, by its "happy modification of Nature," established the standards for art. Theory was good only "in proportion to its reducibility to practice," but in a true genius, like Dickens, theory and practice were inseparable: "the former implies or includes the latter," and "if the practice fail, it is because the theory is imperfect." The mere popularity of *Barnaby Rudge* did not necessarily prove anything, but criticism, by locating the violations of critical rule in the novel, could provide an appropriate measure of artistic value. Excellence as such need not be demonstrated; therefore the traditional opinion that the "beauties" of a work must be pointed out was in fact a concession to imperfection. The critic who described the "errors of a work" did all that was necessary to reveal its qualities. There was no better way to teach "what perfection is" than by "specifying what it *is not*." Accordingly, Poe intended to review Dickens in such a way as to demonstrate how the novelist, with more care, could have achieved an even greater art than that to which the novel itself attested. It goes without saying that in so doing Poe would also indicate to his public the indispensability of a critic who had the capacity to carry the practice of genius back to the theory upon which it was founded. From the works of genius, he had said earlier, a critic could deduce the rules, but even genius sometimes failed to reach the ideal standard. In the book at hand, Dickens did not perform at the level which "his high and just reputation would demand." Therefore it was Poe's duty as a critic to show just where he failed.

Actually, no rules existed for the conduct of a mystery story, but this was no handicap for Poe, who could deduce the theory from the practice. The thesis of a mystery novel, he declared, is derived from curiosity. It is necessary for the secret, or the solution of the mystery, to be kept from the reader until the denouement, but, to obey the self-evident rule, it "becomes imperative that no undue or inartistical means be employed to conceal the secret of the plot." The author does not err if a falsehood which misleads the reader is placed in the mouth of a character who is ignorant of the secret, but when the author himself misleads the reader the rule has been violated. Dickens occasionally exhibited this flaw.

Furthermore, the author fails when his secret is not preserved. Poe modestly supposed that many must have solved Dickens' mystery very quickly, in spite of the false leads, since he himself solved it on the seventh page of the 323-page novel.[17] These defects might seem trivial to the uninformed, Poe admitted, but actually they are violations of principles that are essential to the mystery novel, and it was Poe's duty to exhibit them to the public. A critic must not be blinded by the popularity of a work or by the excellence of previous books by the same author if he is to do justice to the work at hand, and only by rendering justice can he serve as a mediator between the writer and the public. Thus, in his review of Dickens, Poe illustrated the function of the critic which he had described in the "Exordium," the improvement of the public taste by the analysis of the faults of genius, a role sanctioned by tradition and prescribed by Dr. Hugh Blair.

4

Poe had devoted the January and February columns of *Graham's* to an exposition of the proper function of a critic and to the public need for a critic who had the knowledge and the courage to perform this function. Whether he would have continued in precisely this vein is impossible to say, but a personal tragedy slowed the im-

[17] Using the dates of the novel's serial publication, Gerald Grubb has argued that Poe must have had thirteen chapters available when he wrote his first review. If he actually solved the secret by the seventh page, we have only his word for it. See "The Personal and Literary Relationships of Dickens and Poe," 9–11.

petus of his campaign. About the middle of January his young wife Virginia became very ill, and Poe wrote his friend Frederick Thomas of his agonies of fear and grief.[18] Amazingly, he was able to keep up his steady production of book reviews, but we have no way of knowing whether the book reviews that appeared in the March and April numbers were composed before or after Virginia's misfortune. Poe had said in a previous letter to Thomas that the magazine had to go to press one full month in advance of the day of issue. This would mean that his reviews for the March number would have to be ready in January and those for the April number in February. He did manage to publish three reviews in March, two of which represent a continuation of his effort to inform the public of the prevailing errors of the journalistic critics; but these reviews have neither the zest nor the confidence of the January and February reviews.

One of them, a brief notice of Longfellow's *Ballads and Other Poems*,[19] is devoted primarily to an exposition of the fallacy of that "antique adage, *De gustibus non est disputandum*—there should be no disputing about taste." Such an assumption would indicate, Poe wrote, "that taste itself . . . is an arbitrary something, amenable to no law, and measurable by no definite rules." This might be true if there were no psychological science, Poe argued, but he believed that one important use of phrenology would be in the "analysis of the real principles, and a digest of the resulting laws of taste." These principles, he continued, "are as clearly traceable, and these laws as really susceptible of system as are any whatever."

Poe's employment of phrenology as a critical tool has already been described, but we should note here that he used the term "taste" instead of the phrenological word "Ideality." Seemingly an insignificant variation, this change of terminology signals a reversion to an older aesthetic psychology. His use of principles derived from Blair or an equivalent source in his reviews during this period, his view of a work of genius as "nature methodized," and his increasing tendency to invoke reason and common sense in his re-

---

[18] February 3, 1842, in *Letters*, I, 191.   [19] *Works*, XI, 65–68.

views during the next four or five years all show a reaction against romantic criticism. Paradoxically, his teleology of art evidences a romantic idealism like that of Shelley. These contradictions will be examined in due course; it is sufficient to say here that Poe's concern with the psychology of taste was distinctly archaic. His master Coleridge had written a fragmentary essay on taste, but had proceeded little further than to define it as a metaphor for the aesthetic response.[20] The debate about the laws of taste had been carried on in the preceding century, but Poe, having announced that a critic must deduce and apply the rules, needed laws to enforce his standards. The current essay-reviews, whether exercises in literary history or paeans of appreciation, needed no such laws. To almost everyone except Edgar Poe, the rules were obsolete.

In his review of Longfellow, although Poe admitted that he had no space to do it, he proposed to explode the fallacy that the modern poets appealed because of "novelty, . . . trickeries of expression, . . . and other meretricious effects." He would demonstrate that only the kind of poetry written by the romantics "has fulfilled the legitimate office of the muse; has thoroughly satisfied an earnest and unquenchable desire existing in the heart of man." [21] But this demonstration had to wait for the proper occasion, which turned out to be an extensive review of this same book by Longfellow in the April number of *Graham's*.

[20] "Fragment of an Essay on Taste," in *Biographia Literaria*, II, 247–49. Like Poe, Coleridge raised the question of whether there were any fixed principles of taste, but he considered the question of the possible relativity of taste more seriously than Poe did. Every person, Coleridge wrote, is unwilling to consider his own taste as universal, but he does "demand the universal acquiescence of all intelligent beings in every conviction of his understanding." This is as far as Coleridge got.

[21] Probably Poe derived this opinion from his interpretation of Schlegel, who had distinguished between ancient and modern literature on the ground that the poetry of the ancients was that of enjoyment, while that of the moderns expressed the longing of the exile for his distant home. Schlegel, *Lectures*, 26–27. If Poe was remembering Schlegel, however, he was appropriating the letter but not the spirit. Schlegel never undervalued the poetry of the ancients, as Poe was prone to do. Schlegel's distinction was based upon the influence of Christianity in turning man's eyes from earth toward Heaven.

In the only other review in the March number which is pertinent to Poe's effort to demonstrate the proper function of the critic, he simply continued his argument that popularity alone was invalid as a criterion of quality. The book under consideration, *Charles O'Malley, The Irish Dragoon*,[22] had been even more popular than the "inimitable compositions" of Charles Dickens, and the "ephemeral press" had been nearly "unanimous in its praise." The praise, however, had not been based upon specific merits; in fact, it had failed to show that the book had any literary merit whatsoever. Therefore popularity was not, as many people thought, "*prima facie* evidence" of quality. It could indicate instead that the writer had lowered himself to gain mass appeal, and that he had deliberately catered to "uneducated thought," "uncultivated taste," and "unrefined and misguided passion." Still, it was not impossible for a popular book to have elements that would appeal to the discriminating, or, for that matter, for a work of art to appeal to the masses —witness the ingenuity with which Dickens had addressed the general taste. Poe, however, wanted to record his own "positive dissent" from the "usual opinion" that Dickens had done justice to his genius by appealing to the general taste at all. Genius had its office, God assigned. "But that office is not a low communion with low or even with ordinary intellect. The holy—the electric spark of genius is the medium of intercourse between the noble and more noble mind."

The statement above almost has the force of a contradiction instead of a qualification. In two previous reviews Poe had praised Dickens for having the kind of genius that reduced theory to practice and appealed not only to the mass but to the discriminating audience. Now he qualified his position stringently by saying that it was not *impossible* for a popular book to have elements that would appeal to the discriminating, but that a genius should never deliberately address himself to a popular audience. Thus it would appear that Poe had changed his mind and did not want to bring art to the public after all. In the context of his continuing justification of the office of criticism, however, we see that he was merely concluding his argument. The genius owes it to himself to write at the top of

22 *Works*, XI, 85–98.

his bent, and at the top of his bent he will appeal only to like minds. He is lowering himself when he deliberately attempts to reach a mass audience, though it is not impossible for him to do so. It is the duty of the critic, not the literary genius, to be the mediator between the highest products of art and the public, and it is also the duty of the critic "to uphold the true dignity of genius, to combat its degradation, to plead for the exercise of its powers in those bright fields which are its legitimate and peculiar province." The genius should not lower himself to the public; instead criticism should help lift the public taste, insofar as it can be lifted, toward appreciation of the work of genius.

As for the popular *Charles O'Malley*, a brief critical examination would prove that it had no claim to literary merit at all. The plot was loaded with absurdities, incidents were repeated *ad nauseam*, and the structure was anecdotal. Suspense was achieved only by the "silly trick" of "whetting appetite by delay." Even the jokes that could amuse the reader were tactlessly narrated. The whole book was marked by a vulgarity of thought which was reflected in the ungrammatical colloquialism of the language.

The review of *Charles O'Malley* concluded for all practical purposes what Poe had to say about the relationship between popularity and art. He had begun the new year with an exposition of the function of literary criticism, and for three months he had tried to show that a critic not only could guard the public against popular hackwork but also could mediate between a work of art and a public not prepared to appreciate it, thus elevating the public taste. Furthermore, the critic could perform a valuable function for the writer himself by pointing out his idiosyncratic weaknesses, thus forcing him to live up to his innate talent. Next Poe was to engage in a defense of poetry. To him the poet represented the highest type of literary genius, and as a poet-critic he had to inform the public of the intrinsic value of poetry and prove that this value was grounded in the very nature of things, that it was a response to the human need for beauty. He was to make this attempt in his second review of Longfellow's *Ballads and Other Poems*, published in the April, 1842, number of *Graham's Magazine.*

XII · The Province of Poetry

P OE'S reviews during the first five months of 1842 illustrate as clearly as do "The Philosophy of Composition" and "The Poetic Principle" an apparent divergence between his attitude as a literary critic and his attitude as a romantic poet. As a literary critic he attempted to use science and reason in his proofs. As a romantic poet he found value in the experience of a transcendent, visionary beauty. When these two orientations conflicted, his theoretical statements sometimes became obscure and even contradictory, as he attempted to accommodate the vision of beauty to a practical methodology. As a literary critic Poe found it necessary to assume that each event had its rationale, not only in terms of its existence but also in terms of its purpose; the final cause of an event determined its mode of being. Thus, in his criticism he was prone to examine an artistic event not only for its immediate cause but also for its hypothesized place in the scheme of things.

An art work, constructed by man, was thought by Poe to follow the order of nature insofar as it exhibited design, a rational plan to implement a preconceived end. That art did have a place in the universal design was not to be doubted, because God had given man faculties for the production and the appreciation of art. But art was not nature; it was "artificial," made by man, and it had its own final cause and its own mode of being. Art could not duplicate nature, but the human could imitate the divine artist by recognizing the purpose of art and by developing a design that would carry out this purpose.

In April and May of 1842 Poe proceeded from his justification of the function of the critic to the justification of art itself, more specifically the validation of poetic feeling as an innate human need. In this Poe's orientation was toward romantic transcendentalism, particularly its Platonic elements. Had he been guided solely by the aesthetic ideal of the Enlightenment, he would have assumed that the end of art was to create a formal imitation of the order of the universe, and unquestionably this ideal appears in Poe's aesthetics; but in terms of value Poe thought that art must attempt to convey the soul's vision of beauty, for man could not duplicate the Great Design. He could only attempt to reproduce the effect that an intuitive perception of perfect order would stimulate. This concept, though it has its historical origin in Platonic aesthetics, became one of the aspects of the nineteenth-century yearning for absolute experience uncontaminated by the here and now. Among the English romantics it is conspicuous in Shelley's poetry, which helps account for Poe's approval of Shelley. But unlike Shelley, whose *A Defence of Poetry*, published in 1840, could conceivably have influenced him,[1] Poe was determined to devise or discover a rationale of vision and a means for its communication. It is also possible that he was influenced by Friedrich Schlegel, whose *Lectures on the History of Literature* was available in English.[2] Schlegel's statement, "The proper business of poetry is to represent only the eternal, that which is, at all places, and in all times, significant and beautiful; but this cannot be accomplished without the intervention of a veil," reminds us of Poe's insistence that the absolute beauty perceived by the poet could only be rendered in terms of the vague and the indefinite. Yet Schlegel's "veil" has reference to the necessity of a poet's using the national past and present in order to shadow forth the eternal within temporal limits. Poe's purposeful "vagueness" is an expedient to obscure time and place in order to allow the eternal beauty to shine more brightly. Schlegel was writing philosophically. Poe was trying to develop a methodology for the communication of vision. His role as a critic and his Enlightenment orientation demanded it. If the need to enjoy beauty is an aspect of human nature, then there must be a way to insure the fulfillment of this need, and the way must be based upon something permanent in the psyche—a universal psychological princi-

---

[1] See Marvin Laser, "The Growth and Structure of Poe's Concept of Beauty," 69–84.

[2] *Lectures on the History of Literature, Ancient and Modern* (1811) had been translated into English by J. G. Lockhart in 1818. The following quotation is taken from Lecture XII.

ple. Poe's best-known reviews, published in April and May of 1842, are devoted to a description of the human need for the experience of beauty and propositions for a rationale of gratification.

In the March number of *Graham's,* as we have seen, Poe had published a brief review of Longfellow's *Ballads and Other Poems.* His chief point was made in a dogmatic statement that taste could be analyzed and reduced to law: "These principles . . . are as clearly traceable, and these laws as really susceptible of system as are any whatever." Unable to complete his exposition in the March number, Poe continued his review in April,[3] and this continuation contains his most elaborate statement of the nature and final cause of aesthetic feeling. It also contains his most extensive justification for his rule that the didactic has no place in a poem.

Poe opened his April review with an exposition of what he regarded as Longfellow's primary defect, his didactic purpose. This was his usual strategy of selecting an author's characteristic idiosyncrasy as his point of attack. His objection to didacticism had been stated as early as his "Letter to Mr. —— ——," but never before had he undertaken to explain it fully on psychological grounds. Longfellow's aim is wrong, Poe said. "His invention, his imagery, his all, is made subservient to the elucidation of some one or more points . . . which he looks upon as truth."

The aesthetic value which is the proper end of art should not be dissipated by subsidiary values which would be better presented by means other than poetry.

> Now, with as deep a reverence for "the true" as ever inspired the bosom of mortal man, we would limit, in many respects, its modes of inculcation. We would limit, to enforce them. We would not render them impotent by dissipation. The demands of truth are severe. She has no sympathy with the myrtles. All that is indispensable in song is all with which she has nothing to do. To deck her in gay robes is to render her a harlot. It is but making her a flaunting paradox to wreathe her in gems and flowers. Even in stating this our present proposition, we verify our own words—we feel the necessity, in enforcing this *truth,* of descending from met-

[3] *Works,* XI, 68–85.

phor. Let us then be simple and distinct. To convey "the true" we are required to dismiss from the attention all inessentials. We must be perspicuous, precise, terse. We need concentration rather than expansion of mind. We must be calm, unimpassioned, unexcited—in a word, we must be in that peculiar mood which, as nearly as possible, is the exact converse of the poetical. He must be blind indeed who cannot perceive the radical and chasmal difference between the truthful and the poetical modes of inculcation. He must be grossly wedded to conventionalisms who, in spite of this difference, shall still attempt to reconcile the obstinate oils and waters of Poetry and Truth.

Poe's assumption in this passage is what has recently been called by Northrop Frye the greatest fallacy in our present-day concept of literary education, the assumption that prose is the "normal" language of ideas and that the special characteristics of poetry inhibit the efficiency of communication. This error, if it is one, goes back at least as far as Lord Kames[4] and, one must suppose, even farther. It was implicit in the psychology that assigned certain faculties as responsible for feeling and others as responsible for thinking. Characteristically, Poe based his argument on psychology, specifically on the hypothesis that the mental state appropriate for the composition of poetry is different from that which is conducive to the formulation of concepts. It is obvious that Poe's view of style, if anachronistic terminology may be forgiven, was that of a modern positivist. Prose style was valued in terms of its efficiency in communicating facts or ideas, but the style of a poem, insofar as it exhibited imagery, rhythm, and rhyme, was seen as ornamental. In a word, whatever is inessential in the expression of an idea—the gay robes, the gems and flowers—is mere decoration. Poetry, in Poe's

[4] Kames did not ban didacticism from poetry, but he assumed that prose was a more natural form of discourse because it was "not confined to precise rules." The "chief end" of prose was instruction, Kames wrote, and it should be valued accordingly. Using the same metaphor Poe used, Kames argued that we should not undervalue prose because it was in a "plainer dress." *Elements of Criticism*, 291. Poe simply pressed the distinction by making the end govern the means, whereas Kames, who exhibited a neo-classic concern for the utility of art, allowed the artist the Horatian double motive of pleasing *and* instructing.

view, could not have a form which communicated a special kind of knowledge; it was designed only to make us feel.

What Allen Tate has considered a prime aspect of poetic value, the tension that occurs between the logical meaning of figurative language and its rich store of implication,[5] was virtually ignored by Poe. There could not be any consecutive development of a concept in a poem, Poe said many times, without the risk of allegory. He had fumbled with the problem of meaning in previous reviews, and in this particular context he simply referred his readers to his earlier statements: "In our last number, we took occasion to say that a didactic moral might be happily made the *under-current* of a poetical theme, and, in 'Burton's Magazine,' some two years since, we treated this point at length in a review of Moore's 'Alciphron'; but the moral thus conveyed is invariably an ill effect when obtruding beyond the upper current of the thesis itself."

Few would question the validity of Poe's argument here, but the fact that he separated the "currents" of meaning is another indication that he did not escape what Philip Wheelwright has described as the "blind alley of empirical positivism."[6] The positivist tends to obscure the cognitive potential of poetry by regarding it either as fiction or as allegory. Poe actually said elsewhere that a poem might enforce truth only by overturning a fiction, but this opinion appears in the present context only in the form of a definition borrowed from Baron de Bielfeld: poetry is *"l'art d'exprimer les pensées par la fiction."* Poe evidently took this to mean that the fiction, the fable or scene of the poem, had to bear the weight of thought, and that the extension of meaning in the suggestive undercurrent was not really meaning at all but a configuration of congruent affects. If the undercurrent actually became meaning, it obtruded and had the force of a thesis. Poe had said in his review of *Alciphron* that the undercurrent was like an accompaniment in music. It was a "soul-exalting echo." In other words, it had to do

[5] Tate, "Tension in Poetry," in *Reason in Madness* (New York, 1941), 62–81.

[6] Wheelwright, "Poetry, Myth, and Reality," in Allen Tate (ed.), *The Language of Poetry* (Princeton, 1942), 10.

with the stimulative capacity of poetic form and was inhibitory to the communication of ideas. Poe did not describe an interaction between the two kinds of meaning, with each sustaining or qualifying the other; he was more concerned that they should not interfere with each other. Accordingly, symbolic suggestion should not have cognitive value or it would destroy the fable or fiction which was the poem; the undercurrent could only enhance the affective potentiality of the fiction. Such a proposition would remove the possibility of ironic indirection or indeed any other mode of tension in poetic form. To Poe, then, the poet was inevitably a liar, for his poem could not be the vehicle of any kind of truth other than the truth of feeling. With this Keatsian prolegomena, it is not surprising that Poe selected Keats as "the sole British poet who has never erred in his themes." A poem had no heuristic capability except as it might provide a stimulus for that broad range of sentiments which Poe and his contemporaries were pleased to call moral.

Obviously Poe had made great concessions to science. His view of truth was restricted to that which might be conceptualized or represented, and a poem, in consequence, was only a pleasing organization of "inessentials," gay robes and flowers. He had claimed that poetry was his passion, but in reference to truth he called his love a harlot. What, then, remained of poetic value? Actually, a great deal, but Poe had to resort to the psychology of taste to explain:

> Dividing the world of mind into its most obvious and immediately recognizable distinctions, we have the pure intellect, taste, and the moral sense. We place *taste* between the intellect and the moral sense, because it is just this intermediate space which, in the mind, it occupies. It is the connecting link in the triple chain.
>
> It serves to sustain a mutual intelligence between the extremes. It appertains, in strict appreciation, to the former, but is distinguished from the latter by so faint a difference, that Aristotle has not hesitated to class some of its operations among the Virtues themselves. But the offices of the trio are broadly marked. Just as conscience, or the moral sense, recognizes duty, just as the intellect deals with truth; so it is the part of taste alone to inform us of BEAUTY. And

Poesy is the handmaiden but of taste. Yet we would not be misunderstood. This handmaiden is not forbidden to moralize—in her own fashion. She is not forbidden to depict—but to reason and preach, of virtue. As, of this latter, conscience recognizes the obligation, so intellect teaches the expediency, while taste contents herself with displaying the beauty; waging war with vice merely on the ground of its inconsistency with fitness, harmony, proportion—in a word with *to kalon*.

The first thing to be noticed in this passage is that Poe had renounced the jargon of phrenology and was using the traditional terms for the faculties, retaining the separation of the faculties in regard to function which was characteristic of the older psychology. In this context, two quotations from Thomas Jefferson bear repeating for their immediate relevance:

The *To Kalon* . . . is founded in a different faculty, that of taste, which is not even a branch of morality. We have indeed an innate sense of what we call beautiful, but that is exercised on subjects addressed to the fancy through the eye in visible forms . . . or to the imagination directly. . . .

When any signal act of charity or of gratitude . . . is presented to our sight or imagination, we are deeply impressed with it's [*sic*] beauty and feel a strong desire in ourselves of doing charitable and grateful acts also. On the contrary, when we see or read of any atrocious deed, we are disgusted with it's [*sic*] deformity, and conceive an abhorrence of vice.

This is the substance of Poe's argument: taste "wages war" against vice by enabling us to distinguish between the beautiful and the disgusting in human behavior. The second half of the combined quotation above was contained in a letter written in 1771, shortly after the publication of Kames's *Elements of Criticism*, a book Jefferson considered authoritative. In "Exordium" Poe too had attested to the validity of Kames's principles. Our interest here, however, should not be in the location of another probable source for Poe's ideas, but in the use he made of an outmoded psychology to validate his argument. According to the faculty psychology, strictly interpreted, the only way in which the sense of the beautiful could implement morality was by an imaginative depiction of virtuous acts for their hedonic value. Beauty pleases; deformity disgusts. Far from introducing a new concept of poetic value, Poe merely reverted to the old, differing only in his polemically emphatic language.[7]

A significant change from the doctrine expressed in the review of Drake and Halleck is observable. In the earlier review Poe had attributed the value of certain lines from Shelley to their expression of moral sentiment. This was understandable in terms of the phrenological classification of Ideality as a moral sentiment. According to the strict separation of the taste from the moral sense in the older psychology, however, moral feeling derived from the conscience, not from the taste. Poe gave evidence of this distinction in statements that qualified his admission of a moral thesis as a secondary motif in art: "In common with all who claim the sacred title of poet, he [Longfellow] should limit his endeavors to the creation of novel moods of beauty, in form, in color, in sound, in sentiment; for over all this wide range has the poetry of words dominion. To what the world terms *prose* may be safely and properly left all else." This should be clear enough, but Poe wanted to eliminate any possible misunderstanding. Trying to be fair, he praised Longfellow's ballad "The Luck of Edenhall" extravagantly, in spite of the "pointed moral with which it terminates," because the moral was "perfectly fluent from the incidents." Yet it was through images rich in physical rather than moral beauty that such a ballad made an appeal to the imagination: "It is chiefly . . . amid forms of physical loveliness (we use the word *forms* in its widest sense as embracing modifications of sound and color) that the soul seeks the realization of its dreams of BEAUTY."

In this qualification Poe did not violate the principles of the taste psychologists; he simply carried the implications of a separate faculty of taste further than would have been possible for Kames and Stewart, or for their American disciple, Thomas Jefferson. The Scottish philosophers had not wanted morality to become a mode

[7] See Chapter I, Section 2, of this book for the pertinent historical discussion.

of aesthetic gratification, as it appeared that Shaftesbury had permitted; instead, they had tried to show how the sense of beauty could serve the conscience. Poe, by the evidence of this review, would use precisely the same psychological principles to show that morality, properly depicted, could serve the sense of beauty. His analysis of the faculties and their function allowed him to proceed to his validation of the aesthetic end. If a poem attempted to communicate directly either the concepts of the intellect or the precepts of the conscience, it would fail because these faculties would usurp the office of the taste. The means would not be adapted to the proposed end. Aesthetic appreciation of the symmetry, harmony, and proportion of nature and of art was the sole function of the taste. This faculty was a link between the human and the divine because of the natural human yearning for perfect beauty: "An important condition of man's immortal nature is . . . the sense of the Beautiful." Why immortal? Because no beauty on earth fully satisfies man's longing for beauty. If this "thirst unquenchable" exists, it must have an explanation in terms of its cause. God has given it to us as a sign of our "perennial" existence. It is a token of a future life beyond the grave. If what we have here and now were all, man would not have dreams of something more beautiful beyond. But man does have such dreams, which proves that longing for this beauty was divinely established in human nature. Thus the true sentiment of poesy (by which Poe meant the fine arts) is "not the mere appreciation of the beauty before us." Instead, he continued, "It is a wild effort to reach the beauty above. It is a forethought of the loveliness to come. It is a passion to be satiated by no sublunary sights, or sounds, or sentiments, and the soul thus athirst strives to allay its fever in futile efforts at *creation*. Inspired with a prescient ecstasy of the beauty beyond the grave, it struggles, by multiform novelty of combination among the things and the thoughts of Time, to anticipate some portion of that loveliness whose very elements, perhaps, appertain solely to Eternity."

When we encounter this rhapsody, we are immediately reminded of romantic Platonism. Love of beautiful earthly forms is only a preparation for love of ideal beauty, eternal and absolute.

This quasi-religious emotion is, according to Poe, an aspect of the natural constitution of man. As he expressed it: "Poesy is thus seen to be a response—unsatisfactory it is true—but still in some measure a response, to a natural and irrepressible demand. Man being what he is, the time could never have been in which Poesy was not. Its first element is the thirst for supernal BEAUTY—a beauty which is not afforded the soul by any existing collocation of earth's forms —a beauty which, perhaps, *no possible* combination of these forms would fully produce."

The poetic imagination, then, is not a means of communicating intuitions of moral or metaphysical truth, say of the kind expressed by religion or myth. It is the artistic faculty of creating a beautiful composition, a re-ordering of the given, "the things and thoughts of Time." The given is the same for every artist; it is the stuff of experience, and the only originality the poet can achieve inheres in his compositional effects. Even here, Poe was only rephrasing what Archibald Alison had said before him:

> The forms and the scenery of material nature are around them [the artists], not to govern, but to awaken their genius—to invite them to investigate the sources of their beauty; and from this investigation to exalt their conceptions to the imagination of forms and compositions of form more pure and more perfect than any that Nature herself ever presents to them. It is in this pursuit that ideal beauty is at last perceived, which it is the loftiest ambition of the artist to feel and to express; and which . . . is capable of producing emotions of a more exquisite and profound delight than nature itself is ever destined to awaken.[8]

Platonic idealism was common property. Were this all that Poe shared with Alison, the quotation above would be pointless, merely another in the list of possible sources, which already include Coleridge, the Schlegels, Shelley, and perhaps actually Plato himself. The significance of Poe's reversion to the eighteenth-century psychology of taste and its teleology of art is that it offered him a way out of the dilemma imposed by his interpretation of Coleridge. If the imagination actually created something new out of elements

[8] *Essays on Taste*, 453–54.

alien to human experience—which appears to be Poe's interpretation of Coleridge—then the empirical approach would have to be discarded and the poet would not be an artist but a prophet or seer—a Moses on the mount or a Saul on the road to Damascus— and poetry would become revelation. In a very few years Poe was to employ his most pungent invective in discrediting the transcendental hero, the poet-seer,[9] but in this review he accomplished his object by placing a limitation on the purpose of art. By making "Poesy" (understood in its generic sense as "art") the "handmaiden" of the faculty of taste, Poe limited its function, as Alison had done, to the production of exquisite delight. Yet this delight itself was blended with and productive of moral feeling, Alison had said, for admiration of the beauty of earth inevitably led the soul toward the author of that beauty and resulted in religious feeling. Poe went beyond Alison only in the emphasis achieved by his rapturous rhetoric. Alison did not specify that the artist had a vision of absolute beauty, but he implied it when he required the artist to investigate the source of temporal beauty in order to imagine forms and compositions "more perfect" than any in nature. The proposition is the same. Aesthetic delight leads the mind toward the source of that delight; and the artist, with his exquisite sensibility, his refined taste, will not be satisfied with any ordinary gratification—the sights and sounds that greet all mankind; he will be content only with perfection itself.

However much Poe may have drawn from the aesthetic of high romanticism, as represented by Shelley, he still imposed the old psychological limitation upon the artist. He was the man of taste, not the legislator for all mankind, and his vision was limited to the imagination of perfect beauty. He could improve on nature in his composition of forms, but he would never truly create; he would only invent new combinations of old forms. The second element of poetic feeling was an attempt to satisfy the thirst for beauty which was the first element. The poet would attempt to satisfy his thirst

[9] For a discussion of the transcendental view of the artist as redeemer, see Morse Peckham, *Beyond the Tragic Vision* (New York, 1962), 161– 226 *passim*.

"by *novel* combinations among those forms of beauty which already exist—or by novel combinations of *those combinations which our predecessors, toiling in chase of the same phantom, have already set in order.*" Thus, he went on, we "clearly deduce the *novelty*, the *originality*, the *invention*, the *imagination*, or lastly the *creation* of BEAUTY (for the terms as employed are synonymous) as the essence of all Poesy." [10] Certainly Poe was implicitly extending the refutation of Coleridge which he had introduced in the review of *Alciphron*. Like Coleridge, he saw imagination as the essence of poetry, and, like Coleridge, he considered two aspects of this essential power. Yet Coleridge's primary imagination was a mode of perception, common, in greater or lesser degree, to everyone. His secondary imagination was the esemplastic power which brought the many into one. Poe's first element was not the imagination but the taste, the appreciation of beauty which induced one to desire even greater beauty; Poe's second element was imagination, but, as is obvious in the passage above, the imagination in its creative aspect was equated with invention, as was customary in the eighteenth century. An ordering of the forms experienced in nature and a re-ordering of previous artistic "combinations" were equally valid as imaginative art. Poe had taken the statement he had found in Bielfeld, that the mind of man can imagine nothing new, as irrefutable psychological doctrine.[11] Yet presumably man can imagine whatever exists, even if it exists only in the mind of God, so man can imagine absolute beauty. The trouble is, he cannot invent it. The visionary capacity of the imagination far exceeds its creative capacity.

By whatever source it may have been transmitted, it was the *Symposium*, that marvelous parable of the soul ascending the lad-

[10] The text in *Works* omits the very important statement in this quotation that a poet may make new combinations "among those forms of beauty which already exist." Without this choice, the poet is limited to previous works as a source for his materials.

[11] Poe had first quoted Bielfeld in a footnote in his review of Drake and Halleck. See *Works*, VIII, 283. He had also paraphrased Coleridge in the same note without perceiving what later he took to be a contradiction. In his review of *Alciphron*, however, he quoted Bielfeld again in order to refute Coleridge's description of imaginative creativity. *Ibid.*, X, 62.

der of beauty until it is able to grasp the idea of beauty, that influenced Poe. Art, like religion, led *toward* Heaven, but not all the
way. All things on earth, natural or artificial, are imperfect; thus
the relative and contingent beauty of any combination, however
novel, will be at last unsatisfying, for the soul, in its aesthetic as
well as its moral aspect, can rest only in its immortal home.

But Poe had also read the *Republic,* and he knew that in the
sphere of social utility all poets were liars; the beauty of their vision
was true, and yet it could be expressed only by a fiction, or what
the men of fact called a fiction. Accepting the positivist's version of
truth, Poe could defend the poet's lies only by affirming that they
were necessary lies; they served a basic human need. The fiction of
beauty which the poet created would be recognized as nearly true
only beyond the grave, after man experienced the reality of the absolute.

All of Poe's speculations about the value of the taste were not
expressed in this review, no doubt because he limited himself to
what he could support by a traditional aesthetic psychology. Yet in
his philosophical fantasy, "The Colloquy of Monos and Una,"
published in *Graham's* the previous August,[12] he did make a pro-
visional allocation of redemptive potential to the poet's mind. Poetic truth could have saved mankind, had man listened to the poets
instead of the scientists. The scene in the "Colloquy" takes place
after the destruction of the earth by fire. The fable is a retrospective survey by an angel, Monos, and of course must be accepted as
true in the only way in which a fiction can be true. Monos accounts
for the destruction of the earth as a cleansing or purification. Man
had cultivated his practical reason instead of his poetic instinct and
had infected the earth with his partial knowledge. Among other errors, he had attributed value to scientific progress and to a mani-
festly unnatural condition known as universal democracy; this was
a defiance of nature and of nature's God, but in his pride man did
not submit to nature. Instead, he attempted to enforce "dominion
over her elements." He would have been saved had he been guided
by his taste instead of his practical reason:

[12] *Ibid.,* IV, 200–12.

Occasionally the poetic intellect—that intellect which we now feel to have been the most exalted of all—since those truths which to us were of the most enduring importance could be reached by that *analogy* which speaks in proof-tones to the imagination alone, and to the unaided reason bears no weight—occasionally did this poetic intellect proceed a step farther in the evolving of the vague idea of the philosophic, and find in the mystic parable that tells of the tree of knowledge, and of its forbidden fruit, death-producing, a distinct intimation that knowledge was not meet for man in the infant condition of his soul. And these men, the poets, living and perishing amid the scorn of the "utilitarians"—of rough pedants, who arrogated to themselves a title which could have been properly applied only to the scorned—these men, the poets, ponder piningly, yet not unwisely, upon the ancient days when our wants were not more simple than our enjoyments were keen—days when *mirth* was a word unknown, so solemnly deep-toned was happiness—holy, august, and blissful days, when blue rivers ran undammed, between hills unhewn, into far forest solitudes, primeval, odorous, and unexplored.

In his fantasy, where he was not burdened with polemic necessity, Poe permitted the poet to discover truth through the perception of analogies, a cognitive mode not different in principle from that employed by Emerson. Significantly, the poet's vision projected an unfallen world, the world described in the myth of the garden. In a fallen world, however, the only paradise that the poet could imagine was that beyond the grave. Applied science had created "huge, smoking cities," and "the fair face of Nature was deformed as with the ravages of some loathsome disease." [13] Cultiva-

[13] Leo Marx mentioned Poe only once in his provocative study of the reaction of the American romantics to the machine, yet his discussion applies as well to Poe as it does to Hawthorne and Melville, provided that it is limited to Poe's creative work. See especially the discussion of Hawthorne's "Ethan Brand," in Marx, *The Machine in the Garden* (Galaxy ed.; New York, 1967), 265–77. Like Hawthorne, Poe took the Enlightenment ideal of knowledge as unpardonable sin and found value in "pastoral harmony," but perhaps even more clearly than Hawthorne, Poe realized that a restoration of the pastoral state would require a "reversal of history." As was observed in the first chapter of this study, Poe's version of the pastoral in "The Domain of Arnheim" owes a great deal to his Southern origin.

tion of the aesthetic sense, which the "majestic intuition of Plato" had seen as man's salvation, would have made man "beautiful minded," and he would have been able to dwell forever in an earthly paradise.

Poe's "fiction," then, allowed the truth of myth which his psychology denied, for Monos affirms the value of the "mystic parable" of Genesis. Yet with hard common sense Poe knew that his audience relied on scientific procedures rather than the perception of analogies for the production of truth. Besides that, the history of mankind showed that very few were interested in becoming "beautiful minded," so Monos can only cry, "Alas for the pure contemplative spirit and majestic intuition of Plato!"

In his very first poems Poe had associated art with the paradisal vision. In "Al Aaraaf" he had located the artist's paradise in a wandering planet, and in his "Sonnet—To Science" he had described the way in which reality vanquished dream. Yet however true these "fictions" were under the aspect of eternity, his proofs had to be accommodated to time and place. Shelley had erred when he claimed that the poets were the unacknowledged legislators of the world. If they were unacknowledged, they could not legislate. A conditional capitulation is the best defense when one is outnumbered. Then one at least has a voice in the terms of the surrender. Poe could use an accepted psychology to limit the poet's province to the aesthetic. Art created the beautiful. Everyone admitted that. Accordingly, let the poet at least be the man of beauty, or, in terms of the faculty psychology, the man of taste. Let his sole function be the giving of pleasure, but then assert, with an authority stemming from Plato but reiterated down through the centuries, that the pleasure in beauty is a necessary pleasure—indeed, that the aesthetic response is a link between earth and heaven. Allow science and reason to have what they had already successfully claimed, the truth, but leave the poet his gems and flowers. The great romantics, in assigning poetry the province of truth, had demanded more territory than the world would allow and in effect had isolated the poet-prince from his people. Poe, on the other hand, claimed only the province of beauty, a province he could defend with the very weapons of the enemy, the laws of nature and the constitution of the human mind. It is for this reason that he used familiar proofs in his review of Longfellow, carrying them only the one step farther that was necessary to validate his own ends.

If Poe learned anything from the science and reason that he deplored in his fictions, it was that means had to be adapted to ends, and that a theory was only as good as its practice. In the remainder of his review, Poe attempted to show that Longfellow had failed because he had misconstrued the purpose of poetry in using didactic themes. The test for appropriate themes was elementary; the poet asked himself if the matter could not "be as well or better handled in prose." [14] If it could be, it should be left alone. When we examine Poe's actual judgments of Longfellow's poems, we see that his chief objection was to moral statement, not moral feeling. He commended "The Skeleton in Armor" almost without reservation because it exhibited "the beauty of bold courage and self-confidence, of love and maiden devotion, of reckless adventure, and finally of life-contemning grief." These were beautiful sentiments to Poe, but they were also what his age called moral sentiments. Poe was more conventional in what he liked than his pro-

[14] Poe may have derived this test from Blair's *Lectures*. At least they used the same term, "province," to describe the subject matter of literature. Blair cited the separation of poetry from other genres as historical fact. It no longer embraced history, philosophy, and persuasion (oratory) but was a "separate art, calculated chiefly to please, and confined generally to such subjects as related to the imagination and passions." *Lectures*, II, 322. Blair took it for granted that an author who wished to communicate facts or concepts would use prose and that anyone wishing to persuade would compose an oration. The "province" of poetry to Blair as to Poe was defined by the taste, and Blair, like Poe, thought instruction secondary: ". . . the primary aim of a Poet is to please, and to move; and, therefore, it is to the Imagination, and the Passions, that he speaks. He may, and he ought to have it in his view, to instruct, and to reform; but it is indirectly, and by pleasing and moving, that he accomplishes this end." *Ibid.*, 312. Poe's "heresy of the didactic" only states in more emphatic terms a commonplace of criticism, and, as his reference to "ordinary opinion" in support of his view indicates ("Nor is this idea so much at variance with ordinary opinion as, at first sight, it may appear"), he was catering to the common sense of his reader.

clamation of the "heresy of the didactic" would imply. For all of his assertion that it was chiefly in physical beauty that the soul found its dreams fulfilled, he prized moral beauty as highly as anyone else,[15] so long as it was implicit in the fable and not explicit as an apothegm. In fact, Poe was more tolerant of Longfellow's didacticism than most of us are today.

Less defensible is his application of the test of affective value. Any critic who uses the test of effect must assume that his own reaction should be taken as universal. What he feels, everyone should feel. This is patently not the case, as Coleridge himself asserted in his fragmentary essay on taste. Poe's reliance on normative psychology, which assumed a mechanical relationship between feelings and their causes, would lead him to this error. He made little allowance for individual differences in response because he assumed that human nature in its optimum development was always and everywhere the same. For instance, melancholy was much admired in Poe's time, and aspects of the grave were considered poetic; accordingly, much of the "beautiful sentiment" in Poe's own poetry was expressed by what today we consider a morbid preoccupation with the grave. Yet, astonishingly, Poe objected to what he considered to be the feeling of horror evoked by the poem "The Wreck of the Hesperus," in the lines, "The salt sea was frozen on her breast, / The salt tears in her eyes." Such a description, Poe

---

[15] An extremely able exposition of Poe's aesthetic moralism appeared as I was preparing to send the final revision of this study to the press. Joseph J. Moldenhauer has properly taken account of Poe's use of psychology in his assessment of the way in which Poe considered taste productive of virtue; and though he has ignored the background of Poe's concepts in eighteenth-century taste psychology, his conclusions are the same as my own. I disagree in some respects with his application of Poe's central concept to the short tale, but, unfortunately, the necessities of meeting a deadline prevent me from what, in view of Mr. Moldenhauer's amassed evidence, would have to be an elaborate attempt at a refutation of the point that to Poe unity is *both* death and art. Philosophically and psychologically, the equation is valid, but I consider it alien to Poe's premises of composition. It must be taken as an unconscious predisposition toward *Thanatos* on Poe's part. See Moldenhauer, "Murder as a Fine Art: Basic Connections Between Poe's Aesthetics, Psychology, and Moral Vision," *PMLA*, LXXXIII (1968), 284–97.

claimed with what was probably an unconscious play on words, arouses "a chilling sense of the inappropriate." Thus to him, and perhaps to his audience, a description of a painful death, which was "unpoetic," was better treated in prose. It was perfectly all right to describe the grave of a beautiful woman and the "life-contemning" grief of her lover, but under no circumstances should one go into detail about the death agonies. The salt-encrusted corpse of the maiden made Poe feel disgust, so he assumed that everyone else would feel the same way, just as he assumed that any reader would feel the sentiment of beauty in the "childlike confidence and inno-cence" of the girl and in "the father's stern courage and affection." When poetry is judged simplistically by the sentiments it ex-presses, critical standards are disallowed. Poe was more effective when he examined Brainard's poems by his rules.

Because in this review Poe's argument, based as it is upon psy-chological assumptions no longer considered valid, obscures the aesthetic principles that he advanced, it will be helpful to sum-marize his conclusions, which are implied if not always stated: (1) Art is a means of gratifying a natural and irrepressible human need for aesthetic experience. (2) The gratification of this need is formative in that it reinforces our sense of the harmonious. (3) Overt statement of any kind of truth is inappropriate in poetry, since precepts or facts may be more clearly communicated in prose. (4) Feelings that inflame or disgust are inappropriate in poetry.

Of these principles only the last is questionable, and eventually Poe recognized the seriousness of the limitation. Some years later he defined the imaginative process in such a way as to allow it to include the deformed. Yet this was in theory alone. Ordinarily Poe restricted the artist to the use of conventionally poetic raw materi-als. This was his greatest weakness as an apologist for poetry. He could find value only in the way poetry made us feel. Even if we grant that in his own fictions he was able to locate a form of truth in myth, he was able to justify the poetic enterprise to his public only by severe reductionism. To an audience still indignant at the "atheist" school of Shelley and perplexed by the obscurities of Coleridge, it was necessary for him to use the proofs of science and common sense. The enemy, Poe had said in "The Colloquy," was the scientific reason; but in his reviews he infiltrated the ranks of the enemy in the service of art. Poe called his theoretical pronouncements from this time forward the "commonest of common sense," and it is difficult to understand his approach as anything other than a strategy of defense. It required him to repudiate Coleridge, at least superficially, and eventually to dispense with Schlegel and to speak pejoratively of Shelley's "wild abandon."

XIII · *Art as Stimulus: The Single Effect*

POE's greatest difficulty in developing a theory of poetry arose, as we have seen, from his attempt to prove that a transcendental vision could be transmitted, at least in part, by an empirical method. He was not the only theorist who recognized the problem; it was central in the aesthetics of high romanticism, and it was solved, insofar as it can ever be solved, by critics like Coleridge who advocated a symbolistic technique which enabled the artist to transmit his intuitions of universals by showing the correspondences between things and thought. To Poe, however, if the object depicted retained its authenticity as a thing, the artist was trying to achieve truth by a representation of reality. Though Poe is often considered a symbolist, he employed symbolism in a very special sense. In "The Colloquy of Monos and Una" he had invoked analogy as a mode of cognition, but his analogies were drawn from the cosmos as a whole and not from particular objects. This is why Allen Tate, in a perceptive essay based partly on "The Colloquy," described Poe as having an angelic instead of a symbolic imagination.[1] Poe used symbolism in the manner of a musician. Morse Peckham's description of the symphonic form of Berlioz would apply equally well to Poe's work: "The reappearance of the theme made it unmistakable that behind each 'scene' or movement was an individual who was organizing the material in order to symbolize his attitudes. It was not, like eighteenth-century music, saying: 'This is love, this is nobility.' Rather, it said, 'This is the joy, this is the sorrow, this is the ecstasy of the same person.'"[2] Such a symbolic mode was the result of Poe's initial concept of poetry as music with an idea. Words were used for their affective and not their referential value.

[1] "The Angelic Imagination," in *The Forlorn Demon*, 56–78.
[2] Peckham, *Beyond the Tragic Vision*, 203.

Yet Poe was concerned with principle, with law, and when he counseled following nature, he meant first, observation of human nature and of the Great Design, and then the application of natural laws to human art. Not in the individual object but in the sweep of the planets about the sun, in the reciprocity of cause and effect as exhibited in the adaptation of a form of life to its surroundings, and in the periodicity of the seasons did he see the laws that could be applied to human art. An imitation of nature's variety, fecundity, vitality, and growth was alien to Poe's concept of art. To him aesthetic value was received by the poet as feeling, a feeling inspired by existing forms of beauty but not satisfied by them. Since ideal beauty was beyond life, the poet had to place minimal reliance upon sense perception. The feeling could be adequately symbolized only by the whole poem, just as the beauty of God's design could be realized only by an apprehension of the whole universe, not its minute particulars. Unlike Emerson, Poe could not see the universal in the particular. Phenomena described in a poem had to be transformed imaginatively into something not common to sense experience, something ideal. Not only symbols which retained their authenticity as objects but also similes and metaphors should be eliminated, because they referred to the actual, and Poe wished to stimulate the response he considered attendant only upon vision. The whole should stimulate the poetic feeling, and in order to stimulate strongly, the poem had to achieve a unity of emotional effect.

Although in poetry only aesthetic feeling could be rendered with propriety, Poe thought that prose had no such limitation. It could make use of a wide variety of effects. Prose, in Poe's opinion, had a lower purpose than poetry because it did not make its appeal exclusively to the soul; it was a more flexible instrument and could be used artistically to arouse a unified emotional effect. During the same fertile period in which Poe produced his review of Longfellow, he wrote his most significant theoretical statement about the short tale in the context of a review of the tales of Nathaniel Hawthorne.[3]

[3] *Works*, XI, 104–13.

The concept of unified effect that Poe developed in his theory of poetry was applied with equal stringency to the short tale. The April number of *Graham's* contained a brief notice of Hawthorne's *Twice-Told Tales*,[4] which was perhaps composed during Virginia's illness. But just as he had done with Longfellow's *Ballads*, Poe announced that because of lack of space he would treat the subject more fully in a subsequent issue. This he did in the May number. Poe needed space because he wanted not merely to evaluate Hawthorne's stories, but to establish a rationale of the short tale by which an evaluation could be made. Just as he had validated the function of the critic and the purpose of poetry, now he intended to validate the short story as an authentic literary genre.

In this attempt Poe was able to reduce theory to practice more successfully than he had done in his review of Longfellow's poetry because he did not think it necessary to establish transcendent aesthetic value for the short tale. Prose, not appealing exclusively to the aesthetic sense, could evoke terror, passion, horror, mirth, or even stimulate the reason:

> The writer of the prose tale, in short, may bring to his theme a vast variety of modes or inflections of thought and expression—(the ratiocinative, for example, the sarcastic, or the humorous) which are not only antagonistical to the nature of the poem, but absolutely forbidden by one of its most peculiar and indispensable adjuncts; we allude, of course, to rhythm. It may be added here, *par parenthese*, that the author who aims at the purely beautiful in a prose tale is laboring at great disadvantage. For Beauty can be better treated in the poem.

Poe tended to continue his theoretical arguments from review to review, and we can see that here he was reinforcing the claim that he had made for poetry in the review of Longfellow's *Ballads*. Poetry, in Poe's opinion, produced transport, or vision. Rhythm was indispensable because of its hypnagogic effect in detaching the senses from external reality and making the mind receptive to emotional stimuli. Of course one might argue that prose can do the same thing. Prose like that of Sir Thomas Browne can often be scanned,

[4] *Ibid.*, 102–104.

but Poe, in theory at least, considered highly rhythmic prose as merely inefficient poetry.[5] Rhythmic prose does not rhyme, and rhyme, with its repetition of sound, reinforces the hypnagogic effect of rhythm. Although he could write good blank verse himself, Poe was not overly fond of the form because it failed to use rhyme, one of the tools at the poet's command.

Poe's strategy in this review was to elaborate his concept of the unified effect, which he had touched on briefly in his review of Longfellow and in earlier reviews, and to apply it to the short tale. He based his concept upon empirical psychology, which served his purpose here as had the theoretical physiology of the brain in the review of Longfellow. Now he developed his famous doctrine of the single sitting, and he claimed that it applied equally to poetry and to fiction:

> Were we bidden to say how the highest genius could be most advantageously employed for the best display of its own powers, we should answer, without hesitation—in the composition of a rhymed poem, not to exceed in length what might be perused in an hour. Within this limit alone can the highest order of true poetry exist. We need only here say, upon this topic, that, in almost all classes of composition, the unity of effect or impression is a point of the greatest importance. It is clear, moreover, that this unity cannot be thoroughly preserved in productions whose perusal cannot be completed at one sitting. We may continue the reading of a prose composition, from the very nature of prose itself, much longer than we can persevere, to any good purpose, in the perusal of a poem. This latter, if truly fulfilling the demands of the poetic sentiment, induces an exaltation of the soul which cannot be long sustained. All high excitements are necessarily transient. Thus a long poem is a paradox. And without unity of impression, the deepest effects cannot be brought about. Epics were the offspring of an imperfect sense of Art, and their reign is no more. A poem *too* brief may produce a vivid, but never an intense or enduring impression. Without a certain continuity of effort—without a certain duration or repetition of purpose—the soul is never deeply moved. . . . Ex-

---

[5] It goes without saying that Poe was inconsistent. He wrote several "prose-poems."

treme brevity will degenerate into epigrammatism; but the sin of extreme length is even more unpardonable.

This quotation represents Poe at his most pragmatic, extracting rules for poetry from empirical psychology. The state of transport cannot be long maintained; hence a poem must be brief. On the other hand, if it is too brief, the hypnagogic effect of rhyme and rhythm is diminished, and the soul is not deeply moved. Poe accepted the Longinian concept of transport as the test of poetry, but, like Coleridge, he would not allow the title of poem to a composition which contained a series of striking lines or passages. It was the unified effect of the whole which counted, but the length of the whole had to be adjusted to what Poe considered to be the duration of ecstasy—arbitrarily about an hour.[6]

Poe had broached the subject of unity of effect as far back as 1836, but then he had used the requirement to attack Mrs. Sigourney's habit of prefixing an epigraph to her poems. He had previously indicated a distaste for long poems, but in his review of Moore's *Alciphron*, which was a long poem, his strategy had been to examine the poem for evidences of the fancy and the imagination and he had made no objection to its length. Now, however, the theoretical portion of his review was devoted to a discussion of unity of effect and the psychological need for such unity.

The rule of unified effect was in Poe's system applicable to all purely literary genres except the novel, and Poe had his doubts that the novel was really an art form. The reader had to be in a situation in which stimuli could operate without interruption, and for this the single sitting was necessary. To guard against disturbance, a reading time for the tale of no more than two hours was prescribed; this was Poe's estimate of the length of time a person could screen himself from "worldly interests" and give the tale his undivided attention.

How, we may ask, could Poe have been so naïve as to ignore the different reading rates of his projected audience and the differences

[6] It was the current romantic notion, more common in German than in British aesthetics, that art should produce an ecstasy that could not be long endured. Abrams, *The Mirror and the Lamp*, 89–90.

in leisure time available for reading? Probably because in this review he was thinking in terms of a mass audience, and his purpose was to prescribe a desirable length for journalistic fiction. It is difficult to separate Poe the journalist from Poe the artist. He had a given medium, the monthly magazine, and his problem was to create an art form for this medium. He believed that reading would eventually be confined largely to magazines. The increasing complexity of life would create a public demand for short fiction. Poe had learned from his own experience that collections of short tales sold poorly, however publishable they might be in magazines. If, however, the tale could be established as an art form, it would be properly reviewed, and the critics, mediating between the author and the audience, would make the audience aware of the suitability of the form to their needs. Poe's concern about the reading time of a prose narrative represents journalistic expediency as well as practical psychology. Brevity in the tale was not as psychologically necessary as it was in the poem, but it was a sort of rule of thumb which would enable the tale-writer to make the greatest impression on his reader.

Since theory had to be reduced to practice, Poe next proceeded to explain how an author might evoke a unified response within the limits of two hours' reading time.

A skilful literary artist has constructed a tale. If wise, he has not fashioned his thoughts to accommodate his incidents; but having conceived, with deliberate care, a certain unique or single *effect* to be wrought out, he then invents such incidents—he then combines such events as may best aid him in establishing this preconceived effect. If his very initial sentence tend not to the outbringing of this effect, then he has failed in his first step. In the whole composition there should be no word written, of which the tendency, direct or indirect, is not to the one pre-established design. And by such means, with such care and skill, a picture is at length painted which leaves in the mind of him who contemplates it with a kindred art, a sense of the fullest satisfaction. The idea of the tale has been presented unblemished, because undisturbed; and this is an end unattainable by the novel.

We notice immediately that in this passage Poe speaks of both effect, which we might presume is the emotional effect, and idea, which could be construed as an appeal to the intellect. In Poe's theory the tale could appeal either to the emotions or to the reason, and emotion and thought had to reinforce each other to achieve a totality of effect. He considered the tale superior to the poem, not in the quality but in the range of experience it yielded to the reader. The tale, like his own detective stories, could combine horror and an exercise in deduction, or, if we take some of his own tales as examples, it could present philosophical ideas. Consequently, Poe concluded rightly, it would have more appeal to the "mass of mankind." Critics who made disparaging comments against the "tales of effect" (horror, etc.) were simply mistaken, for these tales "were relished by every man of genius: although there were found many men of genius who condemned them without just ground."

In his argument to establish the short tale as a serious art form, Poe's grounding in British empirical psychology served him better than it did in his attempt to methodize the poetic vision. The only source he ever acknowledged for his concept of totality of effect was Augustus William Schlegel, but it is not difficult to locate what he had learned from other writers on the subject. Kames, Blair, Alison, and Coleridge—not to mention the phrenologists— had served Poe in his development of a theory of poetry, but it was chiefly Kames and Alison who stood behind his principle of unity of impression, the single effect of the short tale.

Lord Kames had stated, "Emotions that are opposite or extremely dissimilar, never combine or unite: the mind cannot simultaneously take on opposite tones." [7] Therefore, if one wanted to create a strong impression, he should be careful not to promote confused reactions. He should preserve the "harmony of emotions." Alison gave this requirement of emotional harmony still greater emphasis, making it a first principle of composition and its recognition a criterion of taste: "In all the Fine Arts, that Composition is most excellent, in which the different parts most fully unite in the produc-

[7] *Elements of Criticism*, 68.

tion of one unmingled Emotion, and that Taste the most perfect, where the perception of this relation of objects, in point of expression, is most delicate and precise." [8] Alison stated the requirement much more strictly than did Poe's acknowledged source, Schlegel, who had called only for a unity of interest in the drama. Poe reflected Alison's emphasis when he wrote "that in almost all classes of composition, the unity of effect or impression is a point of greatest importance." Hence it should not be too surprising that when four years later Poe published his "The Philosophy of Composition," illustrating the practical application of his literary principles, he claimed that after deciding upon the proper length of his poem (invoking his doctrine of the single sitting) his second consideration was the choice of the effect to be rendered. "The Philosophy of Composition" will be discussed in a later chapter; it contains little that Poe had not already advanced in his reviews of Longfellow and of Hawthorne—the limitation of the poem to beauty, the doctrine of the single sitting, and the necessity of a single emotional effect. In this context it is appropriate to say only that the mechanical mode of composition described in "The Philosophy of Composition" was a logical development in the light of Poe's effort to shape art for the needs of a mass audience while at the same time retaining its appeal for the elite. Alison had said that even a man of ordinary taste would recognize confusion in expression, whereas a man of refined taste would be able to recognize the most delicate shades of relatedness.

The question immediately arises, were Poe and Alison discussing the same kind of unity? Is Poe's "single effect" equivalent to the "single emotion" of Alison, or is it the "totality of interest" of Schlegel? An examination of the terms themselves will not provide an answer, but an interpretation of the presuppositions that lie behind the terms will be helpful. Schlegel's unity is organic unity, "the idea of life" which is intuited from the perception of a living thing. Hence in a drama, the requisite unity is not merely formal relatedness of parts to a whole but a "joint impression" on the mind which is productive of a felt or intuited unity.[9] It is the unity

[8] *Essays*, 106.   [9] Schlegel, *Lectures*, 244.

of the manifold, the impression of life in all of its relatedness held within a single organic form. The work of art, then, is a microcosm in reference to the biosphere.

Alison's unity of impression, however, derives from an organization of congruent associations. The mixture of elements which Schlegel admired in Shakespeare was deplored by the Scottish critic. Alison assumed that each object had its characteristic expression; that is, each object was productive of a simple emotion in the mind of the observer through the process of association. A complex of simple, congruent emotions constituted the emotion of taste, which could be described in terms of beauty or sublimity. Incongruous or conflicting expressions should not be joined in a composition, or the unity of idea (feeling and thought) would be lost. Accordingly, the artist must combine elements that produce an unmingled response. If beauty is the object, then elements that express beauty must be combined. If sublimity is the object, then elements which express sublimity must be chosen. In Poe's terminology, when the effect is chosen in advance, all elements must combine to produce that effect.

It is obvious that Poe's "single effect" is more nearly Alison's "unmingled emotion" than it is Schlegel's (and Coleridge's) unity of the manifold which is recognized in the intuition of "life." All Poe added to Alison was the doctrine of the single sitting. Not even the undercurrent of meaning, a requirement which Poe attributed to Schlegelian aesthetics, was absent from Alison, for Alison conceived of the associative activity of the imagination as always adding something to the objects of perception which the objects themselves did not express. "Our minds, instead of being governed by the character of external objects, are enabled to bestow upon them a character which does not belong to them; and even with the rudest, or the most common appearances of Nature, to connect feelings of a nobler or a more interesting kind than any that the mere influences of matter can ever convey." [10] With Alison as with Poe, it was for the suggestion of something "more pure and more perfect" *beyond* that art was valuable, and this suggestion

[10] *Essays*, 450.

was managed not by the coalescence of the diverse but by the elimination of the incongruent.

When Poe listed his effects, it is clear that he was referring to the production of a single emotion, which might be admiration of the reasoning power of a detective, or "terror, or passion, or horror"; in his own tales, say "The Fall of the House of Usher," the requirement of the single emotion was strictly observed. From the very first sentence to the last, the tale evokes a species of terror. Other effects are possible, of course, including "the sarcastic, or the humorous," but what Alison called the unity of expression had to be preserved. Terror, for instance, does not combine well with humor, so there is no humor in "Usher"; and even in "Ligeia," which could be interpreted as a story of passion, the passion is subordinate to the overall impression of psychic terror. Alison's theory predicted Poe's practice and serves us better than Schlegel's as an explanation of the single effect. That Poe was thinking chiefly in terms of sensation, or emotional effect, is evident from his admiration of the "tales of effect" in *Blackwood's*. Critics should not hold sensation stories in contempt, Poe argued. "The true critic will but demand that the design intended be accomplished, to the fullest extent, by the means most advantageously applicable."

This statement admits no ambiguity. The critic does not demand a compelling insight into human nature. He does not demand thought, nor does he demand that a work of art possess the vitalistic quality revered by Schlegel; he demands only skill in execution, technical virtuosity. Like Alison, Poe thought taste was manifested in a delicate and precise perception of the relatedness of elements in producing an unmingled effect.

To those who require a work of art to do something other than move us, Poe's reductionism is alarming, for fiction loses all ethical and social value under the doctrine of the single effect. Yet as a prescription for technique, it has had astonishing success. Even in the twentieth century, some manuals on short story writing have quoted Poe approvingly. The prescription of the single effect requires the beginning writer to make an effort at a certain kind of unity, yet the pertinent question in this context has to do with how well Poe's rule serves the purpose of criticism. An examination of his comments on Hawthorne's tales will provide the answer.

2

Poe began by describing the emotional effect of Hawthorne's tales in general. It is that of "repose," a feeling of tranquillity, but there is "a strong under-current of *suggestion* . . . beneath the upper stream of the tranquil thesis." The presence of this suggestiveness, as Poe had said in earlier reviews, indicates imagination, but Hawthorne's imagination was somewhat "repressed by fastidiousness of taste, by constitutional melancholy and by indolence." [11] In other words, Hawthorne's temperament kept him from attempting the strong effects that Poe himself relished. This did not mean that Hawthorne was not a genius, and that his art did not serve his genius well. His "distinctive trait is invention, creation, imagination, originality—a trait which, in the literature of fiction, is positively worth all the rest." Here, of course, Poe equated imagination with invention, or the power of making up new fables or images, as he had in his review of Longfellow, but he extended his concept of originality to include novelty of tone as well as novelty of matter. Hawthorne displayed originality both in his choice of materials and in his tone.

Of the individual tales, Poe had little to say. Of most of them he approved, but the superficiality of his concept of meaning was evident in his interpretation of "The Minister's Black Veil." "The *obvious* meaning of this article will be found to smother its insinuated one. The *moral* put into the mouth of the dying minister will be supposed to convey the *true* import of the narrative; and that a crime of dark dye, (having reference to the 'young lady') has been committed, is a point which only minds congenial with that of the author will perceive." Here one is compelled to say that if Hawthorne's tale is a crime story, only minds congenial with Edgar Poe's will perceive it. Remembering the review of *Barnaby Rudge,*

[11] About the only flaw that Poe customarily attributed to genius was a predisposition toward indolence!

we can see that Poe was looking for clues and that he considered Parson Hooper's declaration of a universal and hidden guilt only as a false lead. To Poe, the reported shudder of the "dead maiden" conveyed the true import of the tale,[12] even though Hawthorne was only using the familiar device of Irving to mitigate the supernatural by having the report come from a "superstitious old woman." Poe was no descendant of the Puritans, and his mind was less congenial with Hawthorne's than he supposed. In fact, what Poe called the undercurrent of meaning was actually the kind of meaning a literalist would discover in looking for the minister's motivation in wearing the veil. Because the minister *states* the moral significance of his veil, Poe assumed that the imaginative artist, Hawthorne, could not possibly mean what he said; and he remained blind to Hawthorne's symbolic portrayal of universal guilt.

This same superficiality may be observed in Poe's comment about another tale: " 'The White Old Maid' is objectionable, even more than 'The Minister's Black Veil,' on the score of its mysticism. Even with the thoughtful and analytic, there will be much trouble in penetrating its entire import." In this passage Poe used the term "mystic" pejoratively, although in an earlier review he had used it in reference to the undercurrent of meaning which evidenced imagination. The only possible conclusion is that Poe demanded a fairly obvious meaning in the short tale, but one which was suggested, not stated. If it were stated, then it was a thesis, or the surface meaning. There should be no ambiguity, no unresolved potentialities of interpretation. The fable should bear the meaning, and suggestion should be limited to the manipulation of event and

---

[12] The minister, having donned his symbolic black veil, bends over to look into the face of an unnamed "dead maiden." The veil hangs in such a way that the girl would have been able to see his face, if she had been alive. Hastily the minister pulls the veil back over his features, but a superstitious old woman claims to have seen the corpse shudder when the minister's face was disclosed. This event is the basis for Poe's interpretation, although it occurs early in the tale. Nothing else in the story supports the theory of crime except an exclamation from the minister of an adjoining parish who attends Father Hooper's deathbed.

scene in terms of the single effect. Accordingly, we should not be surprised that Poe selected "The Wedding Knell," "Mr. Higginbotham's Catastrophe," and "Dr. Heidegger's Experiment" as Hawthorne's best tales, for these offer relatively little in the way of ambiguity. The aspect of Hawthorne's work that has been most interesting to modern critics was the most objectionable to Poe.

Poe's generalizations about Hawthorne are more defensible. The monotony of tone, "a tone of melancholy and mysticism," should have been avoided. There should have been more variety of subject matter, because Hawthorne was too great an artist to limit himself to only one kind of appeal. In his own tales Poe attempted to achieve variety by appealing to the imagination, to the reason, and to the sense of humor; so to him Hawthorne's lack of versatility was censurable. Even though Poe listed these defects, he accorded the New England writer a high place as an artist and apologized that the limitations of space had prevented him from paying the "full tribute of commendation" that Hawthorne deserved.

Unfortunately, this same lack of space prevented Poe from explicating Hawthorne's tales in full. This in turn bars us from evaluating the quality of his insight. His general remarks about Hawthorne have stood the test of time, but his examination of particular tales is disappointing. We would grant today that Hawthorne had imaginative power and purity of style, that he sometimes succeeded in making every word count, but we would be likely to admit, as Hawthorne did himself, that his range was narrow. We would be less disposed than Poe to find fault with Hawthorne's obscurity and ambiguity, but today we are prepared to recognize and approve of complexities that Poe's theory could not assimilate. And we should remember that even so astute a critic as Henry James objected to the "superficial symbolism" of *The Scarlet Letter* and found that the characters functioned primarily as representatives of a "single state of mind." Poe, of course, was not proceeding from a basis of realism as was James, but he recognized at least one of Hawthorne's limitations, the tendency toward allegory which prevented a thorough incorporation of meaning into the symbolic texture of his narratives. Hawthorne was prone to tell us the import of his symbols, although his telling, as Poe perceived, did not exhaust the possibilities of interpretation.

That the requirement of the single effect has minimal value as a critical principle is obvious.[13] Focusing as Poe did upon technique, he was unprepared to explore ambiguities or paradoxes. If they existed at all, they were technical flaws. The principle of the single effect demanded that the theme or idea of a tale be as open to the comprehension of a reader as a painting is open to visual perception. In this review, as in his previous reviews of *Undine* and *Alciphron*, Poe showed uneasiness when confronted with the problem of symbolic import. The management of symbols could not be adequately prescribed in his simplistic formulae; and although he allowed the tale to express truth, he evidently meant by truth an illustration of the reasoning process, or a way of arriving at the truth. Both tale and poem are fictions. They have value in their stimulative capacity but little cognitive value. Although his own tales reveal psychic terror, Poe failed to recognize that Hawthorne's greatest achievement was his exploration of the human psyche under conditions of guilt. He saw Hawthorne only as a master of tone and a manipulator of effects, unfortunately restricted by his temperament to a tone of melancholy and mysticism and an effect of tranquillity.

[13] There are a number of critical studies of Poe's theory of unity of effect which draw upon Schlegel and upon Poe's metaphysics for assistance in interpretation. Obviously my own interpretation confines Poe's principle within much narrower limits by treating it as a rule for composition or for judgment. For various other interpretations, see Kelly, "Poe's Theory of Unity," 34–44; Walter Blair, "Poe's Conception of Incident and Tone in the Tale," *Modern Philology*, XLI (1944), 228–40; and Moldenhauer, "Murder as a Fine Art," 284–97.

XIV · *Politics and Poetry*
The Problem of Meaning

THE reviews of Longfellow and Hawthorne were Poe's most impressive theoretical statements during his editorship of *Graham's Magazine*. From January through May of 1842 he had made an attempt to validate the role of the critic, the function of poetry, and the right of the short tale to be considered as an art form; but his most characteristic reviews, as distinguished from his statements of theory, had been those of Brainard and Dickens. In the first he had demonstrated the faults of Brainard's verse by using conventional rules of rhetoric; in the second he had attempted to show that a good novel could have been better had the author made use of a sound method to implement his natural genius. Genius, in Poe's view, did not automatically produce perfection.

Poe's connection with *Graham's Magazine* was severed probably around the first of April, 1842; and the criticism in the May number was his last in the journal that represented editorial prerogative. From that time on he was a contributor, not an editor. The review of *Zanoni* in the June number was included by James A. Harrison in Poe's *Works*, but Poe indignantly denied its authorship in a letter to his friend Joseph E. Snodgrass.[1] His post at *Graham's* was taken by Rufus Wilmot Griswold, whose anthology, *The Poets and Poetry of America*, was reviewed in the June issue. Griswold was hired at a larger salary than that which Poe had received, but the story that he was employed without Poe's knowledge and that Poe walked in one day to find Griswold in the editor's chair is not true, although it has been revived recently.[2] The reasons for Poe's

[1] June 4, 1842, in *Letters*, I, 201–203. In this letter Poe composed a virulent repudiation to be published in Snodgrass' magazine, together with a statement that Poe had "retired" from *Graham's*. The repudiation was to appear as if it were an editorial comment by Snodgrass himself.

[2] See William Bittner, *Poe: A Biography* (Boston, 1963), for a repetition of this story. Actually Poe had retired from *Graham's* early in April, and

resignation are obscure, but they probably had to do with his desire to establish his own magazine. He had hoped that Graham would back him, but, since Graham refused, Poe sought other backers and alleged that his employer had held out false hopes of support.[3] At any rate Poe did resign from the best post he had ever had.

In September of 1842 Poe wrote to his friend Frederick Thomas stating that Graham had made him a good offer to return, not being "especially pleased" with Griswold. For the moment Poe considered the proposition seriously and even said that if he did return he would try "to bring about some improvements in the general appearance of the Magazine, & above all, to get rid of the quackery which now infects it." [4] He also told Thomas that Griswold had tried to bribe him into writing a favorable review of *The Poets and Poetry of America* by promising to guarantee the publication of the review. Poe did write the review, but he claimed to have written it "precisely as I would have written it under ordinary circumstances." Then Poe boasted that Griswold did not dare read the review in Poe's presence and that he had serious doubts that

---

Graham did not contact Griswold until April 20. Griswold began work on the magazine early in May. This information is documented in *Letters*, I, 203 n., and in Hull, "A Canon," 292–93.

[3] Poe wrote to Snodgrass on September 19, 1841, saying that it was "not impossible that Graham will join me in The 'Penn.'" *Letters*, I, 183. In a letter to Frederick Thomas dated October 27, 1841, he said that "Graham holds out a hope of his joining me in July." *Ibid.*, 185. By February 3, 1842, Poe was beginning to find fault with Graham and with the magazine itself. Poe to Thomas, *ibid.*, 192. In a letter to Thomas dated May 25, 1842, Poe gave as his reason for resigning his "disgust with the namby-pamby character of the Magazine—a character which it was impossible to eradicate—I allude to the contemptible pictures, fashion-plates, music and love tales." *Ibid.*, 197. Obviously Poe could not be content with what was essentially a family magazine, although one of very high quality. In a letter to David Bryan, dated July 6, 1842, Poe claimed that he had remained with Graham only because the publisher had promised to help him start the *Penn*, Poe's projected literary magazine, within a year. Poe claimed to have had a subscription list of a thousand to start with. *Ibid.*, 205. For all of Poe's wishful thinking, it seems unlikely that Graham would have wanted to back a magazine that would be at least in partial competition with his own.

[4] *Ibid.*, 211–12.

Griswold would publish it once he inspected its contents. The review appeared in the *Boston Miscellany* in November, and it should not have made Griswold angry unless he thought he had purchased unqualified commendation. Griswold's extreme hostility toward Poe in later years should not have been inspired by this particular review,[5] and the matter is mentioned here only to indicate that Poe's privately expressed opinion of a work or an author was not always duplicated in his reviews. He was a journalist out of work, and he had to live on his sales. The contempt of Griswold that his letters reveal might have cost him the opportunity to publish in *Graham's* if it had appeared in his reviews. As it was, he continued to publish occasionally in the journal for the next few years. Poe was courageous and frequently vitriolic, but sometimes he had to restrain himself because of financial necessity. Undoubtedly this was one of the reasons he wanted his own magazine, so that he would not have to cater to editors and literary cliques who could cut off his income if they were offended.

One other review Poe published in *Graham's Magazine* in 1842 is worth attention.[6] It shows him descending from the high theoretical plane of the review of Longfellow in order to examine the means by which ordinary poetry could succeed or fail. He had written a harsh review of Rufus Dawes for Burton in 1839, but Burton

[5] The virulent review that undoubtedly had something to do with Griswold's malice toward Poe appeared on January 28, 1843, in the Philadelphia *Saturday Museum*. It is probably not by Poe, although he may have had a hand in it. See Quinn, *Edgar Allan Poe*, 354 n. Both the *Boston Miscellany* review and the *Saturday Museum* review are printed in *Works*, XI, 147–60, 220–43. The first is a fair review in Poe's judicious manner; the second is a viciously sarcastic attack in which invective is allowed to supplant wit. It does repeat some of Poe's principles, but it is doubtful that even in 1843 Poe would have claimed that Longfellow was the best poet in America and that his poems were full of "ideality."

[6] "The Poetry of Rufus Dawes—A Retrospective Criticism," in *Works*, XI, 131–47. In a letter to me listing Poe's contributions to *Graham's*, Professor T. O. Mabbott failed to include this review, but I agree with Hull and others that it is Poe's. The review refers specifically to Poe's "A Chapter on Autography" as written by "ourselves," and it seems unlikely that Charles J. Peterson, who also reviewed for Graham, would have taken such a liberty, even though Graham had persuaded Poe to "speak well" of Peterson in the "Autography."

had not published it. Possibly the review in *Graham's* was the old one, revised for the occasion. If Poe revised it, he removed very little of its bite. His strategy was his customary one of asserting that the poet in question had a high reputation and then demonstrating by analysis that he did not deserve it. But before he devoted himself to the destruction of Dawes, he made some generalizations that could surprise anyone who had read no more of Poe's criticism than the review of Longfellow's *Ballads* and his lecture "The Poetic Principle." In his theoretical statements he asserted that the value of poetry was in the glimpses it afforded of a perfect beauty beyond appearances. As a practicing critic, however, Poe was insistent that the poet's vision was valueless unless it was communicated, and that communication required method: "The wildest and most erratic effusion of the Muse, not utterly worthless, will be found more or less indebted to *method* for whatever of value it embodies; and we shall discover, conversely, that, in any analysis of even the wildest effusion, we labor without method only to labor without end."

Difficulties, Poe affirmed, did not spring from the principles upon which composition and criticism were based, because these principles were "founded in the unerring instincts of nature" and were "enduring and immutable." Difficulty in composition or in analysis came from a faulty application of those principles; hence a knowledge of method was indispensable. Using the correct method, a critic would have no difficulty in demonstrating the good or bad qualities of a particular poem, and, furthermore, he would be able to correct the errors of the poet himself, which Poe immediately proceeded to do in the case of Rufus Dawes.

Dawes's longest poem, "Geraldine," Poe asserted, was a "servile imitation" of Byron's *Don Juan*. Imitation itself was a serious error, because it deprived the poet of a chance for originality, but even more serious was tactless imitation. Dawes imitated Byron's method—systematic digression—but Byron knew the limits of digression and used it purposefully. Dawes did not know what he was doing, and the result was "a mere mass of irrelevancy, amid the mad *farrago* of which we detect with difficulty even the faintest vestige of a narrative." To prove his point Poe made one of his devastating satirical summaries of the narrative, quoting lines occasionally either to ridicule their sense or to parody their style. Frequently he used prose paraphrase to show that the quoted passages were logically absurd. "It is impossible," Poe wrote, "to put the latter portion of it [the stanza quoted] into intelligible prose."

Why should a poem, we are entitled to ask by Poe's own criteria, be reducible to prose? He had stated in his review of Longfellow's *Ballads* that nothing which could be better communicated by prose should be handled in verse. The contradiction can be resolved if we note the kind of poem that Poe was examining. "Geraldine" is a narrative poem; hence it should have an intelligible sequence of events. If in a narrative poem extended metaphors or conceits are used, they should be analyzable in terms of what the poem has to say—its total import. If they are not connected with the narrative meaning, then they represent pointless difficulties for the reader. Poe quoted case after case to prove that the entire narrative was "pervaded by unintelligibility."

Remembering Poe's review of Morris, we will understand that he allowed a lyric poem a certain license. Since its aim was to evoke the aesthetic response and not to tell a story, it could be forgiven for some of the obscurity caused by difficult conceits and metaphors. A narrative, on the other hand, should be judged at least in part by its story value. "Simplicity, perspicuity, and vigor, or a well-disciplined ornateness of language, have done wonders for the reputation of many a writer really deficient in the higher and more essential qualities of the Muse. But even upon these minor points of manner our poet has not even the shadow of a shadow to sustain him." It is evident that in demanding simplicity and clarity Poe was invoking what he would have called the "lower qualities" of the Muse, the ability to tell a story in verse. There was no point in judging Dawes by any higher standard. *Sic transit* Rufus Dawes.

Although it is not readily apparent from his reviews, Poe did not have the highest regard for narrative poems, either epic or romance. He wrote to James Russell Lowell in 1843 saying that the highest poetry must "eschew narrative," because the merely narrative portions were prosaic.[7] This is the reason why he put Dawes's poem to the test of a prose paraphrase. A narrative poem could be reduced to prose, in Poe's opinion, and its principles of composition were scarcely different from those of the tale. It should have a unified effect; there should be an undercurrent of meaning that was not too obscure for comprehension; and the narrative movement should show the connectedness of a good plot. In such a poem clarity and orderly development were essential.

2

Poe's personal difficulties during the remainder of 1842 and through 1843 and 1844 are not the concern of this study but will be summarized briefly to indicate the conditions under which he published a few reviews as a free-lance journalist. He was, of course, without a regular salary and had to support himself by writing. He even tried through Frederick Thomas and through Rob Tyler, a minor poet who was also the son of President Tyler, to obtain a sinecure at the Philadelphia Custom House, but he did not succeed. In 1843 he seemed confident that at last his own projected magazine, now to be called the *Stylus*, would come into being. He wrote Thomas that he had secured a partner with ample capital and that he himself would have "the entire control of editorial conduct," which of course was what he had always wanted. The backer was one Thomas C. Clarke,[8] but either the capital was insufficient or badly managed, because Poe continued trying to interest President Tyler in his project. Since both Clarke and Poe apparently felt that political patronage was necessary, for a time Poe professed a great interest in Whig politics. He even wrote to Dr. Thomas Holley Chivers, whose support he was also soliciting, that he was assured of government patronage if he admitted "occasional articles" in support of the administration.[9] In March of 1843 it was

[7] October 19, 1843, in *Letters*, I, 238–39.
[8] Quinn, *Edgar Allan Poe*, 368–70, describes the agreement between Clarke and Poe.
[9] September 27, 1842, in *Letters*, I, 214–16.

arranged for Poe to go to Washington, make some lectures, visit various government departments, and have an audience with the President. Poe, Clarke, and Poe's friends Frederick Thomas and Jesse E. Dow were very optimistic about his prospects. Poe wrote Clarke from Washington on March 11 that he believed that he was making a "sensation which will tend to the benefit of the magazine." [10] Unfortunately he made too much of a sensation. His Washington indiscretions ended his chances for patronage, though he and his friends continued to seek it. The agreement with Clarke was dropped, [11] but throughout the remainder of the year Poe kept alive his own hopes for publishing his magazine.

It became increasingly apparent, however, that there was nothing for Poe in Philadelphia, unless he returned to *Graham's*. By early 1844 he decided to go to New York, hoping to have better luck than he had had in 1837. In an effort to establish connections in New York, he began to court the politico-literary group headed by Evert Duyckinck and Cornelius Mathews. Toward this end he wrote a conciliatory letter in March of 1844 to Mathews, whose *Wakondah* he had tomahawked in *Graham's* in 1842. Professor Quinn has called this letter a "manly apology," [12] but Poe was not ordinarily given to apologies, manly or otherwise. In the letter Poe described his own review as "impudent and flippant." [13] This it was, but it was also a trenchant condemnation of a worthless poem. Poe even went so far as to praise Mathews' novel, *The Adventures of Puffer Hopkins*, which he had previously disposed of with a slightly veiled sneer. [14] The apology was only the desperate

[10] *Ibid.*, 227.
[11] See Poe to James Russell Lowell, June 20, 1843, *ibid.*, 234.
[12] Quinn, *Edgar Allan Poe*, 402.
[13] March 15, 1844, in *Letters*, I, 245.
[14] Poe mentioned *Puffer Hopkins* in his review of *Wakondah*. Perry Miller has described Mathews' attempt to create a Dickensian picture of New York but declared that the novel "was and is unreadable" (*The Raven and the Whale*, 93). Poe could scarcely have referred to the novel as admirable, as he did in his letter, without temporarily misplacing his literary conscience. Curiously enough, in 1845 Poe *did* say that Mathews was unreadable. See "Fifty Suggestions," *Works*, XIV, 184–85

expedient of a man out of work and with a sick wife to gain allies who would support him against Lewis Gaylord Clark. Poe had to suppress his pride, repudiate his own opinions, and mollify Mathews out of necessity.

Poe moved to New York in April of 1844, and his work from this time on rarely approached the standards he had called for in *Graham's*. Virginia's worsening condition, journalistic controversy, poverty and overwork, together with his own declining energies, resulted in inferior critiques, in which he often repeated earlier reviews or indulged in pointless vituperation. Of Poe's later criticism only those reviews which illustrate shifts of emphasis in his literary theories or changes in his tactics will be examined. He did engage in a new enterprise, however; he reviewed live drama, and these reviews too will be examined.

3

Poe published a number of reviews between the time of his resignation from *Graham's* in 1842 and his joining the staff of the *Broadway Journal* in 1845. His March, 1843, review of Thomas Ward,[15] a minor poet who published in Clark's *Knickerbocker*, is in Poe's satirical manner, what he called his "funny" criticism, but it does analyze the defects of Ward's poetry according to the rules of rhetoric. Mixed metaphors, lapses from good taste, inappropriate language, shifts of tone, and unpronounceable consonant combinations were Ward's defects. Most damaging of all in Poe's opinion was Ward's attempt to communicate matters in poetry that should have been confined to prose: "He descends into mere meteorology —into the uses and general philosophy of rain, &c . . . ." However "funny" Poe's review may be, he employed his usual criteria for condemnation, and his animus against the *Knickerbocker* shows itself only at the end of the review, where he announced that the Whig journal had praised and published an incompetent poet.

In August of 1843 Poe reviewed the poetry of William Ellery

[15] "Our Amateur Poets, No. I—Flaccus," *Works*, XI, 160–74.

Channing,[16] nephew of the famous Unitarian minister of the same name and an inferior poet whose style Thoreau had described as "sublimo-slipshod." Poe's prejudice against New England was to become more obvious and it is possible that in this review he was identifying himself with the New Yorkers, who sneered at the transcendentalists. At any rate Poe was to rail against the obscure and the metaphysical as stridently as did the *Knickerbocker* and the *American Review*, both Whig publications. Certainly Poe was not catering to the prejudices of his enemies—it would have been impossible for him to curry favor from Lewis Gaylord Clark—but from 1842 on Poe did show a conservative strain in his literary opinions. He assailed "undue profundity" and objected to difficult symbols and recondite metaphors.

In the case of Channing, Poe found that the New Englander erred in imitating Tennyson's "quaintness." Quaintness, Poe affirmed occasionally, could be an adjunct to the beautiful, but it should not be used excessively. Tennyson could be quaint, but he was never obscure. A more grievous error lay in Channing's imitation of the obscurities of Carlyle. Carlyle was an ass, Poe said, because he took all possible pains to keep himself from being understood. Channing in turn had tried to set himself up as "a poet of unusual depth" by imitating Carlyle. Such an attempt alone would be enough to prove that Channing was no poet, but he had also used the loosest of rhythms. It was impossible to scan his lines, and his grammar was far from perfect.

Poe ended the review with a satirical diatribe accusing Channing of borrowing the fame of his illustrious uncle to gull the public; but one suspects that not the least of Channing's faults was his affiliation with the transcendentalists. Poe associated him ironically with the "logic" of Emerson and the "Orphicism" of Bronson Alcott. Poe's quarrel with New England and especially with the transcendentalists was to grow, and no unprejudiced judgment of their writings could be expected in his reviews.

[16] "Our Amateur Poets, No. III—William Ellery Channing," *ibid.*, 174–90.

In September, Poe appeared again in *Graham's* with an essay on Fitz-Greene Halleck,[17] whom he had previously examined in the *Messenger* in 1836. Poe used the essay to introduce a discussion of metrics. William Cullen Bryant had reviewed his friend Halleck favorably and had praised his metrical skill. As far back as the 1820's Bryant had argued for trisyllabic substitutions in iambic verse to relieve the monotony of the iambic measure. Therefore Bryant considered it a merit when Halleck introduced occasional roughness in his meter. Poe, with his predilection for smoothly fluent verse, challenged Bryant immediately. Monotony was not relieved by deliberate roughness, Poe claimed, but by discords. These discords "affect only the time—the harmony—of the rhythm, and never interfere . . . with its smoothness or melody. The best discord is the smoothest."

To Poe the supreme test of the quality of versification was ease of pronunciation. Surprisingly, however, he admitted that the sense of a poetic passage was its most important element. If there was a choice between sound and sense, it was the sound which had to go. Nevertheless, a skillful poet should not find it necessary to make such a choice. The colloquial emphasis necessary for a natural reading should always tally with the chosen rhythm, and in this Halleck had failed. It was impossible to give a natural reading to some of his lines. The remainder of Poe's essay was adapted from his *Messenger* review and advanced no new opinions. If journalistic politics were involved, the evidence is slight. Bryant was a prominent New York Democrat, and Halleck had virtually retired from writing. It is likely that Poe, having become aware of Bryant's metrical theories, seized the opportunity to publicize his own. In his review of Bryant in 1837, published in the *Messenger*, Poe gave no indication that he knew of the elder poet's advocacy of trisyllabic substitution in iambic verse, so he may have considered it necessary in the 1843 essay to make the proper discriminations.

[17] *Ibid.*, 190–204. This is not a review but an essay in a series that *Graham's* was running on various contributors. Poe summarized Halleck's literary career before he disputed Bryant's opinion of Halleck's metrics. The essay concludes with a revised excerpt from Poe's *Messenger* review of Halleck.

Otherwise, the public might have assumed that he was merely following the lead of Bryant, then considered America's foremost prosodist.

4

Poe's reviews during 1843 and 1844 have literary significance only as he continued to address himself to the problem of meaning, and they reveal various reallocations of emphasis as he attempted to accommodate conceptual value to forms designed to please. But these reviews must also be viewed in relation to his efforts to survive in journalism. Only necessity can explain one of the strangest reviews, in respect to his usual theories and practices, that he ever wrote. In March of 1844 Poe published in *Graham's* a long review of *Orion*,[18] an epic by the British poet Richard Hengist Horne. Horne was affiliated with the Spasmodic School of poets, who were strongly influenced by Byron and Shelley.[19] It is possible that Poe was attracted to Horne because he believed, along with the Spasmodics, that the divinely inspired poet had a right to indulge in egocentricity and self-contemplation. As a younger man Poe himself had displayed these attitudes, but they had not proved to be viable in the hard world of competitive journalism, and they were especially unwelcome among those conservative gentlemen, the New York Whigs. Philip J. Bailey, one of the Spasmodics, had published in 1839 an epic-drama called *Festus*, which had annoyed the Whig *American Review* with its obscure symbols and analogies.[20] The Spasmodics were prone to use metaphors, conceits, and extended analogies in abundance. Furthermore, none of them

[18] *Ibid.*, 249–75.

[19] For an account of the Spasmodics and Horne's relationship with the group, see Jerome H. Buckley, *The Victorian Temper* (Cambridge, 1951), 41–65.

[20] Poe reviewed *Festus* in the *Broadway Journal* for September 6, 1845. See *Works*, XII, 241–42. He confessed, however, that he had not read the entire poem and commented only on the excitement it had aroused: "The poetical and critical world of England were . . . violently agitated (in spots) by the eruption of 'Festus,' a Vesuvius-cone at least—if not an Aetna—in the literary cosmos."

seemed capable of constructing a poetic whole. Undisciplined and careless, they often neglected what Poe called the unity of effect in order to exploit feelings quite at variance with the dominant mood of the poem. When they were good, they were good only in selected passages. In short, Poe should have been as severe with Horne as the *American Review* was with Bailey, even more severe, because *Orion* purported to be an epic. Its purpose was truth, and its method was allegorical.

Poe's review can possibly be explained by the maneuvering he was engaged in at the time. He wrote to Cornelius Mathews for the address of Mathews' "friend" Horne, stating that he wished to send Horne a "letter and a small parcel." [21] The parcel was Poe's tale "The Spectacles," which he wanted Horne to publish in England. Mathews, apparently on his own initiative, sent Horne a copy of *Graham's* containing Poe's review, and though Horne did not agree with Poe's strictures, he felt that since they appeared "amidst such high praise" it would be ungrateful of him to attempt to justify himself in detail. Horne offered to send Poe copies of his own works and expressed his "obligations to the boldness and handsomeness of American criticism," [22] meaning Poe's.

It is obvious that Poe was attempting to ingratiate himself with Horne. He should have condemned *Orion* out of hand because it violated all of his own rules. He admitted this (even quoting from his review of Longfellow's *Ballads*) to the effect that truth had no place in a poem. Then, rather than concede directly that Horne was in business as a transcendental seer, he attacked Horne's admirers and burlesqued a "transcendental" review—one that might have been written by a Spasmodic:

> "Orion" is the *earnest* outpouring of the oneness of the psychological MAN. It has the individuality of the true SINGLENESS. It is not to be regarded as a Poem, but as a WORK—as a multiple THEOGONY—as a manifestation of the WORKS and the DAYS. It is a pinion in the PROGRESS—a wheel in the MOVEMENT that moveth ever and goeth always—a mirror of SELF-INSPECTION, held up by the SEER of

[21] March 15, 1843, in *Letters*, I, 245.
[22] See Horne to Poe, April 27, 1844, in *Works*, XVII, 167–69.

the age essential—of the Age *in esse*—for the SEERS of the Ages possible—*in posse*. We hail a brother in the work.[23]

Poe's tactics in this burlesque are clever. He called the alleged reviewer an Orphicist, thus associating him with Bronson Alcott, at least to the American mind, but perhaps reminding erudite readers of the ancient Orphic doctrine that time produced an egg from which the gods proceeded. The Orphic religion was ecstatic and transcendental, affirming that the progress of time would liberate man from his earthborn limitations. The modern Orphicist also believed in the progressive liberation of the soul, and Horne's poem used the ancient myth of Orion to affirm the necessity of progress. Atypical of the nineteenth century in his denial of progress, Poe also satirized the transcendentalists by burlesquing a poet-prophet who was made to speak as follows: " 'I am a SEER. My IDEA—the idea which by providence I am especially commissioned to evolve —is one so vast—so novel—that ordinary words, in ordinary collocations, will be insufficient for its comfortable evolution.' " [24] Then Poe proceeded to chastise the hypothetical seer with his customary sarcasm:

> Very true. We grant the vastness of the IDEA—it is manifested in the sucking of the thumb—but, then, if ordinary language be insufficient—ordinary language which men understand—*a fortiori* will be insufficient that inordinate language which no man has *ever* understood, and which any well-educated baboon would blush in being accused of understanding. The "SEER," therefore, has no resource but to oblige mankind by holding his tongue, and suffering his IDEA to remain quietly "unevolved," until some Mesmeric mode of intercommunication shall be invented, whereby the antipodal brains of the SEER and of the man of Common Sense shall be brought into the necessary rapport.[25]

While mounting this attack upon the transcendentalists in the name of common sense and clear English, Poe managed to apologize for Horne by alleging that the British writer was "unhappily infected with the customary cant of the day—the cant of the

[23] *Ibid.*, XI, 251.   [24] *Ibid.*, 252–53.   [25] *Ibid.*

muddle-pates who dishonor a profound and ennobling philosophy by styling themselves transcendentalists." [26] Horne had been infected, Poe went on to say, only because sensitive and imaginative intellects were drawn toward mysticism. The poetic intellect was drawn toward the mystic because the unknown and the obscure were associated with the sublime, a legitimate object of poetry. Thus Horne, surrounded by a "junto of dreamers" with intellects far inferior to his own, had fallen into the error of thinking that "a poem, whose single object is the creation of Beauty—the novel collocation of old forms of the Beautiful and of the Sublime—could be advanced by the abstractions of a maudlin philosophy." [27]

And having been taken in by the muddle-headed dreamers, Horne did not do justice to his own high powers by composing a "poem *written solely for the poem's sake.*" Instead he had composed an allegory, "with an under and upper current of meaning." Four years earlier, in his review of *Alciphron*, Poe had said that the presence of a mystic undercurrent of meaning was the mark of an imaginative poem. Had he changed his mind? Probably not. Poe occasionally invented rules to defend poems he liked, and this may have been the case with *Alciphron*, but his seeming shift of position was occasioned by the nature of the poems he was reviewing. As has already been indicated, Poe did not regard narrative as the highest form of poetry. Both *Alciphron* and *Orion* are narrative poems. Given the narrative form, however, there must be an infusion of thought to prevent it from being a barren account of events. Thought, merely suggested, formed the undercurrent of meaning. If the meaning were too obvious, then the story element was lost, but fortunately Horne was gifted with a poetic sense which "softened this allegory . . . to keep it . . . well subject to the ostensible narrative." Whenever his desire to enforce his allegorical message overpowered Horne's poetic sense, the result was the kind of "bombast, rigmarole, and mystification" to be found in the last "paragraph" of the poem.[28]

Thus, throughout the entire first part of his review Poe maintained his theoretical position. The unusual aspect of the critique is

[26] *Ibid.*   [27] *Ibid.*, 254.   [28] *Ibid.*, 258.

that he made excuses for Horne as a man of genius who had fallen into error. Then he proceeded to examine Horne's poem and found passages in it to which he gave the most extravagant praise he ever tendered any author:

> This "Hunter of shadows, he himself a shade," is made symbolical, or suggestive, throughout the poem, of the speculative character of Orion; and, occasionally, of his pursuit of visionary happiness. For example . . . Orion, possessed of Merope, dwells with her in a remote and dense grove of cedars. Instead of directly describing his attained happiness—his perfected bliss—the poet, with an exalted sense of Art, *for which we look utterly in vain in any other poem,* merely introduces the image of the tamed or subdued *shadowstag,* quietly browsing and drinking beneath the cedars . . . .
>
> There is nothing more richly—more weirdly—more chastely— more sublimely imaginative—in the wide realm of poetic literature.[29]

By this statement we see that Poe did not object indiscriminately to meaning, particularly in a narrative poem which was worthless without it, but he did specify the mode by which it should be rendered. The tamed stag in Horne's poem symbolizes the subduing of the animal nature of Orion by love. Yet Poe admitted that Horne was by no means successful in his method, for the reader "is always pausing, amid poetical beauties, in the expectation of detecting among them some philosophical, allegorical moral." The burden of a search for an allegorical thesis, Poe thought, prevented the reader from feeling the unique effect of poetry.[30] All of Horne's errors sprang from his original error of

[29] *Ibid.,* 267–68.

[30] In this context Poe digressed from his subject in order to discuss the incompatibility of poetry and passion. *Ibid.,* 255. He referred to Coleridge as his authority. To establish the psychological basis of his distinction, he described the "sentiment of the beautiful" as a "divine sixth sense." Even if his usage is metaphorical, rt reminds us of the old description of the taste as an inner sense. Probably Poe's reference to Coleridge was derived from Chapter XV of the *Biographia Literaria* (II, 15–16), where Coleridge praised Shakespeare's ability to portray animal passion in such a way as to preclude sympathy, maintaining that the poet himself was aloof from the emotions he depicted. In this particular case Coleridge gave a more

conception, when he chose truth instead of beauty as his object. This was unfortunate, because "in all that regards the loftiest and holiest attributes of the true Poetry, 'Orion' has never been excelled." Indeed, Poe continued, "we feel strongly inclined to say that it has never been *equaled*. Its imagination—that quality which is all in all—is of the most refined—the most elevating—the most august character." [31] High praise indeed for a transcendental allegorist! But Poe had his reasons for not attacking Horne too ferociously, and he had preserved his standards by pointing out both the beauties and the faults of the poem. Furthermore, although he shared the distaste for allegory which was common among romantic symbolists, Poe's objection was to the genre *as* genre. When he was required to review an allegory, he examined it as a poem according to his rules for the management of meaning.

These rules had been stated concisely some months earlier in Poe's review of "Death; or Medorus' Dream," an allegorical poem by Robert Tyler.

> These allegorical subjects are faulty in themselves, and it is high time they were discarded. The best allegory is a silly conceit, so far as the allegory itself is concerned, and is only tolerable when so subjected to an upper current of obvious or natural meaning, that the moral may be dispensed with at pleasure—the poem being still good, *per se*, when the moral, or allegory, is neglected. When this latter is made to form an under-current, that is to say when an

---

valid account of the psychological process of composition than did most romantic critics, for Shakespeare did not *identify* himself with Venus and Adonis but analyzed and depicted their feelings. Coleridge did not declare that passion was alien to poetry but made it subject to the artistic will: "There must be not only a partnership but a union; an interpenetration of passion and of will, of *spontaneous* impulse and of *voluntary* purpose." *Ibid.*, 50. Eventually Poe, as did Coleridge, described the way that raw emotion was transformed into something else by the imaginative process.

[31] *Works*, XI, 266. As if this praise were not enough, Poe claimed that Horne's description of the palace of Vulcan was superior to Milton's description of Hell, and he concluded his review with the statement that "every man of genius" would admit *Orion* "to be one of the noblest, if not the very noblest poetical work of the age." *Ibid.*, 271, 275. It is not surprising that Horne was pleased with the review.

occasionally suggested meaning arises from the obvious one—then, and then only, will a true taste endure the allegorical. It can never properly be made the main thesis.[32]

In contrast to *Orion*, in which the allegorical meaning was subordinated, Tyler made it into the "main thesis," and Poe condemned the poem without reservation. The allegorical import was "handled in the crudest, most inartificial, and most commonplace manner." The only excuse that Poe could make for the poem was that it was intended as "a philosophical essay in verse," but this was really no excuse because there should be "no such anomalies." Thus, in terms of its object and its technique, "Death" was indefensible; but after making this judgment Poe proceeded, just as he had in his review of *Orion*, to examine the poem in detail, pointing out its few excellences and its many defects.

The relative severity of Poe's criticism of the poem of Robert Tyler, the President's son, could be explained on the grounds that the Tylers had disappointed him. Yet to claim that Poe was seeking revenge would not be fair. He used precisely the same method in reviewing Horne. By Poe's rules for the management of meaning, *Orion* was superior to "Death," and it was a far better poem in general. Since Poe usually reserved his extravagant praise for poets like Keats and Shelley, however, he may be suspected of lavishing superlatives upon Horne in order to remove the sting of his satire against Horne's admirers. He wanted an English audience, and for a time it appeared that Horne could help him.

5

The review of *Orion* was the last criticism of any importance that Poe wrote for Graham, and despite any element of self-serving it may have had, it shows that he was still concerned with the problem of symbolic technique. This review, read along with the reviews of *Alciphron*, *Twice-Told Tales*, and "Death," express just about all that Poe had to say about narrative import. It is clear that

[32] *Graham's Magazine*, XXIII (December, 1843), 320.

to Poe's mind little pleasure could be gained from a tale or poem whose chief object was to make one think, yet meaning was necessary to prevent a narrative from being a barren sequence of events. The only way to manage meaning in this form, he concluded, was to allow an occasional symbolic suggestion. If this suggestiveness were systematic enough to overpower the story element, then the narrative became allegory, disgusting, Poe had said, to every man of taste. If his own tales yield a systematic symbolic import, it would appear that he could not have been fully aware of it, for he liked tales of effect, and certainly he wrote them. Some have considered Poe's tales of terror as mechanical psychodramas devised to stimulate sensation, yet Poe was a better artist than his theory implies, or at least he appears to be according to modern methods of exegesis.

One other review published in 1844 deserves comment, not because it was first-rate criticism but because Poe picked up a topic he had introduced gratuitously in the review of *Orion* and enlarged it. For the first time he explained why he considered passion discordant with poetry. The poems of Mrs. Amelia Welby were not worth extended analysis, but they did give Poe an opportunity to explain his position: "True passion is prosaic—homely. Any strong mental emotion stimulates *all* the mental faculties; thus grief the imagination: but in proportion as the effect is strengthened, the cause surceases. The excited fancy triumphs—the grief is subdued—chastened—is not longer grief. In this mood we are poetic, and it is clear that a poem now written will be poetic in the exact ratio of its dispassion. A passionate poem is a contradiction in terms." [33]

This insight into the creative process shows that Poe, for all of the mechanistic procedures he occasionally recommended, knew what happened in an artist's mind in the act of composition. Unquestionably he had learned something from Coleridge's account of the way the imagination was subjected to the artist's will so that the strong feeling that was the subject did not dominate the expression of the subject. If it did, the moans or cries which are normal manifestations of intense feeling would be proper in a poem.

[33] *Works*, XI, 277.

Poe also knew, as did Wordsworth and Coleridge, that the presence of metrical form, one could say *any* artistic form, changed the expression of intense feeling into an expression of something else. Wordsworth, thinking in terms of his audience, had said that the regularity of metrical form subdued painful feelings and provided the necessary pleasure that art was supposed to produce.[34] Coleridge, shifting the emphasis to the poet's mind, had described the way in which the imaginative process separated the poet's feelings from those which he analyzed and depicted. One of the marks of poetic genius, Coleridge wrote, was the "alienation, and . . . the utter aloofness of the poet's own feelings, from those of which he is at once the painter and the analyst." [35] Poe's position was similar. It prefigured what T. S. Eliot said in "Tradition and the Individual Talent," that it was not the intensity of the feelings but the intensity of the artistic process that was significant. If it was still necessary in 1917 to make such a statement, we can estimate the persistence of the romantic notion that feeling was all that counted.

Poe had previously banned passion from poetry on the ground stated in the first sentence of the quotation above: that it was "prosaic—homely," unsuited to the ideal. This is naïve aesthetics and, if taken literally, means that a poet can never write about any intense feeling, but when Poe finally explained that a poem could not imitate passion directly because the activity of the imagination transformed the passion into something else, his psychology of art was sound. The poetic mood and the passionate mood are incompatible. It may be noted that Poe's description of what happens in the poet's mind is not equivalent to Wordsworth's "emotion recollected in tranquillity." Instead, it has to do with the necessary activity of the imagination in transforming natural expression into artistic expression. By such a means, he would invalidate the cries of simulated anguish all too prevalent in inferior romantic verse. Mrs. Welby's verse, Poe explained, would usually be taken as passionate verse because of her elegiac subjects. Elegies, he continued,

[34] The statement is in Wordsworth's preface to the second edition of the *Lyrical Ballads* (1800).
[35] *Biographia Literaria*, II, 15–16.

should not treat grief directly, but should either express melancholy regret "interwoven with a pleasant sense of the natural loveliness surrounding the lost in the tomb . . . or dwell purely on the beauty (moral or physical) of the departed—or, better still, utter the notes of triumph." This "latter idea," Poe claimed, he had used "in some verses which I have called 'Lenore.' " [36]

Poe drew upon the conventions of the elegy, of course, but his psychological principle is broader than the specific illustration of the moment. It is an apt description of the way in which the imagination transforms natural emotion into aesthetic feeling. That Poe intended such an interpretation is revealed by a generalization: "the higher order of genius should, and will combine the original with that which is *natural*—not in the vulgar sense, . . . but in the artistic sense, which has reference to the *general intention of Nature*." His idiom is that of the eighteenth century and can mean only that the artist purifies or exalts nature, a commonplace of eighteenth-century aesthetics. He meant this, but also something more, and we can understand what else he required by examining his concept of originality in the context of this review. He found fault with Mrs. Welby's poems, not because they reverberated with howls of anguish, but because her elegies simply served up the conventional sources of melancholy—the night, the grave, the roses and forget-me-nots. All of these are natural as the furniture of melancholy, appropriate in their associative value, but they are unoriginal. The "general intention of Nature" has to do with the power of

[36] Poe's "Lenore" was published in 1831, and it contains in the last stanza the conventional consolation of an elegy, the "notes of triumph." It is perhaps significant that this is rare in Poe's verse, and comparatively rare in Southern elegiac laments for beautiful dead women. As a rule, he preferred his first alternative—to interfuse thoughts of beauty, "moral or physical," with melancholy regrets. Of his poems that may with some latitude be called elegies, "Lenore" is the only one that actually utters "notes of triumph." "The Raven," "Ulalume," and "Annabel Lee" dwell upon the beauty of the dead girl and the anguish of her lover. "To One in Paradise," written in his youth, is conventionally Byronic in the expression of blighted hopes, but the melancholy lover finds a kind of satisfaction in an aesthetic vision. The loveliness of the dead girl is perpetuated in "ethereal dances" by "eternal streams."

the imagination, an aspect of *human* nature, to transform *natural* materials, which are inevitably commonplace, into art by a new or original mode of expression. A poet can "rejuvenate" the "common fancies" by "grace of expression, and melody of rhythm." In other words, it is the artistic process which transforms nature. When Poe referred to the "intention" of nature in the context of the psychology of art, he meant the way in which nature intended the mind of the artist to work.

XV · *The Universal Audience*

IN April of 1844 Poe and his wife Virginia left for New York and
found a place to live in an old and "buggy looking" house at 130
Greenwich Street. He had no salary and depended for his income upon the articles he sold to magazines and newspapers.
One outlet was a small newspaper called the *Columbia Spy*, published in Columbia, Pennsylvania. Poe's letters to the *Columbia
Spy* have little interest for this study except for his reiteration of his
high opinion of *Orion* and a mildly disparaging remark about
Nathaniel Parker Willis,[1] from whom he was to receive his first
regular employment in New York.

In effect, Poe was the New York correspondent of a small-town
newspaper, and most of his letters were designed to give the country people impressions of life in the metropolis. In the meantime
he was trying to get his stories and poems published in book form
and even sought to have Harper's publish his stories without any
royalties.[2] His correspondence during this period indicates that he
had never abandoned his hope of starting a magazine of his own. In
October, 1844, he wrote to James Russell Lowell, who had been
damaged financially in his own abortive publication, the *Pioneer*,
that a coalition of literary men should get together and form a

---

[1] Poe, *Doings of Gotham*, ed. Jacob E. Spannuth (Pottsville, Pa., 1929),
24, 34.

[2] Poe to Charles Anthon, before November 2, 1844, in *Letters*, I, 271.
Anthon, a professor of Arabic languages at Columbia University, had assisted Poe previously by translating some lines of Hebrew in connection
with Poe's review of a travel book by J. T. Stephens. Later Poe occasionally
presented the translation as if it were his own. At Poe's request Anthon
attempted to persuade the Harper brothers to publish Poe's collection, but
he wrote Poe, "The Harpers . . . have *complaints* against you, grounded
in certain movements of yours, when they acted as your publishers some
years ago." November 2, 1844, in *Works*, XVII, 193. These "complaints"
show how easy it was for a writer to alienate a publisher. Whether they
were based upon Poe's own erratic behavior or upon reviews the Harpers
considered damaging to their own interests is not clear.

350

stock company to publish a journal of high quality. Each member would take a hundred dollars' worth of stock, and each would contribute, if necessary, one article a month.[3] Nothing came of Poe's proposal, and it was necessary for him to find a position in New York. Free-lance journalism was too precarious.[4]

Poe's aunt and mother-in-law, the indefatigable Mrs. Clemm, had come to New York to take care of Virginia, and she took the initiative to set things right. Nathaniel Parker Willis, who had joined with George Pope Morris in reviving the New York *Mirror*, received a call from Mrs. Clemm, who told him that Poe was ill and in serious financial straits. Had Willis been as vindictive as some of the other authors Poe had reviewed unfavorably, nothing would have come of her plea. In his *Messenger* days Poe had ridiculed Willis and had charged him with affectation, and one month after he arrived in New York he had said in one of his letters to the *Columbia Spy* that while Willis was "well-constituted for dazzling the masses—with brilliant agreeable talents," he had no profundity and no genius. Willis was good-natured enough to accept these strictures without animosity, for he found a place for Poe in spite of the fact, as he revealed some years later, that he "had been led by common report to expect a very capricious attention to his

[3] *Letters,* I, 265. In a letter dated March 30, 1844, Poe had proposed a similar plan, except that each member of the elite literary group was supposed to contribute two hundred dollars to the enterprise. *Ibid.,* 247. These letters describe Poe's concept of an ideal literary magazine. It should be a monthly instead of a quarterly, should be well printed on good paper, should adhere to high standards, and should express independent opinion. Such a magazine, Poe thought, would be "irresistible" to the public and would protect writers against inept or unscrupulous publishers. It would not be the organ of any particular group but would represent the best writers, regardless of political or sectional affiliations. Needless to say, Poe's dream was not realized in his own time and only provisionally by the *Atlantic Monthly* during the second half of the century.

[4] Poe's letter to Anthon (see Note 2, above) speaks of the "sad poverty & the thousand consequent [ills] . . . which the condition of the mere Magazinist entails upon him in America." The chief reason he wanted a collection of his work published was that a journalist would inevitably be judged by occasional pieces, some of them "mere extravaganzas," rather than by his total achievement. Poe was correct. Not often has he been evaluated by his work as a whole.

[Poe's] duties, and occasionally a scene of violence and difficulty." Because he had only the highest admiration for Poe's genius, he would let that "atone for more than ordinary irregularity." [5]

By October of 1844 Poe had joined the staff of the *Mirror*, which was published in two formats, the *Evening Mirror*, a daily, and a supplement called the *Weekly Mirror*. Poe published in both. It is somewhat ironic that he was now employed by the same journal he had challenged in 1835 with his review of Fay's *Norman Leslie*. Both Willis and Fay had been associate editors of the journal at that time, and Morris had been the publisher. But apparently Morris was no more disposed than Willis to hold a grudge against Poe, perhaps because Poe had lavishly praised his book of songs in the *Gentleman's Magazine* in 1839. At any rate, the editorial management of the magazine was now left up to Willis, and Willis did not scruple to make use of Poe's capacity for controversy. He prefaced a series of articles by Poe called "Author's Pay in America" with this comment: "We wish to light beacons for an author's crusade. . . . We solemnly summon Edgar Poe to do the devoir of Coeur de Leon—no man's weapon half so trenchant." [6] Willis intended to get full advertising value from Poe's reputation for being a scathing critic, as is clearly revealed by a notice he published of a lecture Poe was to deliver:

> The decapitation of the criminal who did not know his head was off till it fell into his hand as he was bowling, is a Poe-kerish similitude, but it conveys an idea of the Damascene slicing of the critical blade of Mr. Poe. On Friday night we are to have his "Lecture on the Poets of America," and those who would witness this fine carving will probably be there. Besides the division of sensitive membrane, however, there will be many a bright flash from the keen temper of the blade itself, and altogether the feast will be epicurean to all but the sufferers.[7]

Willis also gave some reinforcement to Poe's plan to establish his own journal, for in January of 1845 he wondered in print why some enterprising New York publisher did not "establish a

[5] Quoted in Quinn, *Edgar Allan Poe*, 434.
[6] Quoted in Hull, "A Canon," 402.
[7] *Evening Mirror*, February 20, 1845, quoted in Hull, "A Canon," 408.

Monthly Review, devoted exclusively to high critical purpose."
Poe, he continued, "has genius and taste of his own, as well as the
necessary science, and the finest discriminative powers; and such a
wheel of literature should not be without axle and linch pin." [8]
The statements above were published about the time Poe was preparing to leave the *Mirror* for the *Broadway Journal*. If Willis knew
of his plans, which was likely, he may have been motivated more
by a desire to help Poe than to advertise his own paper. Perhaps it
disturbed him to see that "wheel of literature," Edgar Poe, turning
for a daily and weekly newspaper. In later years Willis described
Poe's pedestrian position on the paper:

> It was his business to sit at a desk, in a corner of the editorial room,
> ready to be called upon for any of the miscellaneous work of the
> moment—announcing news, condensing statements, answering cor-
> respondents, noticing amusements—everything but the writing of a
> "leader" or constructing any article upon which his peculiar idio-
> syncrasy of mind could be impressed. Yet you remember how abso-
> lutely and how good humoredly ready he was for any suggestion,
> how punctually and industriously reliable, in the following out of
> the wish once expressed, how cheerful and present-minded in his
> work when he might excusably have been so listless and abstracted.[9]

Regardless of the good grace with which he carried out his regular assignments, Poe had little chance to write for the *Mirror* the
kind of reviews he considered valuable. A newspaper column is no
place for an extended analysis, but there is room for disparagement.
Poe's "Damascene slicing" was displayed in a review of Lowell's
Conversations with Some Old Poets and in one of Longfellow's
anthologies of neglected poems quaintly entitled *The Waif*. In spite
of the fact that he and Lowell had been friendly and had exchanged favors, Poe deprecated Lowell's ability as a critic, a fact
that was not lost on the young New England poet.[10] His review of
The Waif intimated that Longfellow, in his capacity as editor, had
carefully avoided including in his anthology any poets "who may be
supposed especially to interfere with the claims of Mr. Longfel-

---

[8] *Ibid.*   [9] Hull, "A Canon," 404.
[10] Lowell to Charles F. Briggs, January 16, 1845, in H. E. Scudder, *James
Russell Lowell* (Boston, 1901), I, 163.

low." Poe's conclusion was that *The Waif* was "infected with a moral taint." In earlier reviews Poe had suggested that Longfellow was imitative to the point of plagiarism, but now he made a more damaging charge. Longfellow's friends took up the challenge, and the "Longfellow War" was on, mostly to Poe's discredit.[11]

Poe's association with the *Mirror* lasted only from September, 1844, to February, 1845, but during this period he was also writing for other journals, chiefly the *Democratic Review*. By the time Poe contributed to the *Democratic Review*, it had relaxed somewhat from its initial position of trying to be a voice for the radical Democrats and was steering a moderate course, but it is doubtful that political affiliation had anything to do with Poe's contributions. He sold what he could where he could. In November of 1844 he began in the *Democratic Review* a series he called "Marginalia," allegedly made up of notes he had made while reading books. Actually these notes, as published in the *Democratic Review* and later in *Godey's Lady's Book, Graham's Magazine,* and the *Southern Literary Messenger* contain, in addition to brief statements on various topics, excerpts from his published reviews. In the context of this study the "Marginalia" will not be considered as a separate publication but will be used to extend or qualify statements Poe made in his reviews or his essays. Occasionally an item from the "Marginalia" states in dogmatic terms a position that he had established tentatively elsewhere, and will serve as a clarification of his opinions. He said in his introduction to the series that he was only talking to himself, so it may be supposed that he was being sincere. There is no evidence to the contrary except that some of his notes are plagiarisms.[12] He continued the publication of his "Marginalia" for the rest of his life, the last installment appearing in September of 1849, a month before his death. Poe's financial

[11] The review of Longfellow's *The Waif* is not in Poe's *Works*, but his editorial replies to "Outis," Longfellow's defender, may be found there. *Works*, XII, 41–106. The fullest account of this controversy is in Moss, *Poe's Literary Battles*, 157–82.

[12] See George E. Hatvary, "Poe's Borrowings from H. B. Wallace," *American Literature*, XXXVIII (1966), 365–72. Most of the plagiarisms from Wallace occur in the later installments published in the *Southern Literary Messenger*.

difficulties made him publish whatever he had at hand, and it is reasonable to suspect that such forced publication was responsible not only for his occasional plagiarism but also for his use of excerpts from previously published reviews. At least we know from the "Marginalia" that Poe thought some of his opinions worth republishing out of the context in which they originally appeared.

Poe was able to leave the *Mirror* because of a recommendation from Lowell to Charles F. Briggs, editor of the *Broadway Journal*, a weekly which began publication in January of 1845. Lowell, a friend of Briggs, sent contributions to the new paper and recommended Poe as a contributor,[13] and Poe wrote reviews for the first and second numbers of the *Journal* while he was still on the staff of the *Mirror*. Briggs paid him only a dollar a page, however, and if Poe was to work for the paper he had to have more money. Accordingly, in March of 1845 Poe was announced as an assistant editor of the *Journal*; he was to receive one-third of the editorial profits, the other two-thirds going to Briggs and to Henry C. Watson. Watson was the music critic for the magazine, and Briggs and Poe took care of the other editorial duties. The publisher was John Bisco.

This alliance was a strange one for many reasons. Briggs, who had won local fame with his *The Adventures of Harry Franco* and *Working a Passage* (semi-autobiographical novels), had published in Lewis Gaylord Clark's *Knickerbocker* for many years.[14] Furthermore, Briggs's Knickerbockerish dislike for certain aspects of romanticism that Poe had at one time defended would have been irritating had Poe not begun to have second thoughts about romanticism himself, an attitude which his first reviews in the *Broadway Journal* reveal. At least his affiliation with Briggs offered him a measure of editorial authority, although Briggs wrote to Lowell that "Poe is only an assistant to me and will in no way interfere with my own way of doing things." He went on to say that Poe had left the *Mirror* because "Willis was too Willisy for him." [15]

[13] Woodberry, *The Life of Edgar Allan Poe*, II, 115–23. See also Lowell to Poe, December 12, 1844, in *Works*, XVII, 194–95.
[14] Miller, *The Raven and the Whale*, 47–58.
[15] Briggs to Lowell, March 8, 1845, in Hull, "A Canon," 492.

Much of Poe's criticism in the *Journal* sheds light only upon his journalistic wars, but some of his reviews furnish evidence of a change in his literary allegiances and an increasing concern with universal appeal, marked by a growing insistence that a literary work avoid obscurity and profundity. Although while still with *Graham's* Poe had objected to obscurity, particularly in some of the tales of Hawthorne, the first striking evidence that he had begun to associate this quality with transcendentalism had appeared in his review of Horne's *Orion*. He continued the attack upon transcendental mysticism in a two-part review in the *Broadway Journal* of Elizabeth Barrett's *The Drama of Exile*, published in January, 1845. In reviewing Miss Barrett, Poe was placed in the same peculiar position that he had been in when he reviewed Horne. He had praised *Orion* extravagantly, but to be consistent he had had to deprecate its length, its didactic purpose, and its occasional obscurity. In *The Drama of Exile* he could admire certain passages that created what he considered the proper effect by management of rhythm, rhyme, and symbolic suggestiveness, but he deplored the tendency toward allegory, the effort at mysticism, and the disregard of what he considered poetic law. Reviewing Miss Barrett was a delicate problem, because she was a woman. He had just admitted in the November, 1844, installment of the "Marginalia" that "there seems to be but one course for the critic" in reviewing women—"speak if you can commend—be silent, if not; for a woman will never be brought to admit a non-identity between herself and her book . . . ." [16] Poe had learned his lesson in 1836 from his tiff with Mrs. Sigourney. Accordingly, he prefaced his review of Miss Barrett by making an apology for treating her as a poet instead of as a mere female. This was a compliment, Poe implied, for he intended to speak the truth, which no other American reviewer had done.[17]

Miss Barrett had announced in a prefatory note that *The Drama of Exile*, though based upon the expulsion of Adam and Eve from the Garden of Eden, had been modeled after Greek tragedy. Poe, who believed in the progress of literary art and who

[16] *Works*, XVI, 12.   [17] *Ibid.*, XII, 2–3.

was stringently to condemn the use of ancient models within the next few months, reproved Miss Barrett accordingly:

> It would have been better for Miss Barrett if, throwing herself independently upon her own very extraordinary resources, and forgetting that a Greek had ever lived, she had involved her Eve in a series of adventures merely natural, or if not this, of adventures preternatural within the limits of at least a conceivable relation—a relation of matter to spirit and spirit to matter, that should have left room for something like palpable action and comprehensible emotion—that should not have utterly precluded the development of that womanly character which is admitted as the principal object of the poem. As the case actually stands, it is only in a few snatches of verbal intercommunication with Adam and Lucifer, that we behold her as a woman at all. For the rest, she is a mystical something or nothing, enwrapped in a fog of rhapsody about Transfiguration, and the Seed, and the Bruising of the Heel, and other talk of a nature that no man ever pretended to understand in plain prose, and which, when solar-microscoped into poetry "upon the model of the Greek drama," is about as convincing as the Egyptian Lectures of Mr. Silk Buckingham—about as much to any purpose under the sun as the *bi presto* conjurations of Signor Blitz.[18]

This harsh assessment of the mystical aspects of Miss Barrett's dramatic poem reveals that Poe had begun to emphasize more than ever before what he called a natural art: simple, comprehensible, and even to an extent realistic. As we shall see shortly, he demanded a realism in drama that he did not require in lyric poetry because drama was a mimetic art. Miss Barrett's poem was dramatic, and Poe required probability in the dramatic and narrative forms. He had just written "The Raven," and in "The Philosophy of Composition" he declared that he had stayed within the limits of the real throughout the narrative phase of the poem.

More clearly than anything else, this review shows that Poe was changing with the times. Certain aspects of romanticism had been opposed by most critics in America during the 1820's and 1830's, but Poe had defended romance during his early career as a critic.

---

[18] *Ibid.*, 4–5.

By the 1840's a new attack upon romanticism was being mounted by the Victorians. John Stuart Mill, Macaulay, Carlyle, and even Tennyson objected to various aspects of early romanticism. Tennyson found that Wordsworth was too "diffuse and didactic." Macaulay spoke of Wordsworth's *The Prelude* as having "the old crazy, mystical metaphysics." Mill found Byron full of the complaints of a worn-out hedonist.[19] Poe, although he would have rejected any opinion from Mill (he detested Mill's utilitarianism) and from Carlyle (a transcendentalist), admired Tennyson and Macaulay. Increasingly stressed in Victorian aesthetics was the social and moral value of art, conceived, as Jerome Buckley has pointed out, in terms of the capacity of art to communicate full experience in the idiom of universal emotion.[20] Only part of this generalization is applicable to Poe. By 1844 he had begun to emphasize as never before the duty of the artist to use an idiom of high emotional value, but one which did not involve the reader in the difficulties of philosophical concepts. Poe's view of the social value of art was more limited than that of the Victorians, yet it was closer to Victorian moral aestheticism than it was to the transcendentalist concept of hieratic value. Then, too, he resembled the Victorians in demanding technical discipline in poetry. Like Tennyson, he declared his allegiance to the beautiful rather than the good. Tennyson, in the poems then available to Poe, had displayed consummate artistry, and few of his poems were overtly didactic. This made Poe think that at last a poet had appeared who had technical skill and a proper sense of audience. Poe showed, as always, a tendency toward aestheticism, but not of the art-for-art's-sake variety.

Poe's concept of the nature and purpose of art bears a resemblance to that of certain British critics whose aesthetic, like his own, developed out of the premises of the eighteenth century. Like Sydney Dobell and Charles Kingsley, he thought that the purpose of art was to evoke the perfection of the ideal and prefigure the beauty beyond. Like the Scots critics David Hay and John G. Macvicar, Poe thought that the principles of beauty could be derived from the laws of nature, and like Hay and John Addington

[19] Buckley, *The Victorian Temper*, 17–18.   [20] *Ibid.*, 159.

Symonds (the elder), he thought that the "great harmonic law of nature" could be described mathematically.[21]

In conceiving of a static perfection which art could imitate but never copy, Poe revealed his heritage from classic aesthetics. His is a philosophy of being, not of becoming, yet for all of Poe's references to Plato, his artist does not draw unmediated inspiration from the absolute. The cosmos itself is his model, and the cosmos is characterized by invariable laws, whether manifested by the regularity of planetary orbits about the sun or by a hierarchy of life forms unchanging in respect to the human sense of time. The discoveries of science become the foundation of artistic rule, not the shaping power of the imagination working on the materials thrown up from the unconscious mind. To use Morse Peckham's terms, "positive romanticism" makes the form of an art work inevitable in that the intuition of a truth provides the "shape" of the work that reveals the truth. The imagination creates by bringing out the indwelling form. As a consequence, each work of art is unique and the old subspecies of art become meaningless as vantage points for the critic.[22] To Poe, however, the imagination could not create, because to the human time-sense all forms were fixed; they could only be rearranged. Accordingly the genres, although they could be modified in terms of the needs of a given culture, were still operant as universal types. They were arranged, by Poe's laws, in a hierarchy of value according to the appeal offered by each. Of the lowest value were those forms which imitated phenomenal flux or the character of a particular object. The highest forms were those which conveyed an impression of a harmony imperceptible to man's unaided senses.

Richard P. Adams' essay, which describes Poe as exhibiting what Peckham called "negative romanticism," is correct,[23] but a general essay is not the place for discriminations. "Negative romanticism," as offered by Peckham, is the "expression of the attitudes, the feelings, and the ideas of a man who has left static mechanism but has

---

[21] *Ibid.*, 144–45.

[22] "Toward a Theory of Romanticism," *PMLA*, LXVI (1951), 5–23.

[23] "Romanticism and the American Renaissance," *American Literature*, XXIII (1951–52), 431.

not yet arrived at a reintegration of his thought and art in terms of dynamic organicism." Yet Poe could not relinquish his premise of a universe static in human time; nor could he abandon the mechanistic approach conditioned by this premise. He did endeavor to incorporate a dynamism of process into his "new" cosmology, *Eureka*, whereby man's consciousness of Being evolved through the millennia, but he envisioned the end as catastrophic, neither a running down by energy loss nor an achievement of some ultimate perfection. Throughout his life Poe framed his theories according to the premise of a static universe. This topic will be discussed more fully in relation to Poe's philosophical ideas, but in this context it serves as an introduction to the aesthetic conservatism that characterized the criticism of his later years in respect to every form except the drama. Cosmic Toryism prefigures genre criticism, invariable rules that represent an ideal standard for every form of art. It views the universe in terms of physics instead of biology. To use Lovejoy's terms, it is the view that promotes "uniformitarianism" instead of "diversitarianism." Poe employed genetic criticism in his theory, examining each art form in terms of its mental origin and its purpose, but in his applied criticism he was something of a genre critic, basing his standards for each genre partly on tradition and partly on rules he invented for himself.

Poe, like some of his Victorian contemporaries, wanted to develop a science of beauty according to natural law, but he did not restrict himself to physics or the mathematically demonstrable; he also employed the empirical psychology that had been handed down from the preceding century, for to his mind the constitutive principles of human nature were laws too, and they had to be obeyed by an artist who wished to command an audience. Thus Poe bypassed some of the more revolutionary developments of romantic aesthetics and formed a connection between late eighteenth-century and Victorian aestheticism. His principles differed from those of the Aesthetic Society of Edinburgh,[24] founded in 1851, chiefly in his greater emphasis upon subjectivity, particularly in regard to the emotional receptivity of an audience.

[24] Cf. Buckley, *The Victorian Temper*, 145.

In a way his aestheticism was a moral aestheticism, in that he valued art because it aroused a sense of harmony and order as a corrective to vice, but he looked to science as a guide to method.

By the year 1845, although he had not lost his admiration for certain aspects of romantic idealism, Poe was becoming increasingly critical of the expressivist tendencies of romanticism, and he was insisting that art serve the need of the public for aesthetic experience. Poe's brief account of the history of English poetry since Shelley, done in the context of his review of Miss Barrett, reveals not only how closely he kept in touch with developments abroad, but also the first principle of his current criticism: that an artist should make a conscious effort to achieve universality of appeal.

> From the ruins of Shelley there sprang into existence, affronting the Heavens, a tottering and fantastic pagoda, in which the salient angles, tipped with mad jangling bells, were the idiosyncratic faults of the great original—faults which cannot be called such in view of his purposes, but which are monstrous when we regard his works as addressed to mankind. A "school" arose—if that absurd term must still be employed—a school—a system of rules—upon the basis of the Shelley who had none. Young men innumerable, dazzled with the glare and bewildered with the *bizarrerie* of the divine lightning that flickered through the clouds of the Prometheus, had no trouble whatever in heaping up imitative vapors, but, for the lightning, were content, perforce, with its *spectrum*, in which the *bizarrerie* appeared without the fire. Nor were great and mature minds unimpressed by the contemplation of a greater and more mature; and thus gradually were interwoven into this school of all Lawlessness— of obscurity, quaintness, exaggeration—the misplaced didacticism of Wordsworth, and even more preposterously anomalous metaphysicianism of Coleridge.[25]

In this passage Poe was probably referring to the Spasmodics. Since the "school" did not develop its rules until the 1850's,[26] he was somewhat premature in saying that they had a system, yet his adverse criticism of the group is not unlike that of Professor Buckley, who may be quoted in comparison:

[25] *Works*, XII, 33.   [26] Buckley, *The Victorian Temper*, 43.

More consistently than their greater contemporaries, they dreamed of a Victorian epic ample enough to embrace the manifold aspiration of the nineteenth century. Yet none possessed an architectonic sense at all commensurate to his high vision; and none would submit to the formal discipline requisite for the proportioning of an epic structure. Uncertain of their ultimate design, they neglected overall theme and action to magnify isolated emotions, to embroider random sentiments often quite irrelevant to the given mood. . . . Though they often produced striking figures of speech, compelling metaphors, suggestive similes, they were repeatedly carried away, like some of the Renaissance poets whom they revered, by their own embellished images, their own laborious conceits.[27]

Poe had pointed out similar faults in his review of Horne's *Orion*, although he considered it the finest modern epic (we should remember that he thought all epics faulty). He had blamed Horne's errors upon his connection with the "Orphicists," which was no more than affirming that the Spasmodic doctrine of inspiration was a gross error. Horne's own connection with the Spasmodics was primarily his acceptance of their inspirational aesthetic,[28] but this alone would have been enough to annoy Poe. A poem should have an intelligible design, a requirement the Spasmodics grandly ignored.

Elizabeth Barrett also had her connections with the Spasmodic School (through Horne), and so did Tennyson, as Poe was quick to point out, perhaps recognizing some of the Spasmodic "passion" in "Locksley Hall." [29] As Poe put it,

Matters were now fast verging to their worst, and at length, in Tennyson, poetic inconsistency attained its extreme. But it was precisely this extreme (for the greatest error and the greatest truth are scarcely two points in a circle)—it was this extreme which, following the law of all extremes, wrought in him—in Tennyson—a

[27] *Ibid.*   [28] *Ibid.,* 46.
[29] *Ibid.,* 61–62, 78. Poe was uncomfortably aware that Tennyson's poem had displayed intense passion, and he had mentioned it in his review of *Orion*. Considering the conditions under which he worked, it is remarkable that Poe knew as much as he did about contemporary developments in England, but in New York he possessed advantages he had not had before of participating in the international literary dialogue.

natural and inevitable revulsion, leading him first to contemn and secondly to investigate his early manner, and, finally, to winnow from its magnificent elements the truest and purest of all poetical styles. But not yet even is the process complete; and for this reason in part, but chiefly on account of the mere fortuitousness of that mental and moral combination which shall unite in one person (if *ever* it shall) the Shelleyan *abandon*, the Tennysonian poetic sense, the most profound instinct of Art, and the sternest Will properly to blend and vigorously to control all . . . has the world never yet seen the noblest of the poems of which it is possible that it may be put in possession.[30]

Thus Tennyson had shown admirable artistic awareness in perceiving and correcting his own stylistic faults. This, to Poe, was a proper development. The trouble with imitating Shelley was that the great romantic poet had no sense of audience. He wrote simply to please himself and exercised no control over his idiosyncrasies. Those without his special genius would merely ape his mannerisms, for Shelley's "art" was unconscious and therefore inimitable.

For all of Poe's frequently expressed contempt for the mob and the mere popularizer, he thought that a writer had a duty to his public; at the very least, his works should be felt and understood. Tennyson had developed a "pure poetical style," which to Poe meant that he had avoided overt didacticism, that he had disciplined rhyme and rhythm, and that he had achieved a limpid clarity of import. Tennyson's *Poems* of 1842, from which Poe would have formed his opinion, were addressed to the public, not to a select audience of dreamers, either transcendentalist poet-priests or alienated aesthetes. Even though Tennyson did not have Shelley's natural gift of song, he was a craftsman, and this made his effects available to both the naïve and the sophisticated reader. Poe still cited Shelley as a type of the inspired genius, but he thought that inspiration had to be controlled by taste and by a sense of audience limitations. Only by being aware of his audience's capacity could an artist have any effect in making his readers mindful of beauty, and this, to Poe, was his divine task.

[30] *Works*, XII, 34.

As with Tennyson, so with Elizabeth Barrett, who had imitated Tennyson's early manner. No doubt her choice of the wrong models originated in her secluded life—she was relatively out of touch with the literary world [31]—Poe wrote with a New Yorkerish air of sophistication. Provincial no longer, he proclaimed the value of the up-to-date. Miss Barrett had a fine native poetic sense, but it had been contaminated by the obsolete. Her imagination was more vigorous than Tennyson's, and, if she had studied his later style, she would have avoided the turgid, the obscure, and the mystical. She would have been able to use the later Tennyson as a bridge to cross "the disgustful gulf of utter incongruity and absurdity, lit only by miasmatic flashes, into the broad open meadows of Natural Art and Divine Genius." [32] Poe's metaphor is significant. The Muse no longer explores the dark caverns and subterranean corridors of the sublimely terrible. The gulfs that had figured so prominently in his own tales and poems, the hidden meanings that flash up in murky light from the depths, the incongruities that arouse sensations of horror, are all declared disgusting. The Muse romps in the sunlit meadows of classic art, or, as Poe would prefer, in the simplicity and clarity of nature.

2

Poe's attack upon the "school" of Shelley, his warning against imitating the inimitable, signals an attempt on his part to adjust his view of the imagination to his increasing emphasis upon the public duty of the artist. Shelley had imagination in excess, yet his "rhapsodies" were but "the stenographic memoranda of poems." The problem was, how could a poet share his vision with the world at large?

Throughout most of his career Poe had had difficulty in arriving at a definition of imaginative power that would serve as a criterion of the highest value and at the same time offer something for the

[31] Poe's assumption here is nearly correct. During the early 1840's Elizabeth Barrett had kept in touch with current movements at least partly through correspondence with Horne.

[32] *Works*, XII, 35.

undiscriminating who could not reach the higher levels of perception. At first he had followed Coleridge and Schlegel in associating imagination with the presence of reverberations of symbolic meaning, but this test involved him in a dilemma. If the presence of imagination in a poem was signaled by a mystic meaning, then a highly imaginative poem could not be universal. It would appeal, as Shelley himself had said, only to "the selectest of the wise of many generations." It was not that Poe did not recognize this melancholy fact, but that he did not believe that it was a law of nature. A poet should have some appeal to everyone. Yet if imagination were marked by meaning, and if this meaning were so simple and obvious that all could understand, then a poem would become an allegory, a didactic form that did not reside in the province of taste. The poems of both Horne and Miss Barrett exhibited mystic meaning, or imaginative power, and yet they could not be understood. They were either imperfect allegories or defective poems. As we have seen, Poe treated them in both ways by saying that the allegorical purpose made them defective as poems. But this was no solution. The imagination had to be redefined so that mysticism and obscurity could no longer be mistaken for evidence of poetic value.

Poe's occasion was a review of the achievement of Nathaniel Parker Willis as a prose writer.[33] It did not matter that Poe should have been analyzing prose style instead of discoursing on the imagination; he made his statements of theory in whatever context he could, and his excuse was that Willis, both in poetry and in prose, was a man of fancy, not imagination. Poe's brief essay—it was not really a review—was published in the *Broadway Journal* of January 18. He was still a subeditor of the *Mirror* and probably did not wish to say anything derogatory about his employer, but he remained consistent in refusing to accord Willis the highest honor—that of imaginative genius. Actually Poe used Willis' work in this review merely as a point of departure, for he made no examination of Willis' writings but proceeded to make discriminations among the mental qualities evidenced in composition at large.

Poe was not unconsciously shifting his ground in this essay, for

[33] "American Prose Writers, No. 2. N. P. Willis," *ibid.*, 36–40.

he paraphrased his refutation of Coleridge from his review of Moore's *Alciphron* and then proceeded to re-evaluate Moore on the basis of a new description of imaginative power. Showing his increasing antipathy toward the obscure and the metaphysical, he found that the test of the imagination was the harmony of combination of the various elements of which any work was composed. In this view the imagination has little to do with creation or with meaning. Instead, it is a discriminative agent guided by the aesthetic sense. It chooses the elements of a composition that may be "harmoniously" combined, and its combinations appear obvious and inevitable.

The fact seems to be that Imagination, Fancy, Fantasy, and Humor have in common the elements Combination and Novelty. The Imagination is the artist of the four. From novel arrangements of old forms which present themselves to it, it selects only such as are harmonious;—the result, of course, is *beauty* itself—using the term in its most extended sense, and as inclusive of the sublime. The pure Imagination chooses, *from either beauty or deformity*, only the most combinable things hitherto uncombined;—the compound as a general rule, partaking (in character) of sublimity or beauty, in the ratio of the respective sublimity or beauty of the things combined—which are themselves still to be considered as atomic— that is to say, as previous combinations. But, as often analogously happens in physical chemistry, so not unfrequently does it occur in this chemistry of the intellect, that the admixture of two elements will result in a something that shall have nothing of the quality of one of them—or even nothing of the qualities of either. The range of Imagination is therefore, unlimited. Its materials extend throughout the Universe. Even out of deformities it fabricates that *Beauty* which is at once its sole object and its inevitable test. But, in general the richness or force of the matters combined—the facility of discovering combinable novelties worth combining—and the absolute "chemical combination" and proportion of the completed mass—are the particulars to be regarded in our estimate of the Imagination. It is this thorough harmony of an imaginative work which so often causes it to be undervalued by the undiscriminating, through the character of *obviousness* which is superinduced. We are apt to find ourselves asking *"why is it* that these combinations have never been imagined before?"

This account of the imagination indicates that Poe's previous refutations of Coleridge were nothing more than an attempt to reconcile conflicting assumptions in his own theory. He wished to attribute to the poetic imagination the power to penetrate the veil of appearances to the beauty beyond, yet his concept of a universe in which all forms are given denied the implicit creativity of the imaginative vision. A reproduction in finite terms of the beauty of the absolute would necessarily be creation, for no such beauty could be perceived by the senses. Heretofore, as we have seen, Poe wriggled out of this dilemma by invoking Platonic metaphysics: all human creations are imperfect imitations of the transcendental ideal. But even this was too metaphysical for Poe, for to him the source of the artist's feeling was not the absolute but a yearning inspired by beautiful earthly forms for a still greater beauty. This is Platonic enough, but it is also the Alisonian aesthetic of taste. The poet's refined taste rejects imperfection, so he must ceaselessly combine the objects of sense perception in order to create combinations so harmonious that his taste will be fully gratified. There is a perfect beauty somewhere, for one can imagine it, but a poet will never create it. He can only rearrange the given according to his innate sense of harmony. When he is most nearly successful, he produces works which reflect in some measure the universal harmony, and these works are natural. The harmony is obvious, because it is so agreeable to the constitutive laws of the taste that the naïve are prone to underestimate the artistry of the imagination in selecting and combining raw materials, just as the insensitive are blind to the artistry of the creation itself. The great thing, however, is that the artistry will be felt, even if it is not recognized for what it is.

Poe did not completely neglect that "mental chemistry" valued by the romantics as the agent of a dynamic organicism, but he depressed its value. The "something else" which is not inherent in the quality of the poet's materials must be accounted for, but Poe did not tell what this "something else" was; and his test of imagination is not the presence of an excess quality, but the harmony of combination. We may only presume that the "something else" appears when the artist combines "deformities" in order to produce beauty. This, of course, might appear to be Coleridge's reconciliation of opposites, but we should not forget that in Coleridge's system beauty is a means toward the end of truth, whereas in Poe's system harmony, order, and the relatedness of part to whole exist in terms of their appeal to the taste. The "something else," then, is an added dimension of beauty not predictable from the quality of the materials used by the artist. It has little to do with meaning, as such. Since Poe's analog of the artistic process was physical chemistry, he was being consistent. Whatever is produced in a chemical compound is produced by physical law, the reaction of one element with another.

It is interesting that T. S. Eliot used the same analogy when he compared the creative process to what happens "when a bit of finely filiated platinum is introduced into a chamber containing oxygen and sulphur dioxide." [34] Eliot was specific whereas Poe generalized, but both indicated that the mind of a poet might combine the elements of experience in such a way that the compound might contain no trace of the experiences themselves. The only difference is that Eliot implied that this was a *test* of the poetic mind, but Poe thought that traces of the raw material would *normally* be found. The most Poe would say about the metamorphosis of the materials into something else is that it sometimes happened. Yet, like Eliot, he knew that the transformation which is art *should* take place, for the proper end of artistry is a work of art, not a revelation of personality. [35]

[34] Eliot, "Tradition and the Individual Talent," *Selected Essays, 1917–1932* (New York, 1932), 7.
[35] See Eliot's statement, "the more perfect the artist, the more completely separate in him will be the man who suffers and the mind which creates; the more perfectly will the mind digest and transmute the passions which are its material." *Ibid.*, 7–8. To the best of my knowledge, Poe has been given credit for this valid insight into the artistic process only by Emerson Marks, "Poe as Literary Theorist: A Reappraisal," *American Literature,* XXXIII (1961), 302. Mr. Marks has noted the anticipation of Eliot, citing different evidence.

During his critical examination of *Undine, Alciphron, Orion,* and *The Drama of Exile* Poe had evidently begun to have serious doubts as to whether a didactic theme, however subordinated, could ever be reconciled with an aesthetic end. If the most active mental power of a poet was evidenced by meaning, it could be argued that truth was the final cause of a poem. On the other hand, if the imagination were only a selecting and harmonizing agent, as Poe claimed it was, then it would serve the sense of beauty, and its sole function would be the selection of the proper elements of art and the fabrication of those elements into a work that would arouse the aesthetic response. In this, his last description of the activity of the imagination, Poe finally broke free of Coleridge and made his own psychological theory consistent. Beauty was the province of art, and the imagination was the agent that erected harmonious structures throughout this province.

Poe's description of the materials with which the imagination works is much broader in theory than his previous criticism would allow us to recognize. Now he stated that the imagination might combine elements of deformity as well as those of beauty, whereas in many of his reviews he had objected to unpleasant or inappropriate materials because the end was beauty and because it was a law of nature that an effect would inherit the character of its cause. Now, at least in theory, he permitted the ministry of the imagination to transform even unpromisingly ugly elements into something beautiful. This freed the artist from the necessity of choosing inherently "poetic" materials. Yet even this freedom was limited. Poe qualified his statement by claiming that the combination, *as a general rule*, would "partake" of the "sublimity or beauty of the things combined." To be on the safe side, it appears, the poet would feast his mind on beauty, not on deformity: Lord Jeffrey had said as much over thirty years earlier.

We should not overlook the stress that Poe placed upon novelty in his description of the imagination. During this period Poe used "novelty" more frequently than "originality," possibly because his theory really outlawed originality. To originate something, in the strict sense of the term, would be to create it, and the artist could only combine. The love of novelty, however, was an "indisputable element of the moral nature of man." [36] Since the artist had to meet human needs, his combinations had to be new, although their elements would be common to human experience. Poe made little allowance for the light that never was on land or sea, for "the mind of man can imagine nothing which does not exist."

Though less significant than his account of the imagination, Poe's description of the operation of the fancy deserves some comment, because it gives further evidence of his shift from his earlier position. In his review of *Alciphron* in 1840 he had admitted that imagination was not the chief characteristic of Moore's poetry, but that he possessed the power in "no little degree." He claimed to have found imaginative passages in *Alciphron*; in fact, he said he was "bewildered" by the beauty of the poem and could think of no poem which greatly excelled it.

In 1845, however, having decided that the imagination was a harmonizing power instead of an agent of meaning, Poe removed Moore from the high place he had originally assigned him: "When Moore is termed a fanciful poet, the epithet is precisely applied; he *is*. He is fanciful in 'Lalla Rookh,' and had he written the 'Inferno,' there he would have been fanciful still: for not only is he essentially fanciful, but he has no ability to be anything more, unless at rare intervals—by snatches—and with effort. What we say of him at this point, moreover, is equally true of all little frisky men, personally considered." Poe probably had Willis in mind when he made the remark about "little frisky men," but he was condemning Moore on the basis of his new definition. If Moore were imaginative at rare intervals, and then only by effort, then one could

---

[36] The love of novelty is often associated with nineteenth-century romanticism, but this, like so many other categorical assignments, may be misleading. Lord Kames had devoted an entire chapter to novelty, alleging that it had more capacity to "raise emotion" than any other stimulus. Kames attributed the effect of novelty to curiosity, "a principle implanted in human nature for a purpose extremely beneficial." *Elements of Criticism*, 131. Poe, in his employment of "principles," did not hesitate to invoke the traditional psychology which assumed that the *proper* gratification of any basic human need was beneficial, according to the premise of a benevolent God.

scarcely call him imaginative at all, because one does not become imaginative by effort. The appearance of effort belongs to the fancy: "when the harmony of the combination is comparatively neglected, and when in addition to the element of novelty, there is introduced the sub-element of *unexpectedness*—when, for example, matters are brought into combination which not only have never been combined, but whose combination strikes us as a *difficulty happily overcome*—the result then appertains to the FANCY—and is, to the majority of mankind more grateful than the purely harmonious one—although, absolutely, it is less beautiful (or grand) for the reason that *it is* less harmonious."

The problem for Poe here, in respect to his opinion that an artist should be able to reach a universal audience, was to explain why a merely fanciful writer should have a broader appeal than an imaginative one. He knew that the fanciful Moore had been more popular than the imaginative Shelley. Why? His answer was that an imaginative poem, constructed according to the harmonic laws of the universe, appeared so right, so inevitable in its combinations, that the crowd, titillated by the unexpected and incapable of appreciating the artistry of a harmonious design, would be drawn to the ingenuities of a fanciful writer rather than to the natural art of an imaginative writer. Yet, as always, Poe did not think that this condition necessarily had to obtain. A combination of the natural genius of a Shelley and the artistic skill and audience sense of a Tennyson would produce a poem that would please both the crowd and the *cognoscenti*. Poe had said this in his review of *The Drama of Exile*, and he was to attempt to prove it in "The Philosophy of Composition," but in the review of Willis he was mainly concerned with establishing the imagination as the power which enabled the poet to imitate the harmonies of the universal design, or, in Poe's words, to develop a natural art. Fancy was unnatural because it gave the appearance of conscious effort; one could detect the artist's intention to force elements together which did not belong together. Elsewhere Poe characterized the metaphysical conceit as a product of the fancy, no doubt following Dr. Johnson's description, in his *Life of Cowley*, of the "*discordia concors:* a combination of dissimilar images, or discovery of occult resemblances in things apparently unlike." Dr. Johnson had complained that the thoughts of the metaphysical poets "are often new, but seldom natural; they are not obvious, but neither are they just; and the reader, far from wondering that he missed them, wonders more frequently by what perverseness of industry they were ever found."

Like Johnson, Poe commented disparagingly upon the appearance of effort and the lack of naturalness, but he differed in thinking that the surprise effect of unusual combinations would please the reader. Johnson had said that the reader would sometimes "admire," but would be "seldom pleased." Poe's account of the fancy is somewhat closer to Johnson's definition of wit than it is to Coleridge's description of the fancy, but Coleridge too had characterized Cowley as being fanciful.[37] Both Johnson and Coleridge prefigured Poe's definition.

Perhaps to outdo his predecessors, Poe extended his discriminations to include still other predispositions or capacities.

> Carrying its errors into excess—for, however enticing, they *are* errors still, or Nature lies,—Fancy is at length found impinging upon the province of *Fantasy*. The votaries of this latter delight not only in novelty and unexpectedness of combination, but in the *avoidance* of proportion. The result is therefore abnormal, and to a healthy mind affords less of pleasure through its novelty, than of pain through its incoherence. When, proceeding a step farther, however, Fantasy seeks not merely disproportionate but incongruous or antagonistical elements, the effect is rendered more pleasurable from its greater positiveness; there is a merry effort of Truth to shake from her that which is no property of hers;—and we laugh outright in recognizing humor.

Poe intended his distinctions to be applied in criticism, as is evidenced by his review of the poems of Thomas Hood some seven months later. In this review he placed Hood in "a kind of border land between the Fancy and the Fantasy." Since fantasy was abnormal, he claimed that Hood's work was "the result of vivid

[37] *Biographia Literaria*, I, 62.

Fancy impelled, or controlled,—certainly tinctured, at all points, by hypochondriasis." [38]

Surprising as it may seem in view of his own neurotic tendencies, Poe regarded genius as a reflection of perfect mental health which operated in accordance with nature's laws. The alleged irritability of the genius, Poe claimed, sprang from his sensitivity to disorder and deformity. The genius shuddered at imperfection; a work of art produced by a genius would have harmony and proportion as its leading features, because the mental equipment of the genius, his faculties, were balanced in their development and operation. Therefore fantasy would not be employed by a genius. Certain aspects of Hood's works left a "painful impression," for they represented "the hypochondriac's struggles at mirth—they are the grinnings of the death's-head." [39]

As far as Willis was concerned, however, Poe still had a problem of tact in rescuing him from the category of "little frisky men" in which he had placed him by implication. Poe's tact was tactless enough, even at best; but in this case he softened the impact of his implications by exalting Willis' qualities: Willis' "well merited popularity" came from his "brilliant FANCY," with which his prose style "perpetually scintillates or glows." But, unlike Moore, Willis did not possess merely fancy, "to the exclusion of qualities more noble" (an implication that Willis had imagination also). Furthermore, Willis possessed fancy "to an extent *altogether unparalleled*, and of a kind both relatively and intrinsically the most valuable, because at once the most radiant and the most rare." No doubt Willis was undisturbed by this comment because it was loaded with honorifics. Yet fancy was an error, "or Nature lies." The products of the fancy were never art; they represented artifice. The purest art was a microcosm that reflected the cosmic harmony and as such was a human effort to imitate the art of God. Works of fancy, fantasy, and humor could be enjoyed, but they did not appeal to the aesthetic sense. In the hierarchy of forms they descended, grade by grade, from the natural and the beautiful.

[38] *Works*, XII, 216.   [39] *Ibid.*, 215.

During this period Poe emphasized harmony, control, and order
—which he called "simplicity" and "nature." Almost from the first
he had demanded that the artist control his materials. In 1836 he
had required control of effect, but he had said little about the nature of that effect. Now in 1845 he was stressing the artist's ability
to discriminate among his materials and to impose artistic form
upon his carefully selected raw elements of beauty. There is no
difference between the concept of aesthetic value he expressed in
1836 and that expressed in 1845, if we judge only by the broad predetermined end of pleasure; but there is a signal difference in his
description of the psychological process by which this end is
achieved. In 1836 he had naïvely proclaimed, after Coleridge, that
imagination was the soul of art and had then asserted blandly that
a poet who possessed the "metaphysical" faculty of "constructiveness" did not need imagination. Now, eschewing metaphysics, even
the "metaphysics" of phrenology, he made imagination once more
the soul of poetry, but it was not, as in Coleridge, the agent of the
intuitive reason; it was a discriminatory power vested in the taste.
It neither created nor enabled us to know anything we did not
know before, but it made harmonious combinations that appealed
to the sense of beauty. Poe's reversion to the older psychological
idiom, first evidenced in his review of Longfellow's *Ballads*, now
permitted him to disallow the transcendental as the Scottish philosophers had disallowed metaphysical speculation. He began to
use the terms "reason" and "common sense" increasingly in his reviews. These were the faculties that kept the artist in touch with
reality and prevented him from soaring with Shelley into the white
radiance of eternity, where no one but an Orphicist would even attempt to follow. The taste, Blair had said, must be corrected by the
reason. With a significant change in implication which made him
even less romantic than Blair, Poe was soon to assert that the taste
had to be guided by the reason and common sense, at least in respect to those forms which had a right to be called natural. And in
a higher sense, even the poem and pure music were natural in that
they fulfilled the intention of nature in giving man the aesthetic
value he needed in a world in which pleasure was the necessary

concomitant of pain. The purest of art, adjusted to the receptive capacity of the human mind, was the most exquisite pleasure that man could experience.

"Positive romanticism," in Morse Peckham's words, was characterized by "radical creativity," and it could be observed in the work of the poet-philosopher who not only brought "new artistic concepts into reality," but also new ideas.[40] Certainly no positive romantic, Poe in his last phase is not accurately described by the term "negative romanticism," either. In the reviews to be discussed next he proclaimed, almost boastfully, that he followed the precepts of common sense. If any descriptive term fits his attitude in these reviews, it would have to be "anti-romantic."

[40] "Toward a Theory of Romanticism," 12.

XVI · The Progress of Art

I
N July of 1845 Poe and Bisco, the publisher of the *Broadway Journal*, succeeded in forcing Briggs's resignation, leaving Poe in charge of the literary editorship of the paper. By October, Poe had bought the journal from Bisco on borrowed money and had undertaken the strenuous task of running it largely by himself.[1] Whether because of personal problems or because of his tremendous work load, his reviews deteriorated in quality. Those that were not simply cribbed from his previous work were often tendentious or ill-tempered, as he used them in his skirmishes with the New England transcendentalists or the New York literati. For the most part these reviews fail to perform what he had considered in 1842 to be the high function of the critic: the mediation between the writer and the public with the end of elevating the public taste. Instead, he all too frequently made dogmatic statements about the rules of literary compositon without much attempt to validate the rules.

An exception to the general mediocrity of his criticism of this period, however, was his commentary upon the drama. Poe had been interested in the drama almost from the beginning of his career as a critic, but never before had he reviewed live theater. Now, as editor of the *Broadway Journal*, he received passes to Broadway productions and made the most of his opportunity. Poe's dramatic criticism and his knowledge of the drama has been examined in detail by N. Bryllion Fagin [2] and will not be explored in this study except as his reviews reflect a shift in his concept of composition.

Poe thought that each literary genre should be examined in terms of its purpose and its mode of being. The drama was by its

---

[1] For an account of Poe's acquisition of the *Broadway Journal* see Mott, *A History of American Magazines*, 757–62, and Woodberry, *The Life of Edgar Allan Poe*, II, 141–46.
[2] *The Histrionic Mr. Poe*, 103–32.

very nature mimetic, and its purpose was to hold the mirror up to nature. Yet Poe, a stickler for the distinction between what was nature and what was art, declared that a dramatic production was not nature itself. It was a fiction, an imitation of nature that had to observe the general proprieties of art and the necessities of stage production. In his first extended review of live drama, Mrs. Anna Cora Mowatt's comedy of manners, *Fashion*,[3] Poe deplored her use of the conventions of the theater: "Their hackneyism is no longer to be endured," Poe wrote. "The day has at length arrived when men demand rationalities in place of conventionalities." Mrs. Mowatt's play was "theatrical but not dramatic," because it used stage tricks instead of observing "the natural laws of man's heart and understanding." Then Poe proceeded to attack the stage conventions of the soliloquy, the reading aloud of private letters, and "preposterous asides."

In brief, Poe demanded on the stage the verisimilitude that in previous years he had applauded in the novel. Dramatic action, he insisted, should give an illusion of reality to the audience; and the conventions that dramatists of the past had used to overcome the handicaps of stage presentation were simply "monstrous inartisticalities," which any "person of common ingenuity" could dispense with if he observed nature instead of imitating the old dramatists.

One thing that the playwright would have to do if he followed nature would be to consider the reactions of his audience and refuse to fatigue their understanding by complexity of plot. Undue complication would prevent the play from having its intended effect. This had been the trouble, Poe said, with the Spanish dramas of intrigue, which were the "worst acting dramas of the world."[4]

Considering the affinity of the romantic poets for closet drama,

---

[3] "The New Comedy by Mrs. Mowatt," in *Works*, XII, 112–21.

[4] At every opportunity Poe paraded this bit of knowledge about the Spanish drama, probably derived from Schlegel's *Lectures* but expanded by his own reading of Calderón, Lope de Vega, and Cervantes. As early as 1836, Poe appears to have read Cervantes' *The Destruction of Numantia*, for he cited it in a note to his review of Drake and Halleck. For Poe's knowledge of dramatic literature, see Fagin, *The Histrionic Mr. Poe*, 96–102.

it may seem surprising that Poe insisted that all plays be actable, but such a requirement was logical in his teleological approach. The purpose of a play was to be presented on the stage. Therefore any author of common sense would accommodate his technique to the needs of an audience. Man had progressed in his understanding of human nature, Poe thought, and the art of the drama would have made progress too had it not been for slavish imitation of the ancient conventions. Now that man had more knowledge, he should use it rationally instead of copying the errors of the past. If he did use this knowledge, there would be a revival in the drama. It had declined simply because of the spirit of imitation. This spirit, characteristic of the dramatic medium, had so affected playwrights that they did not follow nature itself but merely did what had been done before them.

The drama of the future, Poe ventured to predict in a second re-view of Mrs. Mowatt,[5] might be "neither tragedy, comedy, farce, opera, pantomine, melodrama, or spectacle"—those traditional types that modern authors were too prone to imitate—but it might include elements of all "while it introduces a new class of excel-lence as yet unnamed because as yet undreamed-of in the world." [6] In Poe's new emphasis upon the science of composition, grounded on reason and common sense, he was prepared to abandon all precedent and create an art unshackled by tradition and conven-tion, a somewhat startling development in the critic who had said only a few years earlier that the principles of Kames, Blair, and Johnson would not be invalidated until nature itself expired. It was not really a contradiction, however. The principles remained the same; art progressed in terms of the progressive discovery of those principles. The arts should progress, even as man's knowledge of science and human nature had progressed.

In his revolt against the past Poe had an opportunity to review a revival of Sophocles.[7] The *Antigone*, as it had been anciently per-

[5] "Prospects of the Drama.—Mrs. Mowatt's Comedy," *Works*, XII, 124–29.

[6] Only in this statement did Poe lapse from his customary genre criticism.

[7] "The Antigone at Palmo's," *Works*, XII, 130–35.

formed at Athens, might have been satisfactory to the relatively primitive Greeks, but the play was marked for a modern audience by "an insufferable baldness, or platitude, the inevitable result of inexperience in Art . . . ." The alleged virtue of simplicity in the Greek drama, unlike that of ancient Greek sculpture, was not the simplicity of nature, but the simplicity of ignorance. "In a word, the simple arts spring into perfection at their origin. The complex as inevitably demand the long and painful progressive experience of ages." Only a pedant, Poe claimed, would insist upon producing a Greek play before a modern audience. Even if a modern producer could present the play as it had been presented at Athens in the vastness of a Greek amphitheater, it would still be a "monstrous folly," but to present it on a restricted modern stage such as that at Palmo's made it seem like a burlesque, and only as a parody could it be well received by a modern audience.

Unlike such Hellenists as Matthew Arnold, Poe was unwilling to concede that the grandeur of the action of the Greek drama made it a universal model. If it seems strange that Poe, conservative in respect to the industrial and social progress that enchanted many nineteenth-century Americans, should plump for progress in the arts, it should be recognized that in his special field he was a journalist, very much a man of his times. For all of his romantic enthusiasm for the poetic ideal, the beauty beyond the grave, Poe never lost sight of the necessity of contemporaneity. He believed that the advance in psychological knowledge and the increasing sophistication of the public required new techniques. A simple art for a simple people; a sophisticated art for a sophisticated people.

Insofar as Poe was developing a thesis in his reviews during 1845 and 1846, it was that art, like science, had to be progressive. He had said as much in his review of *The Drama of Exile*, and he repeated it with polemical exaggeration in his reviews of the drama. The drama existed only in terms of its appeal to a mass audience; accordingly, it should be guided by reason and common sense directed toward uncovering the basis of its appeal. As always with Poe, the effect was the thing, not merely the play.

Perhaps Poe was influenced in his rejection of the past by his temporary affiliation with Young America, his allies against Lewis Gaylord Clark and the Whig *Knickerbocker,* but the fact is that he remained Whiggish himself in his social and political opinions. His demand for a revolution in drama had no relation to politics. It was a logical development from his premise that art must be adjusted to the requirements of a changing culture.

In Poe's last extensive article on the drama, he emphatically demanded a revolution in the dramatic arts.

> The great opponent to Progress is Conservatism. In other words —the great adversary of Invention is Imitation. . . . Just as an art is imitative, is it stationary . . . . Upon the utilitarian—upon the business arts, where necessity impels, Invention, Necessity's well-understood off-spring, is ever in attendance. . . . No one complains of the decline of the art of Engineering. Here the Reason, which never retrogrades, or reposes, is called into play. . . . Where Reason predominated, we advanced; where mere Feeling or Taste was the guide, we remained as we were.

> Coming to the Drama, we shall see that in its mechanisms we have made progress, while in its spirituality we have done little or nothing for centuries certainly—and, perhaps, little or nothing for thousands of years. And this is because what we term the spirituality of the Drama is precisely its imitative portion—is exactly that portion which distinguishes it as one of the principal of the imitative arts. . . . We wish now to suggest that, by the engrafting of Reason upon Feeling and Taste, we shall be able, and thus alone shall be able, to force the modern Drama into the production of any profitable fruit. . . . [There is a] tendency in all imitation to render Reason subservient to Feeling and to Taste . . . and it is clear that only by deliberate counteracting of the spirit, we can hope to succeed in the drama's revival.

> The first thing necessary is to burn or bury the "old models," and to forget, as quickly as possible, that ever a play was penned. The second thing is to consider *de novo* what are the *capabilities* of the drama—not merely what hitherto have been its conventional purposes. The third and last point has reference to the composition of a play (showing to the fullest extent these capabilities), conceived and constructed with Feeling and with Taste, but with Feeling and

Taste guided and controlled in every particular by the details of Reason—of Common Sense—in a word, of a Natural Art.[8]

This quotation has been given at length because it is a striking illustration of the change in emphasis in Poe's criticism. In his first critical document, the "Letter to Mr. —— ——," he had enthusiastically championed a spontaneous art—a poet should protest, not think. In 1836, however, he had declared that the ability to analyze cause and effect was more important in a poet's mental equipment than imagination. In 1842 he had claimed that art was the handmaiden of the taste, making the imagination the servant of the aesthetic sense. In 1845 he still considered taste necessary in the choice of the raw materials of art, and the imagination, its agent, combined those materials into an aesthetic object; but these

[8] "The American Drama," *ibid.*, XIII, 33–37. The fact that this essay was published in the *American Whig Review* has some significance. This was a new journal established to counter the influence of the *Democratic Review*, and George H. Colton, who had published a poem, "Tecumseh," in honor of the Whig hero General William Henry Harrison, was the editor. At last it appeared that Poe's Whig affiliations were bringing a reward. This cannot be entirely the case, however. Lowell had suggested to Colton that Poe be accepted as a contributor, and Poe continued to publish in the *Democratic Review*. His chief concern was price per page. *Godey's Lady's Book* gave him five dollars a page, Colton three dollars, and the *Democratic Review* only two. Poe to Philip Pendleton Cooke, April 16, 1846, in *Letters*, II, 314. For several years Poe continued to publish with Colton, apparently running into difficulty only with "The Rationale of Verse," which Poe claimed would have involved Colton in embarrassment with his "personal friends in Frogpondium" (Boston). See Poe to George W. Eveleth, January 4, 1848, and February 29, 1848, *ibid.*, 354, 360, for his account of his relationship with the Whig editor.

Poe had become hostile to Young America, particularly Mathews, whom he associated with Margaret Fuller and the transcendentalists. It might appear that the progressivist doctrine in "The American Drama" would not have appealed to the conservative party, but the *Whig Review* featured dramatic criticism and Poe's call for progress was founded on "reason and common sense," an approved Whig premise. Progress based upon some kind of mystic intuition of a democratic deity who unfolded himself in the creation was less palatable. Poe displayed his Whiggish attitude in his contempt for "Orphic" rant. See Mott, *A History of American Magazines*, 750–56, for a sketch of the *American Whig Review* and Poe's relationship with Colton.

intuitive faculties had to be guided and controlled by reason and common sense.

This shift of emphasis does not mean that Poe had changed his mind about the purpose of art; it does mean that he had begun to emphasize method, particularly as method contributed to audience appeal. Poe's demand for rational control was extreme during the middle years of the 1840's, and it was during these years that he deplored the inspirational aesthetic of the romantic period and the expressionistic purpose of much romantic art. Only the short lyric remained for Poe the pure expression of the soul. All other forms of composition had to submit to the control of the intellect. The conventionalities of the past had to be cast off, and new forms created.

To serve this revolutionary end, Poe considered an objective criticism necessary. The critic had to survey the dramas of the past not as history but in terms of the qualities of each play as an autonomous construct, irrespective of time and place:

> It is obvious . . . that towards the good end in view, much may be effected by discriminative criticism on what has already been done. . . . We propose, therefore, in a series of papers, to take a somewhat deliberate survey of some few of the most noticeable American plays. We shall do this without reference either to the date of the composition, or its adaptation for the closet or the stage. We shall speak with absolute frankness both of merits and defects—our principal object being understood not as that of mere commentary on the individual play—but on the drama in general, and on the American drama in especial, of which each individual play is a constituent part.[9]

From this statement it is clear that Poe thought that a rationale of dramatic form could be devised and that the "merits and defects" of particular plays could be estimated by their adherence to the rationale, which, of course, would obey the laws of nature.

Poe applied these laws as criteria in an examination of Willis' *Tortesa, The Usurer,* a play he had reviewed briefly in *Burton's Gentleman's Magazine* in 1839. Instead of cribbing from the old

[9] *Works,* XIII, 37.

review, however, Poe pointed out the leading defect of Willis' play, complexity of plot, and proceeded to elaborate his dictum that stage plots should be relatively simple. It was the fault of August Wilhelm Schlegel's "somewhat overprofound criticisms," Poe claimed, that many critics had admired mere intrigue, such as that found in Spanish comedy. Willis had fallen into this trap and had neglected "the dicta of common sense." Common sense would tell anyone that needless complexity of plot would result in fatigue as the mind made an effort to comprehend what was going on, and that this fatigue would deprive the audience of pleasure. When plot elements were developed through "lacquies and chambermaids," the audience would fail to grasp what was going on because they would expect plot development to be confined to the principals of the cast. Such needless mystification was embarrassing, and *ennui* increased in proportion to the embarrassment.[10] A playgoer does not go to a performance to exercise his talent at analysis. He goes to be entertained.

There was such a thing as a perfect plot—and Poe here took the opportunity to repeat his definition of the perfect plot, one from which no element could be detached or disarranged without "destruction to the mass"—but a perfect plot was not essential to the drama at all. It could be appreciated only by the connoisseur of art. The soul of the drama was "life-likeness," and good plots were not found in life, only in art. Pleasure in plot was simply the pleasure found in any exertion of human ingenuity, but after a time such pleasure palled. In a comedy of intrigue, where "underplot is piled upon underplot . . . and all to no purpose," ingenuity was self-defeating.[11]

As usual, Poe in this review was not content to rest his argument upon immediate causes; he had to extend it to ultimate principles, the nature of the universe itself. The only perfect plot was the universe, because God was the artist. To amplify this point Poe quoted a comment he had made in the "Marginalia" upon the Bridgewater treatises. In the Divine plot, there was complete "*mutuality* of adaptation," in which cause and effect were recipro-

[10] *Ibid.*, 44.   [11] *Ibid.*, 46–47.

cal. In human plots, however, "a particular cause has a particular effect—a particular purpose brings about a particular object; but we see no reciprocity." [12] The implication was that in human plotting the artist should always have an end in mind, since his purpose would determine his method. In the drama of intrigue, subplots had the effect of "after-thoughts" and as such were inadmissible.

Poe's chief argument was that the pleasure in drama was derived largely from its mimetic aspect, not from its form. As Bryllion Fagin has stated, Poe's demand for a measure of naturalism in the drama was needed at the time. Drama in America, as Poe recognized, had imitated not life but the old conventions of the stage, and realistic drama was yet to appear. Poe was one of its few harbingers. One qualification, of course, should be made of Poe's views. He did not demand or want photographic realism.[13] Truthfulness to nature should be preserved, he said, but not in the sense of taking a plot directly from life. Instead the artist should combine naturalistic elements in accordance with what Poe usually called the "general intention of Nature." The test was "verisimilitude." In actual fact, a playwright could combine elements that were not closely joined in reality so long as his combinations met this test. Like any other art form, the play was a fiction, and its truth did not consist in the reproduction of natural fact. Even in a mimetic art, the elements of experience had to undergo the transformation that was inherent in the medium. Being true to the general intention of nature, in Poe's idiom, meant obeying the laws of physical and psychological nature.[14]

[12] *Ibid.*, 45. Nowhere did Poe reveal his Enlightenment orientation more than in his first principle of art, that means must be adapted to a preconceived end. He never showed any inclination to accept the romantic aesthetic principle of art as discovery.

[13] Cf. Fagin, *The Histrionic Mr. Poe*, 115–16.

[14] Poe pressed this point in many reviews, but he stressed it in a review of Hazlitt's *The Characters of Shakespeare*. See *Works*, XII, 226–27. Unerringly he singled out the error of romantic criticism as typified by Hazlitt: the character of Hamlet was interpreted as if he had really lived instead of being the creation of Shakespeare's mind. Shakespeare must have known, Poe said, that in certain kinds of excitement there is an impulse to simulate greater agitation than is actually felt. The character of Hamlet was con-

The only other play Poe examined in his article was Longfellow's *The Spanish Student*. This was a closet drama, but to Poe there should be no such thing as a closet drama.[15] A play had to be *acted*, and *The Spanish Student* "could not be endured upon the stage." It was admittedly imitative of Cervantes' *La Gitanilla* and Thomas Middleton's *The Spanish Gypsy*, which deprived it of originality in subject matter, but it also lacked originality in incidents and in tone. Like most of the American dramas of the period, *The Spanish Student* was an imitation of foreign models.

It would have been better as a poem, Poe argued: "Let a poem be a poem only; let a play be a play and nothing more." Longfellow's was neither. Its poetic quality could be admired only when "we separate the poem from the drama." As for the dramatic structure, it failed miserably in plot construction. There were irrelevant incidents that had nothing to do with plot development and "deficiency in the dramatic tact" in the highly important scenes of recognition and reversal. Longfellow made the reversal appear to be accidental, "a happy chance," instead of obeying the rules of necessity and probability. Poe, like Aristotle, would have the change in fortunes of the characters come about not fortuitously but as a necessary consequence of the previous action. Lacking both in originality and in plot construction, Longfellow's play had no dramatic virtue whatsoever. It could be admired, if at all, only for the occasional beauty of the poetic passages.[16]

Thinking as always in terms of effect, Poe demanded more richness of expression and more lifelikeness in detail than the older plays afforded. In his view the drama had to walk a tightrope between the enormous complexity of life and the comprehensible

---

structed on this psychological premise, Poe thought. Shakespeare, knowing that his character would have been driven to "partial insanity" by his father's ghost, exaggerated the insanity for dramatic effect.

[15] In a review of Robert T. Conrad, Poe had written, "A closet-drama is an anomaly—a paradox—a mere figure of speech. There should be no such things as closet-dramas. The proof of the *dramatism* is the capacity for representation. In this view it will be seen that the usual outcry against 'stage effects' as meretricious, has no foundation in reason." *Graham's Magazine*, XXIV (January–June, 1844), 242.

[16] *Works*, XII, 69–73.

form that was necessary for art. Simplicity was demanded, not the simplicity of action of the Greek drama, but the simplicity of nature interpreted as general principles, a few basic laws that governed the interaction of all phenomena. In such a way, Poe thought, a rich simplicity could be achieved. Richness would come from the management of subject, style, and tone within the limits of stage presentation. The play as a whole would be attuned to the psychological limitations of the audience, but even within this limit, Poe thought, the "capabilities" of drama were immense, for all life was its subject. Totality of effect in the drama did not derive from plot construction but from the emotional impact of a felt relatedness of part to part and part to whole. This in Poe's aesthetics was the artistic mode of simplicity. It was not a primitive restriction of action but a conscious manipulation of materials to provide a simplistic response. By such a psychological ordering of his raw materials the playwright would insure the first value of all art—pleasure.

That the arts had to progress along with man's knowledge of the universe was one of the cardinal principles of Poe's aesthetic theory. In trying to justify art, he had concluded, along with many other theorists of the romantic and Victorian periods, that the artist had a responsibility to mankind; but, like most Americans of the nineteenth century, Poe was pragmatic—he was interested in efficiency. Each tool had to perform the function for which it was designed, or efficiency would be lost. Truth was the object of science, and in literature the efficient instrument to convey the truth was prose. Pleasure was the object of art, so art must be made into an efficient instrument to convey pleasure. The only way to justify art as being more than frivolous entertainment was to justify pleasure, certain kinds of pleasure, as being not only a gratification of the senses but also an enabling factor in man's spiritual development. Science and reason could be used to make art a more efficient means of gratification, and only the quality of the gratification should be scrutinized. Art should excite the mind and the spirit, not the passions. It should make us "beautiful-minded," which in turn would make us loathe the disorder represented by the evil in man's experience. To this end Poe developed his strategies of gratification, and to this end he wrote the philosophical essays in which he attempted to ground artistic purpose in the nature of things. These essays will be examined in due course, but first it is necessary to take a brief look at some of Poe's last reviews, reviews which demonstrate vividly how his career as a critic was damaged by the necessity of surviving in a journalistic jungle.

2

With the exception of his criticism of the drama, Poe's book reviews during the remainder of his career as a journalistic critic belong largely to the history of his controversies. Occasionally he did make an evaluation on the basis of his established principles, but often it was done in a captious manner that did not reflect his ideal standard of scientific objectivity in criticism. Of the "Longfellow War," the skirmishes with the Bostonians, and the verbal duels with various New York literati enough has been said by his biographers, by Professor Sidney Moss, and by the late Professor Perry Miller. This examination of Poe's later reviews will be confined to those which illustrate Poe's final positions in regard to the necessity of universal appeal and of a method to insure that appeal. A few reviews will be cited to show that at last Poe declined into the provincialism he had always deplored in an attempt to gain sectional support for his cherished project of establishing a magazine. It is probable that the decline in the quality of Poe's criticism toward the end of his short life can be blamed on circumstances rather than on a deterioration of ability, but the circumstances were such that a decline in mental health would seem inevitable. We can only applaud his courage in fighting against what for a man of his temperament must have been intolerable.

On July 19, 1845, during the same period in which he was publishing his best reviews of the drama, Poe quoted in the *Broadway Journal* an excerpt from a long review by Edwin Percy Whipple, a

Massachusetts critic, with whom Poe declared himself in perfect accord. The quoted passage is a tribute to Tennyson, and the gist of it is that Tennyson was a consummate artist: " 'It seems to us that the purely intellectual element in Tennyson's poetry, has been over-looked, owing perhaps to the fragility of some of his figures and the dreariness of outline apparent in others. Many think him to be a mere rhapsodist, fertile in nothing but a kind of melodious empiricism. No opinion is more contradicted by the fact. Examine his poetry minutely, and the wonderful artistical finish becomes evident. There are few authors who will bear the probe of analysis better.' " [17] No wonder Poe agreed with Whipple. He had always demanded that a work of art be able to stand the test of analysis, and only six months earlier, in his review of *The Drama of Exile*, he had lauded Tennyson as a skillful artist.

Yet not quite a year later, in the context of a review of William Cullen Bryant, Poe seemingly disparaged Tennyson while attacking the "new licentious 'schools' of poetry." The "Tennysonian and Barrettian schools," Poe claimed, had "in their rashness of spirit, much in accordance with the whole spirit of the age, thrown into the shade necessarily all that seems akin to the conservatism of half a century ago."

> The conventionalities, even the most justifiable decora of composition are regarded, *per se*, with a suspicious eye. When I say *per se*, I mean that, from finding them so long in connexion with conservatism of thought, we have come at last to dislike them, not merely as the outward visible signs of that conservatism, but as things evil in themselves. It is very clear that those accuracies and elegancies of style, and of general manner, which in the time of Pope were considered as *prima facie* and indispensable indications of genius, are now conversely regarded. How few are willing to admit the possibility of reconciling genius with artistic skill! Yet this reconciliation is not only possible, but an absolute necessity. . . . The greatest poems will not be written until this prejudice is annihilated . . . .[18]

[17] "Alfred Tennyson," *ibid.*, XII, 182–83.
[18] "William Cullen Bryant," *ibid.*, XIII, 129.

It would appear from this statement that Poe had suddenly repudiated progressivism in art in one context while demanding it in another. Yet a careful reading of the review, with Poe's previous criticism in mind, will clarify his position. For more than a year Poe had been deploring imitativeness—which bred "schools" of poetry. In the review of *The Drama of Exile* he had stated that Miss Barrett had imitated the early Tennyson, who in turn had served his apprenticeship in that "school which arose out of Shelley." Tennyson had revolted against his early manner, but the schools of imitators, though at one remove from Shelley, were still copying the licentiousness of the great model without his compensating genius. The point that Poe was stressing was that the spirit of revolt in itself was valueless, for it condemned even justifiable conventionalities simply because they were established in the past. A skillful poet, such as Bryant, would be undervalued because he was an accurate metricist and obeyed the established conventions of verse. In fact, Poe admitted that he had undervalued Bryant himself and was now disposed to make a correction. He was prepared to do justice to Bryant's skill as an artist without considering him "a genius of the loftiest order." Bryant did have genius, but it was being overlooked by the modern schools because his work was deficient in "those externals which have become in a measure symbolical of those schools." Bryant's work, as described by Rufus Wilmot Griswold, lacked passion, but in Poe's opinion the fact that the emotion in Bryant's poetry was not passionate showed him as a true artist: "It is precisely this 'unpassionate emotion' which is the limit of the true poetical art." [19]

Ever since he had become a literary critic, Poe had consistently denied that passion was a proper element in poetry. In his limitation of poetry to the "unpassionate emotion" of art, he was simply restating his credo that art existed only to serve an aesthetic purpose, not to stimulate emotions that were sensual in nature. To arouse a response to art, the artist had to possess skill. Bryant should be valued because of his consistent devotion to artistry. The very "correctness" which had been undervalued by the "licentious"

[19] *Ibid.*, 131.

schools would help eliminate the current prejudice against artistry that had been the unfortunate influence of the inimitable genius of Shelley, as transmitted through Tennyson and Miss Barrett.

This review, then, should be seen not as a disparagement of Tennyson but as a re-evaluation of Bryant designed to stress the point Poe had been making during his middle period, that the artist should know the laws of his craft. It was the school of the Spasmodics that Poe rightly condemned as licentious, and in spite of his admiration for Tennyson and Miss Barrett, he regretted that some of their verse belonged to what he had earlier called the "school of all Lawlessness" that had magnified the errors of the great romantic poets.

Most of the contradictions in Poe's reviews resulted from his continuing dialectic of art. He sometimes elaborated an argument begun in an earlier review by shifting his approach and modifying his strategy. Sometimes, as in the review of Bryant, he admitted that he had changed his mind, but at other times, although he had not changed his mind, he would modify his strategy and appear to contradict himself. This is the reason it is difficult to assess Poe's critical theories and his practice by examining only a few reviews. His writing desk was his laboratory, in which he discovered, tested, and refined his ideas with the object of developing a consistent theory of art that would serve as a guide to evaluation and composition. Unlike the experiments of the scientist, which are not exposed to the public view until they are perfected, Poe's reviews are open to scrutiny, with all of his procedural errors and modifications of approach pitilessly revealed.

Poe assumed that he had a constant audience which would be aware of the continuity of his argument; accordingly, he referred to previous proofs without repeating his demonstrations. In the review of Bryant, for instance, he refused to explain why he denied passion as a legitimate theme for poetry because he had "repeatedly shown" that passion was ineligible in a pure art form and he did not wish to do his work over again. Instead he referred the reader to his review of Mrs. Welby, published about a year earlier. There he had explained that strong emotion stimulated the imagination, but that when the imagination was stimulated the emotion itself was subdued; thus the artistic imagination would triumph over passion. In this Poe's psychology of art was valid. The imaginative transformation of a strong emotion into artistic form sublimates the emotion itself. Therefore to Poe, "a passionate poem is a contradiction in terms." The emotion that went into the poem was not the emotion that came out of the poem, a valid argument. Poe's reputation as a critic would be greater if he had managed to place his more lucid explanations within the context of his better known essays and reviews. Unfortunately he did not, and his reputation has suffered.

In another essay-review, which must also be considered as a re-evaluation, Poe undertook to explain why Hawthorne, whom in 1842 he had called a man "of truest genius," had failed to win regard from the public at large.[20] With his increased emphasis upon universal appeal Poe found it necessary to explain why an artist gifted with both imagination and skill should fail to please the public. In 1842 he had said that Hawthorne's tales "belong to the highest region of Art—an Art subservient to genius of a very lofty order." In 1847, however, Poe was disposed to make genius subordinate to art. The eccentricities, the mannerisms of genius, had to be controlled in the interest of universal appeal because these very eccentricities would be mistaken for originality, and true originality should always appeal. Thus, to avoid the paradox of asserting that Hawthorne was an original genius who still failed to command a large audience, Poe found it necessary to re-examine his concept of originality in relation to idiosyncrasies which repelled instead of attracted. "It is often said, inconsiderately, that very original writers always fail in popularity—that such and such persons are too original to be comprehended by the mass. 'Too peculiar,' should be the phrase, 'too idiosyncratic.' It is, in fact, the excitable, undisciplined and childlike popular mind which most keenly feels the original. . . . The fact is, that if Mr. Hawthorne were really original, he could not fail of making himself felt by the public." What, then, was true originality? "This true, or commendable originality . . .

[20] "Tale Writing—Nathaniel Hawthorne—," *Works*, XIII, 141–55.

implies not the uniform, but the continuous peculiarity—a peculiarity springing from ever-active vigor of fancy—better still if from ever-present force of imagination, giving its own hue, its own character to everything it touches, and, especially, *self impelled to touch everything.*"

Examined in the light of this Coleridgean definition, Hawthorne, Poe claimed, was not original, and those who credited him with originality simply meant that he differed from the other authors they were familiar with. The alleged unpopularity of original authors, Poe went on to affirm, sprang from the confusion of literary with metaphysical originality. Metaphysical originality, in Poe's sense, meant "combinations of thought, of incident, and so forth, . . . [that] are . . . absolutely novel." Literary originality, on the other hand, "is that which, in bringing out the half-formed, the reluctant, or the unexpressed fancies of mankind, or in exciting the more delicate pulses of the heart's passion, or in giving birth to some universal sentiment or instinct in embryo, thus combines with the pleasurable effect of *apparent* novelty, a real egoistic delight."

If a reader was confronted with metaphysical originality, Poe insisted, the burden upon his intellectual faculties was too great and he was pained instead of pleased. Novelty was of no value unless it was appreciated; hence it was novelty of effect rather than novelty of matter that counted. By striking the common pulse, by giving birth to a universal sentiment that existed only embryonically in the reader, an artist could double the reader's pleasure by giving him the delight of discovery. "He feels and intensely enjoys the seeming novelty of thought, enjoys it as really novel, as absolutely original with the writer—*and himself*. They two, he fancies, have, alone of all men, thought thus. They two have, together, created this thing. Henceforward there is a bond of sympathy between them, a sympathy which irradiates every subsequent page of the book."

This passage shows how far Poe the mature critic had moved from the young romantic tale-writer of the 1830's who exploited the terrible. Now originality was measured by the author's ability to express the implicit universals of the imagination and the emotions so that the audience, recognizing these universals, would share the pleasure of creativity. The audience, Poe felt, could not share an author's idiosyncrasies. These personal elements of feeling, tone, and expression served only as agents of alienation and were at root egotistic, as if the author were proclaiming, "Look! How different I am from all others!" Poe, in his zeal to bring art to the people, thus repudiated the cult of personality and self-expression. Art should appeal to all mankind, and the eccentricities of genius had to be governed by the necessity of universal participation in the experience of art.

Along with his demand that the artist achieve the universal in thought and feeling, Poe praised what he called the "natural style," even claiming that it was an aspect (in a lower degree) of the "true original." The natural style was "but the result of writing with the understanding, or with the instinct, that the *tone*, in composition, should be . . . the tone of the great mass of humanity." When a reader encountered such a style, he was inclined to accept the import of any given passage as representing universal thought, thought which had "occurred to all the rest of the world." Addison, Irving, and Hawthorne had achieved this naturalness of style, but it did not serve to make Hawthorne popular simply because Hawthorne's allegorical method removed him from mass mind and feeling. People do not think in allegorical terms, Poe insisted, nor are their feelings aroused by allegory, because its aim at truth dispels the illusion created by the fiction: "One thing is clear, that if allegory ever establishes a fact, it is by dint of overturning a fiction." Allegory destroys the pleasure that comes from identification with the virtual life, that illusion which is necessary in fiction. This pleasure was denied by Hawthorne, for the allegorical strain was his peculiarity, and he imposed it on his work. Like all writers, Hawthorne wanted to be read, but "the simple truth is that the writer who aims at impressing the people, is *always* wrong when he fails in forcing the people to receive the impression."

At this point in his review Poe described what the short tale should be, but since he merely quoted from his 1842 review of

Hawthorne, a discussion may be omitted. For the first time, however, Poe used sarcasm on the New England author he had admired. In conclusion he stated that Hawthorne possessed all the qualities of authorship—style, taste, scholarship, humor, pathos, imagination, and ingenuity. He had failed only because he had attempted to be a mystic. Poe's advice to the New England writer was simple but pungent: "Let him mend his pen, get a bottle of visible ink, come out from the Old Manse, cut Mr. Alcott, hang (if possible) the editor of 'The Dial,' and throw out of the window to the pigs all his odd numbers of 'The North American Review.'" Except for this jocular conclusion Poe's re-evaluation of Hawthorne appears more as principle than prejudice. For several years Poe had asserted the right of the noncreative public to share the aesthetic pleasures hitherto confined to the few. It was not the duty of the artistic genius to reform the populace or to inform them; it was his duty to make them aware of potential harmony, to give them a sense of form, felt form, through which disorder and deformity could be recognized in whatever guise. To perform his duty the genius would have to express the half-formed thoughts and feelings of mankind in a style devoid of mannerisms and obscurities. His imagination would touch everything and select what could be brought together in a harmony of combination. If he were a true artist, he would express what everyone would *almost* think and *almost* feel for himself, thus giving every person the egotistic delight of apparent discovery. This, to Poe, was the only universality that counted—the appeal to all mankind. Was he only a journalist trying to rescue popular art from the opprobrium of the intellectuals, or did he ascribe to art a redemptive power that should be extended to everyone? An attempt to answer this question has already been made, but the final argument must be reserved for Poe himself, and he made it in his philosophy.

3

After the collapse of the *Broadway Journal* in January of 1846 Poe had no regular outlet for his criticism. Some of his reviews, like the two just examined, were published among the fripperies of a woman's magazine, *Godey's Lady's Book*, and a few others in the *Southern Literary Messenger*. Poe's personal situation, after the bankruptcy of the *Broadway Journal*, was deplorable. His own health was poor, and his wife Virginia was in her terminal illness. Moreover, as he wrote to Thomas Holley Chivers, he was "ground into the very dust with poverty," and he had not been able to write "*one line* for the magazines for more than five months." The articles which had appeared in *Godey's* had been written and paid for much earlier.[21]

In this period Poe was living in a cottage at Fordham, New York, and during the winter of 1846–47 the predicament of the Poe family became more serious. In December the New York *Express* entreated his friends to come to his aid, and the faithful Willis wrote an editorial in the *Home Journal* the same month defending Poe as a person and asking for help. Poe's pride was offended by the publicity given his situation and particularly by a statement in the *Saturday Evening Post* that he was without funds and friends. Accordingly, he wrote a brave letter to Willis claiming that there were a hundred people in New York to whom he could have applied for aid if it had been absolutely necessary.[22]

Virginia died on January 30, 1847, and Poe experienced a nervous collapse. His enemies showed no mercy, however. The *Saturday Evening Post* had published a charge of plagiarism against him, which his correspondent George W. Eveleth brought to his attention, and he was engaged in a suit against the New York *Mirror* (no longer edited by Morris and Willis) for slander. The *Mirror* had published a vicious attack by Thomas Dunn English that accused Poe of forgery. The occasion of English's attack was a series called "The Literati of New York City," which had been published in installments in *Godey's Lady's Book* during 1846. Poe's opinions of the lesser authors of New York, sometimes malicious, are interesting, but they are not criticism. In fact, Poe himself wrote to Eveleth that he had to drop the series because

[21] Poe to Chivers, July 22, 1846, in *Letters*, II, 325–27.
[22] December 30, 1846, *ibid.*, 338–39.

"people insisted on considering them elaborate criticisms when I had no other design than critical *gossip*." [23] But his gossip was sometimes offensive, and English had retaliated unscrupulously, charging that Poe had obtained money from him under false pretenses and that he had given Poe a "sound cuffing" the last time he saw him. English's charges were slanderous and Poe won his suit. He was awarded $225 plus costs, which afforded at least temporary relief. The money he got from his few articles during this period would have done no more than keep him alive.

After Virginia's death, Poe's health, both mental and physical, was precarious. The few letters he wrote during 1847 were concerned chiefly with his attempts to defend himself against the charges of his enemies. By January of 1848, however, he had recovered enough to start trying to re-establish himself in journalism. He wrote Eveleth that he had resolved to be his own publisher and that he would travel through the South and the West to work up a subscription list for his projected magazine, the *Stylus*.[24] At the same time he was delivering lectures on the "universe," which later became his prose-poem *Eureka*; and his enthusiasm over both his magazine project and his cosmology appeared in his correspondence.[25] Busy with the composition of *Eureka*, his plans for his magazine, and a frenetic love affair with Sarah Helen Whitman, an ethereal and sickly poetess some six years his senior, Poe had no time to write reviews, and the few he did write must be examined in the light of his attempt to gain support in the South. By the end of 1848 he had re-established a connection with the *Southern Literary Messenger* (now managed by John R. Thompson) and proceeded to try to win the South to his cause by exploiting sectional feeling.

There had been a cordial relationship between Poe and James Russell Lowell in 1843 and 1844, with a frequent exchange of letters, and there had been a proposal that the two authors write biographical sketches of each other. Poe had reviewed Lowell favor-

[23] December 15, 1846, *ibid.*, 331–33.
[24] January 4, 1848, *ibid.*, 354–57.
[25] See Poe to Eveleth, February 29, 1848, *ibid.*, 360–62.

ably in *Graham's* for March, 1844, even going so far as to say that Lowell's new volume of poems would put him *"at the very head* of the poets of America." [26] He had objected only to Lowell's didacticism, which by Poe's standards was an objection on principle. But once Poe moved to New York and began writing for the *Mirror*, the relationship became strained and finally was broken. Lowell's description of Poe in *A Fable for Critics* (1848) infuriated him, and he retaliated by reviewing the satire in the *Southern Literary Messenger* for March of 1849. [27] The retaliation, however, was almost exclusively in terms of sectional prejudice:

> Mr. Lowell is one of the most rabid of the abolition fanatics; and no Southerner who does not wish to be insulted, and at the same time revolted by a bigotry the most obstinately blind and deaf, should ever touch a volume by this author. His fanaticism about slavery is a mere local outbreak of the same innate wrong-headedness which, if he owned slaves, would manifest itself in atrocious ill-treatment of them, with murder of any abolitionist who should endeavor to set them free. A fanatic of Mr. L's species, is simply a fanatic in whatever circumstances you place him. . . .
>
> With the exception of Mr. Poe, (who has written some commendatory criticisms on his poems,) no Southerner is mentioned *at all* in this "Fable." It is a fashion among Mr. Lowell's set to affect a belief that there is *no such thing* as Southern Literature. Northerners—people who have really nothing to speak of as men of letters,—are cited by the dozen, and lauded by this candid critic without stint, while Legaré, Simms, Longstreet, and others of equal note are passed by in contemptuous silence.

Poe went on to claim, in answer to Lowell's amusing description of Poe's talking "like a book of iambs and pentameters, / In a way to make all men of common sense d——n metres," that common sense had been the basis on which he had always conducted his criticism, in "contradistinction from the *un*common nonsense of Mr. L. and the small pedants."

Poe's review of Lowell, then, sprang partly from personal pique, but it was intended to rouse Southern opinion in his favor by ex-

---

[26] *Works*, XI, 243–49.   [27] *Ibid.*, XIII, 165–67.

ploiting Southern defensiveness about the lack of recognition of
Southern writers in the North. White had founded the *Messenger*
with the promise to publish Southern writers, and Poe, hoping to
gain backing in the South, was simply demonstrating that he would
serve as a champion of Southern letters. As he wrote to John R.
Thompson, the editor of the *Messenger*, "There are many points
affecting the interests of Southern Letters—especially in reference
to Northern neglect or misrepresentation of them—which stand
sorely in need of touching." [28] Experienced controversialist that he
was, Poe presented himself as just the critic to do it. In a letter to
F. W. Thomas dated February 14, 1849, he damned Lowell, Margaret Fuller, and "her *protege*, Cornelius Matthews [*sic*]," and expressed a desire to "use them up *en masse*." [29]

While exploiting the possibilities of the South, Poe did not neglect the West, as his letters to E. H. N. Patterson, a possible
backer in Oquawka, Illinois, reveal. He had received a proposal
from young Patterson, who had inherited a newspaper from his father, to publish a "cheap" magazine with Poe as editor. Poe, as always, was opposed to an inexpensive publication and wrote to Patterson that only a five-dollar journal could possibly succeed. With
Patterson's money, Poe was able to start on his publicity tour and
left New York for Richmond at the end of June, 1849. In Virginia,
during July and August, he delivered his lecture "The Poetic Principle" to appreciative audiences.

Poe's hopes were never higher. The South had welcomed him
home, and Patterson had promised to support not a "cheap" three-
dollar magazine but the five-dollar journal Poe had demanded, if
Poe could only procure a list of one thousand subscribers. Poe was
to meet Patterson in St. Louis on October 15. The scheduled meeting never took place. Poe left Richmond for New York toward the
end of September and was found in Baltimore on October 3 in a
semiconscious condition. He died on October 7, without ever explaining what had happened to him on the trip.

Of Poe's posthumously published reviews, the only one of any
interest is an essay upon contemporary American critics, in which

[28] January 13, 1849, in *Letters*, II, 415–16.   [29] *Ibid.*, 426–28.

he analyzed the work of William A. Jones and Edwin Percy Whipple.[30] In the review he paid tribute to Macaulay for using "the perfection of that justifiable rhetoric which has its basis in common sense." Poe had continued to push the thesis that he had stressed since 1845, that "the highest genius" would be benefited by "availing itself of that Natural Art which it too frequently despises." Jones and Whipple had imitated Macaulay, which was not to imply disparagement. However, the two critics should not be content with "tamely following" in Macaulay's footsteps, but should endeavor to surpass him in his own method, by following "a path not so much his as Nature's." This odd statement, phrased in diction reminiscent of the eighteenth century, was Poe's valediction to criticism. Since 1842 he had worked to invest criticism with the dignity of an art. It was an art scarcely less significant, to his mind, than the creative art. What man had put together with his creative faculties, man could take apart with his analytical faculties. The analytical faculties were not to be despised, because in a fully developed intellect they coexisted with the creative in that harmonious adaptation which represented the fully realized intention of nature. As Poe had written in the "Marginalia," man's "chief idiosyncrasy" was reason: "The more he reasons, the nearer he approaches the position to which this chief idiosyncrasy irresistibly impels him; and not until he attains this position with exactitude —not until his reason has exhausted itself for his improvement— not until he has stepped upon the highest pinnacle of civilization— will his *natural* state be ultimately reached, or thoroughly determined." [31] The literary genius, be he critic or poet, shuddered at imperfection, and the "*highest* genius is but the loftiest moral nobility." [32] It was the function of genius to "combine the original

[30] "About Critics and Criticism," *Works*, XIII, 193–202.
[31] *Ibid.*, XVI, 6–7.
[32] *Ibid.*, 163. This particular statement in the "Marginalia" is listed by George E. Hatvary among those Poe plagiarized from H. B. Wallace's novel *Stanley*. Yet the mere fact that Poe printed it indicates his agreement with the proposition, even if he had not made similar assertions elsewhere. Since in Poe's ethics sensitivity to beauty created an aversion to vice, the genius would have to be morally noble.

with that which is *natural* . . . in the artistic sense which has reference to the *general intention of Nature.*" [33] This, Poe had maintained during his last years as a critic, could be done only when the beauty recognized by the taste was shaped into expression by the harmonious combinations of the imagination, then adapted to the needs and limitations of an audience by the use of the reason and the common sense. Yet because this combination of intellect and feeling was rarely to be seen, criticism was necessary to point out the common faults of art works and to remind both the artist and the public of the natural principles by which all art should be constructed, the principles which could be discovered by an examination of the nature of the universe and the nature of man. An art work, Poe held, was a construction, and the person who knew how to analyze a construction could also build it. "To say that a critic could not have written the work which he criticises, is to put forth a contradiction in terms." [34]

Such a statement as the last scarcely bears repeating, but in his generalizations Poe usually invoked the ideal. To him the ideal critic, or the ideal artist, could carry the "most shadowy precepts into successful application." [35] Pragmatic to a degree that few Americans in a nation of pragmatists ever were, Poe finally achieved a faith in intellect that is startling. Whatever existed, he maintained, could be understood. No mystery was too deep for the mind to solve, not even the mystery of the creative powers of God and man. It was the duty of the critic to understand whatever was put before him, however mysterious it seemed to the unenlightened. "Now, it is the business of the critic so to soar that he shall *see the sun*, even although its orb be far below the ordinary horizon." [36] Thus it appears that Poe, who as a critic had prescribed unusual limitations for the artist, might have prescribed those limitations because he thought he knew just what the artist could hope to achieve with the means that were available to him. The limitations were two: the imperfection of the artist's materials and the imperfection of his audience. Within these given limitations, Poe thought, all could be understood, all could be analyzed, and all

[33] *Works*, XVI, 57. [34] *Ibid.*, 69. [35] *Ibid.* [36] *Ibid.*, 81.

could be reduced to practice. At the end of his career it would seem that Poe's mind was not that of the romantic artist yearning toward the incomprehensible and the mysterious, but that of the scientist, who knew that the rhythm of the universe and the ebb and flow of human feeling could be described in numbers. The critic had to soar to see the sun, for the laws of planetary motion were the same laws that governed a poetic line. Understanding the universe, the critic could prescribe a natural art that could not fail, because it would be founded on the only enduring principles.

By the very nature of his profession Poe was required to evaluate literary works before he had an opportunity to develop, or at least to express, a theory that would validate his practice. As has been indicated throughout, he had to express his critical theories in his book reviews. Eventually, however, he saw that if he were going to proclaim that he was following nature in his method, he would have to describe the nature that he was following. To some, following nature would have meant imitating the appearances of the phenomenal world, but to Poe this was not art. To others, following nature would have meant emphasizing the intuitional and the inspirational at the expense of method. But to Poe, following nature meant obeying the laws of the physical universe and the psychological laws of man. Accordingly, it was necessary for him to develop a cosmology. This he did during the last ten years of his life, disguising his speculation as fiction but at the same time describing the kind of universe in which his questions could be answered and his conflicts reconciled, a universe which was consistent even in its contradictions.

XVII · *The Plot of God*

POE wanted to be a philosophical critic. He wanted his modes of validation not only to be empirically sound but also to be in accord with a metaphysical system. In his first reviews for the *Messenger,* instead of developing a system of his own, he was prone to rely on authority, citing Coleridge, Schlegel, and Bielfeld to provide theoretical support for his method. Very early, however, he showed an interest in philosophical speculation. Sensitive to the charge that he gave merely the "physique of the horrible" in his tales, he began to preface them with epigrams that intimated a serious metaphysical import in even his most fantastic narratives. Prefixed to "Morella," published in 1835, was a quotation from Plato's *Symposium:* "Itself, by itself solely, ONE everlastingly and single." Since the theme of "Morella" is passionate longing for immortality, the epigram is appropriate because in the *Symposium* the cause of sexual love is seen as the human desire to be immortal. People begot children because they lived in their offspring. Poe simply pushed this idea to its logical extreme by having Morella's soul pass into the body of her daughter.

Three years later he published another tale on the same theme. The epigram to "Ligeia," attributed spuriously to Joseph Glanvill, implies that death can be conquered by the will: "And the will therein lieth, which dieth not. Who knoweth, the mysteries of the will, with its vigor? For God is but a great will pervading all things by nature of its intentness. Man doth not yield himself to the angels, nor unto death utterly, save only through the weakness of his feeble will." This quotation, wherever Poe got it, was germinal to his metaphysics; he eventually ascribed pleasure to the free exercise of volition and pain to its frustration. In the tale "Ligeia" the power of the will overcomes death, and Ligeia not only invades the soul of her successor but transforms the body also, accomplishing an absolute transmission of identity.

In these tales Poe of course was writing fiction, and by his own theory a fiction was never to be taken as a truth. Yet the tales reveal his almost obsessive concern with the horror of death, particularly the loss of personal identity after death.[1] During the early 1840's he envisioned a personal immortality and in his "philosophical" tales he attempted to imagine the quality of life after death.

"The Conversation of Eiros and Charmion," published a year after "Ligeia," describes the fiery end of the world after it collides with a comet, but the two "angels," Eiros and Charmion, retain not only the attributes of personality but also their memories of precatastrophic existence. Soon, however, Poe began to explore in his fiction the possibilities of pantheism, which carried him close to the position that the soul after death would be absorbed into the World Soul. In "The Island of the Fay," published in 1841, he struck a Wordsworthian note by having his narrator look at the objects of the landscape and say, "I love to regard these as themselves but the colossal members of one vast animate and sentient whole . . . ." One might dismiss this little fantasy about the death of a fay as simply Poe's exploitation of a familiar motif,[2] except that the idea of the nature of God advanced in the story was later given as an "imagined truth": "As we find cycle within cycle without end —yet all revolving around one far-distant center which is the Godhead, may we not analogically suppose, in the same manner, life within life, the less within the greater, and all within the Spirit Divine?"[3] The phrase "life within life, . . . and all within the

---

[1] For a persuasive interpretation of the meaning of Poe's "horror," see Davidson, *Poe: A Critical Study*, Chapter IV. I must disagree, however, with Professor Davidson's description of Poe's view of nature as a "chaos wherein nothing exists according to any law or order that man can know." Such an interpretation may easily be derived from Poe's poems and fiction, but it is alien to his philosophical thought.

[2] In a recent article Burton R. Pollin implies that this tale should not be taken seriously as a symbolic narrative because it was a "plate story" written to interpret an engraving made by J. B. Martin for *Graham's*. See Pollin, "Poe as Probable Author of 'Harper's Ferry,'" *American Literature*, XL (May, 1968), 169–70.

[3] The last three phrases of this sentence were repeated verbatim in the conclusion of *Eureka*. See *Works*, XVI, 315.

Spirit Divine" was Poe's epilogue to the drama which had been presented in "Ligeia," the tragedy Man, with its hero the Conqueror Worm. Ligeia's dying question to God, "Are we not part and parcel in Thee?" is answered affirmatively in "The Island of the Fay." Everything is part and parcel of God.

Poe's speculation about the nature of God is related to his teleology of art. As early as 1836, in his first "philosophical review," that of the poems of Drake and Halleck, he had claimed that aesthetic feeling—"the sentiment of Poesy"—was one of man's greatest pleasures in life and that this feeling engendered a hope of a greater "Intellectual Happiness" after death. His phrase "Intellectual Happiness" obviously did not mean the satisfaction of the reason alone. As he put it somewhat ineptly in the review, "mingled up inextricably with this love and this admiration of Heaven and of Earth" was the "unconquerable desire—*to know*." Thus we can be justified in assuming that Poe's "Intellectual Happiness" should not be confused with the satisfaction that one feels from having arrived at the truth by a logical process. Instead it is an unmediated cognition, an intuition that has the force and immediacy of our recognition of beauty.

In his review of Drake and Halleck, Poe had claimed that God had given man the capacity for aesthetic feeling not only to provide happiness for his creatures but also, since Poe conceived of God as an artist, to insure admiration for God's art, the creation itself. Presumably then, the "unconquerable desire—*to know*" was associated in Poe's mind with the desire to understand the source of our pleasure, the nature of the universe. Aesthetic pleasure, if perfected, would spring from comprehensive cognition of the aesthetic object, yet this was not possible to mere mortals. The passive "sense of taste," or the artistic sensibility, merely stimulated a desire for such knowledge.

Within five years after the publication of the review of Drake and Halleck, Poe began to grapple with the question of why nature, viewed as art, would always appear to be imperfect to the unaided senses of man. In other words, if the primary attribute of God as evidenced by his creation were his artistry, why did the creation exhibit deformity, pain, and death, those flaws in the artistic design? Poe did not ask this question in his book reviews during this period, but he did ask it in his philosophical tales, and of course he had as much trouble with the answer as metaphysicians have always had in their theodicies. It was difficult for him to explain why an omnipotent artist would create an apparently imperfect art, and it was also difficult to explain why there was a human need for an experience of beauty more satisfying than that furnished by unaltered nature. Poe explored, but could not maintain, the romantic notion that the earthly paradise before the Fall would have fully gratified the sense of beauty.[4] His eventual solution was to bring God into the world in a state of comparative imperfection. Poe's God was not the transcendent and eternal One whose being was absolute, nor was he the benevolent but distant architect of the Deists who created a perfect design for the physical universe but allowed his creatures to suffer for no apparent reason. Instead Poe, like Schelling, whom his narrator cites in "Morella," began to view God as a World-Spirit or a Life-Force limited by his temporal existence.

Poe had difficulty in reconciling the Newtonian universe of perfect order with the phenomenal disorder he observed on every side. His characteristic solution was to bring in the artist as mediator, which of course was in keeping with the romantic tendency to regard the artist as the transcendental hero who would save us all. But to do this Poe found it necessary to formulate a concept of nature, of God, and of man that would allow the creature to improve the work of the creator without surpassing it, a logical impasse. Poe solved the problem, to his own satisfaction at least, by denying man the power of apprehending the creation as a whole and by assigning to the artist the duty of adapting the raw materials of art to the human condition. His speculation after 1841, whether disguised as fiction or expressed in letters to friends, was related to his purpose of validating the artist as the creator of microcosmic totalities that would gratify the sense of taste and at the same time not

---

[4] For an account of this exploration, see my article "Poe's Earthly Paradise," *American Quarterly*, XII (1960), 404–13.

exceed the human capacity for cognition. If the human art work could be simple in design and limited in scope, and if its details exhibited the harmony and symmetry of nature taken as a whole, then the human mind could experience the pleasure of totality, which to Poe meant not only the immediate pleasure that came from beautiful sights and sounds but also the pleasure that the artistic sensibility experienced when confronted with a perfect design. This dual pleasure should be immediate; it should be an effect. One should not have to think about it, as in analyzing a work of extended scope, for reasoning about it lessened the pleasure. The critic could analyze, but the analysis should take place after the experience, and whatever pleasure derived from the exercise of the reason was an impure pleasure unrelated to the gratification of the taste. The taste could be fully gratified only by an almost instantaneous recognition of design, with part related to part and to the whole in perfect symmetry. God's art, however it pleased the senses in some of its details, was too vast in scope to be known as a whole. It could be apprehended as a whole only as a concept, not by an immediate intuition of the relatedness of its parts.

In "The Colloquy of Monos and Una," published in 1841, Poe's attempt to validate the role of the artist as mediator between the divine and the human is obvious. His narrator, the angel Monos, interprets the Fall in the Garden not as an immediate catastrophe but as a progressive alienation of the human soul from the order and beauty of nature. Moral evil, as distinct from natural evil, was brought into the world by man's pride in his reason and in his practical accomplishments. Man "stalked a God in his own fancy" and laid claim to dominion over nature. By using his practical reason and by neglecting the intuitions of his poetic faculty, man came into disharmony with the creation. The poetic mind could still apprehend the beauty and harmony of the creation and would have used these qualities as a guide for human behavior, but the intuition of the poets was scorned by the utilitarians, the rough pedants, who could see nature, to use Emerson's term, only as commodity.

In "The Island of the Fay" Poe had toyed with the idea of a cosmic democracy, speculating that all objects in the universe might be equal in the eyes of God. In "The Colloquy," however, Poe discovered the implication of the Chain of Being. He declared that "gradation" was the order of nature and that man's "wild attempts at an omni-prevalent Democracy" based upon the concept of "universal equality" was "in the face of analogy and of God . . . ." In this way he was able to reconcile his Whiggish conservatism with pantheism. God was in everything, Poe thought, but in different degrees. Each form of life had its place in the scale of being in relation to consciousness and even within each link of the chain there was a hierarchical order. Organic life varied from inferior to superior in terms of mental endowment.[5]

God's plan, Poe asserted, was for man to live forever in an earthly paradise, but in exercising his reason man had not followed the intention of nature and nature's God. Instead he had applied his scientific knowledge to subvert the natural order. In the cultural crisis that ensued, Poe speculated, "taste alone could have led us gently back to Beauty, to Nature, and to Life." The taste, in Poe's system, was the faculty that supplied intuitions of God in his purest attribute, beauty. A culture that gave priority to the practical reason frustrated the divine plan and of necessity had to be destroyed.

In 1841, then, Poe granted the poet the capacity for imaginative insight into God's plan because the poet could perceive analogies between the natural order and the ideal moral order. In this Poe was at one with the transcendentalists, both European and American, who found correspondences between natural law and moral law. His great difference, however, was in his interpretation of the analogies. To Emerson, the poet's insight into the universal as manifested in the particular was ground for hope that man would be able to attune himself to the higher laws and come out from under the dominion of the law of things. Pessimistically viewing the history of mankind, Poe had no confidence that the world

[5] Cf. *Eureka*, in *Works*, XVI, 309–14. Life forms that possessed the highest sensitivity were the forms closest to God, since God experienced his "life" only in the pleasures and pains of his creatures.

would ever be guided by the poet's vision. To Poe, the history of man as interpreted by the "disenfranchised reason" of Monos after his death, was a record of sickness, of infection that could be purified only by death: "for the infected world at large I could anticipate no regeneration save in death. That man, as a race, should not become extinct, I saw that he must be 'born again.'" Ruin was the price of civilization because man had devoted himself to the utilitarian arts instead of the cultivation of the "sentiment of the natural"—which to Poe meant a feeling for the order of nature. Only by some visionary system of education such as that proposed by Plato in *The Republic* could man have become "beautiful-minded." If man's soul had been formed by the experience of music—which Poe defined as "the general cultivation of the taste" —he would have assimilated into his own condition the harmonies of the universe; he would have dwelt forever in an earthly paradise. But instead, he had cultivated the "harsh mathematical reason of the school" and had "scarred" the surface of the earth with "rectangular obscenities." "The fair face of Nature was deformed as with the ravages of some loathsome disease." Only a purification by fire would supply the antecedent condition for the earthly paradise.

Thus there was no help for man in his present condition, Poe maintained. Paradise lay behind and ahead, and in its temporal condition the world was a vale of tears. If, then, the poet had been rejected as a legislator of the world, what could be his significance in human affairs? Only to resurrect memories of the perfection that had once existed and to supply a foretaste of the perfection that was to come. Thus the poet had no business aiming at the truth which could be discovered by the reason or the senses. His only duty was to supply some pleasure in a painful world and to stimulate hope of a return to paradise.

Paradise could not be enjoyed, however, unless there were memories of suffering. In Poe's economy of value, pleasure could be achieved only by paying for it with pain. Accordingly it was necessary for the mind, after death, to be cognizant of previous pain, even of the pain of the transitional stage between flesh and spirit. Monos recites the history of the world and of his own death to Una because the "memory of past sorrow" is the aliment of "present joy." The transition between the temporal and the eternal was not unrelieved anguish, however, for there was some pleasure as the soul effected its release from the body. The boundaries between the "organs of sense" were gradually erased, and the mind could delight in undifferentiated sensation. As the five senses became one with the decay of the body, a sixth sense, "all perfect," arose. This sixth sense was the sense of duration,[6] and it conferred a "wild delight" in which the understanding had no part. It "was the first obvious and certain step of the intemporal soul upon the threshold of the temporal eternity." Man's mind, after death, gradually became conscious of "entity," and his only feeling was that of duration. As the matter of the body decayed, the sense of *being* dominated the mind until the soul departed, and then for the body there remained only the sense of time and place—the grave.

Monos dwells upon the horrors of the grave because these memories are necessary for the enjoyment of immaterial existence. Monos and Una are perfectly happy in the "temporal eternity," but only because they are able to contrast their heavenly state with their antecedent earthly condition.

One striking thing about "The Colloquy" is that Monos experiences pleasure from the derangement of the senses, a condition most of us would regard as the threshold of madness. Yet we are aware that synaesthesia was exploited by the French symbolists and that Poe preceded them in suggesting that a deliberate derangement of the senses might be a source of pleasure. He once claimed that the orange ray of the spectrum affected him in the same way as the buzzing of a gnat.[7] Thus it would appear that he correlated one of the delights of poetry with the imagined process of transi-

[6] This should not be taken as an anticipation of Bergson's *durée*. Poe in his melancholy awareness of human limitations believed that we are aware of time only through events. "Marginalia," *Works*, XVI, 22. The experience of duration, or the sense of time as a quality, would have to be preceded by the decay of ordinary sense experience. The soul had to leave the body in order to experience pure quality; the sense of duration was the first step.

[7] *Ibid.*, 17–18.

tion between the temporal and the eternal. No longer limited by the organs, the mind could experience all sensation unitarily and eventually would sense duration. The poem, in a limited way, could duplicate this experience by coalescing sense impressions and by abstracting the mind from the "movements" by which we are aware of time.[8] The poem that successfully "excited" the soul would provide a brief escape from temporality into eternity.

By 1844 Poe was ready to describe in more specific terms the pantheism he had introduced in "The Island of the Fay." In the tale "Mesmeric Revelation" his strategy was to allow ultimate questions to be answered by a subject under hypnosis. Mesmerism, Poe thought, might free the mind from the bondage of the senses and exalt the reason so that unmediated cognition would be possible. So long as the mind was dependent on the senses, one could know only what the senses perceived and could deduce causes only by an examination of effects. The hypnotic trance was a "sleep-waking" condition in which the sensory apparatus was quiescent and vision or perfect cognition was possible.[9]

The subject of the mesmeric experiment, Mr. Vankirk, who suffers from phthisis, is fond of metaphysical speculation. He has read all of the "abstractions" of the philosophers but feels that abstractions take no hold on the mind and cannot induce belief. One cannot look upon qualities as things, so abstractions have no meaning to minds that know the world only through sense perception.

[8] For a psychological explanation of *synaesthesis*, see C. K. Ogden, I. A. Richards, and James Wood, *The Foundations of Aesthetics* (New York, 1922), 72–91. Poe's demand for totality presupposes the aesthetic state which Ogden, Richards and Wood called "equilibrium." As they explained it, "sets of impulses are felt in relation to other sets, which, unless both were already active in the equilibrium, would not occur." Perception is not limited to a single agency in such a condition, and "we are less dependent upon . . . particular impulses."

[9] The Fowler brothers, American phrenologists, accepted Poe's "Mesmeric Revelation" as scientific fact. See Madeleine Stern, "Poe: 'The Mental Temperament' for Phrenologists," *American Literature*, XL (1968), 162–63. Poe, however, claimed that the story was pure fiction. "Marginalia," *Works*, XVI, 71. Disguising his speculative thought as fiction was Poe's way of protecting himself against matter-of-fact critics, but his fondness for hoaxes may have had something to do with it.

The mind can know qualities only if they are experienced as directly as the senses experience phenomena. Free from its organic dependency, the mind can know itself. Accordingly, Mr. Vankirk asks to be put in a hypnotic trance, believing that in such a state he can attain "profound self-cognizance." Thus cognition of identity —Poe would say "of the soul"—can be achieved only when mind is not subservient to matter.

Once under hypnosis Vankirk answers questions about the nature of God and man and describes the state of immortality. He can answer such questions because the mind of man is part of the mind of God and in knowing itself also knows God. God exists, Vankirk reveals, as universal mind. This mind is not spirit, for spirit is an abstraction and hence nothing. God is but the "perfection of matter." Perfect matter is "unparticled," and permeates all things and impels all things. Thought is this matter in motion. Being unparticled, this matter is too rarefied to be perceived by the senses, but the mind can conceive it simply by extending the range of analogy from substances already known, from the least to the most rarefied. If atomic matter exists in a range of density, say, from metal to the "ether" of outer space, then by extrapolation we can assume a nonparticled matter, or a state of perfect unity. This nonatomic matter is what people ordinarily call spirit.

God exists as nonatomic matter, the creation as atomic matter. The thought of God is motion in the nonatomic matter, and this motion creates the material universe. Thus the entire universe in its unceasing motion is invested with the mind of God: "To create individual, thinking beings, it was necessary to incarnate portions of the divine mind. Thus man is individualized. Divested of corporate investiture, he were God. Now the particular motion of the incarnated portions of the unparticled matter is the thought of man; as the motion of the whole is that of God." Obviously Vankirk is able to "know" the mind of God because the hypnotic trance takes him outside of himself. He knows God because in the trance he *is* God.

Even after death man will have a body, Vankirk reveals, but it will no more resemble his "rudimental" earthly body than a worm resembles a butterfly. It was the design of God for man eventually to have a perfected life, but perfection was impossible so long as mind was subject to the conditions and laws of atomic matter. In the perfected life man would no longer have the organs of the body. Existing as mind, he would enjoy "nearly unlimited perception," knowing everything except the mystery of God's will. In the rudimentary life we know on earth, however, the "organs are the cages necessary to confine" our perceptions. Each organ has its assigned province or area of operation. Such is the natural constitution of the human mind.

In his rudimentary condition man had to obey physical laws, the laws of the material universe. In the "inorganic life" beyond the grave, there would be only one law, the "Divine Volition." Organic life—constituted of matter—acted as an impediment to the Divine Will, so, paradoxically, even God's will was hampered by the laws of his own creation—the laws of atomic matter. When God's will was impeded, as it was in the sensible universe, the result was "imperfection, wrong, positive pain." Thus Poe solved the problem of evil by asserting that it was the result of the resistance of matter to the will of God. Somewhat like Mary Baker Eddy, Poe regarded matter as error, but he did not believe that matter could be subservient to mind so long as mind existed in its "corporate investiture." Even God in his temporal manifestation had to obey the laws of the physical universe. These laws were necessary because through them the wrongness of matter was "rendered, to a certain extent, practicable."

In brief, Vankirk's revelation was that the life of what we call the spirit would be, eventually, perfection, but perfection was a negative state—"negative happiness." Positive happiness could be enjoyed only if it could be measured against misery. Imperfection was necessary before we could appreciate the perfect. "The pain of the primitive life of Earth, is the sole basis of the bliss of the ultimate life in Heaven." Pain merely provided the variety in God's otherwise monotonous existence.

That Poe intended the metaphysics of his fiction to be taken seriously is indicated by his letter to James Russell Lowell in July of 1844.[10] In this letter Poe summarized the revelations of Van-kirk but prefaced them with conclusions that denied progress and perfectibility:

> I have no faith in human perfectibility. I think that human exertion will have no appreciable effect upon humanity. Man is now only more active—not more happy—nor more wise, than he was 6000 years ago. The result will never vary—and to suppose that it will, is to suppose that the foregone man has lived in vain—that the foregone time is but a rudiment of the future—and that the myriads who have perished have not been upon equal footing with ourselves—nor are we with our posterity. I cannot agree to lose sight of man the individual, in man the mass.

It is easy to connect these conclusions with Poe's speculation. If every soul, or mind, is a portion of the mind of God in "corporate investiture," all souls must be on an "equal footing." Yet perfection cannot be achieved because it is the result of the free operation of the Divine Volition, and the Divine Volition is impeded by matter. Each individual must be considered separately because identity is conferred by the body. Although Poe, like Emerson and Whitman, could conceive of a sort of cosmic democracy because the mind of God was in everything, he differed in his interpretation of natural law. Emerson could acknowledge that man was subject to the "law of things," but he could envision mind as being superior to "Fate." Whitman, while proclaiming that the body was equal to the soul, exulted in the perfection of the laws of nature and in his "cosmic consciousness" was prone to see pain and evil diminishing through the process of emergent evolution.

In *Eureka* Poe too gave evidence that evolution might be God's way of moving man *toward* perfection, but there was no perfection in matter, and the laws of matter were merely necessary and expedient, making organic life possible or, as he put it, "practicable." [11] The very existence of matter as a "cage" for the spirit was

---

[10] *Letters*, I, 256–57. A portion of this letter also appears in a letter to Thomas Holley Chivers, July 10, 1845, *ibid.*, 260.

[11] For an illuminating discussion of Poe's evolutionary theory against the background of current scientific thought, see Frederick Conner, "Poe's

a limiting factor. Man, like all the other creatures of the universe, was subject to the laws of matter. Man might progress in knowledge of the natural laws, but he could not progress in wisdom, for wisdom meant the mind's perfect comprehension of itself. Above all man could not progress in happiness so long as he possessed a body tributary to the pain and frustration that were necessary conditions in the organic life. They were part of the Divine Plan. Otherwise the joy of immaterial existence would be unrecognized.

Neither God nor man could call back a thought, Poe claimed in "Mesmeric Revelation." It was the nature of thought to be irrevocable. God's thought was creative, and once it had created material forms, these forms would remain the same until the metamorphosis of death. Poe could not imagine God as having afterthoughts and then interfering with his plan. Consequently he did not temporalize the Chain of Being. The law of gradation was the law of nature, and however man might seek to alter his physical environment, this law would prevail. Attempts to evade the law, as he claimed in "The Colloquy of Monos and Una," would merely increase the wrongness of man's temporal condition. Emerson and Whitman could celebrate the perfection of the Divine Plan, but Poe saw imperfection structured into the universe as part of the plan. In man's flawed condition only intuitive glimpses of the inorganic life beyond the grave could provide hope of perfect happiness. These glimpses were provided by the artist's imagination, and the end of art was properly pleasure. Neither practical knowledge nor exemplary conduct could bring happiness. Only the hope of perfect awareness unimpeded by the brutish atomic constitution of our physical bodies might alleviate our present pain. Therefore the artist, more than the priest and more than the philosopher, was God's agent, for he brought us the beauty of the idea, not pure, not perfect, but as nearly perfect as the human condition would allow.

Poe's last attempt to formulate a consistent theory of the universe that would correlate with his aesthetics came toward the end of his life in what he called a poem, even though it was in prose. In

Eureka: The Problem of Mechanism," *Cosmic Optimism* (Gainesville, 1949), 67–91.

the preface to *Eureka* Poe made his final apology for art, in which
he intimated that only what was beautiful was true:

> To the few who love me and whom I love—to those who feel
> rather than to those who think—to the dreamers and those who
> put faith in dreams as in the only realities—I offer this Book of
> Truths, not in its character of Truth-Teller, but for the Beauty
> that abounds in its Truth; constituting it true. To these I present
> the composition as an Art-Product alone:—let us say as a Romance;
> or, if I be not urging too lofty a claim, as a Poem.
>
> *What I here propound is true:*—therefore it cannot die:—or if
> by any means it be now trodden down so that it die, it will "rise
> again to the Life Everlasting."
>
> Nevertheless it is as a Poem only that I wish this work to be
> judged after I am dead.[12]

By claiming that his prose treatise was a "Romance" or a
"Poem," Poe discarded all of his previous limitations of poetic
form. In a sense he abdicated as a critic, for if he wanted *Eureka* to
be judged as a poem, all of the criteria he had elaborated during
fourteen years as a practicing critic would have to be disallowed.
Most of *Eureka* is concerned with "scientific" proof of Poe's hy-
potheses; there is no unity of tone—the beginning is satirical, the
middle is scientifically objective, and the end is ecstatic. Thus, by
Poe's usual standards, unity of effect would be lost, particularly the
totality of effect derived from the single sitting.

The only concession Poe made to his previous position as a critic
was his affirmation that the beauty of his system made it true. Why
should his system be regarded as both beautiful and true? Because
"a perfect consistency can be nothing but an absolute truth," [13]
and apparently a perfect consistency had to be beautiful. The
beauty would be the beauty of design, the pattern discernible in
chaos, or, as Henry James put it, the figure in the carpet. Poe could
claim that *Eureka* was an art-product because he had imagined a
cosmogony. He could consider it true because he had "proved" the
consistency of his theory by Newtonian physics. Thus he was able
to associate himself by implication with Johannes Kepler. Kepler

[12] *Works*, XVI, 184.   [13] *Ibid.*, 196.

"guessed" the "three omniprevalent laws of revolution," but the truth of his guess was "subsequently demonstrated and accounted for by the patient and mathematical Newton." [14]

It seems that Poe was now equating the poetic imagination with the scientific imagination. Already he had stated that the imaginative mind worked by the perception of analogies; now he assumed that it also had the power of extrapolation, or the ability to project or extend known data into a conjectural knowledge of the unknown. In his romantic youth he had deplored science as the agent which had replaced his dream with dull realities; now he applauded science because the increase of scientific knowledge extended the range of analogies open to the poetic imagination. Yet Poe still considered himself to be avoiding the "Cloud-Land of Metaphysics." [15] To him metaphysics was deductive reasoning based upon a priori assumptions—self-evident truths—but he believed that *"no* truths are *self*-evident." Nor did he consider his method inductive, for induction consisted only in the examination of phenomena to develop general laws.[16] The only way science had advanced was by intuitive leaps from the already known, by "guesses." The ability of the scientist to proceed from the known to the unknown on the basis of an assumption of continuity or regularity was to Poe true evidence of the imagination. The poet or scientist started with empirical data and then launched his mind on a journey into the unknown, "intuitively" certain that one system prevailed throughout the universe. If a perfect consistency could be discovered, it had to be the absolute truth, and this truth would be susceptible of mathematical demonstration.

Poe had at last reached the point where truth and beauty became one. Beauty was the design of the universe itself, wherein each atom surged into being with the thought of God, diffusing outward from the center "in furtherance of the ultimate design— *that of the utmost possible Relation,"* until full heterogeneity would be realized. The diffusive energy, or repulsion, was the

[14] *Ibid.,* 279.
[15] *Ibid.,* 261. See also "A Chapter of Suggestions," *ibid.,* XIV, 191–92.
[16] *Ibid.,* XVI, 188–89.

thought of God, which created the universe. The gravitational attraction, or the tendency to return to unity, was the characteristic of matter. "No other principles exist." The only way in which matter could be "manifested to Mind" was by its properties of attraction and repulsion. The natural tendency of matter to draw together into one was the physical law; the tendency of mind to shape matter into an inconceivable variety of forms was the spiritual principle. The universe, then, represented a balance of two principles, the law of mind and the law of matter, and thus it would remain until the volition of God should be withdrawn. Then all atoms would draw together into the *ur*-stuff, the primal particle. Its property of resistance to mind would no longer be operative, and mind would recognize it no longer. Nothing would be left but mind, or unparticled matter, and the laws of the physical universe would rule no more. The beauty of the universe was the beauty of the plan—the utmost conceivable variety of parts held together in a unitary system. Consequently, the old aesthetic formula that beauty was unity in variety described the universe as an aesthetic object. In it there was "an absolute reciprocity of adaptation," in which cause and effect were indistinguishable from each other. Only the universe showed a perfect organic relationship, part being related to part and every part being related to the whole, and all in accordance with the purpose of God. The universe was a perfect plot. There were no "interposed incidents external and foreign to the main subject"; all events sprang out of the "bosom of the thesis," and every particle existed in terms of the preconceived end. "The plots of God are perfect. The Universe is a plot of God." [17]

What was man's destiny in the plot of God? The individual mind was but a portion of the mind of God, incarnated in matter. Dreams, visions, experiences during "sleep-waking" or hypnotic trances were true because in such experiences the mind freed itself from its organic cage and knew itself as the mind of God. All of God's creatures possessed "more or less conscious" intelligence. They were conscious first of their mortal identity and next, "by faint indeterminate glimpses," of an identity with God. As God's

[17] *Ibid.*, 292.

plan fulfilled itself temporally, the consciousness of mortal identity would grow weaker and the consciousness of an identity with God would grow stronger until individuality would be lost and the collective consciousness of the universe would once more be the mind of God. "In the meantime bear in mind that all is Life—Life—Life within Life—the less within the greater, and all within the Spirit Divine." [18]

At last Poe had returned to the pantheism of "The Island of the Fay." No longer did he think that the perfect plot of the universe was designed to promote the happiness of God's creatures. God became a hedonist who wished only to promote his own pleasure, and it was possible for him to do this only by varying the nature of his existence. The universe represented God's "expansive" existence, and He "feels his life through an infinity of imperfect pleasures—the partial and pain-intertangled pleasures of those inconceivably numerous things which you designate as his creatures, but which are really but infinite individualizations of Himself." When God withdrew his volition—the repulsive force that caused the *ur*-stuff of the universe to radiate from the center—then God would resume his "concentrated" life as One, his existence as pure mind. God passed all eternity "in perpetual variation of Concentrated Self and almost Infinite Self-Diffusion." [19] The plot of God was solely for the purpose of giving him pleasure.

2

It is beside the point to debate whether or not Poe intended his cosmogony to be taken as truth. Its beauty, as he had claimed in his preface, was in its consistency. His intuition of the nature of God and the universe was a "romance" that made use of the laws of physics as he understood them. This was enough. Nevertheless, he was disturbed when he lectured on the subject and found that his audience misunderstood him. Patiently he undertook to simplify his system to one of his correspondents,[20] and he defended himself

[18] *Ibid.*, 315.   [19] *Ibid.*, 314.
[20] Poe to George W. Eveleth, February 29, 1848, in *Letters*, II, 360–62.

in a letter to Charles Fenno Hoffman, editor of the *Literary World*.[21] Poe hedged a bit in saying he had not meant to ridicule the Aristotelian or Baconian modes of reasoning; he merely wished to defend intuition as "a conviction arising from those *inductions* or *deductions* of which the processes are so shadowy as to escape our consciousness, elude our reason, or defy our capacity for expression." He went on to claim that he did not mean to assert that "each soul is its own God—its own Creator," but that "each soul is, *in part*, its own God—its own Creator." Poe knew quite well that he could be called "a pantheist, a polytheist, a Pagan, or a God knows what," but he professed not to care unless someone dubbed him "a Student of Theology." It was a student of theology who had challenged him in the pages of the *Literary World*.

Obviously Poe's audience did not take him at his word. They could not consider *Eureka* as a poem or a romance which was beautiful because it was consistent and true because it was beautiful. Poe had made God into an artist, and America would accept Him only as a moral judge. America was not ready for religion to be turned into an aesthetic exercise. The question before us in this study, however, is not Poe's capacity for metaphysical speculation but the correlation between his metaphysics and his teleology of art.[22]

Poe proposed that God was an artist and that the universe existed as a perfect plot designed for God's pleasure. Therefore the divine principle, insofar as it was exhibited in God's incarnation, was aesthetic pleasure. Man was serving God's purpose when he worked as an artist insofar as he made beauty his end. The artist-God enjoyed beauty more than anything else, so the sum total of all the pleasure men took in beauty was the pleasure of God in his expansive existence.

The artist-God also took pleasure in creativity and his thought was creative, resulting in the utmost multiplicity of form. Yet cre-

---

[21] September 20, 1848, *ibid.*, 379–82.
[22] On this topic see Davidson, *Poe: A Critical Study*, 223–53; and Carol H. Maddison, "Poe's *Eureka*," *Texas Studies in Literature and Language*, II (1960), 350–67.

ativity was limited after the incarnation because the mind in its mortal cage could not think things into being. It had to confine itself to the manipulation of the already created elements of the universe, making new combinations of them in imitation of the symmetry and harmony of the system. On the other hand, direct imitation of the objects themselves was not creative, because God had already thought them into being precisely the way they should be. All things existed in a perfect reciprocity of adaptation, and since it was the nature of God's thought to be irrevocable, he would not "re-think" the universe. In his human incarnation, the most the artist-God could do was strive to make his art "ideal." The artist's mind could not overcome the resistance of matter, but he could idealize it, that is, adapt it to thought. Hence all art should spring, as Poe had said in his review of Drake and Halleck, "*apparently* . . . from the brain of the poet." If the artist merely imitated the sights and sounds that were common to all mankind, Poe claimed in "The Poetic Principle," he would "fail to prove his divine title."

The divine principle in man, which Poe located chiefly in the aesthetic sense, had nothing to do with the truth that came from an exercise of the practical reason. This truth was merely expedient, for it dealt with man's use of nature. In fact, the reason was highly limited in its application, for the great discoveries, both in science and in poetry, had come from intuition. Truth could serve the aesthetic sense, Poe said in "The Poetic Principle," only if "through the attainment of a truth we are led to perceive a harmony where none was apparent before." If we learn something about the nature of God's perfect plot through the attainment of truth, then the aesthetic sense could be served indirectly, but generally speaking the practical reason was the agent of utility. Poe believed that science served the artist by extending the "range of analogy," by which he meant the correspondences that signified a unitary system. In other words, the more the artist knew about the harmony of the Great Design, the more effectively he could plan his microcosmic work of art in accordance with the laws of nature.

However, the work of art itself could not serve science because it was a fiction. The reason, then, could be pressed into the service of art for planning and a posteriori analysis, but art itself could not be utilitarian.

The third mental faculty Poe cited in "The Poetic Principle" was the moral sense. He admitted that there was a long and authoritative tradition, beginning with Aristotle, that associated beauty and virtue. Virtue was beautiful, but the moral sense or conscience in its cognitive function recognized virtue only in terms of duty, whereas the taste or aesthetic sense recognized virtue in terms of beauty. It is clear, then, that Poe's teleology of art was grounded upon a rudimentary epistemology which in turn developed out of the faculty psychology which limited the various modes of cognition. In Poe's thinking, we have an intuitive knowledge of our duty because we have an inner sense called the conscience. We arrive at the truth through an exercise of the practical reason. We feel or intuit beauty because we have an inner sense called the taste. Each faculty is related to the other two in one way or another, but the office or function of each faculty is clearly marked, and each provides a different kind of knowledge.

In the interest of cognitive efficiency, and Poe would be nothing if not efficient, the three different modes of knowledge should be observed in any form of communication. Those aspects of a poem which appealed to the aesthetic sense—meter, metaphor, and rhyme—simply got in the way of the communication of truth. Poe assumed that poetry was at least a way of knowing, but he could not consider it a better way of communicating knowledge than prose. When truth was the object, poetry was inefficient. Similarly, poetry was less efficient than a sermon in appealing to the conscience.

It is obvious that Poe was trying to demonstrate to a utilitarian age and to an audience concerned with practicality that it was more practical to assign each faculty its own province than it was to promote a confusion of purpose. His strategy was based upon his pessimistic assumption that his American audience, accustomed to impure art which justified itself by teaching or preaching, would never disallow these functions unless it could be proved "scientifically" that art was ineffective in its appeal to the reason and the moral sense. The poet-priest, as Poe intimated in "The Colloquy of Monos and Una," had been displaced by the "rough pedants" in the public esteem and would never be able to assume his rightful role unless the public could be persuaded of two things: (1) that the way of knowing that poetry represented contributed a pleasure that could not be experienced in any other way, and (2) that this pleasure was divine in origin and formative in its moral effect. Poe's philosophy of art was thus intended to persuade the public that aesthetic pleasure allowed us to know God in his purest aspect, that of creator or artist, and that other cognitive modes were merely expedients which allowed man to cope with the contingencies of his organic or rudimentary life. The reason enabled us to deal with the world about us. The moral sense served as a guide to behavior, and benevolent behavior was necessary for society. The sense of beauty, however, enabled us to know a God who created the universe as a work of art. Like Jonathan Edwards, Poe reveled in the beauty of the creation and saw earthly beauty as a shadow of the divine; but unlike the worthy Puritan he could not conceive of a God of judgment who would endow each man with a divine soul that yearned for celestial beauty and then arbitrarily cast most of these divine souls into the hideousness of hell. To Poe, existence itself was hell enough, and the divine pleasure which could momentarily alleviate the pain of existence could come only from the artist, who would prove his divine title by adapting the given, the raw materials of art, to the limitations of man's cognitive apparatus in such a way that the pleasure would be as pure as possible. To do this the artist had to be relieved of the burden of truth. Truth enabled us to get along in the world, but it had little to do with our apprehension of the beauty of the creation. This beauty could only be felt, and it was the artist's duty to make us feel it. This was Poe's message in "The Poetic Principle," and it was the summation of his teleology of art.

3

In his role as a practical critic Poe was fond of asserting that inspiration or intuition had no part in the composition or construction of a work of art, yet unless we understand his cosmogony we are likely to conclude that he was perversely contradicting his statements that imagination was the "soul" of poetry and that the artist was a visionary who strove to express his own dreams. Yet by reducing God to the limitations of the physical universe, Poe removed him as a source of inspiration. Poe's artist, unlike Emerson's, was not the passive servant of the Oversoul, because there *was* no Oversoul. In Poe's system there was no consciousness greater than the mind of man. Nature represented God extended in the unconscious or partly conscious, and the presence of God's thought in nature was recognizable by the mind only as the laws of motion. The life of God in his "expanded" existence was only the life of his creatures and was subject to the same limitations. Vision came as a "memory" of the unparticled existence of God before his incarnation. But since such vision was already "there" in the mind—it came to the surface in trance or in what Poe called the "sleep-waking" condition—it had nothing to do with the process of composition. It merely provided an intuition of perfect harmony, or rather a *memory* of a condition in which God's volition was unimpeded by matter. Fragmented and caged within material organs, God as man could not create by merely thinking things into existence. He had to work with the given. As Poe said in his "Marginalia" and again in *Eureka*, in "human constructions a particular cause has a particular effect; a particular intention brings to pass a particular object." The poetical instinct of man was the "instinct of the symmetrical," [23] but in achieving the symmetrical the human artist had to employ the principles of causation in order to fulfill his creative intention.

Composition was a deliberate process. The artist had an intui-

[23] *Eureka*, in *Works*, XVI, 302.

tion of perfect symmetry. This intuition sprang from the soul, or the indwelling divinity, but, as Poe stated in the "Marginalia," there was a difference between the capacity to be a visionary and the capacity to produce a work of art. There were many geniuses, but few works of genius. Genius, as Poe saw it, simply represented a superior consciousness or sensibility—a superior capacity to appreciate.

> But the person appreciating may be utterly incompetent to reproduce the work, or any thing similar, and this solely through lack of what may be termed the constructive ability—a matter quite independent of what we agree to understand in the term "genius" itself. This ability is based, to be sure, in great part, upon the faculty of analysis, enabling the artist to get full view of the machinery of his proposed effect, and thus work it and regulate it at will; but a great deal depends also upon properties strictly moral—for example, upon patience, upon concentrativeness, or the power of holding the attention steadily to the one purpose, upon self-dependence and contempt for all opinion which is opinion and no more—in especial, upon energy or industry. So vitally important is this last, that it may well be doubted if any thing to which we have been accustomed to give the title of a "work of genius" was ever accomplished without it; and it is chiefly because this quality and genius are nearly incompatible, that "works of genius" are few, while mere men of genius are, as I say, abundant.[24]

Often it appears that Poe agreed with Emerson and the other transcendentalists that genius was the divine element in man. Where he differed was in his concept of divinity. Poe's artist-God was creative when he thought the universe into being, but after his incarnation into the universe he became a mere aesthete, enjoying the variety of his expansive existence. He did not exist as a source of inspiration outside of the human mind, and the human mind itself was subject to the mechanical laws of the universe. The human body, like all material objects, was a mechanism. Its machinery provided sensations to the mind, and the mind knew the external

[24] "Marginalia," *Works*, XVI, 67.

world only through sensations. Vibrations moving through the nervous system to the brain provided our only knowledge of the world without. A superior consciousness could be intuitively aware of the symmetry of the whole by its "poetic instinct," but this awareness could not be communicated to the duller consciousness except as an emotional effect. Vision could not be communicated, only the effect of vision, the feeling that attended the "memory" of unparticled existence. The transmission of feeling, however, was subject to the laws of matter, or, in this case, the psychological laws that governed man's perception in his organic life. Accordingly, analysis took over where vision failed, and the ability of the artist "to get full view of the machinery of his proposed effect" was necessary for him to produce a work of genius. He had to have a firm grasp of his intention, he had to know the machinery of the human brain, and he had to have the self-discipline to enforce his will. Thus only by a conscious, willed organization of the raw materials of art could the artist transmit to the dull sensibilities of the mass audience something of the emotional effect he had experienced when his "divine soul" had disengaged itself from its fleshly cage and remembered the perfect unity and harmony of the "immaterial" or "concentrated" life of God. The genius should not attempt to give to an audience what they could experience for themselves, the sensations of phenomena. His proper duty was to give them what they could not experience unaided, the feeling attendant upon the intuition of symmetry. The work of art was a microcosm, but it could not possess the fullness or variety of creation; it could only present a minute totality by organizing percepts and concepts to create a unified impression.

In the light of Poe's metaphysics it is not surprising that he was more concerned with compositional method than he was with interpretation. Many of his book reviews are commentaries on method, but since these have already been discussed, the concluding chapter of this study will be limited to those essays in which Poe attempted to demonstrate how the artist could impress the less sensitive minds of the common run of humanity. It was the artist's divine function to adapt the materials of art to the receptive capacity of the mass audience. In such a way he mediated between the expansive existence and the concentrated existence of God, serving God by providing aesthetic pleasure, the "excitement of the soul" that was a foretaste of the "glory beyond the grave."

XVIII · The Plots of Man

IF the universe as a whole was the perfect plot of God, the great question, as Poe saw it, had to do with how the human artist, hampered by the resistance of matter to thought, could create microcosms that would reflect something of the perfection of the whole and thereby give a temporal experience of divine pleasure. Frequently in his book reviews and in the "Marginalia," Poe had described the pleasure that attended the recognition of artistic design. He had said that perfection of plot was a "rigidly artistic merit" to be appreciated only by the sophisticate. In his view a perfect design was not even desirable in those genres which based their appeal upon the imitation of life—the novel and the drama. Going still further in *Eureka*, he stated that perfection of plot was impossible in "human constructions": "The pleasure which we derive from any display of human ingenuity is in the ratio of the *approach* to this species of reciprocity. In the construction of *plot*, for example, in fictitious literature, we should aim at so arranging the incidents that we shall not be able to determine, of any one of them, whether it depends from any one other or upholds it. In this sense, of course, *perfection* of *plot* is really, or practically unattainable— but only because it is a finite intelligence that constructs." [1] Plot construction, then, was not an instinctive process but the ordering act of the intelligence limited on the human level by the resistance of matter to thought. The predicament of the human artist was that the desire for perfect order, which the God in him knew was "right," would always be frustrated. Objects did not yield themselves readily to the metamorphosis which the artist wished to impose.

A practical solution to this problem was for the artist to represent, not the objects themselves, but the ideas and feelings the objects inspired. A "finite intelligence" could not transfer a sensa-

[1] *Eureka*, in *Works*, XVI, 292.

tion from one mind to another without duplicating sensory stimuli, which was impossible. Therefore he should endeavor to arouse the effect of the stimuli without attempting some crude approximation of sensory experience in words. Poe knew, as many of his generation did not, that an artistic experience could never be an equivalent of sensory experience. The traditional psychology had taught him that sensations were vivid and that ideas were shadowy and indefinite. But whereas Locke's psychology had impelled some writers to try to increase the vividness of their work by the use of concrete imagery, Poe, with his dedication to efficiency, refused to permit the artist to attempt the duplication of sense experience. Truth in description was impossible, even in sculpture, the most imitative of the arts. Therefore it should not be attempted.

If nature could not be duplicated by human art, the only way the artist could create microcosms would be by composition, or the arrangement of the raw material of art in a preconceived design, knowing in advance that his design must be limited by the ability of other minds to take it in. Poe's clearest description of the artist's role in adapting the raw materials of nature to the finite intelligence appears, strangely enough, in two essays upon the principles of landscape gardening. The first of these, "The Landscape Garden," was published in 1842 but was expanded and printed as "The Domain of Arnheim" in 1847. That Poe took landscape gardening as a fine art was indicated by his statement in "The Poetic Principle" that the poetic sentiment could "develop itself in various modes—in Painting, in Sculpture, in Architecture, in the Dance—very especially in Music—and very peculiarly, and with a wide field, in the composition of the Landscape Garden."

Although it is usually classified among Poe's tales, "The Landscape Garden" is really a dissertation upon the imitation of nature in the fine arts. In his literary criticism Poe had denied that an artist should attempt to imitate nature directly, and he employed the same principle for the gardening art. Accordingly, he disparaged what his contemporaries called the natural garden, which was supposed to duplicate the "wilderness" of nature, and described the art as an effort to improve the composition of the landscape. Poe's landscape gardener, Ellison, achieves happiness by constructing a garden that adapts nature to the finite intelligence by arranging it in an order that can be taken in by the human mind.

Before constructing his garden Ellison finds it necessary to distinguish between nature and art. He concludes that nature does not give us complete aesthetic satisfaction because of the limits of our perception. To "angels," unlimited by the organs of sense, the "great landscape garden of the whole earth" might appear to be perfection, but men are not angels, and it is the duty of the mortal artist to adapt the natural scene "to the eyes which were to behold it on earth." Only in such a way can Ellison succeed in the "fulfillment of his destiny as Poet." [2]

Poe carried the speculation of Ellison a step further in "The Domain of Arnheim" by giving a teleological explanation of the "apparent" deformities of nature. He also restated the principles of the gardening art and illustrated the principles by giving a description of Ellison's perfect garden.

It must have been the original intention of God, the narrator surmises, to have "so arranged the earth's surface as to have fulfilled at all points man's sense of perfection in the beautiful, the sublime, or the picturesque," but "geological disturbances" had altered form and color grouping. Yet to admit that natural occurrences could frustrate the intention of the God who created nature would be absurd, so Ellison suggests that the apparent imperfection of nature is the sign of mortality—"prognostic of death." The earthly immortality of man was God's first intention, and the "primitive arrangement of the earth's surface had been adapted to his blissful estate, as not existent but designed." The disturbances, then, "were the preparations for his subsequently conceived deathful condition." [3] Thus Poe's God had changed his mind. Ellison does not mention the Fall in the Garden, but it is obvious that Poe was still using the myth of the Fall as he had in "The Colloquy of Monos and Una." Paradise was behind and ahead. The art of the

[2] "The Landscape Garden," *Works*, IV, 265–71.
[3] "The Domain of Arnheim," *Works*, VI, 184.

Creator could still be recognized in the universe as a whole, but it was "apparent to reflection only." It lacked immediacy of effect, just as the design of an overly complex drama or an overly long poem could be discovered only by analysis, not by an immediate intuition of the whole. Only in landscape gardening, Poe claimed, could nature be improved, and then only by composition:

No such paradises are to be found in reality as have glowed on the canvas of Claude. In the most enchanting of natural landscapes, there will always be found a defect or an excess—many excesses and defects. While the component parts may defy, individually, the highest skill of the artist, the arrangement of these parts will always be susceptible of improvement. In short, no position can be attained on the wide surface of the *natural* earth, from which an artistical eye, looking steadily, will not find matter of offence in what is termed the "composition" of the landscape. And yet how unintelligible is this! In all other matters we are justly instructed to regard nature as supreme. With her details we shrink from competition. Who shall presume to imitate the colors of the tulip, or to improve the proportions of the lily of the valley? The criticism which says, of sculpture or portraiture, that here nature is to be exalted or idealized, rather than imitated, is in error. No pictorial or sculptural combinations of points of human loveliness do more than approach the living and breathing beauty. In landscape alone is the principle of the critic true; and, having felt its truth here, it is but the headlong spirit of generalization which has led him to pronounce it true throughout all the domains of art. Having, I say, *felt* its truth here; for the feeling is no affectation or chimera. The mathematics afford no more absolute demonstrations than the sentiment of his art yields the artist. He not only believes, but positively knows, that such and such apparently arbitrary arrangements of matter constitute and alone constitute the true beauty. . . . Let a "composition" be defective; let an emendation be wrought in its mere arrangement of form; let this emendation be submitted to every artist in the world; by each will its necessity be admitted. And even far more than this:—in remedy of the defective composition, each insulated member of the fraternity would have suggested the identical emendation.[4]

[4] *Ibid.*, 182–83.

This quotation reveals both Poe's strength and his weakness as a theorist. He was aware, as every landscape painter is, that the beauty of nature lacked composition. Furthermore he was aware that the experience of an art object was different from the experience of the "living and breathing beauty," so that the true beauty of art—that which appealed to the "fraternity" of the artists—was in the artistry itself, the "apparently arbitrary arrangements of matter." His mistake, as has been emphasized in this study, lay in his assumption that a highly developed taste was infallible. The sense of beauty, Poe thought, would recognize an error in design as easily as normal eyesight would distinguish between white and black. Therefore all true artists would see the same errors and suggest the same corrections. This is perhaps the reason why Poe was so deeply pained when his own attempts to point out errors were greeted with charges of personal bias and ill temper. No one had the right to make moral judgments of a critic who described errors and suggested corrections any more than one should make a moral judgment of a mathematician who demonstrated that two and two were not five.

As for the improvement of nature by art, the only way nature could be improved was by "arrangement." The details of nature could not be improved; they could only be imitated, and even then the imitation would be imperfect. Imitative arts were at best only poor substitutes for nature. Yet since physical loveliness appealed to all mankind, the landscape garden, or the composition of nature in an art form, would have a wide appeal. Ellison, the "poet of the landscape," undertakes to supply a design and to infuse this design with a meaning that will be transmitted by the association of ideas. His design is so vast "as to convey the sentiment of spiritual interference," as if the "Almighty design" were "one step depressed" and "brought into something like harmony or consistency with the sense of human art . . . ." The garden must "assume the air of an intermediate or secondary nature—a nature which is not God, nor an emanation of God, but which still is nature in the sense of the handiwork of the angels that hover between man and God." [5]

[5] *Ibid.*, 187–88.

In 1847 as in 1842, Poe envisioned the possibility of an earthly paradise created by the human artist and adapted to mortal limitations; but before this vision could be realized the artist would have to be given power. Even in a fallen world, a poet could recover some of the joys of the lost paradise. He could develop a composition neither too great nor too complex for the human mind to grasp as a whole and yet great enough so that his art would seem to the uninitiated to be supernatural in origin. Allen Tate has described perceptively Poe's concept of the angelic imagination, but he overlooked the pessimism with which Poe surveyed the possibility of angelic creativity. Happiness might be possible on earth, Poe admitted, if a sensitive and imaginative person were given health, love, "contempt of ambition," and an object of unceasing pursuit. Furthermore, he would have to have freedom from distraction. Ellison, the landscape poet, has such freedom only because of his four hundred and fifty million dollar inheritance. In a materialistic culture, the only power available to the poet was the power of money. Given the resources, the poet could do something about the alienation of man from God by re-ordering nature in an approximation of the beauty of the Great Design. His work would *seem* to be a product of the angelic imagination to ordinary eyes. All great art seems miraculous to the naïve, but to the sophisticated even the greatest work of art would give evidence of its human construction. The paradise of Arnheim would be constructed by the conscious intelligence employing thoroughly mundane principles of craftsmanship.

It is interesting to note Poe's conditions for mastery of art: good health, leisure, and money. How much these requirements reflected his own situation of having to do journalistic hackwork under conditions of psychic and physical misery is open to conjecture. Yet it is certain that he thought the artist could be and should be the master of his means. Even vision could be controlled and manipulated into expression, Poe thought, provided that the visionary were in a favorable mental and physical condition.[6] Great

[6] Cf. "Marginalia," *Works*, XVI, 88–89. Poe described his ecstatic fancies as "a glimpse of the spirit's outer world" and went on to say that he had

art did not spring from neurotic compulsion but was the end product of a balanced mind, with the intellectual faculties guiding and controlling the urgencies of expression.[7] This view explains Poe's objection to Hood's hypochondria; he claimed to have caught the intimation of the "death's head" in Hood's attempts to convey the comic. For all of his own fictional accounts of neurosis, Poe's theory of composition demanded the *mens sana in corpore sano.* Compulsion, whether from the divine madness of inspiration or from the agony within, had to yield to the control of the artistic will.

2

The poet of the landscape was limited to the materials of the physical universe and had to arrange these materials so as to suggest ideas. The poet of words, however, could use ideas directly because words appealed to the mind and were ineffective in conveying sense impressions. Words could evoke mental states, in Poe's psychology of art, without referring to the flux of phenomena that assaulted the external senses. A "made-up" landscape would evoke feeling better than a description of a natural one because such a description, however specific in detail, would be inferior to an imag-

---

conducted experiments to control the condition of these fancies so that he could make them occur at will: "I mean to say . . . that now I can be sure, when all circumstances are favorable, of the supervention of the condition, and feel even the capacity of inducing or compelling it . . . ." If the vision was experienced, it could be communicated: "Now, so entire is my faith in the *power of words,* that, at times, I have believed it possible to embody even the evanescence of fancies such as I have attempted to describe."

[7] Cf. "Fifty Suggestions," *Works,* XIV, 175–78. One flaw that Poe found in the artistic genius has to do with his sensitivity. He has an exquisite sense of beauty and will be depressed by the "deformities" of the world about him. As a consequence he will frequently lack motivation: "Give to genius a sufficiently enduring *motive,* and the result will be harmony, proportion, beauty, perfection . . . synonymous terms." "Marginalia," *Works,* XVI, 121. However, such enduring motivation "has . . . fallen *rarely* to the lot of genius." Poe's landscape gardener, Ellison, illustrates a genius with an enduring motive.

ined composition in which all elements would combine to create a total effect, an effect never found in the experience of nature. Accordingly, it was appropriate that Poe's essay on method, "The Philosophy of Composition," should begin with a consideration of effect.

Poe's most complete account of the "preconceived design" had been given in his review of Hawthorne's *Twice-Told Tales;* he merely applied to the narrative poem the principles he had previously advanced for the short tale. The fact that he began his exposition of how he wrote "The Raven" with a summary of his principle of plot development indicates that his essay is what he called it, the "philosophy" of composition, "philosophy" being understood here in one of its secondary meanings as a theory underlying a particular activity. "Nothing is more clear," Poe wrote, "than that every plot, worth the name, must be elaborated to its *dénouement* before anything be attempted with the pen," for, he continued, "it is only with the *dénouement* constantly in view that we can give a plot its indispensable air of . . . causation, by making the incidents, and especially the tone at all points, tend to the development of the intention." Every element should contribute to the development of the intention, for only by such a total organization could the artist succeed in conveying a unified impression. Obviously Poe did not regard the writing of a poem as a process of discovery. His mechanistic view of the intellect presupposed a mechanistic method, and the author of a narrative poem, like a builder, had to have a blueprint in advance before he could put together members that would support each other. Poe's artist was both architect and builder. The poetic faculty—the capacity for feeling beauty—had to be implemented by a knowledge of the means of transmitting this feeling to others before a poet could count on the appropriate response. Without such knowledge, he would evoke the response only by accident. Poe proposed to demonstrate that in a *good* poem nothing happened by accident: "It is my design to render it manifest that no one point in its composition is referable either to accident or intuition—that the work proceeded step by step, to its completion, with the precision and rigid consequence of a mathematical problem." The plotting of a poem had to proceed in terms of cause and effect, and a causal relationship among parts could exist only when the poet knew in advance what he wanted to do. As Poe had said in his criticism of the drama, undue complexity of plot was frequently the result of afterthoughts which modified the preconceived design. The human artist, like the divine, should not have afterthoughts, for such afterthoughts would be likely to make the design inconsistent. Inconsistency of design, like a mistake in mathematics, would indicate the incompetence of the designer.

If Poe's mechanistic theory seems absurd in the light of our knowledge of the part the unconscious mind plays in composition, we should remember that Poe, throughout most of his career and particularly during the period between 1842 and 1846, was attempting to refute the idea that artistic genius and skill were incompatible. Thus, as he always did in his literary campaigns, he tended to overstate and to underline. His qualifications, when he was willing to make them, existed in the context of his evaluative judgments, not in his theoretical statements. Thus he was able to praise Dickens for having genius that made the rules, but at the same time he pointed out instances wherein superior skill could have saved Dickens from errors. He had claimed that Shelley's soul was law, but he deplored Shelley's tendency to write only to himself.[8] To record the experience of vision solely for oneself was quite different from the process of transferring the emotional effect of the vision to the "unvisionary" mind. It was only vanity, he thought, that caused an author to claim that he was the instrument of some higher power.

> Most writers—poets in especial—prefer having it understood that they compose by a species of fine frenzy—an ecstatic intuition—and would positively shudder at letting the public take a peep behind the scenes, at the elaborate and vacillating crudities of thought—at the true purposes seized only at the last moment—at the innumerable glimpses of idea that arrived not at the maturity of full view—at the fully matured fancies discarded in despair as un-

[8] "Marginalia," *Works*, XVI, 148–49.

manageable—at the cautious selections and rejections—at the painful erasures and interpolations—in a word, at the wheels and pinions—the tackle for scene-shifting—the step-ladders and demon-traps—the cock's feathers, the red paint and the black patches, which, in ninety-nine cases out of the hundred, constitute the properties of the literary *histrio*.

This is a valid description of the process of composition as it ordinarily occurs, much more convincing even than Poe's reconstruction of his own method. Yet if Poe overstated the case for deliberate procedure, it was because he had to use everything he could to combat the transcendentalists, who made the artist the passive vehicle of Divine Truth. The artist was divine, Poe had claimed in *Eureka*, but it was only because God himself was an artist. Every man was divine, but only the creative man carried out his divine function. What the poet saw, if he were indeed a poet, was the beauty of the divine plan, but it required human technical virtuosity to convey some portion of the feeling attendant upon vision to the less acute sensibility of an audience.

Since Poe's concept of response involved a more or less mechanical associative process, it would appear that his preplanned effects would arouse only stock responses. Unfortunately they often do when his theory is applied as a formula by less able writers. A stock response depends upon psychological norms, and Poe used a normative psychology. His premise of normative reactions lay behind his assertion that a writer had no excuse if he failed to create the desired impression.

Poe's "subjects" consisted of his magazine audience and himself. He believed that the "mob" could be misled by dishonest critics, but he assumed that his own reaction was a reliable norm and that when a poem or a tale failed to impress him there was something wrong with it that could be revealed by analysis. Accordingly, much of his criticism was directed toward the end of showing the public the origin of their invalid responses in something like the way that I. A. Richards analyzed the responses of his students. A poem which properly marshaled emotional effects should appeal to both the popular and the critical mind, Poe thought. "The Raven" had exhibited this kind of universal appeal; it was his most popular poem and had earned plaudits from the sophisticated in America and in England. By analyzing his method of composition, Poe was demonstrating that this happy result could be brought about deliberately. Like Richards, Poe wanted fresh responses, which was the chief reason he stressed novelty. Yet Poe was more concerned with novelty of effect than with the freshness of experience that Richards found in a re-ordering of our impulses.[9] Even here, however, the difference is not so great as might be supposed. Poe attributed the highest value to the poet's transmission of a felt harmony. An intuition of order, if successfully transmitted to others, enables them to have an aesthetic experience, an experience which probably contributes as much to the ordering of impulses as do the moral and social imperatives that are obeyed under protest.

Early in his career as a critic Poe had concluded that there must be unity of impression to produce the desired effect of an artistic whole; hence, on an empirical basis he decided that a poem should be short. The single sitting which permitted an undiluted effect was obligatory. Yet a poem should not be too short, or it would not have the weight and momentum to create a strong effect. If the poem did what Poe thought it could do, detach the spirit from its mortal home by its incantatory and evocative qualities, then it must exhibit a certain "duration or repetition of purpose" for its powers to work. All safeguards must be taken to prevent the breaking of the spell. Arbitrarily he decided that a poem short enough to be read in one-half to one hour would not fatigue even the most delicate sensibility. Furthermore, it could probably be read without interruption; and it would be extensive enough to provide the sophisticate with the pleasure of recognizing a design of some complexity. On the other hand, if the poem were too long, the spell would be broken as far as feeling was concerned, and even a cultivated taste would be unable to take in the total design without an effort of the abstracting and organizing reason. Poe, like many of his contemporaries, did not believe that one could feel intensely and think at the same time. Therefore, if structural analysis had to

[9] Richards, *Practical Criticism*, 268–71.

be carried on while the poem were being read, the effect would be lost. Such labor would be unnecessary in a short poem, however, for the totality of the poem could be appreciated without undue strain on the cognitive faculties.

Given his premises, Poe's argument is sound. Edmund Wilson affirmed in *The Triple Thinkers* that Poe was correct in his prediction that a long poem would never be popular again, but Wilson argued that it was because verse technique had passed out of fashion in all genres except the lyric. Wilson ignored, as Poe did not, the limitations of the mass audience, who would not recognize technique if they saw it. Poe made allowance for the increased tempo of an industrial civilization, the duration of the attentive span, and the incapacity of a semiliterate audience to recognize a complex structure. He erred only in that he thought the duration of attention and response was predictable. They are, as experimental psychology has shown, but not within a range that would be particularly useful to a poet.

It would not do to say that Poe was completely unaware of the variation of response possible even within a given audience, but he thought it possible for an artist to appeal on all levels. He planned "The Raven," he said, to take account of "that degree of excitement which I deemed not above the popular, while not below the critical taste . . . ." The poem demonstrated the universal appeal that in his later reviews he had claimed entirely possible.

The remainder of "The Philosophy of Composition" embodies the practical rules Poe had already advanced in his reviews.[10]

---

[10] I consider the debate about whether Poe actually wrote the poem as he said he did irrelevant. Kenneth Burke has made the most sensible statement on this question: "He [Poe] really did ask himself, as a *critic*, what principles he found (or thought he found) implicit in his act as poet . . . . In effect, he thus formulated the aesthetic principles (including a theory of beauty and of lyrical effects) which seemed to him the conceptual equivalent of the principles that had implicitly guided him in the writing of the poem." Burke went on to say that Poe "tricked himself" into explaining his act in "terms of a purely 'genetic' (narrative, temporal) series" and left himself open to the distrust that followed. Even so, Burke said, we should "recognize what an admirably sound critical procedure was struggling for

Beauty was the only proper effect for a poem, but beauty must not be considered as a quality of the object. It was recognizable only as a response. If an audience did not feel the beauty of a work of art, it was not beautiful. One could not argue with feelings; one could only stimulate them. In this Poe was not far from the position of Henry James, who admitted that one could not abolish the primitive test of liking or not liking a given work.

Poe's next choice of a necessary condition for universal effect was tone. In this he displayed a tendency to accept the taste of his times. An audience in Poe's time liked melancholy; therefore, it was the most nearly universal tone: "all experience has shown that this tone is one of *sadness*." Poe's tendency to accept the sentiments of his age as universal was his greatest weakness as a theorist. The Victorian sensibility might have been moved to tears by beauty, but modern aestheticians are prone to regard the response to a work of art as cold. Aesthetic appreciation has to be learned, and today we attempt to elevate the mass audience by offering classes in music and art appreciation. Poe, a practical journalist, recognized that there was little evidence that the education of the taste would ever be carried on as a public enterprise, except by the literary critics, and concluded, somewhat like Jonathan Edwards in respect to religion, that devotion to art could be stimulated on the mass level only by moving the emotions. The art object might impress the connoisseur with its perfection, above and beyond all desire, but to Poe a brief glimpse of perfection stimulated a yearning to experience it fully; and unless this yearning were stimulated, the work of art failed. As he wrote in "The Poetic Principle," "when by Poetry, or when by Music, . . . we find ourselves melted into tears, we weep then, not . . . through excess of pleasure, but through a certain petulant, impatient sorrow at our inability to grasp *now*, wholly, here on earth, at once and for ever, those divine and rapturous joys . . . ." Poe did not consider a mass audience capable of a pure aesthetic response, disinterested and serene. People were like

expression there." Burke, "The Principle of Composition," *Poetry*, XCIX (1961), 46–53.

children, petulant and impatient to possess whatever they enjoyed, whether it was an experience or an object. The important thing for an artist was to make his audience desire the appropriate aesthetic experience, not the passion of sexual love, nor the pangs of conscience, nor the exhilaration of intellectual exercise. The divine function of the poet was to make his audience desire a beauty greater than any that could be experienced through ordinary activities, thus stimulating a hope for the future and a concomitant dissatisfaction with the gratifications of phenomenal existence. The *contemptus mundi* theme, though indirectly expressed in Poe's work, was unquestionably there. The poet was a priest, but only in his own way, anticipating for his audience the glory beyond the grave while demonstrating the evanescence of all earthly joys. The raven is correct in replying "nevermore" to the lover who hopes to clasp his Lenore in heaven, for sexual love cannot exist beyond the grave.

If we explain Poe's requirement of melancholy in terms of *Eureka*, we see that it was the yearning of the God in man for his former estate, and even if the unimaginative man could not experience this yearning unaided, it was potential in his soul and could be awakened by the magic of verse. Presumably even the dullest would feel melancholy at the death of a beautiful woman, and presumably even the sensual man might be stimulated to an awareness that the soul could not content itself forever with dreams of sexual delight.

Such an argument would seem to Poe only the commonest of common sense, and he had the contemporary popularity of elegiac poems as empirical evidence. The journals were full of mournful lyrics lamenting the deaths of fragile ladies with names such as Lenore, Isabella, and Rosalie Lee. If the beloved woman were unequivocally dead, then the poem would not be marred by sexual passion, which Poe claimed was alien to the true poetical effect. Poe applied the steps toward ideal beauty that he had learned from the *Symposium*, but he introduced into his application the pessimism of experience. Man will not naturally gravitate from the love of one beautiful form to the love of all beautiful forms and then to

the love of the idea of beauty itself. Instead, frustration and pain
—the loss of the loved one—will lead him to a yearning for beauty
absolute and eternal. Man is dominated by his senses, and detach-
ment from the senses is achieved only by what today we call sub-
limation. Thus the "meaning" of "The Raven," which Poe claimed
to have poured into the poem toward the end almost as if he were
pouring condiment into a stew, has to do with the predicament of
a lover who is so infatuated with an earthly love that he lives
throughout his life with "mournful and never ending remem-
brance." By implication, the only hope for him is the "glory beyond the grave," which he will never glimpse so long as his mind is
captive to the passion of the heart. Poe used the same theme with a
different strategy in his "Ulalume," published two years later. In
"Ulalume" the poet is tempted by Astarte, the goddess of fleshly
love, to forget the dead Ulalume, even though his soul protests
against the temptation. Only by encountering the tomb of
Ulalume and by remembering the horrors of the grave, which Poe
vulgarly illustrated by a reference to ghouls, can the poet rise above
sensuality and experience the beauty of the idea. The last stanza of
the poem is confusing because Poe endowed the ghouls, ordinarily
the eaters of the dead, with the quality of pity. It appears that the
"pitiful, the merciful ghouls" are responsible for conjuring up the
vision of Astarte to keep the poet from remembering the horrors of
the grave. Yet it is only by remembering the evanescence of earthly
love, its frustration and pain, that his soul can be freed for its
search for heavenly beauty. The ghouls, eaters of flesh and thus associated with the inevitable destruction of the body, exhibit a mis-
placed mercy, for they tempt the poet to fall in love all over again
and once more experience the pangs of loss. Poe, as poet-priest,
was once more telling us what he had intimated in "The Raven,"
that the frustration of earthly love forces us to seek something immutable and imperishable, something we experience only partially
on earth, but which we must yearn for as the emotional attribute of
our divinity.

There is no need to examine in detail Poe's explanation of the
more mechanical aspects of his strategy in "The Raven." Whether

we accept his philosophy or not, he was perfectly clear about his method. Starting with the assumption that he wanted to write a narrative poem, he described a procedure which would observe the "laws of human nature." These laws are displayed by the morbid self-torture of the bereaved lover as he deliberately asks the raven questions which must invariably be answered by "nevermore," since this is the only word the raven knows. Poe claimed that he had not overstepped the "limits of the real" in the narrative incidents, but in accordance with his theory that a narrative was merely an "array of incident" unless the incidents had some meaning, he proceeded to introduce a metaphorical expression, "Take thy beak from out *my heart*," that would stimulate the reader to seek a symbolical suggestiveness in the events of the narrative which would give the tale that "*richness* . . . which we are too fond of confounding with the *ideal*."

This last statement invites comment. In Poe's reviews of *Undine* and *Alciphron*, he had himself confused the undercurrent of meaning with the ideal, but by 1845 he had clarified his own interpretation of the term. The ideal, as Poe interpreted it in his later years, was to be found only in music or in lyric poetry. It was something that happened in the mind and could only be recognized as a psychic response. Meaning that could be rendered in a prose redaction was not ideal. The ideal could only be felt, but the feeling could be deliberately stimulated. If, however, the feeling could be attributed to any cause other than the poem itself, then the poem was not ideal. The poem need have no transferable meaning, as such; it was simply an experience. Thus the sentiment of "ideality" could be evoked, but it was unrelated to anything that happened outside of the experience of the poem.

By this definition, Poe did not regard "The Raven" as a highly imaginative poem. It was a narrative designed to appeal on two levels. A naïve audience could understand the grief of a bereaved lover and could learn that earthly joys end with the grave and are not to be renewed in Heaven. The sophisticated could appreciate the form of the poem and interpret the symbolic suggestion contained in the single metaphor that occurs near the end, perhaps even rereading the lines with the symbolic meaning diffusing its richness throughout the poem.

For all of his insistence upon the needs of the mass audience, Poe had doubts that a purely ideal poem would ever be popular, because participation in the experience of such a poem required a highly developed sensibility. This did not mean, however, that the poet had to ban himself forever from popular approval. If he knew his audience psychology, he could compose a poem that would gratify both the vulgar and the sophisticated taste, but he would have to aim deliberately at a lower level of appeal than the purely imaginative, while at the same time evidencing enough artistry to please the aesthete.

"The Philosophy of Composition," then, was illustrative of Poe's contention in his later criticism that the artist should not neglect the man in the street. Scornful though he was of popularity as an end in itself, he felt that it was the duty of the artist to educate the public in beauty, while at the same time pleasing the critically minded. His account of how he wrote "The Raven" shows how it could be done. It was the application of his theoretical statements. Whatever the claim of the romantic genius that he wrote only to please himself, Poe knew that a poet wrote to be read, and he had little patience with the artistic flower that was born to blush unseen.

3

Poe never wrote an essay on method for the short lyric as distinguished from the narrative poem, probably because he thought no method could be prescribed. The lyric, originating in the "soul" or "mind" of the poet, had to obey only the general laws of composition: it must not exceed the human capacity to sustain poetic feeling; it must have an aesthetic purpose; it must obey metrical rules; and it must create a unity of effect. Poe had advanced these propositions in his reviews and essays, concerning himself more extensively with validating the aesthetic purpose of the lyric than with any other requirement. Even his metaphysics was simply an elaboration of his teleology of art, so we may properly regard Poe's efforts to develop a theory of poetry as being directed toward the end of instructing the public; the enjoyment of beauty was not only a permissible but even a necessary element in human experience. Poe's concern with the more technical aspects of verse was displayed in his reviews, particularly in his 1837 review of the *Poems* of William Cullen Bryant, but he was not prone to elaborate his theories of prosody in an ordinary review. After all, it was a technical subject and Poe was not writing to an audience of specialists. Usually in his reviews he confined himself to the rules that would be recognized by any schoolboy who had studied his textbook in rhetoric.

As early as 1835 Poe claimed in a letter to Beverley Tucker that he had made a special study of prosody; this study was centered on the relation of music to poetry. Not until 1843, however, did Poe publish an essay on prosody, and in this essay, "The Rationale of Verse," he attempted to show that the laws of rhythm were structured into the universe and would be the same everywhere regardless of variations in language and verse conventions. Linguistically naïve, Poe would have thought that a poem written in Bantu or Chinese should employ the same metrical system and have the same effect on the ear as a poem written in English. Accordingly, he attempted to develop a system of scansion for verse as accurate as that of musical notation. Music was the "universal language of the soul," and in Poe's opinion verse should be a universal language, as far as the effect on the ear was concerned. All human ears are constructed the same way, Poe argued; the universe itself exhibited periodicity and balance. Therefore all of the poets in the world should employ the same metrical system.

It goes without saying that Poe did not understand that a metrical system involved something more than rhythm.[11] He ignored linguistic discriminations and cited the law of nature as his princi-

[11] Although his own prosody was based upon a similar principle, Sidney Lanier dismissed Poe's essay with scant courtesy, saying that Poe erred in assuming that stress makes a syllable long. "Preface," *The Science of English Verse*, in *Sidney Lanier*, Centennial Edition (Baltimore, 1945), II, 11 n.

ple in prosody just as he claimed it was his principle in all other aspects of his literary theory. "Verse originates," Poe wrote, "in the human enjoyment of equality . . . ." By equality he meant "similarity, proportion, identity, repetition, and adaptation or fitness." The human enjoyment of music came from the recognition of "equality of *sounds*," [12] and this enjoyment could be increased by experience. The "practised ear" could enjoy complex patterns of sounds, detecting similarities even though intervals of time separated them. The musically naïve would fail to appreciate complex patterns of sounds because they could not recognize the repetition of a theme amidst its variations. In terms of enjoyment, then, undue complexity encountered the law of diminishing returns. Only the "scientific" ear could apprehend the unity of a pattern when the variety was too extensive; therefore there was no "intrinsic merit" in "scientific" music.[13] Since music should appeal to everyone, the simpler harmonies were best.

Once again Poe employed the criterion of universality. The enjoyment of art should be for everyone. In his 1839 review of Morris' *Songs* and in "The Poetic Principle," Poe had found great merit in the ballad, and now we see why: "Unpractised ears can appreciate only simple equalities, such as are found in ballad airs." Thus when Poe stated in his review of Morris that he would rather have written the best song of a nation than its noblest epic, he was simply stating his credo that art should be for the public. Like Vachel Lindsay, who absorbed Poe's poetry through his very skin, Poe preached the gospel of beauty throughout the land. Though he was an intellectual snob in many ways, he never thought that the experience of beauty should be confined to the elect. It should be a formative influence on the hearts and minds of the people.

[12] Poe did not understand that the recognition of equality by the ear is only proximate, and that the human voice in reading verse never approaches the exactness of duration achieved by the reproduction of notes on a musical instrument. Lanier fell into the same error. See Paull Franklin Baum (ed.), "Introduction," *The Science of English Verse*, xli–xlii.

[13] By scientific music, Poe apparently meant an extended composition technically accurate according to the laws of harmonics; the scientific ear would be that of a trained musician.

Without going into the details of Poe's metrical system, which was adequately summarized by Gay Wilson Allen over thirty years ago,[14] this discussion will center on the correlation between Poe's prosody and his theory of the universe. To Poe the universe was the great machine described by Newton's physics. Regularity was the law. Man's mind was not able to apprehend the complexity of the great machine, but by knowing that the design was perfect he could extrapolate from the observable periodicity and assume that balance or equality was the law of nature. The regularity of the seasons, the alternation of day and night, attraction and repulsion—all proved that the "omnipresent law of laws" was the law of periodicity. Thus, if prosody were to follow the law of nature, it had to embody equality or balance. Each long syllable should be balanced by two or more short ones within a line, each long line by two or more short lines within a stanza, and stanzas should be balanced with each other throughout the poem. The complexity of the microcosmic poem would vary with the skill of the poet, but it should be limited by the capacity of the audience to "remember" equivalent sounds and temporal units.

Poe's metaphor describing the pleasure experienced from the metrics of a poem is revealing. To him it was like the pleasure obtained from examining a crystal. "We are at once interested by the equality between the sides and between the angles of one of its faces; the equality of the sides pleases us, that of the angles doubles the pleasure. On bringing to view a second face in all respects similar to the first, this pleasure seems to be squared; on bringing to

---

[14] *American Prosody* (New York, 1935), 56–61. Professor Allen discounted Poe's prosodic theory because Poe did not recognize the accentual basis of English verse. Poe's system of scansion would have to be like musical notation. Such a method would appear to have limited value because the duration of a given syllable in oral delivery depends upon interpretation, a subjective factor. No one reads to the beat of a metronome. Yet even in the twentieth century the late Morris W. Croll developed a system of scansion by musical notation. See his "The Rhythm of English Verse," in J. Max Patrick and Robert O. Evans (eds.), *Style, Rhetoric, and Rhythm* (Princeton, 1966), 367–429. Poe, Lanier, and Croll are only a few of the many prosodists throughout history who have sought to establish a more accurate mode of scansion upon a temporal base.

view a third it appears to be cubed, and so on." Arguing from the premises of a mechanistic psychology, Poe had no doubt that the amount of pleasure derived from meter could be calculated with mathematical precision. He would perhaps have agreed with Edna St. Vincent Millay that Euclid alone saw beauty bare. Unlike some of his contemporaries among the romantic poets, Poe took no pleasure in the fecundity, the variety, the growth and development, the sheer plenitude of biological nature. He retained the attitude of the previous century that one of the greatest pleasures to be enjoyed by the human mind was the perception of order and regularity within the inconceivable variety of temporal flux.

In his essay on metrics, Poe illustrated his theory that the work of art should be a microcosm which adapted to the human perceptive apparatus those laws described by the physicists and astronomers of the past two centuries. He identified the poetic imagination with that of the scientist; it was an ability to perceive equivalent relationships within a world of phenomenal diversity. Thus the artist, glorying in his perception of a perfect system, would mediate between the "imagined" cosmic order and the disorder that assaulted the senses. He would not imitate the complexity of the Great Design; he would reduce it to a simplicity that could be taken in by the ordinary human mind. In such a way he would anticipate, here on earth, the beauty of eternity, wherein all relatedness would disappear and the soul would glory in the experience of perfect unity.

4

Edgar Poe was unique among nineteenth-century American critics because he not only evaluated literary works but also developed an aesthetic theory and a theory of nature to support it. It has sometimes been said that Poe developed his theory of literature merely to defend the kind of poetry and fiction that he wrote. Even if true, this charge is not necessarily a basis for damnation. Most poet-critics work out a theory more favorable to their own practice than to anyone else's. As a rule the practice comes before the theory. Cases like that of T. E. Hulme, who wrote poetry to illustrate the kind of poetry he thought should be written, are rare. The question we should ask when evaluating Poe as a critic is whether his theory yields a larger return than the validation of his own work. In this respect Poe will inevitably be judged as inferior to Coleridge, whose pronouncements, open as they are to varying interpretations, have been seminal in the development of modern organicism. Poe made his own contribution to organicism, chiefly in connection with the short narrative, but since the short narrative has not yet achieved the status of the novel or the poem, Poe's contribution, though recognized, has not been awarded high value. Nor has his limitation of the purpose of poetry to beauty been highly regarded within the English tradition, however much it has appealed to the French. Henry James once remarked of the British novel that it had been too self-consciously engaged with the moral purpose. To a certain extent the same thing is true of English verse. For all of the protests of poets like Archibald MacLeish and Allen Tate that poetry is its own excuse for being, our critics have wanted poetry to bear some responsibility for the human condition. Few have agreed with Walter Pater that to burn with a hard gemlike flame is success in life. And even Pater is being rescued from the "art for art's sake" category by critics like Walter Jackson Bate, who sees Pater as coming close to the great humanistic tradition of art for life's sake.

Critics in the English tradition have wanted poetry to engage in some way with our problems and give us insights if not solutions. Poe's notion that poetry should merely arouse poetic feeling is considered decadent,[15] and his qualification that poetic feeling has an indirect bearing upon behavior has been largely ignored. Yet this is one of the more significant aspects of Poe's theory of art as it relates to society. He did think that the experience of beauty was

[15] Elio Chinol, in an essay published in 1946 but translated and republished recently, rightly claimed that Poe should not be classified among the decadents because his aesthetic remains within the English tradition and his "poetry is still far from dissolving into mere musical atmosphere." Elio Chinol, "Poe's Essays on Poetry," trans. B. M. Arnett, *Sewanee Review*, LXVIII (1960), 390–97.

formative, and with typical American enthusiasm he thought that such experience should be made available even to those who seemed least susceptible. In this Poe was as innocently American as Walt Whitman or, in later days, Vachel Lindsay.

It should not be argued that Poe counseled the artistic genius deliberately to cater to a mass audience. Yet he did think that an artist failed in his public responsibility if he did not consider the needs and limitations of his audience. More than anything else, Poe contested the right of the genius merely to express himself. No matter how valuable we think our thoughts and feelings are, Poe maintained, they serve no purpose unless we can communicate them at large. If the poet deserves to be honored, he must make himself felt; and he will never make himself felt unless he stirs the commmon heart of humanity. More than any other critic of his time, with the possible exception of Hazlitt, Poe sought to bring art to the people without lowering its quality to such an extent that it would be offensive. In his own way he succeeded, though his art still offends many.

Poe expended relatively little effort in the criticism of criticism, though he did not hesitate to challenge any critic, even one as great as Coleridge, when he detected a shaky premise or an unwarranted conclusion. A theory to Poe was worthless unless it could be reduced to practice. In this, more than in anything else, he showed himself in the American grain. His reduction to practice was often faulty, because he was inhibited by some of the older rules of rhetoric and by his reliance upon a rudimentary psychology that was decidedly primitive in its analysis of cognition. Yet, given the tools he had to work with, Poe's evaluation of his contemporaries has stood the test of time in most cases. Only his overpraise of Richard Hengist Horne is likely to cause much astonishment today.

More damaging to Poe's reputation as a critic was his tendency to undervalue the great works of the past. Basing his opinion upon the premise that no work was great unless it could appeal to an audience other than the one for which it was composed, Poe was inclined to think that Greek tragedy was primitive. He reasoned similarly about the epic. *Paradise Lost* would appeal only to the academic few who had the leisure and the interest to work out Milton's vast design, and even then the pleasure would be more that of an intellectual exercise than the pleasure of taste. A general audience would have neither the capacity nor the time to appreciate an epic. Since in Poe's system a poem was effective in terms of its appeal, and since he believed that a skillful artist could always manage to appeal, he declared that *Paradise Lost* and all other epics proceeded from an imperfect sense of art. Poe's chief failure as a theorist came from his simplistic test of effect, yet this test, however we scorn it, is inescapable. A work does not live in the public domain unless it gives pleasure to a great many people. Anyone who claimed that a work could live because of its message or because of its technical perfection Poe would classify as a pedant who spoke only for his own class.

Poe earned the disapproval of the elite when he claimed that art was or should be a public affair, and yet he saw more clearly than most the alienation of the artist that would occur if he neglected his public function in the interest of self-expression, if he engaged in technical frolics that would appeal only to the aesthete, or if he plunged into obscurities that only the philosophically apt could comprehend. Poe would have approved of *Finnegans Wake* or Pound's *Cantos* no more than he approved of *Paradise Lost*.

Poe is a crucial figure in the history of literary criticism, not because he oversimplified important issues, but because he raised a question that still has not been answered satisfactorily: Can art *as* art ever be brought to the general public? Ortega y Gasset has claimed that the dehumanization of modern art has alienated it from the masses because mass appreciation depends upon the recognition of human elements in the art work. Astonishingly, Edgar Poe went very far in eliminating the human element from the art work—and made the public like it. Poe argued that a fiction was a fiction and nothing else. It was not life, and it had no business with the truth that applies to our everyday affairs, except indirectly. He knew that it was impossible to imitate the reality of the thing with words, sounds, shapes, or colors, something that William Hazlitt, for instance, never appeared to find out. Yet we are still so much inclined to seek the living reality or the inspiring insight in an art work that we are inclined to dismiss Poe as a charlatan or a sleight-of-hand performer.

Poe did not demand art for art's sake. He demanded art for the soul's sake, but he mitigated his demand by recognizing that art would have to be impure to reach the public,[16] even going so far as to provide us with a formula for popularity. He knew that a composition devoid of the human element would appeal only to the trained sensibility, and yet, with a certain optimism, he engaged in the act of criticism in the belief that the public mind could be educated to respond at least to the simpler artistic forms. He thought throughout his career that a critical journal of high quality would gain public approval, and he believed that an artist who understood psychology could wring an appropriate response even from a dull sensibility. We cannot declare unequivocally that he was wrong.

His own work occasionally approaches the abstract, the dehumanized. His tales are "arabesques," heavily pictorial, with characters who represent ideas, not human beings. Few of us can empathize with Poe's suffering heroes or even recognize the nature of their suffering without excursions into abnormal psychology. The beauty of Poe's Ligeia is not a human beauty. His women are not drawn from the "living, breathing" reality admired by Hazlitt. They are art objects. The tales in which they appear do not permit the pleasure of identification, yet the popularity of these tales would seem to support Poe's theory that novelty of characterization, even when pushed beyond the limits of the natural, would meet the test of public approval when that novelty was exhibited under conditions that allowed assent.

Similarly with Poe's poems. They, too, exhibit a measure of that dehumanization we find in pure poetry, but many of them are impure, and Poe knew it. He recognized the impurity of his most popular poem, "The Raven," and claimed that he deliberately invoked the natural to appeal to the public taste. Yet in theory more than in practice Poe advocated a poetry that avoided the materials of nature and, so far as possible, all emotions except that attendant

[16] Cf. *ibid.*, 394–96.

upon the recognition of beauty. Ortega y Gasset has stated that Mallarmé was the first poet in the nineteenth century who wanted to be nothing but a poet.[17] Poe started with the idea of being nothing but a poet; he became a fiction-writer and a critic out of necessity. But as he engaged in the act of criticism he began to think about poetry rather than write it, a predicament which is certainly not unusual. In his criticism at least, he held up before the public the proposition that a poet might worthily be a poet and nothing else, and he assigned to the critic the task of making the situation of poet *as* poet possible. Poe's concept of the task of the critic must always be reckoned with, for he imposed upon the American critic a new duty. Before his time American critics had felt that they had to protect the public from the rakehell voluptuosities of Europe or the dangerous ideas of the political revolutionary. Poe, with a vehemence unmatched in his time, declared it the duty of the critic to protect the public from bad writing and to remind the writer that he had a public responsibility to live up to the genius with which nature had endowed him. The poet could be a poet and nothing else, in Poe's book, so long as he wrote good poetry.

Poe was remarkable in his time and place for his argument that art could exist only as the result of an aesthetic purpose. His mistake, as far as the application of his theory is concerned, sprang from his assumption that by deliberately avoiding external reference the poet could force his poems to appeal only to the "soul." Adding to his confusion, at least in respect to the lyric, was his premise that music, since it was nonreferential, was a pure art. He failed to recognize that the kind of music he admired was as expressive of human feeling as the most passionate poem, and that its universal appeal originated in its expression of feeling. He betrayed his own cause when he advocated the ballad as the most appealing form of poetry. This choice proves that Poe, if he really intended to champion a pure art, had only the vaguest notion of what it was, for the ballad is the most human, the least abstract, of all poetic

[17] *The Dehumanization of Art* (Doubleday Anchor ed.; New York, 1956), 29.

genres. The only conclusion that may be drawn is that Poe was not an aesthete at all. He wanted art to be *expressive* of human feelings, but not *representative* of human feelings, for representation was not art.

Poe's devotion to musicality set up a conflict in his theory of poetry that he was never able to resolve. He attached great value to the apprehension of an art object as a completed design, an achieved purpose, but the design itself was not the purpose. To stimulate feeling was the purpose, and value was attached to the quality of the feeling; it had to be love without passion, melancholy without grief, or virtue without an object. Such to Poe were the sentiments of the soul, the sentiments expressed in music. Yet in his zeal to bring art to the people he had to advocate the expression in poetry of feelings they could understand, the grief of a bereaved lover or the passion of a betrayal, feelings frequently expressed in the ballad. In the final analysis it must be said that Poe effected the democratic compromise: give art to the people, but only so much art as they can stand. He could never reconcile himself to the alienation of the artist from the public that art for art's sake entails. Could he have fled to Europe, as did Henry James, perhaps he could have remained secure in his dedication to the artistic idea; but he would have had to recognize, as did James, that most people would "agree that the 'artistic' idea would spoil their fun." As it was, Poe became the advocate of an impure art, while at the same time striving to remove as much excess baggage as possible from the artist's motivational load.

We can credit him with one significant accomplishment. He described the purpose of the artist in terms which would make a purer art possible, and for this reason he has been more honored in France than in any country that follows the English tradition. He never became what Ortega y Gasset called the "pure nameless voice" of lyricism, but he entertained the possibility. Whether he be honored for it or condemned, Poe was the first critic in America to speak out boldly for the aesthetic purpose, even though he understood it imperfectly.

Index